# SUING GOVERNMENT

# SUING GOVERNMENT

## CITIZEN REMEDIES FOR OFFICIAL WRONGS

*PETER H. SCHUCK*

*YALE UNIVERSITY PRESS*

*NEW HAVEN AND LONDON*

Designed by Sally Harris
and set in Caledonia type by
Northeast Typographic Services, Meriden, Conn.
Printed in the United States of America by
Halliday Lithograph, West Hanover, Mass.

Portions of this book appeared in earlier form in *The Supreme Court Review*,
volume 1980 (Chicago: University of Chicago Press).

Library of Congress Cataloging in Publication Data

Schuck, Peter H.
   Suing government.
   Includes bibliographical references and index.
   1. Government liability—United States. 2. Administrative responsibility—United
States. 3. Remedies (Law)—United States. I. Title.
KF1321.S38 1983      342.73′088      82-48907
ISBN 0-300-02957-8

10  9  8  7  6  5  4  3  2  1

*For Bruce Ackerman—playful antagonist, intellectual agent provocateur, and colleague extraordinaire*

# CONTENTS

Acknowledgments                                                          ix
Introduction                                                             xi

PART I   COMPLICATING THE PROBLEM                               1
    1   A Framework for Thinking about Remedies   3
    2   The Evolution of American Public Tort
        Remedies                                        29

PART II   THE CASE FOR REMEDIAL REFORM                          55
    3   Official Liability for Damages: The Power
        and Perversity of Incentives                    59
    4   Distributing the Costs of Official
        Misconduct                                      82
    5   Toward Remedial Justice: Expanding the
        Damage Remedy against Government                100

PART III   INSIDE THE BUREAUCRATIC
         BLACK BOX                                      123
    6   Mobilizing Organizational Change: How
        Will Agencies Respond to Governmental
        Liability?                                      125
    7   The Courts and Specific Deterrence: The
        Judge as Bureaucratic Reformer                  147
    8   Conclusion: A Remedial System for the
        Future                                          182

Appendix 1   Volume of Federal Court Litigation against
        Governments and Public Officials                199
Appendix 2   Governmental and Official Liability-Im-
        munity Doctrine in the Federal Courts           203
Appendix 3   Sovereign Immunity in the States                206

Notes    209
Index    257

# ACKNOWLEDGMENTS

Although scholarship is an unusually solitary activity, it invariably reflects the contributions of individuals and institutions other than the author. This book is no exception, for I have shamelessly exploited the generosity, industry, and insights of others.

The Yale Law School has provided much nourishment: a triennial leave during the spring of 1982, financial support, stimulating students, challenging colleagues, and an environment that fosters, indeed demands, intellectual growth. The Center for Health Studies, part of Yale's Institution for Social and Policy Studies, contributed support during the summers of 1980 and 1981 under a grant from the Henry J. Kaiser Family Foundation.

A number of individuals read and criticized earlier drafts of much or all of the manuscript; Bruce Ackerman, Robert Cover, Owen Fiss, Jerry Mashaw, George Priest, and David Reiser were especially generous with their time and ideas. Regular participants in the faculty seminar on regulation at the Center for Health Studies reviewed an early draft of chapter 7, as did Geoffrey Hazard, Drew Days, Dick Murnane, Ted Eisenberg, Steve Yeazell, Don Horowitz, and Dick Craswell. I also benefited from outstanding research assistance from Yale Law School students George Wyeth and Eben Moglen; their colleagues Alice Miskimin and Theresa Glennon were helpful in more limited roles. Pat DeLucca, whose sunny disposition and zest for hard work are legendary at Yale, demonstrated why word processors will never replace talented secretaries. Marian Ash at Yale University Press provided welcome encouragement.

I dedicate the book to Bruce Ackerman, whose robust intellectual energies, buoyant spirits, and high aspirations evoke the best from all who are fortunate enough to be touched by them.

# INTRODUCTION

Lawbreaking is endemic to government. Madison, a republican without illusion, viewed this as perhaps the most problematic aspect of political life:

> But what is government itself but the greatest of all reflections on human nature? If men were angels, no government would be necessary. If angels were to govern men, neither external nor internal controls on government would be necessary. In framing a government which is to be administered by men over men, the great difficulty lies in this: you must first enable the government to control the governed; and in the next place oblige it to control itself. A dependence on the people is, no doubt, the primary control on the government; but experience has taught mankind the necessity of auxiliary precautions.[1]

Madison taught that the toll of official wrongdoing is not fully measured by harm to individual citizens, that abuses of public power fundamentally threaten the integrity of the legal order itself, eroding the values of a law-abiding people. Mr. Justice Brandeis recognized this larger danger:

> In a government of laws, the existence of the government will be imperilled if it fails to observe the law scrupulously. Our government is the potent, the omnipresent, teacher. For good or ill, it teaches the whole people by its example. Crime is contagious. If

the government becomes a lawbreaker, it breeds contempt for law; it invites every man to become a law unto himself; it invites anarchy.[2]

We know little about the amount or character of official wrongdoing in America, now or in the past. No reliable measures exist or are likely to be devised. Criminal prosecutions and convictions of public officials are increasingly common,[3] but we do not know whether this reflects changed public attitudes toward official behavior, post-Watergate prosecutorial zeal, or growth in actual criminal activity. Civil actions in the federal courts against public officials have increased exponentially in the last twenty years, as shown in appendix 1. These statistics, however, reveal only broad, undifferentiated statutory categories, not specific patterns of official wrongdoing. The explosion of such litigation since 1960 certainly reflects the extraordinary proliferation of public law rights and remedies during that period, an evolution traced in chapter 2. But it does not necessarily signify that lawless attitudes among officials are more common.

Still, the rule of law is probably more precarious today than when Madison, or even Brandeis, wrote. Activist government breeds official misconduct on a large scale. Many more individuals wield governmental authority today, of course; thus the number of potential lawbreakers has grown correspondingly.[4] But the many new affirmative functions of government, and the qualitatively greater difficulties it faces, also multiply the occasions and opportunities for official misconduct. In the past, government simply maintained order, administered the currency, built physical infrastructure, delivered the mail, collected revenues, educated the young, controlled deviance, protected established property rights, and fought foreign wars. Official wrongdoing had limited scope.

Today, government is ubiquitous. A breathtakingly complex system of social welfare programs requires low-level officials to evaluate the characters and circumstances of tens of millions of individuals rapidly, with little information and under chronic budget constraints. Far-reaching new regulatory programs delegate enormous powers to front-line inspectors and other field operatives, creating numerous risks of error and abuse. Legislative enactments and court decisions require officials to dismantle traditional school systems, reshape housing patterns, deliver social services to previously underserved populations, redesign criminal justice systems, and protect environmental values.

Often, their only tool for molding these large social changes is a regulation, court order, or resistant bureaucratic apparatus.

Official wrongdoing reflects the number and character of legal rights and available remedies against government, not simply the state of official morality. Since the early 1960s, legislatures and courts have created new substantive claims on public resources and new procedural entitlements to secure them. Whether the rights are those of handicapped children to a "mainstream" educational experience, elderly citizens to nursing home benefits, welfare recipients to pretermination hearings, or factory owners to permits, the activist state is directed to act affirmatively. When it fails to act or when it implements rights incompetently or incompletely, government becomes a law-breaker.

The highly technical, uncertain, and rapidly changing rules that today's officials must often apply facilitate much illegality. The complexity of economic regulation, for example, reflects the diversity and dynamism of the reality that it attempts to control.[5] Rules governing permissible search procedures and regulations implementing civil rights law are often opaque, and their meanings emerge only gradually through case-by-case adjudication. Increasingly, common sense unaided by detailed legal analysis is a poor guide to what public law requires. Official wrongdoing is less *malum in se* than *malum in prohibitum*. Sometimes, so much law issues from so many sources—legislatures, agencies, courts, private agreements, and informal administrative practices—that uncertainty increases rather than lessens. Discordant, dispersed messages often produce Babel-like confusion and incoherence.

The bureaucratic form of the activist state also nurtures official illegality. Efficient, highly structured decision processes and articulated decision rules can achieve relatively predictable, accurate decisions consistent with explicit program objectives. But this same bureaucratic rationality may systematically sacrifice other values, such as individuation of decision, human dignity, and professional judgment, and these are values that the law increasingly protects.[6] Activist government's "mass justice" ambitions make procedural due process more costly and difficult to provide. Professionalization, specialization of function, organizational complexity, and fragmented administration threaten to render conventional bureaucratic controls ineffective, introducing sharp cleavages between agency leaders and their low-level operatives, between front-office command and front-line performance.

These relationships between post-New Deal government and official lawbreaking are not ephemeral but enduring. They will survive the Reagan administration's best efforts to curtail activist government. Indeed, some of these efforts, launched against a backdrop of well-entrenched procedural and substantive rights, may themselves be illegal. A recent court decision invalidating the administration's repeal of the air-bag regulation is an example. Other administrative proposals, especially the so-called New Federalism, would not so much eliminate public activities as simply transfer their loci to state and local government, which are at least as prone to violate the law as the federal government. Governmental "reform," it seems, often means little more than requiring officials to discharge the same functions with fewer dollars. In such cases, compliance with laws premised upon a greater budgetary commitment will often become more difficult.

A final linkage between the activist state and official wrongdoing is especially ironic. By proliferating public programs, the activist state stimulates (and sometimes actually creates) new institutions with political, professional, ideological, programmatic, economic, or other incentives to expose and challenge official misconduct. Whether these public and private watchdogs are equal to the enlarged task of control that the activist state necessitates remains unclear, but their efforts certainly render official misconduct more visible and vulnerable.

*Public Tort Law in the Activist State*

If the activist state poses a fundamental challenge to the concerns voiced by Madison and Brandeis, it is one to which the American legal system has responded with stunning speed and creativity. In particular, the federal judiciary has fundamentally reshaped our public tort law, transforming the relationship of citizen to government in the process. This legal revolution—no less dramatic word will do—has largely been the work of litigants and judges.

Public tort law is the system of substantive norms, procedural rules, and remedial opportunities that citizens may invoke to redress harm that public officials cause to their person, property, or other noncontractual interests. This book is chiefly concerned with civil remedies for public torts. These are lawsuits brought by citizens against officials individually ("official liability") or against government itself ("governmental liability"): such lawsuits seek any of three kinds of relief —monetary damages, an injunction prohibiting or requiring certain official actions, and a declaratory judgment that simply declares the rights and liabilities of the parties.

The legal convulsion in public tort law, spawned by the school desegregation cases of the 1950s, is only now beginning to abate. It left
three major doctrinal shifts in its wake; each culminated during the late
1970s, although some began or were prefigured earlier. The first,
*substantive* in nature, was characterized by a profusion of newly
created rights against federal, state, and local governments. The publicly subsidized benefits that Charles Reich envisioned as "the new
property"—for example, health and income support entitlements;
services for · the handicapped, elderly, and children; student and
homeowner loans; contractual opportunities[7]—created unprecedented
and widely diffused social, political, and legal interests in controlling
official illegality.

A second major shift concerned *procedural* rights. Stimulated by the
Warren Court's expansion of criminal procedure protections as well as
the Great Society's creation of substantive entitlements, this shift possessed an independent vitality. As the activist state conferred new
benefits, expectations, and opportunities, it usually surrounded them
with procedural rights designed to safeguard public and private interests in decisional accuracy, fiscal soundness, programmatic integrity, and fair process. The federal courts, especially after the Supreme
Court's epochal decision in *Goldberg* v. *Kelly*,[8] found many procedures inadequate under the due process clause of the federal Constitution. The courts thereupon constructed an impressive arsenal of
procedural weapons with which citizens might defend not only the new
substantive rights, such as medical benefits, but also the expectations
associated with certain traditional statuses, such as criminal suspect,
criminal defendant, prisoner, parolee, pensioner, and government
employee.[9]

The third shift was *remedial*. Congress accompanied many of the
new substantive and procedural rights with private remedies designed
to secure official accountability to citizens.[10] The federal courts, for
their part, not only shaped the contours of the new legal rights but
transformed the nature, scope, and efficacy of the relief that individual
citizens could obtain to vindicate those rights. This remedial transformation is so recent that its implications remain largely unexplored.

## The Inquiry: Goals, Themes, and Limitations

This book undertakes that task. In the course of doing so, I hope to
construct sturdy intellectual foundations for thinking about the problem of governmental wrongdoing and its control and to justify some

specific reforms in the present system. These goals—the one analytical and conceptual, the other normative and reformist—are also efforts to isolate choice-of-remedy as a distinctive problem worthy of intellectual attention and policymaking concern, and to illuminate and perhaps answer questions like the following: What purposes should public tort remedies serve? How should those purposes relate to one another? How do they affect officials' behavior? What roles do immunity rules and other risk-shifting mechanisms play? What are the advantages and disadvantages of particular remedies, and under what circumstances should they be used? What would a socially optimal system of public tort remedies look like? What should the roles of court, agency, and legislature be? And how can we best get from here to there?

To address these questions coherently, we must lift the subject of public tort remedies out of the narrow technical mold in which it has usually been cast and instead locate it in a larger, more complex behavioral setting. Public tort remedies touch upon four legal specialties: tort law, administrative law, constitutional law, and civil procedure. Like many cross-specialty subjects, it resides in limbo, languishing in a kind of academic no-man's-land. Standard courses and texts in tort law, for example, focus upon disputes between private parties under state law. Public tort remedies are marginal topics for study, momentary excursions to the rapidly vanishing realm of common law immunities. The leading torts treatise, over 1,000 pages in length, contains not a single reference to 42 U.S.C § 1983, the remedial fountainhead of today's public tort law.[11] Administrative law texts and scholars usually treat the public tort action as an exotic, mutant form of judicial review, peripheral and ancillary to traditional direct review of administrative decisions under the Administrative Procedure Act.[12] Constitutional scholars are far more concerned with substantive conceptual and doctrinal developments than with their remedial underpinnings. Proceduralists, who do study remedies as such, seldom analyze them from a comparative or extraprocedural perspective.[13] To them, damage remedies are far less interesting than injunctions, and immunities are of little interest at all.

A more fruitful approach, I think, would consider public tort remedies from the larger perspective of social policy and regulatory technique. From this prospect, each remedy is a discrete arrangement through which society pursues collective ends; each creates different incentives and implicates different institutional interests. Private tort law, true to its distinctively individualistic and decentralized premises,[14] leaves the initial choice of remedy and defendant to individuals pursuing their strategic self-interest. In public tort law, these choices, like society's choice between alternative regulatory tools (for example, command-and-control regulation, taxes, subsidies, or liability rules), should instead be regarded as fundamental public policy decisions that also require careful, self-conscious weighing of social advantages and disadvantages by courts, legislatures, and administrative agencies.

In this book, I hope to isolate the crucial considerations that ought to guide these institutions as they shape this remedial system. Private tort law has much to teach us. In public tort law, private law notions such as enterprise liability, contractual risk-shifting, strict liability, punitive damages, and the efficiency criterion have been slow to take root, and compensation of victims has been subordinated as a goal. I shall argue that a more complete assimilation of some of these private tort law concepts is long overdue, even though some features of public torts, particularly the contexts in which certain low-level officials act, seem to call for distinctive legal and institutional responses. This tension, this convergence and divergence between the private and public tort systems, constitutes a central theme of my analysis.

The book chiefly concerns how public tort law remedies affect an important subset of officials, those to whom Michael Lipsky has felicitously referred as "street-level bureaucrats."[15] They include police officers, schoolteachers, social workers, inspectors, prison officials, drug enforcement agents, workers in institutions for the mentally disabled, and the like. Whatever their differences, these officials share three common characteristics. They personally deliver basic governmental services directly to citizens. They occupy the lower rungs of their bureaucratic ladders. And despite low bureaucratic rank, they exercise substantial discretion in their daily work. No bright line, of course, separates these officials from others whose misconduct is also of public concern, such as political appointees, mid-level bureaucrats, or those who do not provide direct services. Still, there are good reasons for this narrower focus. Street-level officials are far more numerous. Because social scientists have devoted far more attention to them than to their superiors back at headquarters, we also know more about them.[16]

Impressionistic evidence also suggests that most defendants in public law damage actions in the federal courts are street-level officials and their immediate superiors. (Reliable data are lacking, as appendix 1 reveals.) They are more vulnerable to damages liability than "policy-level" executives. This may seem anomalous. High-level supervisory or policymaking officials tend to be more visible, financially capable of satisfying a judgment, and well positioned to change official policy. Moreover, their "greater power," as the Supreme Court has observed, "affords a greater potential for a regime of lawless conduct."[17]

The Supreme Court, however, has made high-level officials poor targets for damage actions. It has tended to absolve them from personal liability, absent proof of direct, personal involvement in the wrongful conduct.[18] It has also suggested that broader immunity ought to be accorded officials who bear broader responsibilities.[19] Most important, it has repeatedly refused to hold governmental entities liable for their employees' torts.[20] In private tort law, where such liability is well established under the common law principle of enterprise liability (or more generally, *respondeat superior*), victims almost always sue the relatively well-financed employer rather than the employee. In public tort law, however, immunity doctrines relegate many victims to a damage remedy only against individual, low-level officials.[21]

Street-level officials are not a homogeneous group, of course. It is doubtless simplistic to wedge the disparate circumstances of, say, policemen and teachers into a single analytic pigeonhole; only journalists and pollsters fancy that they can speak intelligibly of the "typical" street-level official. But law itself is often simplistic in this sense, speaking in broad, categorical terms.[22] Fact-dependent and context-specific legal categories tend to be technical, inflexible, costly to administer, and difficult to apply—yet if we make them more general and encompassing, they grow cruder and less discriminating. Law always seeks the appropriate level of category-specificity. In fact, as chapter 3 shows, street-level officials seem rather similar in certain relevant respects and can usefully be generalized for our limited analytical purposes.

This book focuses upon *civil* remedies under *federal* law. It largely ignores tort remedies under state law and criminal sanctions. Whereas state tort law varies across jurisdictions, making generalization difficult, public tort law in the federal courts is uniform and has become far more visible and important. The omission of criminal sanctions deserves additional comment. Some official behavior may be so intentionally malevolent, so likely to harm, that only criminal prosecution can adequately express society's abhorrence. The police action that led to the Supreme Court's 1961 decision in *Monroe* v. *Pape*, described in chapter 2, was probably such a case.[23] The Watergate era provided other examples. But most official misconduct probably cannot be dealt with effectively by the existing criminal justice system. Tort and administrative remedies are more promising techniques of legal control.

Consider some familiar examples. State mental hospitals fail to provide adequate care to patients. Welfare departments improperly calculate benefits. Probation services revoke probation without providing adequate hearings. Social workers remove children from their homes prematurely. Schoolteachers improperly search students' lockers for narcotics. Police officers use firearms unnecessarily to apprehend fleeing burglars. Such illegality is usually caused by honest error, simple neglect, excessive zeal, poor judgment, unconscious bias, legal uncertainty, deficient execution, and inadequate training or supervision. It tends to be more routinized and repetitive, more deeply embedded in the standard operating procedures and adaptations of public office, than the illegality in *Monroe* v. *Pape* or Watergate. It persists at relatively low levels of visibility and self-consciousness. The duration of these practices, their consistency with formal or informal agency norms and the incentive structures that surround and reinforce them, may legitimate them to officials and even to citizens. They may come to be seen as inseparable from the intractable operating realities of government, necessary evils of our public life.

This moral camouflage encourages officials to lay the blame for misconduct elsewhere—on politicians who lack courage to make difficult decisions, on inadequate budget or support structure for doing the job properly, or on other actors whose interference or noncooperation makes unconventional or illegal tactics necessary. Fault may even be found in the character of the victims. Policemen who patrol high-crime neighborhoods, teachers who must maintain discipline in troubled schools, prison guards who tend potentially violent inmates under incendiary conditions, managers who cannot run their units efficiently without bending the civil service system—these otherwise law-abiding public servants may take comfort and find justification in continuing to do what they have always done, even if it is illegal. Unless aggravating circumstances exist, prosecutors may be reluctant to file criminal charges in such cases.[24] Juries seldom convict and almost never incarcerate, and if they do, chief executives may feel obliged to pardon.[25] In these situations, tort sanctions—less severe in principle than some criminal penalties but controlled by citizens and capable of being used to compensate victims—may actually be more damaging to defendants and more important in the larger remedial scheme of things.

*The Structure of the Argument*

In what follows, I argue that our existing system of public tort remedies frustrates its own purposes and should be reconstructed but that, hap-

pily, the essential elements of reform are well within reach. This argument consists of three linked parts. In part I, I present conceptual and
historical frameworks for thinking about how to control official misconduct through tort remedies. Chapter 1 explores this question at an
abstract level, isolating three aspects of the problem—the sources of
official misconduct, the forms and purposes of public tort law, and the
nature of rights and remedies—as a prelude to an evaluation and redesign of the remedial system. Chapter 2 traces the evolution of our
public tort remedies from their antecedents in medieval English common law, emphasizing the broad and historically anomalous pattern of
sovereign immunity for federal and state governments that has persisted to the present day and has left a significant remedial void.

In part II, I argue that reliance upon official liability for damages
to fill that void is unsound remedial policy and urge that a much-
broadened regime of governmental liability consistent with private law
principles supplant it except in the most unusual circumstances. Chapter 3 grounds this argument in a model of official behavior in which
fears of litigation and personal liability generate personal risk-
minimizing strategies that systematically neglect social consequences.
Chapter 4 considers the immunity doctrines and other arrangements
that help officials to avoid these risks by shifting them to their government employers or back to their victims. It concludes that far from
solving the problem of official self-protection, these risk-shifting arrangements actually have some perverse effects. Chapter 5 contrasts
expanded governmental liability with the current system, demonstrates that it would achieve our remedial goals at a far lower social cost,
and analyzes specific changes needed to produce such a regime.

Taking the proposed governmental liability system as a baseline, I
analyze in part III the conditions under which it might need to be
augmented by other modes of deterrence involving specific interventions into the low-level decision processes and I propose how government ought to go about this. Chapter 6 considers two possibilities: that
even a reformed system of governmental liability might not activate
internal bureaucratic controls over low-level misconduct and that even
if it did, they might not be wholly effective. It then suggests how
agencies themselves might intervene to strengthen those controls. Injunctive relief is an essential deterrent in public tort law, and chapter 7
argues that in its most intrusive forms, especially the "structural" injunction, extremely difficult problems of both implementation and
legitimacy confront courts. The concluding chapter suggests how injunctive remedies against government should be integrated into a re-

formed remedial system and argues that Congress, not the courts, should play the leading role in structuring and institutionalizing the remedial system for the future.

# PART I

## COMPLICATING THE PROBLEM

If we would design a just and effective system of public tort remedies, we must first ask ourselves how we wish to be governed. Some answers seem obvious enough. If the rule of law means anything, it means that in our political household, public servants are bound by the constitutional, statutory, and other rules that citizen masters have adopted to guide their affairs. As President Lincoln said, "It is as much the duty of Government to render prompt justice against itself in favor of its citizens as it is to administer the same between private individuals."[1] A credible and fair legal system should stand ready to remedy every significant invasion of rights; citizens injured by officials who violate established legal standards should be made whole. Errant officials should be obliged to pay for their transgressions, encouraging them to be more law-abiding, careful, and solicitous of the public they serve. Courts should enforce these obligations.

Although these norms may be taken as moral axioms from which our inquiry can proceed, they are actually poor and incomplete guides to the design of public remedies. In the first two chapters, I try to reveal their limitations by introducing two kinds of additional complicating considerations, one conceptual and analytical, the other historical and doctrinal. Together, they can help to lay the intellectual foundations for understanding both the defects of our present system and the possibilities of reform.

# 1:  A FRAMEWORK FOR THINKING
# ABOUT REMEDIES

---

A sound system of public tort remedies must take account of three realities, three challenges to the judicial imagination. First, official wrongdoing takes protean forms and springs from diverse sources, each of which demands a discrete, refined, and problem-specific response. I call this the problem of *remedial targeting*. Second, public tort law pursues multiple goals. These goals inevitably compete with one another, and only a delicate balancing of values can resolve the conflicts. Whether and how courts can strike this balance are questions of great policy significance requiring careful analysis. I call this the problem of *remedial form and purpose*. Third, courts conceive many public law rights through different processes from those through which those rights are actually vindicated. Institutional realities often mediate between right and remedy, compromising the one and confounding the other. I call this the problem of *remedial implementation*.

## The Problem of Remedial Targeting

A remedial system must fit the contours of the problem it seeks to ameliorate. So much is obvious, even tautological. What, then, is the morphology of official misconduct and what can it teach us about how public tort remedies should be designed?

We must begin by acknowledging that official misconduct is not one problem but many. Although official misconduct is readily defined—I take it to be an official's failure, whether intentional or not, to comply with a valid legal directive—its forms and sources are legion. In the following discussion, I attempt to reduce this complexity to manageable dimensions by distinguishing four exhaustive categories of causes or sources.[1] I call them failures of *comprehension, capacity, motivation,* and *care*. Here, I explore the logical structure and embedded

3

behavioral reality of each, deferring until part III a discussion of how each might be addressed.

## COMPREHENSION-BASED ILLEGALITY

The official to whom a legal directive is addressed cannot comply unless he understands what is expected of him, what the law requires. Let us view a public law regime as a specialized form of communication. The content of the message or signal consists of substantive norms and information about the circumstances under which sanctions will be imposed if the official violates them. Three features of a message primarily determine its communicative power, the probability that it will in fact be received and understood as the transmitting official or institution intends: the transmitter's ability to secure the target official's respectful attention, the message's amplitude or strength, and its clarity or freedom from distortion.

Any message transmitted to the field must compete with many other stimuli for the target officials' eyes, ears, minds, and perhaps hearts. Success depends not upon the message's importance to the transmitter but its salience to those who receive it. Officials barraged with messages from many sources—peers, clients, professional groups, the larger community, personal intuition—must somehow protect themselves against overload and avoid intolerable levels of dissonance. One form of self-protection is simply to screen out the superior's message. An analysis of the "flagrant noncompliance" with the Supreme Court's ban on school prayer five years after the decision, for example, found that officials "committed themselves to ignoring the Court's mandate as long as possible, apparently develop(ing) perceptual screens which enable them to avoid knowledge threatening or conflicting with the accommodations they have made."[2] The powerful informal culture of police work, because it overwhelms more formal legal norms, is an important source of corruption.[3] Lipsky discovered that many different types of street-level officials subjected to conflicting demands and information devised "coping strategies" to achieve some tolerable level of coherence.[4]

To be heard amid the din created by competing stimuli, a message's strength must persist until it reaches its destination. Like any impulses, however, bureaucratic messages tend to dissipate energy and strength as they pass through media. Journeying through layer after hierarchical layer, they generate friction, losing some of the power and immediacy that propelled them at their source. Thus, a state education agency's gleaming mandate to "mainstream" disabled children reaches the class-room teacher as a dull, routine, bureaucratic instruction to change record-keeping procedures.[5] A sweeping mandate from the courthouse to protect suspects' rights enters the station house as just one more insertion in the patrolman's tattered operations manual.[6] Transmission through bureaucratic strata not only mutes a message's volume and intensity but reduces its clarity. As it passes from promulgation to implementation, migrating from surging current to spent backwater, a message acquires impurities. In the process, a pristine statement of goals can become a lumpy stew of mutually conflicting ends and means. Pressman and Wildavsky, for example, detail how a federal job-creation program foundered on complex "technical details" that were unimagined by those who launched the program but that consti-tuted the operating realities of those down the line who had to carry them out. What they describe as the "separation of ideas from execu-tion" can transform even the clearest message into a confusing and conflicting Babel.[7] But when a message is ambiguous even at its source—as was some recent civil rights legislation, for exam-ple—violations are nearly inevitable, for no one (not even its authors) can be certain about what constitutes compliance.[8]

As a message passes through more hands (or lips), interference and distortion accumulate; recipients find it more difficult to grasp essential meanings. Multiple "clearance points," for example, helped to destroy the coherence and integrity of the jobs program that Pressman and Wildavsky studied.[9] Anthony Downs describes a "leakage of authority" that occurs as messages penetrate the bureaucratic depths; each translator's purposes and resources differ somewhat from those of the individuals above and below him, and each exploits these differences by altering the message.[10] "There are very few orders so precise and unequivocal," Downs maintains, "that they cannot be distorted by a factor of 10 percent" at each level, and for bureaucracies with inher-ently vague and undefined goals, the distortion factor may be far greater. The cumulative effect of many such leakages can be substantial.[11] Separate from the question of a message's qualities as finally received is the question of whether recipients understand it as the transmitter intends. The answer depends not only upon the message's own features but upon the recipients' training, conceptual apparatus, motivation, and environment (including competing mes-sages), as well as the legitimacy that they accord to the message's source and content.

Comprehension-based noncompliance deriving from misunderstanding appears common (or at least is commonly claimed). Small businesses often contend that job safety or environmental requirements are too complex to be understood and complied with. Police officials assert that Supreme Court rulings on arrest and interrogation procedures have rendered the law incomprehensible.[12] Teachers claim ignorance about the legality of disciplinary practices, and state and local governments make similar claims concerning the intricate requirements surrounding federal grants-in-aid.[13] In these domains as in many others, dispelling ignorance is costly.

### CAPACITY-BASED ILLEGALITY

Even officials who understand precisely what is demanded of them may be incapable of performing it. Their incapacity may be rooted in inadequate resources, practical impossibility regardless of the available resources, or both.

Noncompliance based upon insufficient resources is pervasive and assumes different forms according to the types of resources needed by the enterprise. Time, for example, may be a crucial constraint. When Massachusetts sought to implement far-reaching special education reforms, special education teachers could comply with the time-consuming new procedural requirements only by spending fewer hours with the children. In the end, time pressures undermined even formal compliance. As procedures were routinized, the "labeling" practices that the reforms sought to prevent persisted and even increased. Obliged to process more children in less time, teachers employed rules of thumb rather than making the individualized evaluations contemplated by the new law.[14] Information is another scarce resource that low-level officials need to change their *modus operandi*. A mental health or parole agency, for example, may be under a legal mandate to release those who can succeed in a less restrictive setting, but seldom can such agencies provide employees the data that might support reasonable predictions, for those data simply may not exist.

Policy flexibility in the field is often essential to compliance, yet it is a resource in short supply. The federal Office of Civil Rights, for example, wished to shift from its traditional "mailbag" approach, consisting of a sequential processing of complaints received from the public, to a more "proactive" policy stressing targeted compliance reviews of large institutions and other trouble spots. But the agency could not abandon its existing routines because of several factors—a court order mandating complaint-processing according to Draconian schedules, a poorly trained and demoralized staff at the lower levels, and constant accretions of new statutorily imposed responsibilities—over which it had little control at least in the short run.[15] Public employee unions may also inhibit policy flexibility. When the Syracuse police department, criticized for brutality, sought to discipline officers indicted for using excessive force, their colleagues refused to carry their nightsticks on duty and threatened to strike. When the new mayor of Philadelphia ordered the police department to restrict the use of firearms to officers in serious danger, the union sued the department and mobilized strong political oppositon to the new policy in the city council.[16]

Budget, of course, is a chronically scarce resource in most public service agencies, and resulting fiscal stringencies may encourage, even assure, illegal conduct. Welfare departments whose budgets are squeezed may interpret eligibility requirements more strictly or arbitrarily than the law permits. Drug enforcement operatives, unable to purchase the services of informers, may turn to illegal surveillance methods. Inadequate corrections facilities may compel prison officials to permit overcrowding that may violate the Eighth Amendment rights of inmates.[17] It follows that more funds can alleviate or eliminate some kinds of misconduct. If prison guards engage in physical brutality, different kinds of employees can be recruited or old ones retrained. If shelters for the homeless are inadequate, additional budget may purchase enlarged facilities.[18] More money may permit closer supervision of employees, better teaching materials, reduced case loads, and improved employee morale and performance—changes that may be essential to controlling official illegality.

The claim that adequate performance is precluded by insufficient resources, of course, is the first refuge of the harried bureaucrat. Although often true, however, officials' tasks are sometimes not feasible under *any* plausible circumstances. This may be due to inadequate know-how; the state of the art may simply be primitive. Higher education budgets for urban school systems would not assure high-quality instruction to all students, nor could better trained psychiatrists in state mental hospitals predict with perfect accuracy which patients can safely be released and which cannot.[19] Incapacity may also reflect the tendency in complex systems for compliance by one component to be neutralized by the adaptations of others. Enlarging prison facilities, for example, may not reduce overcrowding in the long run if the increased supply of cells creates its own (or fulfills a previously unsatisfied) demand.[20] When racial isolation persists or increases in major metropolitan areas due to busing-induced "white flight" to suburbs or private schools, an analogous effect upon compliance is evident.[21]

Finally, compliance may require a resource that neither time nor money can command. Police fail to provide adequate (or equal) protection in high-crime areas partly because neighborhood residents commonly refuse to cooperate in reporting crime and assisting investigations. If this reticence reflects a loss of trust and confidence in the police, it is not obvious how those feelings can be restored, at least in the short run. Where compliance is thwarted by systemic problems, only system-wide reforms are likely to make a difference. The problem of prison conditions cannot be addressed effectively unless many criminal justice processes, especially sentencing practices, are altered. Yet for many reasons, large-scale changes are seldom initiated in complex systems of this kind.[22]

### MOTIVATION-BASED ILLEGALITY

Officials may comprehend what the law requires and be fully capable of performing it but may nevertheless fail to comply because, all things considered, they do not wish to do so. Many motivations may incline officials toward noncompliance, sometimes decisively so. In chapter 3 I discuss how fear of personal liability or criticism, concern for personal safety or convenience, and sheer indolence may encourage self-protective, rather than dutiful, conduct. Other motives, including malevolence, ideology, peer pressure, avarice, or professional values, may induce similar behavioral effects. If these considerations loom large enough, they may override others that encourage compliance, including fear of sanctions or perceived legitimacy. Hospital administrators frequently instruct physicians not to order "unnecessary" laboratory tests, yet both theoretical and empirical evidence suggests that these directives are not heeded, largely out of fear of malpractice liability.[23]

Other incentives may also overwhelm the bureaucratic habit of obedience. Susan Rose-Ackerman shows that the working environments of certain officials create what amounts to monopoly power; in such cases, the prospect of substantial financial gain may encourage corruption.[24] Ironically, officials' intense commitment to their missions may encourage them to disobey agency directives. For example, many policemen viewed the *Miranda* decision (requiring police to warn suspects prior to interrogation without counsel present) as so drastic, so subversive of police goals as they perceived them, that they tended to ignore or undercut it.[25] Superiors may seek changes that threaten officials' prestige, autonomy, or professional self-image. Many special education teachers, for example, violated a new requirement that parents be intimately involved in assessing and planning for their learning-disabled children; noncompliance preserved the teachers' professional routines and independence from disturbance by untutored outsiders.[26] Similarly, corrections officials sometimes oppose on professional and ideological grounds court orders to release potentially dangerous prisoners from overcrowded facilities.[27]

If officials believe that compliance with a directive, although consistent with their values, would nonetheless have perverse effects, they may disobey it. A public housing authority member, for example, might personally favor racially balanced residential neighborhoods yet conclude that a court order requiring integrated housing projects would in fact impede that goal;[28] principle, in that situation, might tempt him to violate it. Even some policemen who embraced *Miranda*'s goals thought the decision unrealistic and unworkable in the context of actual law enforcement and looked for ways to circumvent it.[29] Of course, misconduct may also be dictated not by principle but by outright obduracy or malice.

Officials' need to create a tolerably pleasant work environment when they are stationed far from headquarters may be so intense that they accommodate themselves to illegality. The Forest Service devotes a good deal of attention to protecting its rangers from that temptation,[30] and federal meat inspectors have sometimes succumbed.[31] Many rookie policemen, despite departmental prohibitions against accepting favors, quickly become inured to the practice when they learn that ostracism by veteran officers can be intolerable.[32]

Paradoxically, fear of punishment may actually induce officials to violate rules, as Sykes's study of prison life illustrates. He observed a delicate symbiosis between guard and prisoner, one based upon mutual favors and threats. Guards almost inevitably violate some prison rules and permit prisoners to violate many others, both to create a web of future obligations and to "bribe" prisoners not to report guards' infractions to their superiors.[33] Similar motives may animate drug enforcement agents who violate rules in the presence of their informers, teachers who do so in the presence of students, and inspectors who enforce regulations selectively.[34] Fear of social and political reprisals caused some school officials to ignore or subvert the Supreme Court's decision banning school prayers.[35]

The perceived illegitimacy of a directive can be a powerful source of motivation-based noncompliance, for officials who regard a rule as lacking moral authority may be inclined to disobey it. Other things being equal, officials are more likely to regard as illegitimate rules that they believe are poorly conceived and personally damaging. Human psychology dictates this much. But legitimacy is empirically and analytically distinct from perceived efficacy and preference. A rule may be viewed as wholly legitimate by one who regards it as incompetent, morally perverse, and personally harmful. Antislavery judges enforced the fugitive slave laws for this reason.[36] By the same token, a rule may be regarded as both efficacious and desirable, yet illegitimate. Those who favor legalized abortion but view the Supreme Court's decision in *Roe* v. *Wade* as an unprincipled judicial usurpation occupy this position.[37]

Even at an analytical level, however, the boundary between non-compliance rooted in perceived illegitimacy and that rooted in perceived ineffectiveness and undesirability often dissolves. When a policeman condemns a judicial decision, it may well be because he believes that the court interpreted the Constitution erroneously; that it exceeded its jurisdiction; that it was unduly influenced by "procriminal" elements; that it failed to understand the real world of law enforcement; that the decision will make not only law enforcement more difficult but failure more likely; or that it can easily be circumvented by conscientious police, transforming otherwise law-abiding officials into criminals. These claims amount to assertions that the decision is incompetent, improperly motivated, uninformed, pernicious in its consequences, foolish in the extreme. At some point, their intensity and cumulative force may well (and with regard to *Miranda*, often did) ripen into something else: a conviction that the decision utterly lacks the elements that give judicial pronouncements their moral claim upon our respect and obedience.[38] Similar claims of illegitimacy, of course, may be lodged against rules issued by legislatures or agencies; statutes depriving officials of the right to strike[39] and police department rules restricting the use of firearms[40] are examples.

It is plausible to believe (though difficult to prove) that field officials sometimes regard directives from headquarters, the legislature, or the courts as not merely ineffective and undesirable but illegitimate. The workdays of the prison guard, meat inspector, patrolman, and classroom teacher have almost nothing in common with those of the officials who formulate the policies they must execute. This disparity of experience is probably highest in an urban police department or troubled school system, in which field operatives routinely confront markedly dangerous, unpleasant, or isolated conditions.[41] Facing fundamentally different and more frustrating realities than their remote bureaucratic superiors, operatives often feel remote and alienated from the source of formal authority in their agency. The cop patrolling his lonely beat, the social worker trudging through tenement after depressing tenement, the teacher cooped up in a room all day with rebellious teenagers—such officials tend to feel that they are doing the "real work" of the agency, while those in the front office are merely "shuffling paper," "playing politics," or perhaps even "selling out" the rank and file. It is the patrolman, not the police chief, who must maintain order, investigate crimes, respond to petty corruption, and interact with prosecutors and courts. It is the ward attendant, not the hospital administrator, who must empty bedpans, deal with sudden violent outbursts, and care for people whom the rest of the world has contrived to forget. It is the prison guard, not the warden, who must subdue and rehabilitate those whom society has already given up for lost.

In these common circumstances, a directive from a court or agency headquarters instructing low-level officials that they have not only failed to achieve an agency norm but have actually subverted it, that they must change their ways or face serious sanctions, and that the claims of outsiders have in effect been preferred to the claims of the agency's shock troops is, to say the very least, unwelcome. It is likely to be received with bitterness, cynicism, and an acute sense of betrayal. It will often seem illegitimate, since it does not rest upon a morally compelling source of authority such as expertise (the "school board has never taught in my classroom or any classroom"), loyalty to the "real" organization ("the chief is more concerned with his pals in City Hall than with us cops on the beat"), realistic understanding of the situation on the street ("if we can't use our informers and protect them, we can't stop the drug traffic"), or consistency with organizational norms and mission ("we're supposed to punish hardened criminals, but the warden says to coddle them"). Orders from the top, then, will often be seen by those at the bottom as ill-informed, insensitive, self-serving, cowardly, disloyal, and unrealistic. They will trigger the resentments and self-justification we feel when we believe that our self-sacrifice and hard work have been ignored, dismissed, or rebuked. Most officials will probably obey nonetheless; their sense of duty or fear of sanctions may be too intense, or their sense of helplessness in the face of authority too abject. But some, perhaps many, will not. As one study of successful organizational change put it:

> Those persons seeking to change the organization . . . must win
> the trust of their colleagues: trust that they will respect the tradi-

tional values and missions of the agency and will not embarrass
their . . . colleagues or reflect poorly upon the organization . . .
Without it, attempts to change will invariably be subverted from
within, irrespective of the formal authority of the change-
seekers.[42]

The problem of motivation-based noncompliance may be recapitu-
lated more generally. Officials ordered to abandon familiar practices
perceive in the mandated change the prospect of incurring costs, if only
the cost associated with having to learn new tricks. Their responses
cannot readily be predicted, even when the costs of compliance and
change seem substantial and the benefits nonexistent. Like all of us,
they possess some "zone of indifference" (to use Chester Barnard's
phrase[43]), some respect for the law and compulsion to duty even when
they pinch. Nevertheless, situations arise—especially in the environments in which many street-level officials work—in which disobedience seems to be the best course, all things considered.[44] Relatively
free of close supervision, they incur little risk of detection. Their misconduct may harm people who are not well situated to invoke sanctions
against them. Their relationships with professional peers whose opinions are unusually salient may sometimes lead them astray. Against this
array of incentives, even effectively communicated and clearly legitimate rules may in the end be disregarded.

NEGLIGENCE-BASED ILLEGALITY

Finally, officials may understand what a rule requires and be both
able and willing to perform it, yet act improperly (or fail to act) through
simple neglect. The many sources of negligence-based illegality have
little in common; they are as varied as the elements of human
frailty—carelessness, forgetfulness, low intelligence, poor coordina-
tion, lack of curiosity, slothfulness, fatigue, tension, passivity, distrac-
tion, and many others. For that reason, I do not analyze them further
here. But it is important to recognize that these are almost certainly the
most common sources of official misconduct. As the courts have steadily expanded public tort remedies for negligence[45] and enlarged the
dimensions of what constitutes negligence,[46] misconduct of this kind
has come under increasing judicial scrutiny. The Supreme Court, for
example, recently invalidated under the due process clause a state's
inadvertent delay in scheduling a fact-finding conference within the
statutorily required time.[47]

In this section, I have explored one determinant of judicial effectiveness—courts' ability to target their remedial weapons on the particular conditions that cause official misconduct. The analysis implies that they are seriously and systematically limited in doing so. Courts cannot significantly improve officials' comprehension of legal rules, except perhaps by reformulating those relatively few rules that courts devise themselves. Nor can they much affect official capabilities; they do not control resources and they cannot make feasible a task that is not so. Courts can influence the motivations of officials to some degree, largely by legitimating controversial directives and increasing the costs of noncompliance through liability rules and injunctive decrees. And they can discourage official negligence through similar means. Each of these levers, as we shall see, is problematic, though for somewhat different reasons. In the next section, I suggest one overarching limitation upon judicial remedies—the effect of remedial form and purpose upon courts' intrusiveness and ability to regulate official behavior.

## The Problem of Remedial Form and Purpose

What social goals do public tort remedies serve? To the lay observer (indeed, to many practical lawyers), this question may seem odd. Remedial doctrine, far more than substantive and procedural law, seems largely self-contained, driven less by exogenous social purposes than by its own rules, internal logic, and systemic necessities, such as consistency with other doctrines, administrative feasibility, and institutional relationships. As chapter 4 suggests, immunity rules exemplify this influence of "internal," system-sensitive factors.

In truth, however, remedies for public torts are predominantly artifacts of public policy animated by public purposes. These purposes seem self-evidently desirable when stated, yet because they tend to conflict, each remains controversial. By shaping remedies in one way rather than in another, we alter the mix of goals advanced and sacrificed as well as the trade-offs between them.

In this section, I present a central theme of this book—that the form of a public tort remedy profoundly affects how a court can use it to influence official behavior. This connection is not obvious. Unlike substantive and procedural rules of public law, which explicitly prescribe how officials ought to behave, remedies prescribe only the form that relief shall take. Not only do they often fail to call attention to their independent behavioral effects; they may deliberately endeavor to conceal them.[48] And even when a remedy does reveal its behavioral content on its face, as with a mandatory injunction, it is the remedy's effect upon the defendant *official* or *agency* that is explicit, not its effect upon the *court*. But a remedy can shape *official* behavior only by first affecting *judicial* behavior; how a remedy influences officials depends not simply upon the court's ability and willingness to invoke it but, more interestingly, upon how the court intervenes in the defendant's decisionmaking milieu. Yet it is precisely these effects upon judges, ultimately so crucial to the control of official misconduct, that are most opaque. It is as if we tried to fully apprehend a musical composition simply by knowing the notes that comprise it without caring whether it takes the form of a march or a scherzo, a rondo or a fugue.

To trace the linkages between the forms and regulatory capacities of public tort remedies, we must first consider how different remedies imply different judicial behavior-shaping capacities and then analyze the social goals of public tort law in light of those implications.

### RELATING REMEDIAL FORM TO JUDICIAL INTRUSIVENESS

The ability of a particular tort remedy to control official misconduct depends upon what a court must know and do in order to effect it. We may usefully approach this question by imagining a remedial continuum, defined by the extent to which a remedy, to be effectively deployed, requires *judicial intrusiveness*—that is, requires the court to comprehend and control either the sources of the particular misconduct or the means to eliminate it (which, as we saw in the first section, are not necessarily the same thing). (The continuum may also be defined according to the reciprocal of judicial intrusiveness, *official freedom*—that is, the extent to which a remedy leaves officials and their superiors free to decide whether and how to reduce or eliminate the misconduct.) By arraying each public tort remedy along this continuum from left to right, depending upon how much judicial intrusiveness the remedy characteristically entails, we achieve a first approximation of this remedial continuum (figure 1):

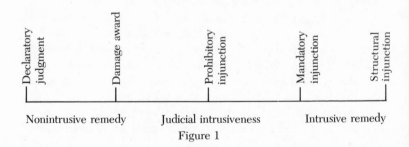

| Declaratory judgment | Damage award | Prohibitory injunction | Mandatory injunction | Structural injunction |

Nonintrusive remedy            Judicial intrusiveness            Intrusive remedy

Figure 1

At the continuum's extreme left end, the nonintrusive pole, we locate the declaratory judgment. This remedy neither prescribes how defendants ought to behave nor compels them to do, or refrain from doing, anything. It merely pronounces particular practices or conditions to be illegal, leaving defendants free to respond as they see fit. Moving toward the intrusive pole, we next encounter the damage award. Although this remedy, unlike the declaratory judgment, has a palpable "bite," the court's only intervention consists of assessing the harm that defendants' misconduct has caused plaintiffs. Once it makes this collective evaluation of the misconduct and imposes this cost upon defendants, however, the court's role is at an end; it need not concern itself with the particulars of how defendants respond. The court prices only the *outcomes* that officials cause, not the particular activities that may have caused them. Damages are assessed only retrospectively; they are an ex post remedy that comes into play only after harm has occurred (although it is intended to deter future harm as well).

At the "intrusive" end of the continuum are the injunctive remedies. The least intrusive of these is the "prohibitory" injunction. Unlike a damage remedy, it does not leave defendants free to continue wrongful conduct even if they are prepared to compensate victims for the collectively (court)-calculated cost of misconduct. Instead, the prohibitory injunction specifies certain conduct as wrongful and prohibits defendants from engaging in it. It leaves defendants free either to choose any *other* course of action, or to purchase plaintiffs' consent to dissolve the prohibition. Thus, a prohibitory injunction supplants the decisional autonomy and initiative of officials or agencies, but only to a limited, specified degree. The court may have difficulty resolving the substantive liability issue (that is, whether a particular official act or practice ought to be proscribed); to decide it, the court may have to understand a good deal about how particular governmental functions are executed. But beyond satisfying itself that its specific prohibition is justified, the court need not know how those functions should be discharged in the future.

The "mandatory" injunction, which requires defendants to take specified affirmative actions, is even more judicially intrusive. In practice, prohibitory and mandatory injunctions may be quite similar; each can be designed to have the same actual effect as the other. In principle, however, the difference is important. With a mandatory injunction, the court does not simply exclude particular choices from defendants' opportunity set, leaving them free to adopt any other; it actually displaces defendants' judgment and substitutes its own. The mandatory injunction therefore requires the court to know much more about the technology for achieving whatever public values are within defendants' keeping.

The difference between prohibitory and mandatory injunctions, in terms of how much a court must know and do to design and implement them, is most apparent when a "structural" injunction is sought.[49] Located at the remedial continuum's most intrusive end, the structural decree is essentially an extreme version of the mandatory injunction, an affirmative regulatory regime in which the judge attempts to transform the behavior of an entire bureaucratic structure—for example, a mental hospital, prison, public housing program, or government agency—through a more or less detailed order.[50] Implementing a structural injunction ordinarily entails an expansive, continuing judicial role in which the court must prescribe, monitor, and sometimes actually perform the administrative activities that might generate the desired outcome. Unlike damages, structural injunctions are prospective and predictive in methodology and preventive in aspiration. To a far greater extent than in mandatory injunctions, the court specifies the particular behavior that will constitute compliance and closely supervises the offending bureaucracy to ensure that it is forthcoming.

It must be stressed that the prohibitory, mandatory, and structural injunction categories are only analytic constructs, useful for illuminating reality but not constitutive of it. No bright line separates them; they occupy segments of, rather than fixed points on, the remedial continuum (another analytic construct) and flow into one another imperceptibly.

RELATING JUDICIAL INTRUSIVENESS TO REMEDIAL GOALS

Public tort law implicates five primary social goals or constraints: to deter wrongdoing, to encourage vigorous decisionmaking by officials, to compensate victims of official misconduct, to exemplify society's moral principles, and to achieve institutional competence and legitimacy. Each remedy affects each of these, as well as the balance between them, somewhat differently; each also taps judicial energies in distinct ways. This implies, then, a sixth goal: to achieve the optimal mix of these other preeminent values.

1. *Deterrence*. Society clearly wishes to discourage official wrongdoing, to reduce the probability that it will occur. This statement does not imply any particular way to attain such an objective. More severe sanctions, for example, may actually reduce deterrence if they discourage the sanctioning authority from imposing them.[51] Deterrence can

be enhanced by encouraging supervision and legal challenge, or blunted by shifting the risks of litigation and liability to others.[52] Which remedies deter particular behavior, then, is ultimately an empirical question, but one that is so elusive that the inquiry must be informed largely by theoretical speculation.

Guido Calabresi has developed a taxonomy of deterrence, distinguishing between "general" (or "market") deterrence and "specific" (or "collective") deterrence.[53] His analysis primarily concerns how substantive liability rules and other regulatory techniques aimed at reducing the costs of accidents ought to be designed. For reasons discussed in chapter 3, Calabresi's prescriptions are somewhat less useful in the public law context. Nonetheless, his categories can help to refine our understanding of the relationship between remedies' forms and regulatory effects. *General deterrence* operates by collectively measuring the costs imposed by an activity without evaluating either that activity or the actor who generated it. It envisions that individuals decide how to behave by calculating the personal benefits of engaging in activities and balancing them against the costs for which liability rules, the engines of general deterrence, will tax them. It contemplates, and counts it a virtue, that different individuals will respond to a liability rule in different ways. In contrast, *specific deterrence* operates through a self-conscious evaluation of particular activities (or actors) as wrongful or undesirable. Rather than leaving the choice of whether to engage in the disfavored activity to individuals, it prohibits the choice ex ante and punishes it ex post.

Each form of deterrence, like each remedy discussed earlier, relies upon a characteristic degree of judicial intrusiveness (and official freedom) and thus generates a distinctive set of behavioral influences. Calabresi's deterrence categories can therefore be useful in augmenting our remedial continuum, adding a dimension defined by the mode of deterrence that each remedy employs. At the nonintrusive end of the continuum are remedies that rely upon general deterrence. In this mode, a court need not second-guess the injurer's judgment or coerce him to make any particular decision. With damage remedies, for example, courts tax injurers with the cost of the injurious activity. Within that constraint, however, potential injurers may select whatever courses of action they believe will minimize the sum of injury and injury-avoidance costs. I say that courts tax "injurers" rather than "cheapest cost avoiders" (Calabresi's term) because in the context of the present discussion the question is not (as it is for Calabresi) whether injurers, victims, or third parties are most appropriately subjected to general deterrence pressures. Here, we assume that a violation of a recognized standard of official conduct has already been established, and the question is which remedy will best secure general deterrence.

Although the deterrence issue focuses now upon the question of public law remedy rather than private law liability, we must still search for the cheapest cost avoider, albeit within a more restricted field. Here, the question becomes which of the possible public defendants—the individual official, the agency, or the government as a whole—can maximize general deterrence and minimize the sum of injury and injury-avoidance costs; our remedial choice is between "official liability" and some form of "governmental liability." From a general deterrence perspective, governmental liability possesses two advantages over official liability. First, it implies minimal judicial intrusiveness. Although deciding whether a substantive violation has occurred may sometimes require the court to consider questions of official means-ends rationality, once the violation is established, the court need not inquire further into precisely how the misconduct is to be prevented in the future or even be able to identify the particular official who misbehaved. Courts need only assess damages accurately—the quintessential common law judicial task. The government, confronted by a new cost, remains free to respond to that constraint as it sees fit. Second, the government is often (though not always) the cheapest cost avoider. Because it can influence many of the incentives, communications, constraints, and conditions that shape officials' behavior on the street, it can deploy a broad repertoire of policy responses.

Consider a damage judgment against a city resulting from an illegal arrest by a police officer. The police department can respond by ordering additional training, new arrest guidelines, more and closer supervision, different recruitment and promotion policies, internal discipline, and the like. It may conclude instead that the benefits of illegal arrests outweigh the costs of anticipated adverse judgments or that in any event, it can protect its budget from being taxed with those costs. In either case, it might decide to seek changes in the law or confine such arrests to situations in which complaints by suspects are least likely. Alternatively, it might issue a warning to officers but take no steps to enforce it.

Thus, the distinctive feature of general deterrence—that it minimizes what a court must know and do in order to achieve compliance while maximizing defendant's ability to adapt creatively to the new incentive—is both virtue and vice. It is a virtue insofar as it encourages efficient allocation of resources, low administrative costs to the regulator (here, the court), responsiveness to changing conditions, and decisional autonomy. It is a vice, however, insofar as the court, by not prescribing or limiting how defendant shall adapt, prevents outsiders (including the court itself) from predicting the actual response. As we shall see in chapter 6, governmental liability magnifies this unpredictability. Large public organizations cannot or will not always control conduct in the field; general deterrence may therefore elicit low-level behavior that confounds both judicial and agency predictions. Society, then, should resort to general deterrence most readily when it is relatively indifferent as to which of the possible adaptations defendant actually selects.

It follows from this analysis that official liability for damages, which also rests upon general deterrence, is somewhat closer to the center of the remedial continuum. This is not because the court's role is significantly different (although official liability does require judicial determination of the perpetrator's identity) but because official liability can elicit a more limited set of responses than governmental liability; thus, in the example of illegal arrests, most of the options I mentioned are simply not available to a solitary officer. This assertion, however, must be qualified in one important respect. Although subject to personal liability, the official may be able to shift that risk to the government either by law or by contract—through provision for immunity, indemnification, insurance, and/or legal defense at public expense. Depending upon how these arrangements are designed, official liability for damages may be more or less judicially intrusive and adaptation-limiting than governmental liability. These matters are analyzed in part II.

At this point, two further refinements should be noted. First, a remedy that in form relies heavily upon specific deterrence and is therefore intrusive and adaptation-limiting on its face—say, an injunction requiring an agency to terminate a certain activity—may in practice be so unenforced and "toothless" that it in fact belongs at the nonintrusive end of the continuum. Doubtless, this is a large set. Second, the details of a remedy's design determine more precisely than its general form where it is located on the continuum—that is, how judicially intrusive it is. A mandatory injunction, for example, may contain few requirements drafted with great generality; similarly, liability rules with which a damage remedy is associated may define a wrongful activity with inhibiting specificity.

With these qualifications in mind, we can complete the remedial continuum, with the injunctive remedies, positioned as in figure 1, occupying the specific deterrence side. Three refinements are appropriate here as well. First, the deterrence that an injunction exerts is made less specific and more general to the extent that defendants are permitted to bargain or buy their way out of the particular obligations it imposes. This possibility depends upon several factors, including the number and inclination of plaintiffs, the degree to which the decree's requirements are viewed as integrated parts of a whole, and the court's willingness to modify the decree when the parties wish to do so. Second, the distinction between governmental and official liability remedies is of little practical importance where injunctions are concerned. Certain immunities available to individual officials in damage actions apparently cannot be claimed in injunction actions,[54] and as I explain in chapter 2, injunctive relief against individual officials has long been used to circumvent governmental immunities.

Before turning to remedial purposes other than deterrence, we can summarize the preceding discussion in a revised remedial continuum (figure 2):

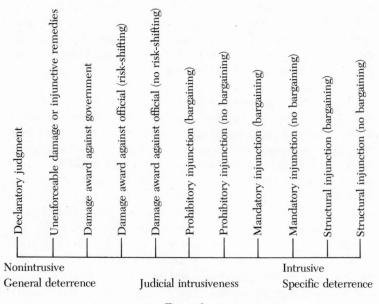

Figure 2

2. *Vigorous Decisionmaking.* We have seen that society's fear of "underdeterrence," its desire to discourage official wrongdoing, generates an array of public tort remedies that secure that deterrence in distinctive ways—sometimes radically different, sometimes only marginally so. We saw that deciding *how* to deter requires choosing among remedies that involve varying levels of judicial intrusiveness into the decision environment. In theory, courts could attempt to minimize misconduct by pricing ex post all harms caused by official wrongs and assessing these damages against the malefactors (perhaps also prohibiting them from risk-shifting). Alternatively they could specify in injunctive decrees all that officials must do, prohibiting them upon pain of contempt from doing otherwise. In practice, of course, courts do neither; the one would paralyze official initiative and permit irreparable or socially unacceptable injuries, whereas the other would be too costly and would produce many incompetent decisions poorly adapted to the realities of governance.[55]

Instead, courts compromise between these two approaches, choosing remedial mixtures that reflect two sets of trade-offs, each of which balances deterrence against another social value that conflicts with it. One conflicting value is society's interest in encouraging officials to act promptly, decisively, and without excessive self-regard or calculation. The other is its interest in encouraging officials to accomplish the public's business in socially efficient, cost-minimizing ways. Taken together, these interests might be expressed as a social purpose—or perhaps more properly, a constraint—to avoid "overdeterrence" of officials. I shall call it the goal (or constraint) of *vigorous decisionmaking.*

Vigorous decisionmaking is a ubiquitous desideratum. We want policemen to follow up on suspicious behavior, teachers to maintain discipline in their classrooms, social workers to act decisively to protect abused children, prison guards to quell disorder, inspectors not to overlook violations, and supervisors to discharge irredeemably incompetent or malingering employees. Vigorous decisionmaking can be threatened from several quarters. One is cognitive or perceptual; the course of conduct that properly discharges official duty often seems indistinguishable as a practical matter from that which may be wrongful and trigger reprisals. Difficulty in distinguishing proper from improper behavior may reflect not only officials' moral obtuseness, low intelligence, or poor training but an error-prone decision environment and indeterminate legal standards. No clear line separates the proper use of force by a policeman in making arrests from that force which is deemed "excessive." Indeed, as that term implies, the conduct does not alter its essential nature or form as its legal consequences change; rather, it becomes wrongful only at the point where it becomes, in a sense, too much of a good thing.

There are other reasons why society cannot leave vigorous decision-making by officials to chance but must instead contrive it. Society's tools for influencing official behavior—liability rules, tort remedies, criminal sanctions, monetary compensation, training, and the like—are quite crude and undifferentiated relative to the nice judgments that the substantive law calls upon officials to make. The danger that manipulating those tools to deter undesirable conduct will also discourage conduct that we wish to permit or even encourage varies with the gap between the complexity and riskiness of the decisions that we entrust to officials and the refinement of our tools for controlling their behavior. Finally, as we shall see in chapter 3, the asymmetric distribution of the benefits and costs of official action means that officials who enjoy broad discretion to choose among different courses of action may use it to minimize personal risk rather than to maximize social welfare.

Vigorous decisionmaking and deterrence, official enterprise and official transgression, can never be wholly reconciled. Although different public tort remedies can combine them to different degrees, some conflict always remains. Society thus faces a fundamental and inescapable issue: How should these values be traded off against one another? This normative question (which conceals some extremely difficult empirical ones) has become particularly urgent in the light of recent Supreme Court decisions[56] that have dramatically expanded the remedial form—official liability for damages (with no assurance of full risk-shifting)—that most completely sacrifices vigorous decisionmaking to deterrence, thus raising the prospect of imbalance most acutely. This problem is fully explored, and a solution proposed, in part II.

3. *Compensation.* In principle, society wishes to compensate all innocent victims of official misconduct, to restore them insofar as possible to their preinjury state. But public tort remedies also serve ends other than compensation; for example, a damage award against a wrongdoer may deter future misconduct as well as compensate the victim. On the other hand, remedies can be devised that would compensate without deterring (e.g., social insurance paid out of general tax revenues) or deter without compensating (e.g., a monetary fine payable to the public fisc).

We value compensation, then, not simply because it can be used to deter illegality or serve corrective justice as between wrongdoer and victim, but because it achieves other goals as well. Compensation spreads losses, distributing the costs of official misconduct from the unfortunate victim to a larger group. Two widely accepted hypotheses in economic theory—that marginal utility to an individual from each additional dollar or other unit of value declines, and that most people tend to be risk-averse—imply that (other things being equal) spreading loss among many people will reduce total happiness less than would leaving one person to bear it. In the absence of a well-defined, socially accepted notion of equity or distributive justice, of course, these propositions cannot demonstrate that *A ought* to share in *B*'s loss—however great the loss to *B*, however trivial the share imposed upon *A*, and however more wealthy *A* is than *B*.

Although there is endless disagreement about whether tort law ought to advance some affirmative conception of a just distribution of wealth, almost everybody would agree that legal rules should not operate to the *systematic* detriment of the relatively disadvantaged in society.[57] Moreover, there is probably widespread agreement that loss-spreading through compensation is singularly justified when citizens are injured through no fault of their own by officials whose capacity (and perhaps even motivation) to injure has been created by the public for public ends. (Weak as these criteria are, the present system of public tort remedies appears to violate them, as we shall see in chapter 5.)

A final reason to compensate victims is to affirm the vitality of the rule of law and the morality of its norms. This purpose is not unique to compensatory remedies; for that reason, I discuss it separately in the next paragraph. Nonetheless, the fact remains that a regime of public tort remedies that consistently failed to compensate many innocent citizens victimized by official wrongdoing would have to be regarded as neither effective nor just.

4. *Exemplification of Moral Norms.* No social or moral order can sustain itself, much less flourish, unless it can affirm, reinforce, and reify the fundamental values that define it. By placing the moral and coercive powers of the state behind those norms, tort adjudication performs these central ritualistic, symbolic functions. When the law immunizes official violations of substantive or procedural rules, leaving their victims without remedy, the integrity and universality of those rules and their underlying public values are called into serious question. Only the weightiest considerations of public policy can be permitted to justify such outcomes. Official immunity, part II will suggest, may be appropriate in some circumstances but governmental immunity is not.

5. *Institutional Competence and Legitimacy.* Society has a funda-

mental interest in ensuring not only that "correct" remedial decisions are made but that they are made by the appropriate decisionmakers. The distribution among governing institutions of decisional power to fashion and implement public tort remedies must of course comport with constitutional norms; Congress may not punish official wrong-doers through bills of attainder and courts may not appropriate tax revenues to support their decrees. The distribution of remedial power should also reflect the distinctive competences and capacities of each institution; remedies are unlikely to be effective if they demand infor-mation, authority, or other resources that their authors are institution-ally unable to supply. Finally, exercises of remedial power should be perceived as morally legitimate by those who must comply with and execute them. The remedy's authority should be grounded in a sense of moral as well as legal obligation; as we saw earlier, this may depend upon its institutional source as well as its content.

Few public tort remedies raise serious issues of institutional compe-tence and legitimacy. These issues are raised most dramatically by structural injunctions, by means of which courts intrude deeply into bureaucratic structures to impose specific deterrence solutions. But they are also raised, though to a lesser degree, by damage remedies, by which courts affect how the incentives to design and locate appro-priate controls within bureaucracies are allocated among institutions. I explore these questions in parts II and III and the analysis leads to a proposed hierarchy of remedies, culminating in a strategy of remedial selectivity, in which the goal of institutional competence and legitimacy shapes how courts ought to proceed in remedying official misconduct.

6. *System Efficiency.* A final integrative purpose of the remedial system is self-evident. Society wishes to achieve as much deterrence, compensation, and moral exemplification as possible at the lowest so-cial cost, which includes any resulting sacrifice of vigorous decision-making and institutional competence and legitimacy. This implies, first, that where the primary goals conflict, we should select that mix that produces the greatest social welfare; and second, that the overhead or system costs of administering public tort remedies should be minimized. But without an agreed-upon social welfare function that can specify how these goals are to be traded off against one another, system efficiency may seem impossible to achieve—or to recognize when and if it is attained. If we cannot say, for example, how much deterrence we should be willing to sacrifice for a gain in vigorous decisionmaking or loss-spreading, how can we conclude that the pres-ent system is better, worse, or equivalent to any particular proposal for

change? Indeed, how can we coherently evaluate the system at all? This is a powerful challenge to an analysis of any system as complex and value-laden as public tort law. By the end of part III, I hope to have met it.

## The Problem of Remedial Implementation

The goals of public tort law remain problematic not because of an insufficiency of substantive and procedural rights but because remedies for effectively vindicating those rights are often elusive. In an ideal world, the distinction between right and remedy would have no significance. Rights, once recognized and defined, would be secure; citizens would enjoy them without the state having to intervene. Remedies would be superfluous, or at least nonproblematic. The law would operate like a mechanical system in which bodies move without friction.

In reality, certain rights do approximate these conditions; once authoritatively established, they are vindicated promptly and without question. A right may be self-actualized if it was created in an authoritative and legitimate fashion, if it is clearly defined, if its violations are both visible and salient to those who can claim it, if its observance requires relatively little change in existing values and institutional practices, and if the costs and benefits associated with those changes are distributed in ways that make enforcement likely.[58] Thus, a criminal defendant's constitutional right to refrain from taking the stand without adverse comment by the prosecution[59] will almost certainly be observed promptly and punctiliously by prosecutors and trial judges alike; similarly, manufacturers are unlikely to market a line of new automobiles that lack a visible safety feature, such as a tinted windshield or seat belt, that Congress has specifically mandated.[60] Here, the existence of a formal remedy strengthens, but is probably not essential to, compliance.

Even when a right is less clearly defined, its infringement less readily visible, and the incentive to cheat significant, a mere declaration of it may be much more than an empty gesture. A right for the violation of which no practicable remedy exists may still under certain conditions induce substantial compliance *ex proprio vigore*. Were this not so, one could not confidently purchase products at the grocery store, drive down a city street, or receive professional services from one's lawyer or physician. It is not the prospect of lawsuits, prosecutions, government investigation, or even loss of reputation that maintains commercial fraud at a tolerable level; in reality, those remedies are (as both parties presumably know) both costly and problematical.[61] Such rights are secured instead by nearly universal respect for the moral claims affirmed by the legal system as a whole.

Vindication of other rights, however, does depend upon an effective remedial regime. Particularly remedy-dependent are public law rights that are affected by decisions of low-level officials whose accountability to citizen right-holders must be mediated by opaque bureaucratic and political processes. It is precisely when adjudicating such cases that courts are most tempted to conflate right and remedy. To affirm that a right exists while furnishing no effective remedy threatens the unique stature, function, and potency of the legal order to which judges have consecrated themselves. The court's institutional power—its capacity to further the goals of the legal system by influencing the behavior and values of other participants—depends not only upon the acceptance of its rights declarations but upon the credibility of its sanctions. The moral content of judicial pronouncements, essential to their legitimacy, is enriched when abstract rights are reified. To the judicial mind, a right without remedy is illogical and a confession of impotence. Any gap between right and remedy, any lacuna in the remedial regime, disturbs the moral and logical symmetry of the legal order and profoundly disturbs its authority.

Yet the truth of the matter is that rights and remedies are utterly different legal phenomena—products of distinct reasoning processes employing distinct sources, methodologies, and decision criteria. Conceptions of justice that deny this disjunction are likely to be deeply flawed. Composing a symphony, after all, is not like designing a bridge; the same creative energies that yield rich sonorities do not necessarily produce soundly engineered structures. The unity of right and remedy fractures on the hard rocks of implementation. This fissure is widest in public tort law, where rights must often traverse broad domains of official and governmental immunity before they can be actualized.[62] Implementation of certain public law rights challenges the moral authority of courts, as we shall see. Yet only recently have courts begun to take that challenge seriously. This judicial insouciance, nourished by theories of judicial activism that treat implementation as little more than a minor detail,[63] also reflects a conventional conceptualization and rhetoric of rights that tends to beguile the judicial mind, encouraging it to underestimate the conflict between implementation of remedy and reification of right.

Although certain theories of law sometimes conceive of rights as nothing more than a contingent balancing of utilities in the pursuit of economic efficiency,[64] it is doubtful that many courts or citizens think of them that way. Most public law rights are instead conceived in abstract aspiration; they are expressed in the uncompromising, unconditional language of absolute entitlement, a visionary vocabulary purified of limiting, qualifying, or prudential impurities. Although often turning upon highly specific factual determinations, these rights invoke juridical relationships and claims based upon general norms. Indeed, precisely because these rights are based upon universalizing principles, being available to anyone who meets prescribed conditions, they enjoy a distinctive moral status. In contrast, remedies are highly particularized, requiring specific defendants to discharge certain obligations to specific plaintiffs and thus giving rights palpable, substantive meaning. Remedies are rooted in the here-and-now, rights in the world-to-be. Rights condemn the status quo and are invoked to initiate its transformation; remedies mobilize the status quo in order to complete it. Rights preoccupy a Don Quixote; remedies are the work of a Sancho Panza.

The reality of our legal system demonstrates that reifying rights is not always its overriding goal. Certain social conditions, such as citizens' ignorance of their legal rights and inability to afford litigation, carve deep chasms between legal entitlement and actualization, rebuking the legal order's claim to fairness and its commitment to secure rights. Other barriers to actualizing rights, such as traditional standing and immunity doctrines, are actually celebrated as bastions of that order. Although the reality of rights often belies their promise, the absolute quality of rights-talk still generates great rhetorical power. To the question "Why must the state treat one in such-and-such a manner?" law and conventional morality usually find the response "Because that is one's right" presumptively sufficient. The legal culture generally recognizes that rights are actually contingent; most judges, after all, were once practicing lawyers steeped in the empirical realities of conflict, cost, contest, and implementation, and they are accustomed to exerting the force of those claims against the remedial fulcrum. But rights remain prima facie immune from incursions by prudence, compromise, and utility.[65] This immunity lies at the heart of our system of law; it defines, as Charles Black has perceptively concluded, our *attitude* toward our fundamental liberties.[66]

Rights-talk, the abstract, elevated discourse of absolute principle, cannot always be translated into remedy-talk, the technocratic argot of utility, trade-off, and means-ends rationality. Even clear violations of right cannot be enjoined unless they first satisfy a series of essentially utilitarian, balancing tests.[67] Although courts insist that a state may not violate a citizen's constitutional rights simply because the legislature fails to appropriate funds necessary to secure those rights,[68] they seldom if ever mandate the appropriation.[69] Even procedurally, courts disjoin right and remedy, bifurcating many adjudications of claims of governmental illegality into liability and remedial phases.[70]

Finally, a right implies a unique end-state that the state is obliged to actualize; to speak of a different prescribed end-state is to speak of a different right. In contrast, a remedy is not uniquely determined but open-textured; it is constructed not through principled elaboration but in the exercise of prudence and policy. Not all remedies, however, are equally discretionary. Indeed, all can be arrayed along a spectrum defined by the extent to which adjudications of right uniquely determine a particular remedial form. At the "unique" pole are actions seeking a declaratory judgment or those seeking monetary damages in which the value of plaintiff's right is objectively quantifiable. At the "discretionary" pole are actions seeking a structural injunction to reconstitute a complex bureaucracy, ones in which "[t]he form of relief does not flow ineluctably from the liability determination, but is fashioned ad hoc."[71] Actions seeking damages for many difficult-to-value constitutional deprivations, and more limited equitable relief, would be located somewhere in between.

In sum, a court does very distinct things when it adjudicates a right and fashions a remedy. It reasons at different levels of abstraction, appeals to different kinds of justifications, employs different conceptual and linguistic strategies, and invokes different criteria of choice. These differences are largely captured in the problematics of remedial implementation. Courts know this, of course, but judges spend most of their time writing and talking about rights, not remedies, and their institutional endowment only confirms and strengthens this abstract preoccupation.[72] For courts as for the rest of us, habit and necessity are easily transformed into virtue. The danger is not simply that courts are too facile with rights-talk but that they will fail to recognize when that particular conversation and the distinctive intellectual style that animates it become inappropriate to the issues at hand. Like Odysseus before the Sirens' song, a judge approaching the remedial realm must anticipate the peril of comfortable but seductive self-delusion and take adequate precautions against it.

# 2: THE EVOLUTION OF
## AMERICAN PUBLIC TORT REMEDIES

The remedies that individuals may invoke against governmental wrongdoing inevitably reflect some normative conception of the relationship between citizen and state, some notion of the legal and political obligations that they owe one another. Remedies give substance to legal obligations by rendering them palpable and enforceable; they do the same for political obligations by structuring one mode of public participation in a political community. As the dominant conceptions of civil life change, new forms of remedies evolve. We should not be surprised to learn, for example, that criminal prosecution in England, a remedy now lodged firmly in the state, was as recently as the 1870s conducted by individual citizens,[1] or that United States citizens' legal standing to challenge administrative decisions has steadily expanded since New Deal days.[2] As the evolution of social reality outstrips our consciousness about that reality, we should expect to find vestigial remedies, shaped by earlier conceptions of justice but ill-suited to our emerging collective purposes. Conversely, remedial changes may advance and perhaps even transform our conceptions of public purpose. This has been most notably true of the civil rights injunction,[3] which I discuss in chapters 7 and 8.

In this chapter, I intend to show that our public tort remedies can usefully be understood in both of these ways—as legal sediment deposited by historical currents and as forces independently propelling those currents. I begin by recounting how subjects' remedies against the Crown and its officials developed prior to the American Revolution and then explore how remedies for federal government torts developed from the Constitutional period to the present. I next discuss liability for state and local government torts, especially the evolution of Eleventh Amendment immunity and of the principal federal court remedy for such wrongs, 42 U.S.C. § 1983. In a final section I consider recent trends in cognate areas of the law that have helped to fuel this remedial transformation.

One historical pattern will be of special interest. The notion that employers are legally responsible for employees' torts committed in the course of their duties, a remedial doctrine known to lawyers as *respondeat superior*, has received very different treatment in private and public tort law. Firmly established as a basis of private enterprise liability for damages by the beginning of the eighteenth century in England, the doctrine never took root in public tort law here; indeed, the Supreme Court expressly repudiated it as recently as 1981.[4] This disparity is all the more remarkable in view of several recent, rather striking convergences between public and private tort law. These include a rapid expansion of substantive liability[5] and a related functional transformation of private tort law from a system for adjudicating essentially private disputes into a self-conscious instrument of public policy in the activist state.[6]

Unfortunately, the precise reasons for this odd pattern of divergence and convergence remain shrouded in mystery.[7] The early rejection of enterprise liability in public tort law probably reflected ancient political conceptions emphasizing the organic unity of state and society. With the rise of nineteenth-century liberalism, which posited a more detached, instrumental relationship between citizen and state, these earlier conceptions gradually came to seem anachronistic, yet certain doctrinal residues remained. These doctrines survived because courts, wishing to remedy wrongs but reluctant to innovate more than necessary, managed to build around them, creatively adapting an old doctrine that discouraged remedies against official wrongs to new social and political conditions that demanded them. As we shall see, however, the emergence of the activist state has rendered the rejection of enterprise liability anomalous. The resulting adaptations, adequate perhaps to the needs of an earlier day, no longer seem defensible.

## The English Common Law Tradition

In 1765, as the storm of American rebellion gathered force, William Blackstone published his magisterial *Commentaries on the Law of England*. In it, he articulated what he took to be the fundamental principle governing legal redress against the Crown: "The King can do no wrong."[8] Part of the received corpus of English legal doctrine at least since Bracton had reported it in the thirteenth century,[9] this maxim was for Blackstone an implication of the royal prerogative, signifying that the Crown could not be brought to account without its consent in any terrestrial court. His concept of sovereign immunity (as the principle was known), which was to strongly influence generations of American lawyers and judges, reflected the dominant conceptions of sovereignty. Although some medieval lawyers thought the king as amenable to judicial process as the lowliest subject,[10] no less an authority than Francis Bacon, the celebrated lord chancellor of England under James I, ridiculed such "old fables."[11] Legal historians have confirmed Bacon's belief that common law writs (the forms of judicial process) never ran against the Crown without its consent.[12]

Victims of wrongs committed by the Crown, however, were not without remedy. From at least the thirteenth century on, any aggrieved individual could petition the king to grant relief through his courts. The king might refer such a "petition of right" to his council for decision; if the petition were granted, relief would issue just as in litigation against a private party. During the fourteenth century, petition procedures were regularized. Some petitions, roughly analogous to today's private bills,[13] were presented to Parliament, and if they fell within its competence and were approved by both Houses and the Crown, they emerged as statutes. Other petitions seeking nonmonetary relief might be referred to the king's chancellor or council. The petition of right thus became the chief instrument for vindicating subjects' claims against the Crown.[14]

A fourteenth-century case illustrates how this remedy worked. Robert de Clifton petitioned the king to redress the harm caused when royal agents flooded his land. After an inquiry was held and damages were computed, he petitioned the king to grant compensation in the form of a feudal grant, and a commission then issued certifying the king's grant.[15] Nineteenth-century commentators on the *de Clifton* and similar cases inferred that the petition of right was a limited remedy, available to challenge wrongful takings of property but not tortious conduct generally.[16] This view, however, failed to recognize that the medieval system, which did not conceive of tort and contract as distinct theories of legal obligation, made real property the locus of a broad range of legally protected interests. In place of a contract to pay money, for example, medieval law granted an annuity or "corody"—interests in the income from land.[17] The real actions of assize of nuisance, *quod permittat*, or *novel disseizin*, prefigured the modern action for nuisance.[18]

From an early period, then, the petition of right remedied many, though not all, officially inflicted injuries that later would be considered public torts. As royal administration became more elaborate and specialized, so did remedies against the Crown. During the fourteenth and fifteenth centuries, several remedies to recover property held by the Crown[19] displaced the petition of right to some degree, leaving its exact contours somewhat obscure.[20] Nevertheless, the petition remained the most important avenue of relief for subjects injured by official conduct.[21] The availability of these remedies certainly colored the meaning of the Blackstonian maxim. It could not have meant, as Blackstone had implied, that the king was above the law; instead, it must have meant only that the king was not privileged to injure his subjects and would not ordinarily suffer wrong to be done to them without remedy.[22]

For purposes of the present inquiry, the important point is that these remedies did not constitute acceptance by the Crown of any general principle of liability for nonproprietary wrongs committed by its agents. Indeed, they allowed the courts to delay for centuries any necessity to consider a broad theory of Crown responsibility in tort, such as *respondeat superior*. They permitted the maxim that "the King can do no wrong" to survive as a credible public law doctrine by minimizing the occasions in which it caused injustices that might call its validity into question.

As feudal tenures were gradually supplanted by commercial relationships during the seventeenth century, the modern development of remedies against the Crown commenced. Much of this development occurred in the Court of Exchequer, the royal organ that adjudicated claims concerning the Crown's revenues. In 1668, that court decided the *Pawlett* case, in which a landowner had sought to redeem a mortgage on his property held by the Crown. The attorney general contended that plaintiff's sole remedy was to petition the king to permit redemption as a matter of grace, but the court instead ordered the redemption, with one judge stating the following ground for equitable relief: "The party ought in this case to be relieved against the King, because the King is the fountain and head of justice and equity; and it shall not be presumed that he will be defective in either. And it would derogate from the King's honour to imagine that what is equity against a common person, should not be equity against him."[23] Equitable relief against the Crown was confined to the Court of Exchequer through the first half of the nineteenth century,[24] but the Glorious Revolution of 1688 nourished other remedial growth. The seminal *Bankers' Case*, which concerned the Crown's default on a secured loan, acknowledged a remedy against the Crown in the Court of Exchequer for contractual undertakings for a sum certain, either through petition of right or through the special writ of *liberate*.[25] With the *Bankers' Case*, then, the English courts began to impose liability upon the Crown for certain contractual violations by royal employees that would have been actionable if committed by private citizens. Official *torts*, however, were treated quite differently.

Holmes later traced the doctrine of *respondeat superior* to the absolute liability of a master for the wrongs of his slave under ancient law,[26] but the doctrine had virtually disappeared by the end of the twelfth century.[27] "*Respondeat superior*," as a term, first appeared in English law in the Statute of Westminster in 1285.[28] It began not as a principle of unconditional liability for the wrongs of one's servant but rather as a kind of surety arrangement, under which the master might be liable only if the servant failed to pay a judgment.[29] For several centuries, *respondeat superior* in private law was limited to situations in which the master commanded, authorized, or ratified the wrong.[30] Gradually, other enclaves of *respondeat superior* were recognized: certain customary liability rules of the law merchant;[31] strict statutory liabilities, such as those of sheriffs and jailers;[32] the common law liabilities of innkeepers, common carriers, and perhaps smiths and surgeons, as well as those of individuals whose servants allowed fires to escape control and injure others;[33] and, by the late sixteenth century, admiralty rules derived from Continental law establishing the liability of shipowners for torts of their crews.[34] On the whole, however, *respondeat superior* in private law remained an exceedingly narrow remedy up to the late seventeenth century; indeed, on the eve of the *Bankers' Case*, a court could still summarize the general rule thus: "If I command my Servant to do what is lawful, and he misbehave himself, or do more, I shall not answer for my Servant, but my Servant for himself, for that was his own Act,—otherwise, it was the Power of every Servant to subject his Master to what Actions or Penalties he pleaseth."[35]

It remained for Sir John Holt, lord chief justice of King's Bench, to transform *respondeat superior* from a doctrinal backwater, consisting of narrow exceptions to the nonliability of employers for damages caused by employees, into a broad remedial mainstream. In a series of private tort cases beginning in 1691,[36] Holt advanced sweeping, unqualified formulations of the principle, drawing support from diverse legal and policy justifications—the master's implied consent; the legal identity of master and servant; the superior deterrent ability of the enterprise; and plaintiff's detrimental reliance upon the servant's apparent authority—while ignoring more traditional grounds for decision.[37] This judicial tour de force was decidedly successful, and by the late eighteenth century enterprise liability was permanently lodged at the center of private tort law both in England and in America,[38] a reception so complete that the Supreme Court in 1852 viewed the principle to be "of universal application."[39]

But if private law assimilated enterprise liability with alacrity, public law found it quite indigestible. Here, too, the doctrine suited Chief Justice Holt's taste, but success eluded him. In *Lane* v. *Cotton*, a 1701 decision concerning postal employees' alleged negligence, the King's Bench affirmed the principle that although the Crown was immune, its servants were individually liable for any wrongs committed in the course of their employment. Holt, however, wished to go further. Appealing to the conservative inclinations of his judicial colleagues, he analogized to the long-standing rule of strict liability of jailers and sheriffs for injury to their charges, concluding that the postmaster general himself should be liable in damages for his employees' negligence: "Such matter is transacted among a multitude of people, and therefore no particular of them can be charged; and therefore the officer ought to be charged, who chuses such inferior officers."[40] To the objection that such broad exposure of supervisors to liability will "ruin the office," Holt asserted that "it will make them more careful."[41] Nevertheless, the majority of judges in *Lane* rejected Holt's invitation to import broad enterprise liability into public tort law, a refusal that continues today. The *personal* tort liability of public officials, affirmed in *Lane*, seemed a workable compromise between the rule of sovereign immunity and the injustice of denying liability altogether. Seized upon as an important circumvention of sovereign immunity, official liability was promptly extended in other cases.[42]

Why was a principle so resourcefully and enthusiastically embraced by private tort law rejected so unceremoniously for public torts? Pending further historical research, we can only speculate as to the answer. Perhaps judges were intimidated by the notion of sovereignty implicit in "the King can do no wrong" or were guided by an intuition that governmental activity was, in ways not then articulated, unique in remedially relevant respects. Perhaps in 1701, a time when the Crown's limited domestic activities occasioned few injuries to subjects and when many government functionaries, such as tax collectors and jailers, were independent contractors rather than employees of the Crown, official liability seemed a serviceable remedy, adequate to the needs of a largely agrarian society. Whether it remains so today, when an activist state is a ubiquitous injurer, is a very different question addressed in part II.

As the English courts were working out their accommodation with sovereign immunity and enterprise liability, a new state was emerging across the Atlantic. Rooted in the soil of English common law, the American bench and bar naturally turned to this tradition for guidance and precedents. What they were to find, however, was a public tort law reflecting a political and legal culture that increasingly diverged from their own.

### The American Sequel: Liability for Federal Government Torts

The Framers of our Constitution did not write on a *tabula rasa*. Many were eminent practitioners of the common law who surely knew that the English sovereign's immunity, though complete in principle, was highly qualified in practice. Yet even then, fundamental discontinuities between the English and American experiences were evident. First, the older system located political sovereignty in the Crown, whereas the newer one placed it not in the state but in the people. Because the government's obligation to the governed flowed from different sources, it came to be defined in different ways. Moreover, English public law was unified, but the American equivalent was far more complex and fragmented, distributed among federal, state, and local systems. In addition, governmental activity in the two societies, and thus the patterns of injurious official conduct, would develop along different historical paths. In England, a tradition of extensive state intervention, which Adam Smith denounced in the very year of American independence, was well entrenched.[43] In America, in contrast, government would remain a limited, reactive institution until industrialization, modern warfare, and massive economic dislocation summoned it to new tasks. Finally, the American judiciary, established by a written Constitution and heir to a tradition in which constitutional review of official conduct by courts was legitimated by its anti-Crown associations,[44] would fashion public law norms and remedies in ways alien to English courts.

Article III of the Constitution extended the federal judicial power to cases between a state and citizens of another state; cases between a state and foreign states, citizens, or subjects; and cases to which the United States was a "party." To lawyers, at least, the meaning of this provision was far from clear. Read literally, it seemed to abrogate governmental immunity altogether, for the text did not expressly distinguish between cases in which governmental entities were plaintiffs and cases in which they were defendants. On the other hand, Article III might plausibly be understood to have incorporated *sub silentio* the English common law tradition of governmental immunity waivable only with government's express consent. (Little is known about immunity doctrines in the colonial courts,[45] but at least one court upheld a state's claim of immunity during the Confederation period.[46])

Although much turned upon which interpretation was correct, the Constitutional Convention did not explicitly debate the issue. Under the Articles of Confederation, the national government had lacked the power to tax and actually defaulted on much of its accumulated debt,[47] whereas the national courts had very limited jurisdiction; indeed, suits against the confederation had to be brought in the state courts.[48] The Constitution clearly envisioned a stronger national judiciary. Article III extended the jurisdiction of the federal courts "to Controversies to which the United States shall be a Party,"[49] but records of the Convention debates shed no direct light upon whether "party" was meant to include party-defendant as well as party-plaintiff, and if it did, whether the duality applied only in those cases in which the United States *consented* to be sued.

In *Chisholm* v. *Georgia*, Chief Justice Jay addressed this question, albeit only in *dictum*. Jay had already argued that the phrase "Controversies between a State and Citizens of another State," by failing to distinguish between cases in which the state was plaintiff and was defendant, implied that jurisdiction extended to *both*.[50] Conceding that the same logic, when applied to the phrase "Controversies to which the United States shall be a Party," seemed to compel the conclusion that the United States was not immune either, Jay pointed to "an important difference" justifying federal, but not state, immunity: "in all cases of actions against States or individual citizens, the National Courts are supported in all their legal and Constitutional proceedings and judgments, by the arm of the Executive power of the United States; but in cases of actions against the United States, there is no power which the Courts can call to their aid."[51] Jay's reasoning has not persuaded his successors; after all, if impediments to implementing a decree implied lack of Article III jurisdiction, many of the Court's most significant decisions, from *Marbury* v. *Madison*[52] to *United States* v. *Nixon*,[53] would themselves have been unconstitutional. Nevertheless, Jay's conclusion that the United States was constitutionally immune was later reaffirmed in *dictum* by Chief Justice Marshall[54] and in the holding of an 1846 decision.[55]

To the Supreme Court of the early nineteenth century, the immunity of the United States rested not simply upon the English precedents, the ascribed intent of the Framers, and the exegetics of Article III. It also reflected firm considerations of governance. Although the Court did not directly address the federal immunity issue until 1846, earlier cases dealing with the legal effect of official delay ("laches") had articulated the "great public policy" underlying immunity:

The government can transact its business only through its agents; and its fiscal operations are so various, and its agencies so numerous and scattered, that the utmost vigilance would not save the public from the most serious losses, if the doctrine of laches can be applied to its transactions. It would, in effect, work a repeal of all its securities.[56]

This notion, penned by Mr. Justice Story, reflected a more general principle asserted in the 1844 edition of the justice's treatise on agency:

The government itself is not responsible for the misfeasances, or wrongs, or negligences, or omissions of duty of the subordinate officers or agents employed in the public service; for it does not undertake to guarantee to any person the fidelity of any of the officers or agents, whom it employs; since that would involve it, in all its operations, in endless embarrassments, and difficulties, and losses, which would be subversive of the public interests.[57]

On the face of it, this policy argument amounted to a non sequitur. Story neither explained what specific types of evils would result from the government's operations nor suggested how, if at all, such consequences differed from those flowing from private conduct concededly subject to the ancient rule of *respondeat superior*. Still less did he justify why, even if his premises were granted, the government should be absolved of responsibility for its agents' wrongs. Story's *ipse dixit*, however, retained unquestioned vitality and authority through the Civil War period, often palliated by the assertion that a legislative remedy, the private bill, was available.[58] Congress had indeed enacted many private bills to relieve victims of federal torts, the earliest of which was passed in 1792 (one year prior to the *Chisholm* decision), compensating a school damaged by American troops during the Revolution.[59] Private legislation, however, was apparently burdensome and subject to political abuses.[60]

So firmly entrenched was the tort immunity of the United States at the time of the Civil War that when Congress established the Court of

Claims in 1863 to adjudicate claims against the United States (an advisory body had been created in 1855),[61] jurisdiction was limited to contract claims; tort claims were explicitly barred.[62] One must admire the lawyerly ingenuity of plaintiffs' counsel in seeking to avoid this prohibition. In *Langford* v. *United States*, for example, federal agents forcibly occupied land claimed by plaintiff. His counsel cited the "King can do no wrong" maxim, contending that the occupation could not have been a tort. If not a tort, he argued, it must have been a taking for which "just compensation" must be paid under the Fifth Amendment. The Court, however, responded with its own gambit: Since "we have no king to whom [the maxim] can be applied," a public tort might indeed have been committed, but the Court of Claims was not empowered to adjudicate it; thus, plaintiff's only recourse was to attempt to secure private legislation.[63]

Such harsh results, of course, could not have been congenial to judicial sensibilities accustomed to remedying established wrongs. The Court found relief in the same fiction that John Marshall had employed against state officials in *Osborn* v. *Bank of the United States* and that Justice Peckham would later exploit in *Ex parte Young*: the metaphorical notion that misconduct strips officials of the authority in which they are clothed, leaving them naked of justification and therefore vulnerable, like any citizen, to liability.[64] But it established three broad exceptions to official liability, exceptions that not only swallowed up much of the official liability rule but that continue to influence today's remedial law. First, the Court preserved immunity in damage actions for officials who erred in the exercise of "judgment and discretion" rather than "ministerial duties."[65] Second, even if an official allegedly acted with malice, the immunity was absolute so long as his action had "more or less connection with the general matters committed by law to his control," rather than being "manifestly or palpably beyond his authority."[66] Third, *respondeat superior* liability was rejected; supervisory officials remained absolutely immune from personal liability for their subordinates' torts.[67]

The immunity of the United States and its officials, then, was substantially complete and absolute by the beginning of this century, the major chink in their armor being officials' liability for purely ministerial acts. Immunity also prospered under state law, being virtually absolute in suits against governmental entities in the absence of a statutory waiver. Official immunity, however, was abridged in some state courts, which developed an elaborate, formalistic, but highly malleable set of exceptions to the immunity rule.* By World War I, the federal role was changing, and the public's conception of government's responsibilities to its citizens was evolving into a distinctively modern view. As government increasingly intervened affirmatively in the economy, expanding its propensity and capacity to harm private individuals, sovereign immunity seemed ever more anomalous. In 1910, Congress consented to be sued in the Court of Claims for patent infringements,[68] and in the 1920s, it consented to suits for admiralty and maritime torts involving government vessels.[69]

Traditional immunity doctrines did not lack for academic critics. Between 1924 and 1928, Edwin Borchard of the Yale Law School published a magisterial survey of governmental liability in tort, examining in exhaustive detail the evolution of the American case law, its English roots, and contemporary British and Continental developments.[70] Borchard's work stimulated a profusion of law journal articles on related topics,[71] and this wave of interest among academic lawyers, perhaps propelled by the federal government's greater activity and visibility after World War I, spurred consideration of a federal tort claims law, a project to which Borchard devoted his energy and expertise. A bill passed the Congress in 1929 but was pocket vetoed by President Coolidge (apparently as the result of a procedural objection by the attorney general).[72] Nevertheless, the 1920s saw a more limited statute enacted, empowering administrative agencies to settle claims under $1,000 arising from employees' torts.[73] But efforts to narrow the immunity of the United States continued. On the bench, Justices Douglas and Frankfurter noted these efforts in broadly interpreting waivers of immunity in statutes establishing New Deal public corporations.[74] In 1938, the administration sponsored a bill,[75] but despite the president's initiative, the Federal Tort Claims Act (FTCA) was not enacted until 1946, when it passed as part of the Legislative Reorganization Act.[76]

While this legislative assault upon governmental immunity was gaining strength, however, the citadel of official immunity remained virtually impregnable in the federal courts. In 1927, they extended absolute immunity to prosecutors[77] and subsequently to the secretaries of the interior and treasury.[78] The new quasi-judicial and regulatory organs of the welfare state were also accorded absolute immunity.[79] Even a special FBI agent performing a ministerial duty was allowed by a lower

---

*For a very brief discussion of the immunity rules under state law, see appendix 3.

court to wrap himself in his superiors' absolute immunity.[80] A much-cited 1949 circuit court decision, *Gregoire* v. *Biddle*, articulated the dominant rationale for making official immunity absolute rather than dependent upon a showing of good faith. Plaintiff, who had been imprisoned for four years as an enemy alien, alleged a malicious Justice Department conspiracy to deprive him of liberty and sued the attorney general and other Justice Department officials for damages. Judge Learned Hand assumed *arguendo* that defendants were motivated entirely by personal spite and knew that plaintiff was being wrongfully held, yet he nonetheless held them to be absolutely immune.

> If it were possible to confine . . . complaints to the guilty, it would be monstrous to deny recovery. The justification is . . . that it is impossible to know whether the claim is well founded until the case has been tried, and that to submit all officials, the innocent as well as the guilty, to the burden of a trial . . . would dampen the ardor of all but the most resolute, or the most irresponsible, in the unflinching discharge of their duties . . . In this instance, it has been thought in the end better to leave unredressed the wrongs done by dishonest officers than to subject those who try to do their duty to the constant dread of retaliation.[81]

Hand's emphasis upon the paramount value of vigorous decision-making, and his implicit premise that only absolute immunity could secure it, were not universally accepted either in the state courts[82] or among academic commentators.[83] A sharply divided Supreme Court, however, adopted Hand's approach in a 1959 decision, *Barr* v. *Matteo*,[84] in which mid-level federal officials claimed that their superior had libeled them in a press release issued by their agency. Since libel claims are expressly excluded from the FTCA,[85] they sued their superior, not the United States. Justice Harlan, whose opinion mustered only a plurality of the Court, conferred absolute immunity. Publishing a press release, Harlan reasoned, was discretionary and "within the outer perimeter of [his] line of duty." Although immunity might permit some injustices to go unredressed, sanctions other than civil tort suits against the official made such forebodings "remote."[86] The vigorous dissenting opinions pointed out that absolute immunity for an official like Barr had large implications; it could immunize "the most obscure subforeman on an arsenal production line who has been delegated authority to hire and fire and who maliciously defames one he discharges."[87]

*Barr* v. *Matteo* was not without its ironies; as one commentator has noted, it took Barr a jury trial, an appeal to the circuit court and then to the Supreme Court, a remand to the circuit court, and a second appeal to the Supreme Court—six years of litigation—to establish that he could not be sued.[88] *Barr*, moreover, was to be a turning point—the high-water mark of personal immunity for administrative officials. During the 1970s, as we shall see, its precedential significance would be limited, if not wholly vitiated, by the Court.[89]

## *The Federal Tort Claims Act of 1946 and the* Bivens *Remedy*

When *Barr* v. *Matteo* was decided, the federal courts had already begun to flesh out the FTCA's meaning. The act effected a limited waiver of the sovereign immunity of the United States, providing a damage remedy for personal injury, death, or property damage caused by the "negligent or wrongful act or omission" of any federal employee acting within the scope of his or her employment.[90] Procedurally, the FTCA allows actions against the United States, the offending official, or both, except for cases concerning motor vehicle accidents, where the remedy against the United States is exclusive.[91] A judgment against the United States bars any action against the offending official, but the reverse is not true.[92] (Double recoveries, of course, are not permissible.) When the United States pays a judgment, it may not seek indemnification from the official whose misconduct caused the judgment.[93]

The substantive coverage of the original act was highly qualified by numerous exceptions, some (such as the exception for most intentional torts and all "discretionary functions") quite broad, others activity-specific. Although the most important of these are analyzed in chapter 5, a conclusion drawn from that analysis may be stated here: Taken as a whole, the FTCA denied—and continues to deny—relief for much, perhaps most, governmental misconduct; as two justices recently noted, it is "hedged with protections for the United States."[94]

Until 1971, victims of federal misconduct not covered by the FTCA had several options, none wholly satisfactory. They might request the introduction of a private bill which, if enacted, would authorize payment of the claim by the United States Treasury. Such relief, however, has always been somewhat remote and adventitious; only claims of special political interest can hope to be prosecuted successfully.[95] They might sue for injunctive or declaratory relief against individual officials accused of wrongdoing, and because sovereign immunity has been of little practical significance in such cases, such a decree might well be effective. But victims who sought damages for past harm rather than relief from threatened future injury could only sue the individual officials and hope that they were personally insured or wealthy.

In 1971, the Supreme Court added a powerful new string to a victim's bow in the case of *Bivens* v. *Six Unknown Agents of the Federal Bureau of Narcotics*.[96] Federal narcotics agents had made an egregiously improper, warrantless raid upon Bivens's apartment, violating his Fourth Amendment rights. Because the agents were federal officials and their tort was intentional, a category of conduct excluded from the FTCA's coverage, Bivens could not sue the United States. Instead, he argued that the Fourth Amendment implicitly conferred a direct private damage remedy for its violation. This theory, which the Supreme Court had managed to sidestep in an earlier decision,[97] was not an easy one to sustain. Congress, after all, had not simply neglected to create a statutory remedy for such torts but had actually excluded from the remedy that it *did* create (the FTCA) a long list of intentional torts, including false arrests, false searches, and other law enforcement wrongs.[98] Nevertheless, a fragmented Court, including Justice Harlan, who had conferred absolute immunity in *Barr* v. *Matteo*, agreed with Bivens; none of the majority justices so much as mentioned the FTCA. In his dissenting opinion, however, Chief Justice Burger had taken the highly unusual step of actually urging Congress to adopt particular statutory changes,[99] and in 1974 Congress responded by amending the FTCA to cover assault, battery, false imprisonment, false arrest, abuse of process, and malicious prosecution by officials empowered to make searches, seizures, or arrests.[100]

In the decade after *Bivens*, the Court enlarged the decision's impact in two ways. First, it extended the *Bivens* remedy well beyond its original domain, construing it to permit a Fifth Amendment equal protection claim against a congressman alleged to have engaged in sex discrimination[101] and to allow inmates to sue prison officials for alleged "cruel and inhuman punishment" violate of the Eighth Amendment.[102] This latter decision, *Carlson* v. *Green*, is remarkable because the plaintiffs could have sued the government under the FTCA, but that remedy was deemed not equivalent to the one available in *Bivens*-type actions.[103] (Indeed, a dissenting justice maintained that *Carlson*'s logic might imply a *Bivens*-type remedy against *state* officials *in addition to* the one already available.[104]) The Court expanded *Bivens* in a second way by curtailing the immunities available to federal executives in *Bivens*-type actions. A 1978 decision, *Butz* v. *Economou*,[105] adopted qualified immunity for nonprosecutorial federal officers (in that case, the secretary of agriculture and other high-ranking Agriculture Department officials) in constitutional tort cases, the same rule that had been established four years earlier for their state and local counterparts.[106] Because federal officials had been assumed after *Barr* to enjoy absolute personal immunity in most cases, the significance of *Economou*'s resurrection of official liability (at least for constitutional violations) became evident in 1982. The Court then held that although the president enjoys absolute immunity from damage actions, his close personal aides can claim only a "good faith" immunity, at least in the performance of most of their functions.[107*]

*Bivens* and its progeny have vastly increased the litigation against individual federal officials. Today, roughly one out of every 300 officials is personally named in pending *Bivens* actions,[108] a development of great concern to the agencies that employ them and to the Department of Justice, which defends most of them.[109] Even when plaintiffs can proceed directly against the United States under the FTCA or another statute, many choose to sue individual officials instead (or as well). Substantive and tactical considerations explain why. First, the FTCA exceptions do not apply in a suit against officials. (On the other hand, officials who are personally sued can claim a "good faith" or absolute immunity denied to the United States in FTCA actions.) Second, victims may recover from officials without establishing that they acted within the scope of employment, a necessary element of proof in FTCA actions. Third, victims may desire a jury trial or an opportunity to prove punitive damages; neither is available under the FTCA.[110] Fourth, victims' access to a competent attorney may as a practical matter be abridged in a FTCA action by the statutory ceiling on the fee that plaintiffs' attorney may charge.[111] No such restrictions exist in a suit against federal officials. Finally, officials who are sued but not represented free by government-provided counsel may be more anxious to settle than they would in an FTCA case, in which the United States is represented by salaried Department of Justice attorneys. Even in the more typical case in which officials are represented by government counsel, their interests and those of the government may diverge in ways that plaintiffs can use for tactical advantage.[112]

## Liability for State and Local Government Torts

Throughout our history, state and local government has posed the

---

*For a brief summary of the current rules governing the liability and immunity of the United States and federal officials, see appendix 2.

greatest danger of official misconduct. The federal system ensures that most street-level, direct service functions, most notably law enforcement, are performed by those governments, and they employ far more civilian employees than the federal government. For this reason, the issue of state and local immunity from tort liability has always been a significant one for those governments and their citizens. As federal law has steadily assumed greater importance to the overall structure of public law, the liabilities and immunities of their employees under federal law have become central questions of national policy.

We have seen that the Constitution was not altogether clear about the survival of governmental immunities under the new regime. Clyde Jacobs has shown, however, that the Framers probably intended to preclude governmental immunity, at least for the states. Many wished to prevent the new state governments from repudiating the substantial debts they had accumulated during the Revolution and Confederation period, many of which were owed to citizens of other states. More generally, a strong national judiciary was viewed as essential to the resolution of interstate conflicts that had festered under the Articles of Confederation. Debates at state ratifying conventions were equivocal on the immunity question; Madison, Hamilton, and Marshall argued that states could not be sued by citizens in federal courts, but other evidence from the state conventions implied the contrary.[113] The Judiciary Act of 1789, which implemented Article III and is thought to reflect the Framers' original intent, was also equivocal.[114]

In any event, the immunity issue arose in the federal courts almost immediately. The very first case docketed in the Supreme Court, a suit brought against the state of Maryland by foreign creditors,[115] raised it but the case was settled before a ruling could be rendered.[116] During the early 1790s other suits were filed against states by aliens and citizens. Inconclusive on the immunity question, these cases nevertheless generated strong protests by the states.[117]

In 1793, *Chisholm* v. *Georgia* came before the Court.[118] Chisholm, a citizen of South Carolina, had sued on a contract that the state of Georgia had allegedly breached, and Georgia had successfully asserted its immunity in the lower court. Chisholm then filed an original suit in the Supreme Court, and when Georgia refused to enter an appearance, the Court proceeded to adjudicate without it. Mr. Justice Iredell alone supported Georgia's immunity, maintaining that American courts did not recognize the petition of right, which he regarded as the sole remedy for Chisholm's claim at common law.[119]

The four other sitting justices, however, upheld the Court's jurisdiction over Chisholm's claim. Justices Blair and Cushing relied upon a literal reading of Article III; the text did not limit jurisdiction to cases in which the state was a party-plaintiff.[120] Justice Wilson and Chief Justice Jay, however, took a far more expansive view, advancing what might be called a "populist" conception of public tort law. In feudal societies like England, they contended, the prince was sovereign and his people were subjects, but sovereignty under our Constitution resided in the people. By ratifying it, the states had consented to be legally accountable as popular sovereignty presupposed, including the classes of cases embraced by Article III. Jay could not imagine why the Framers would have devised a system permitting a citizen to sue the city of Philadelphia but not the state of Delaware.[121] Justice Wilson acknowledged that the states were sovereign insofar as they were self-governing in certain areas but stressed that "[a]s to the purposes of the Union . . . Georgia is NOT a sovereign state" (emphasis and capitalization in original).[122] The British sovereign was indeed immune from suit, Wilson conceded, but this had not always been so; in any event, he added, the British system was "despotic."[123]

*Chisholm* produced swift, intense opposition from the states. Increasingly sued over fiscal claims, title to Loyalist property, and the validity of land grants, the states pressed Congress to reverse the decision. It promptly obliged by proposing the Eleventh Amendment early in 1794. The amendment stated: "The judicial power of the United States shall not be construed to extend to any suit in law or equity, commenced or prosecuted, against one of the United States by Citizens of another State, or by Citizens or Subjects of any Foreign State." It attracted widespread support among Federalists and their opponents alike, and the states ratified it within a year.[124]

*Chisholm* was an action for damages. Although the Eleventh Amendment proscribed both damage and equitable relief against states, its actual preclusive effect was virtually confined almost from the beginning to damage actions against states *eo nomine*. In a century-long series of decisions, whose course was anything but straight, the Supreme Court emasculated the amendment, at least as it applied to injunction actions, by allowing litigants to use the federal courts to challenge state officials in their *individual* capacities, even when acting under authority of state law. So long as the state was not named as a defendant of record and the relief would not in effect extract damages from the state treasury, the amendment would not bar the action.[125] In the 1908 case of *Ex parte Young*,[126] the Court rationalized this in a vivid, metaphorical legal fiction, one prefigured by John Marshall's early opinion in *Osborn* v. *Bank of the United States*.[127] When the errant official, cloaked in state authority by the invalid statute, "comes into conflict with the superior authority of the Constitution, . . . he is in that case stripped of his official or representative character and is subjected in his person to the consequences of his individual conduct. The State has no power to impart to him any immunity from responsibility to the supreme authority of the United States."[128]

Long before *Ex parte Young*, however, the Court had devised other ways to cabin the amendment.[129] Sometimes, states were found to have waived the immunity.[130] Although the amendment had been construed to cover federal court actions brought against a state by its own citizens (contrary to the amendment's language but probably in accord with its intention and policy), even those suits were allowed to be brought against state *officials* under the "federal question" jurisdiction that Congress had conferred upon the lower federal courts in 1875.[131] Even more important, the amendment was held not to immunize counties, cities, or other political subdivisions of a state.[132]

In Eleventh Amendment litigation, the Supreme Court found a valuable weapon for pressing its late nineteenth- and early twentieth-century assault upon state efforts to tax and regulate economic activity. In *Ex parte Young*, for example, the Court enjoined the attorney general of Minnesota from enforcing through the state courts a state program of railroad rate regulation that imposed heavy penalties for selling tickets for a rate higher than the one that had been prescribed. By opening the federal courts to such challenges, especially in injunction actions against state officials, the Court laid an essential foundation for the substantive due process doctrine that it deployed against Progressive-era legislation and would extend well into the New Deal period.[133] *Ex parte Young* represents the last great judicial step in disarming the Eleventh Amendment as a restriction upon the *injunctive* power of the federal courts over state action; subsequent cases essentially worked out the details of the principles elaborated there.[134] Although litigants seeking non-monetary relief can usually circumvent the amendment through artful pleading techniques, it remains fully effective in precluding damage claims against the states;[135] indeed, very recent Supreme Court decisions suggest that the amendment may sometimes pose serious obstacles even when non-monetary relief is sought.[136]

The Supreme Court could not possibly have foreseen that these constrictions of the Eleventh Amendment were destined for service in other, decidedly different campaigns. Indeed, an irony of our legal history is that by thus allowing the federal courts to be mobilized to protect the traditional property rights of bondholders and corporations, the Court made it possible in a later day for welfare recipients and minority plaintiffs to use these same courts to vindicate their "new property"[137] claims against state and local governments. When this movement gained momentum, a half-century after *Ex parte Young*, it found a federal court remedy of vast potential scope waiting to be molded into effectiveness. In the next section I discuss that remedy and its transformation.

## Evolution of § 1983

In 1871, Congress responded to outbreaks of terrorism directed against the recently emancipated blacks, often with the connivance of state and local officials, by enacting the Ku Klux Klan Act. Section 1, now known as "Section 1983," stated:

> Every person who, under color of any statute, ordinance, regula-
> tion, custom or usage, of any State or Territory, subjects, or causes
> to be subjected, any citizen of the United States or other person
> within the jurisdiction thereof to the deprivation of any rights,
> privileges, or immunities secured by the Constitution and laws,
> shall be liable to the party injured in an action at law, suit in
> equity, or other proper proceeding for redress.

On its face, § 1983 might seem a sweeping remedy for official mis-conduct, a *pro tanto* elimination of whatever immunity state and local officials enjoyed from federal court suits and remedies. After all, it empowered anyone to seek any form of civil relief—damages, injunc-tion, or other "redress"—against any "person" who deprived him of any federally protected right "under color of" law. But despite its broad language and scope, § 1983 seemed directed at a particular, time-limited evil: the mistreatment of Southern blacks during Reconstruc-tion. Even within the Ku Klux Klan Act itself, § 1983 was "an *a fortiori* tail wagging along behind the criminal conspiracy section, the power of the President to suppress rebellion, and the suspension of *habeas corpus*."[138] And because it was remedial only, its reach would be narrowly circumscribed so long as the substantive "rights, privileges, [and] immunities secured by the Constitution and laws" remained narrowly defined. Indeed, for almost seventy years, § 1983 seemed to justify that unprepossessing description. It was seldom invoked prior to 1939, and even then was largely confined to challenges of unconstitu-

tional voting restrictions. Between 1939 and 1960, however, the Supreme Court interpreted its key provisions expansively, extending it
beyond constitutional challenges to statutes or voting abuses to cases of
police brutality and due process rights.[139]

A 1961 case brought the Supreme Court to a momentous turning
point in the remedial road. *Monroe* v. *Pape*[140] was decided under the
incubus of compelling facts. The plaintiff, a black Chicagoan, alleged
that police broke into his home at 5:45 A.M., woke him and his wife
with flashlights,

> forced them at gunpoint to leave their bed and stand naked in the
> center of the living room, . . . roused the six Monroe children and
> herded them into the living room. . . . Detective Pape struck Mr.
> Monroe several times with his flashlight, calling him "nigger" and
> "black boy" . . . another officer pushed Mrs. Monroe . . . other
> officers hit and kicked several of the children and pushed them to
> the floor . . . the police ransacked every room . . . Mr. Monroe
> was then taken to the police station and detained on "open"
> charges for ten hours. . . . he was not advised of his procedural
> rights . . . he was not permitted to call his family or an attorney
> . . . he was subsequently released without criminal charges hav-
> ing been filed against him.[141]

In upholding Monroe's right to sue the policemen under § 1983, the
Court ensured that § 1983 would develop into a remedy of awesome
power. To potential plaintiffs, the Court delivered both good news and
bad. The good news was that henceforth the phrase "under color of
[law]" would embrace any official conduct—whether valid under state
law or not,[142] a ruling to which Mr. Justice Frankfurter took vigorous
exception on the ground that § 1983 was intended to cover only misconduct that the state had *authorized*.[143] The bad news was that
§ 1983's opening phrase, "every person," would preclude claims
against the city of Chicago and other local governmental entities; relief
in such cases could be had only against individual local officials, and if
they could not pay the judgment, victims were without federal
remedy.[144] On balance, *Monroe* v. *Pape* was rightly perceived as a
watershed decision, establishing § 1983 as a potent remedy that citizens could invoke affirmatively against official misconduct without the
state's help or indeed in the face of its opposition. It swiftly became the
legal bulwark of the ripening civil rights movement; only two years
after the decision, § 1983 litigation had grown by over 60 percent.[145]

In the 1970s, and into the 1980s, propelled by a series of favorable

Supreme Court decisions, § 1983 litigation experienced a second growth spurt. These decisions narrowed (and in some cases eliminated) the immunities available to individual and governmental defendants in § 1983 actions and extended the statute's affirmative reach. In 1974, the Court held that even the governor of a state, acting in a crisis atmosphere to quell a campus insurrection, was not entitled to the absolute immunity that a 1959 decision had assured even for mid-level federal officials motivated by malice. Instead, the governor could claim only a qualified immunity, available only after a trial on the issue of "good faith."[146] The next year, the Court ruled that the good faith standard required the jury not merely to inquire into the official's subjective attitude but also to evaluate from an objective standpoint what he *should* have known about the state of the applicable law.[147] In 1978 and 1979, the Court overruled the "bad news" portion of its decision in *Monroe* v. *Pape*, allowing § 1983 actions against local government[148] and regional planning agencies.[149]

It was in 1980, however, that the scope of § 1983 reached its zenith. Emphasizing the importance of compensation and deterrence goals, the Court stripped municipalities, which until 1978 had enjoyed absolute immunity, of even a good faith defense.[150] It allocated to officials the burden of pleading immunity and, more important, implied that they would bear the burden of proof as well.[151] It suggested that a state supreme court and its chief justice might be denied the absolute immunity traditionally enjoyed by judges, might be subject to declaratory and injunctive relief, and might even have to pay plaintiff's attorney's fees.[152] The Court also implied that liability under § 1983 need not be limited by state tort law principles of causation.[153] It interpreted § 1983 to apply not only to constitutional and civil rights torts but to violations of the many federal statutes (and perhaps regulations and common law as well) that state and local officials help to administer or enforce.[154]

In 1981, the Court apparently had some second thoughts about its recent handiwork and rejected attempts to sue state officials and agencies in several § 1983 cases. In one, the Court held that Congress, in establishing a comprehensive scheme to regulate water pollution, had intended to preclude private enforcement actions under § 1983.[155] Another decision, which relied upon considerations of comity implied by the Tax Injunction Act, rejected a § 1983 damage action against local tax assessors.[156] A third decision denied a prisoner's negligence claim against prison officials.[157] The significance of these decisions, however, remains unclear; arguably, each was a narrow holding. Stronger clues about the future trajectory of the Court's § 1983 jurisprudence may be offered by a 1982 decision that sidestepped substantial Eleventh Amendment objections in order to hold that plaintiffs need not exhaust administrative remedies before suing under § 1983.[158]

Indeed, one of these cases denying liability planted seeds that may yet germinate into remedial expansion. In *Parratt* v. *Taylor*, an inmate sued state prison officials for $23.50, the value of hobby materials that had been mailed to him but had been lost through defendants' alleged negligence. The case presented an extremely important question that the Court had successfully evaded in earlier cases:[159] Did § 1983 provide a remedy for official *negligence* as well as for intentional harms? If so, as Justice Stewart pointed out in a concurring opinion, § 1983 would cover a vast number of trivial incidents such as ordinary automobile collisions in which a state official drove negligently.[160] Although it denied this plaintiff's claim, the Court ruled that officials' mere negligence might support liability in future § 1983 cases, at least where the state fails to provide an "adequate" remedy for that negligence; the negligence would in that event deprive plaintiff of property "without due process of law," thereby violating § 1983.[161]

The Court did not clarify the circumstances under which state remedies for official negligence might be deemed "inadequate," but a 1980 decision had analyzed this issue in a somewhat analogous context and implied that remedial inadequacy might be readily established.[162] For example, whereas a "prevailing party" in a § 1983 action may recover attorney's fees and litigation costs,[163] state law seldom confers that advantage in simple negligence actions. State law might also be deemed inadequate if it immunizes officials from liability for negligence claims.[164] A recent Supreme Court decision, which found a state tort remedy "constitutionally inadequate" simply because it is apt to be a "lengthy and speculative process" (as indeed *any* tort remedy inevitably is), suggest how weak *Parratt*'s limitation on the potential scope of § 1983 is likely to prove.[165]

Prodded by the civil rights movement and the "due process revolution," the Court has transformed § 1983 into a powerful engine of social control, supplementing and often supplanting state tort law. Not all decisions have enlarged the remedy's scope, of course, and important limitations remain. Thus, although injunctive relief against state and local governments and officials has become commonplace since *Brown* v. *Board of Education*, the Court has held in recent years that § 1983 was not intended to abrogate states' Eleventh Amendment immunity;[166] this precludes monetary relief against state governments and all injunctive and other relief having a similar effect.[167] In addition, officials continue to enjoy broad common law immunities against personal liability,[168] and punitive damage awards against governmental entities are barred.[169]

These continuing barriers to liability are considerable, and yet the overall expansive thrust of the decisions is unmistakable and remarkably persistent. Indeed, a Court now dominated by Nixon, Ford, and Reagan appointees has not yet managed to change its fundamental course. Even when denying claims under § 1983, the Court has opened up new avenues of opportunity for resourceful plaintiffs: the possibility of asserting negligence claims,[170] a potential escape from proximate cause limitations,[171] and the prospect of punitive damages against individual officials.[172] Today, as the Court recently remarked, the risk of liability for public torts under § 1983 "cover[s] a large range of activity in everyday life."[173]*

## The Contemporary Context of Public Tort Remedies

The historical legacy of public tort remedies is a jerry-built structure, a patchwork, a doctrinal stew. It is a pastiche of policies, precedents, and perspectives drawn primarily from three distinctive legal realms but overlaid with features of its own. It is private tort law without *respondeat superior*, administrative law without the Administrative Procedure Act, and constitutional law without much guidance from the Constitution. The current state of public tort remedies—their strengths and weaknesses, dynamic growth, and persistent incoherencies—is the legacy of their legal progenitors.

The tort liability of private actors has expanded relentlessly in recent decades,[174] largely repudiating the earlier notion that losses should ordinarily remain wherever they happen to fall.[175] In private tort law, *respondeat superior*, manifested organizationally as enterprise liability, has played an essential part in the triumph of this meliorative paradigm. It has done so by fastening liability upon entities well situated by reason of their size, insurability, control of risks, and loss-spreading capacity to reduce the social costs of harmful conduct.[176] As I point out in part II, this doctrine is even more compelling when applied to public sector activity. Nonetheless, it remains stunted and even alien there.

Administrative law has also spawned remedial growth. Spurred by widespread perceptions of bureaucratic and regulatory failure[177] and

*For a more detailed summary of the current rules governing the liability of state and local officials and governmental entities under § 1983, see appendix 2.

an increasing mistrust of claims of professional authority and autonomy,[178] courts have claimed a larger role in controlling official discretion and conduct. Judicial supervision has taken many forms:
court-imposed procedures designed to forestall official depredations;[179]
regulatory statutes that rely upon judicially enforced controls;[180] and
the nurturing of nonprofit, "public interest" organizations to influence
policy formulation and implementation.[181] As we have seen, tort actions against officials and governmental entities have also become important instruments by which courts can control administrative behavior. In particular, a damage action "concentrates the mind" (as Dr.
Johnson said of the prospect of hanging) in a way that the possibility of
being enjoined does not. As the Supreme Court recently noted in a
case asserting a damage claim against local tax assessors: "There is little
doubt that such officials, faced with the prospect of personal liability to
numerous taxpayers, not to mention the assessment of attorney's fees
. . . would promptly cease the [unconstitutional] conduct . . . whether
or not those officials were acting in good faith."[182] The attractiveness of
such leverage over administration has surely encouraged courts to expand damage remedies under § 1983 and *Bivens*.[183]

Tort remedies also meet certain technical and professional needs of
courts better than does conventional judicial review of administrative
action under the Administrative Procedure Act. Judicial deference
to official decisions is most complete when those decisions take the
form of general rules not yet particularized through case-by-case
adjudication.[184] General rules are ordinarily predicated upon the kinds
of predictive, intuitive, policy-oriented, "legislative facts" that courts
are reluctant to second-guess. But in a tort action, the concreteness of
the dispute, the particularity of the harm, and the accessibility of
critical "adjudicative" facts appeal to courts' institutional strengths.
They can limit their rulings in such actions to the particular fact situations before them; intervention and impact can be more surgically
precise. Finally, only ex post remedies can reach certain kinds of public
torts, especially low-level, nonrepetitive misconduct.[185] Tort actions,
then, are not simply "mopping-up" operations ancillary to traditional
judicial review of governmental decisions. They are distinctive,
specialized tools for performing administrative law's essential
task—shaping and controlling official action.

Constitutional law, like administrative law, allocates decisionmaking
power among the organs of government.[186] Public tort remedies,
reflecting this parentage, likewise constrain legislatures and bureaucracies, transferring political power and policy initiative from those

branches to courts (especially federal judges) and to private litigants. This fundamental redistribution of influence affects most areas of governmental activity and is so intensely controversial[187] that it has already produced a powerful (though at this writing, still unsuccessful) legislative backlash.[188] At the same time, however, immunities from tort liability weaken the ability of the remedial system to vindicate constitutional values.

As we move in parts II and III to a more systematic evaluation of the remedial structure, it is well to remember that as a matter of historical fact, that structure is a product of extraordinary judicial creativity and chronic legislative neglect. The courts have been obliged to work with singularly unpromising raw materials. The Constitution's only intimation of a governmental duty to compensate, after all, is the takings clause.[189] The Constitution explicitly bars (in the Eleventh Amendment) most federal court actions against the states. Statutory remedies consist chiefly of a long-dormant Reconstruction law and a waiver of federal immunity riddled with sweeping exceptions. Even the common law of public torts was restrictive, recognizing broad immunities, rejecting *respondeat superior*, and barring resort to injunctive and declaratory remedies against government except under "extraordinary" circumstances.[190]

Despite these handicaps, however, the federal courts have managed to fashion a sturdy structure of citizen-initiated remedies for official misconduct. Moreover, they have done so virtually unaided. Like a parent who abandons children without means of support, Congress has created public tort remedies only to leave their care to judicial supervisors poorly equipped to reform them.[191] Not surprisingly, this dubious upbringing has left its marks.

# PART II

# THE CASE FOR REMEDIAL REFORM

It is mentioned, that the Lord Mayor of London, in 1666, when that city was on fire, would not give directions for, or consent to, the pulling down 40 houses, or to the removing the furniture, &c. belonging to the Lawyers of Temple, then on the Circuit, for fear he should be answerable for a trespass; and in consequence of this conduct half that great city was burnt.[1]

In part I, I exposed the purposive, conceptual, historical, and doctrinal underpinnings of public tort remedies, revealing a system that relies heavily, though certainly not exclusively, upon the damage remedy against individual officials. Although history and hoary doctrine furnish powerful support and momentum for this remedy's continuing prominence (and for some harms, primacy), its present importance is in my view neither desirable nor inevitable, and a superior system that relegates it to the sidelines is readily available. In this part, I hope to substantiate this proposition.

Part II advances four central themes. The first, explored in chapter 3's opening section, is that when the remedy of official liability is applied in the unique context in which street-level public officials work and make decisions, it aggravates their natural predispositions to be "risk-averse." Technically, this means that in order to avoid such low-probability adverse outcomes as litigation and liability, officials would be willing to pay a premium beyond the expected (negative) value of those outcomes. More colloquially, it means that they will go to great lengths to avoid what they may regard as personal calamities. The second theme, which is discussed in the rest of chapter 3, is that these officials are well situated to indulge their risk aversion by engaging in self-protective strategies that systematically stifle vigorous official decisionmaking and are heedless of the resulting social costs. Third, I maintain (in chapter 4) that this consequence of the official liability remedy is doubly perverse. For in order to restore and secure the vigorous decisionmaking that the remedy jeopardizes, the system must resort to crude immunity rules and other risk-shifting techniques; these not only reduce compensation, deterrence, and other remedial values, but do so without really eliminating the threat to vigorous decisionmaking that the remedy inevitably poses. Finally, I demonstrate (in chapter 5) that a public tort system centered upon a much-expanded governmental liability would serve our remedial purposes better than do the present arrangements and would obviate the need for official liability in all but the most extreme cases.

These four themes—the tendency of the official liability remedy to stimulate the risk aversion of street-level officials; their flight to self-protection at the cost of vigorous decisionmaking; the decidedly perverse effects of the remedy, when coupled with risk-shifting arrangements, upon other remedial purposes as well; and the superiority of a regime of enlarged governmental liability—serve to underscore yet another theme sounded early in chapter 2: the historically anomalous position of enterprise liability increasingly undermines the integrity of our public law. A premise of the argument, presented in this part, is that private tort law provides a benchmark against which public tort remedies should be evaluated. In this view, the "double standard" that continues to divide these legal systems can be justified, if at all, only by identifying relevant differences between either the contexts. in which they function or the goals they purport to advance.

In fact, the differences between the contexts and goals of these two systems powerfully support the extension of enterprise liability to public torts; the case for this reform thus becomes (in lawyers' jargon) *a fortiori*. My reasons for this strong conclusion will emerge in part II (especially in chapter 3), but it seems appropriate here to mention some more general, systemic differences that reinforce it—differences between the two sectors relating to the nature of the services delivered, the obstacles to managerial control, their compensation systems, and risk aversion.

First, some public officials, such as postal service drivers and Veterans Administration physicians, have closely analogous private sector counterparts, but most do not. Some public services, including education, housing, and personal security, are also sold in private markets, but even these tend to be delivered by public officials to people of generally lower social class who typically possess fewer choices. In those contexts, the adequacy of legal remedies is especially important. Middle-class apartment dwellers who are poorly treated can rely upon

market remedies and take their business elsewhere; most public housing tenants, however, cannot.

Second, public agencies and private firms do share some systematic
difficulties in communicating information and norms, monitoring and
controlling employee conduct, planning for uncertainty, and integrating organizational and subgroup goals,[2] but these broad similarities
mask important differences of detail and degree.[3] Civil service systems
and influential legislative committees sensitive to employee interests,
for example, tend to reduce public employers' managerial authority
below the level enjoyed even by those who run the small minority of
unionized private firms. The relative weakness of these controls in the
public sector, a subject discussed in chapter 6, enhances the importance of tort remedies that effectively compensate, as governmental
liability can and official liability cannot.

Third, public agencies are unable to induce low-level employees to
accept risks of danger or litigation as easily as private firms can. Uniform, often statutorily frozen compensation schedules prevent public
employers from paying risk-sensitive premiums. Governmental liability can serve much the same purpose by attenuating or eliminating
such risks for employees; official liability, however, simply exacerbates
them.

Finally, civil servants probably tend to be more risk-averse with
respect to litigation and liability than individuals generally. Empirical
evidence suggests that most people systematically exaggerate the
likelihood of low-probability events, such as being sued, that would be
personally catastrophic and receive media attention.[4] Whereas private
employees are seldom sued because their employers are ideal litigation
targets and almost universally vulnerable to suit, individual officials are
often the only available defendants due to broad restrictions upon
governmental liability. These restrictions have resulted in an estimated
one out of every 300 federal officials being sued individually in pending
*Bivens* actions.[5] In addition to this heightened sensitivity to litigation,
there is some evidence that officials tend to shun risks more than
individuals who are drawn to the more competitive private sector.[6] If
that is true, a remedy that concentrates risk upon the risk-averse,
rather than one that spreads it, may generate powerful incentives for
self-protection that are simply too powerful to resist.

# 3:   OFFICIAL LIABILITY FOR DAMAGES:
## THE POWER AND PERVERSITY
## OF INCENTIVES

In order to evaluate the present system of public tort remedies, we must have some notion of how it affects the way officials behave. And to predict their behavior, we in turn need a theory, a set of propositions that can identify and integrate the crucial factors that influence what they do and how they do it. Theories of bureaucratic behavior abound, but none enjoys general acceptance. Economic models of bureaucratic decisionmaking, for example, affirm that officials seek to maximize something. But whether that something is budget, political support, autonomy, discretion, some combination of these, or something else entirely, remains a matter of endless, inconclusive debate.[1] Other models of administrative behavior stress more general goals: "Satisficing,"[2] organizational maintenance,[3] "muddling through,"[4] and managing uncertainty.[5] These theories are valuable, for they emphasize familiar and significant features of official life. They conceive of decisionmaking in abstract terms rather than contextually, seeking to illuminate the intellectual and bureaucratic antecedents of decisions rather than either the morphology of the discrete social problems to which decisions are addressed or the specific tasks that officials perform. Some purport to be both positive and normative, describing how decisions *are* made and prescribing how they *ought* to be made.

These models are useful if one's analytical purpose is to understand the scope of rationality in decisionmaking or to evaluate the organization of decisionmaking processes. My project, however, is to predict how tort remedies affect the behavior of officials, especially those in street-level organizations that deliver vital services directly to the public—police, prison officials, teachers and school board members, caseworkers, inspectors, the FBI, drug enforcement agents, mental hospital workers, and the like. James Q. Wilson, a leading student of such organizations, has emphasized that their behavior is determined less by explicit organizational goals or instrumental rules than by the specific tasks that their officials perform and the incentives that such tasks generate. These tasks, Wilson remarks, "are to an important degree the most enduring, hard-to-change elements of the situation; administrative procedures must adapt to tasks, not the other way around."[6] I shall maintain that effective remedies for misconduct, no less than sound administrative procedures, must reflect what officials actually do. This purpose, then, requires a different kind of model, one more sensitive to the distinctive contexts in which these officials work and the incentive systems that develop in these milieus. In this chapter, I attempt to develop such a model. It is extremely simple and is descriptive, not normative, drawing upon empirical findings from studies of street-level government organizations.[7] The model is elaborated in two stages. I first delineate some common features of street-level work, suggesting that these officials and their superiors are exposed to risks of reprisal and litigation to a marked degree. I then consider how they are likely to seek to control those risks. The model is grounded in the conventional behavioral assumption, drawn from price theory, that officials' choices concerning whether and how to act are affected at the margin by the personal risks they perceive in alternative courses of action or inaction—here, the risks of being sued, having to mount a defense, and suffering an adverse judgment.

## The Work Environment

Street-level officials are exposed to litigation-related risks that flow from systematic features of their work. These features include: the character of their interactions with the public; their ambiguous and conflicting goals; their duty to act; the risk of harm from official decisions; their risk of error; the scope of their discretion; and the external constraints upon their decisions.

### OFFICIAL INTERACTIONS WITH THE PUBLIC

Street-level operatives interact constantly and intensively with individuals who are either "clients" or enforcement targets. These interactions implicate significant values and interests. For the citizen, they include physical security, a sense of dignity, protection from personal harm, and access to the life-sustaining benefits of the welfare state. For the official, they include performance of official duty and public service, personal safety and well-being, professional respect, and the obedience-inducing display of authority. These high stakes make the encounter intense and complex, as citizen and official seek to vindicate their respective positions.

These contacts are seldom consensual. In most private law situations (other than traffic accidents), potential injurers and victims can avoid one another unless they perceive some advantage in the contact. In contrast, nonconsensual interactions occur because the state exercises coercive or monopoly powers. When street-level officials discharge functions that only government performs, they deal with citizens not out of mutual desire but simply because there is no alternative. Citizens, lacking any real exit option, must voice their grievances or swallow them; officials, knowing that citizens cannot take their "business" elsewhere, are less pressed to accommodate them.[8] Encounters between policeman and suspect, mental hospital worker and patient, social worker and client, and teacher and student often reflect and exacerbate deep antagonisms, resentments, and fears. Persistent threats of conflict, reprisal, and litigation loom over them like a dreaded incubus.[9]

## THE GOALS OF OFFICIAL CONDUCT

Street-level services are devoted to ends—law enforcement, education, public health, rehabilitation of offenders, care of the ill, and the like—that are subjective and ambiguous, difficult to operationalize or measure, diverse and conflicting. Political consensus as to their meaning tends to coalesce only at the highest levels of generality. Moreover, we can only dimly perceive the extent to which these goals are attained. Our knowledge of techniques to accomplish them is fragmentary and rudimentary, and almost certain to remain so. In an important sense, we come to know and to hold these goals only as a result of making actual, particularized choices that define the terms of trade between them, choices that mediate between the goals and the means for attaining them. That process—because it *is* a process— generates uncertainty, controversy, and misunderstanding, obscuring the standards against which an official's performance should be measured, appraised, and legitimated. "Maintaining order" or "stabilizing troubled families" is not like producing widgets, selling cars, or even practicing medicine. Compared with their private sector counterparts, policemen and social workers can more easily and plausibly be accused of selecting the wrong means or pursuing the wrong ends. Without defined, coherent technologies in which officials can find refuge, these accusations are difficult to overcome—or so officials may fear.

## OFFICIALS' OBLIGATION TO ACT

Private tort doctrine, from which official liability rules largely derive, posits autonomous individuals—free to act, to delay acting, to act in one way rather than another, or to refrain from acting altogether. The choice is theirs, animated by personal commitments and invigorated by idiosyncratic calculations of costs and benefits. Although tort rules are designed to influence those choices, to bring individual self-interest into harmony with the larger social interests, they have nevertheless protected the individual's right to do nothing. Even when one individual could have rescued another from peril at little or no cost to himself, private tort law generally refused to impose any duty to do so.[10] Indeed, the common law rule actually went so far as to deny a remedy against a physician who refused to treat a dying man who had previously been his patient and who had tendered the fee in advance.[11] Only some preexisting "special relationship" or statutory obligation can give rise to a tort law duty to act in another's behalf.[12]

Although this "no duty" rule has its contemporary defenders, utilitarian[13] and libertarian alike,[14] generations of critics have assailed it[15] and its scope has steadily narrowed. Some states, for example, require physicians to assist strangers suffering medical emergencies.[16] Such impositions, however, are unusual, limited to situations in which one could, by acting, almost certainly confer very large social benefits at relatively trivial personal cost. Even these obligations are hedged about with protections, such as granting the rescuer immunity from liability for ordinary negligence and a right to recover costs or the value of rescue services from the victim. Only under these very restricted conditions has society suspended its conviction that individual self-interest is the only motive for action upon which liability may legitimately be based. And even when statutes impose affirmative obligations to act upon a private organization, they seldom extend that duty to individual employees.[17]

Street-level officials, however, must act not in their own behalf but for a diffuse principal, "the public." They are not free to remain passive when that seems the wisest course; they and their organizations are usually under a legal duty to act. Mental hospital administrators must care for mental patients who need treatment and release those who do not.[18] Social workers must remove children from their families when they are in danger and keep them in their homes when they are not.[19] Teachers must not only maintain discipline but educate their students. Because of governmental immunity rules, many victims of official error can proceed only against individual employees, yet when those employees are held liable, they cannot be indemnified by their agencies without benefit of statute even if they acted within the scope of employment and in good faith. And where indemnification statutes exist, they invariably retain important exceptions.[20]

Officials are obliged not only to act, but to act promptly and decisively. Delay, as the Supreme Court has acknowledged, may mean "that action deferred will be futile or constitute virtual abdication of office."[21] When they act, they must often do so coercively; indeed, if they do not coerce others, they may themselves violate the law.[22] They may demand additional compensation for exposing themselves to action-related risks, but civil service wage schedules and agency budgets are too categorical and rigid to respond adequately. Legally obliged to undertake actions that may well cause them to be sued, their realistic options are limited to quitting, accepting the risk, or contriving to avoid or at least minimize it, perhaps in socially perverse ways.

By contrasting the social consequences of official and private inaction, we can better understand why the law imposes a duty to act upon officials but seldom upon private citizens. When society adopts a liability rule, it confers upon $A$ a legal entitlement to be free of conduct that injures certain of $A$'s interests unless the injurer pays $A$ damages.[23] Having done so, society then allows $B$, $C$, . . ., $n$ to decide whether and how to act in light of the risk that their actions will infringe $A$'s entitlement, thus triggering liability. In a crucial sense, society is indifferent to the outcome of this decision. If $B$ decides to act and injures $A$, $A$ can be made whole by the court. Any other decision, however, will not adversely affect interests that society is prepared to protect. A particular individual or group may want others to act and may even be willing to compensate them for doing so. But if the latter nevertheless decline, those who desire the action are not without remedy. Unless those who refuse enjoy monopoly power over the action, the others may obtain substitutes in the market, albeit at some price. Those who refused to act may or may not regret their decisions, but that is not society's affair.

Officials' inaction, however, entails very different considerations. Officials are charged with advancing precisely those collective purposes and values that cannot be readily or accurately priced and thus are not fully vindicated when autonomous self-interested individuals decide whether and how to act. When officials fail to act, neither society in general nor particular individuals harmed by official inaction can ordinarily obtain alternative instrumental actions in the market. Officials' inaction also tends to impose high "opportunity costs"; often, significant benefits would have flowed from the choices foreclosed by their failure to act. A private individual's decision not to act may also jeopardize important values, but his decision implies that on balance he valued inaction more. And because collective interests are not at stake, we presume that he is in the best position to strike that balance.

In contrast, officials are commissioned to act in precisely those situations in which precious but conflicting public values—order, public morality, individual liberty, care of the dependent and vulnerable, personal security, and (to paraphrase Holmes) the social virtues of autonomous individual activity[24]—must be delicately balanced. Society's interest in how officials strike this balance is paramount, for only officials' actions can secure the nonmarketable collective goals at stake. Individual officials would inevitably define and trade off these values idiosyncratically, in radically different ways than would society. Thus, society cannot always count upon them to make the socially correct choice—either the choice between action and inaction or that between action of one kind and action of another. Reluctant to leave this exquisite balancing process either to officials' paralyzing ambivalence or to their untrammeled discretion, public law's solution is to impose a duty to act and to provide remedies for any harm that may result. A dilemma remains, however: the same conditions that make it necessary to require officials to act also make it difficult, perhaps impossible, to specify the content of that duty and to circumscribe their discretion.

### THE RISK OF HARM FROM OFFICIAL DECISIONS

The obligation to act means that street-level officials, far more than private employees, must often risk harm to innocent persons. This propensity to harm springs not simply from the public values implicated by official action or from the number of citizens their behavior affects, but also from the necessity that they wield legitimate coercive authority. As the Supreme Court observed in *Bivens*: "An agent acting—albeit unconstitutionally—in the name of the United States possesses a far greater capacity for harm than an individual trespasser exercising no authority other than his own."[25] When officials err or misbehave, they risk grievous injury to individuals and to the integrity of public authority.[26]

Virtually all official action or inaction makes someone (more likely, many people) worse off than they were before. Most official decisions—decisions to act, to refrain from acting, or to act in one way rather than another—inevitably sacrifice important public values.

That, after all, is what it means to say that officials must strike a delicate balance. Indeed, many decisions are so "close" that officials who pass over the line into the realm of illegality may feel little remorse; even to the law-abiding official, such transgressions often seem justified.[27] Even the police officer who illegally searches one who would be convicted but for the exclusionary rule has advanced some important social values—the apprehension, detention, and perhaps deterrence of a wrongdoer—while flouting others that are thought to override them. Psychological and moral justifications of this kind of illegality have been noted in the behavior and statements of many officials, ranging from police to prison guards to employment service workers.[28]

Many governmental actions not only create winners and losers but pinpoint them with clarity. Traditional adjudication, "pork barrel" legislation, police arrests, and suspension of rowdy students are common examples. Official action and inaction, however, are quite asymmetric in this respect. Police officers who arrest criminals may violate their rights, and they will have a powerful incentive to complain; failure to arrest may neglect the interests of criminals' subsequent victims and of the larger society, but neither victims nor society will know of what did not occur. Officials who discharge subordinates may do so without adequate cause or in violation of procedural rules and the subordinates will have remedies to invoke; failure to fire malingerers may encourage incompetence, impair the morale of co-workers, and injure taxpayers, but these victims are in a poor position to complain. Such asymmetries strongly bias public tort remedies to favor the highly visible victims of official action but to leave the largely invisible and silent victims of official inaction or neglect without recourse.

THE RISK OF OFFICIAL ERROR

Any decision, of course, is subject to error, but the conditions under which street-level officials decide significantly magnify this irreducible "background" risk. Many choices must be made quickly, even instantaneously, about events occurring not retrospectively but in "real time."[29] Inspectors and other law enforcement officials, for example, are obliged to intervene as soon as they detect a violation. The massive case loads of most client-oriented officials and the situational, emergency nature of many public services also ensure that a particular decision will be made far more quickly than the precious values at stake might seem to warrant. Many decisions must be made in virtual ignorance; the scant available information is typically of low quality and costly to improve, and time pressures preclude considering whether investment in obtaining more and better information would be worthwhile.[30] A rational decision strategy, therefore, might emphasize using rules of thumb, cues, and presumptions,[31] but strong legal, professional, and moral norms demand precisely the opposite. Officials are expected—indeed, the Constitution may even require them—to individuate their decisions according to the circumstances of each citizen rather than to generalize on the basis of broad conceptions.[32] This ethos, however, requires a quantity and quality of information simply unavailable to most street-level officials.[33]

RULES AND OFFICIAL DISCRETION

Private tort law expects little of individuals. In general, they need only behave as ordinary persons in similar circumstances would behave; mistakes in judgment are tolerated if they are "reasonable." No special knowledge, insight, or capacity is required. Indeed, private tort principles actually disadvantage one with above-average skills or training.[34] An individual is presumed to know the law, of course, but the law ordinarily has little to say concerning what courses of action may safely be undertaken; it simply whispers "behave reasonably, nothing more."

Street-level officials, in contrast, are usually subject to, and must administer, a plethora of rules[35] designed to guide action, but they are often so voluminous, ambiguous, and contradictory, and in such flux that officials can only comply with or enforce them selectively.[36] Some officials are more rule-bound than others and the nature of the rules that constrain them varies,[37] but the ones they are most likely to violate and be sued about tend to provide the least guidance as to what constitutes compliance. In many situations in which police officers must act quickly, for example, "no guidelines can do much more than restate the law and urge officials to obey that law and, in the gray areas, to use their judgment."[38] Anthony Amsterdam has observed that police officers will always arrest a murderer when they see one, but whether they will do many other things depends largely upon their "mood and inclination."[39] Moreover, legal language cannot supply the certainty and determinacy lacking in the reality to which it applies. Like a physician exercising clinical judgment, officials must often rely in the end upon nonsystematic decision criteria—intuition, experience, and "feel."[40]

Street-level officials, then , are actually awash in discretion. Patterns of informal influence in their agencies mock the distribution of formal legal authority. Indeed, the lower their position in the agency hierarchy, the more de facto discretion they tend to enjoy.[41] This inverse relationship between organizational position and influence over outcomes characterizes the situations of not only police officers but teachers, welfare workers, prison guards, and even inspectors in the most "legalistic," rule-oriented agencies; it primarily reflects their complex tasks and freedom from supervisory observation, and the absence of objective performance criteria.[42] It is no great exaggeration to say that such officials are "the *policymakers* in their respective work arenas."[43]

## POLITICAL, INSTITUTIONAL, AND RESOURCE CONSTRAINTS

Street-level officials may operate far from the gaze of front-office supervisors, but they are not autonomous; indeed, their performance and professional well-being largely depend upon forces beyond their effective control. Legislative committees, courts, pressure groups, the civil service apparatus, the media, employee unions, and other influential organs can and do reward, punish, threaten, and embarrass them. Abjectly vulnerable, pursuing ambiguous and nonmeasurable goals, officials often aspire less to achieving the agency's formal mission than to avoiding personal criticism. The "state of affairs most costly to the police department," Wilson notes, "[is] not a rising crime rate, but revelations of corruption, fiscal malfeasance, and citizen complaints of misconduct."[44] Teachers unsure of what it means to "educate" their students attend instead to test scores, lesson plans, and classroom discipline.[45]

The chronic gap between demand for (and entitlement to) street-level services and the supply of resources for satisfying it adversely affects the information base for decisions, the possibility of individuated decisions, and the recruitment, training, and quality of personnel. The fact that most street-level jobs are at entry level exacerbates these deficiencies.[46] Public services are free to those who consume them and politically valuable to those who supply them; demand therefore tends to expand to meet supply, and any new supply increments in resources are usually devoted to increasing the population served rather than to improving the correctness of individual decisions.[47] When courts mandate expanded public services or procedures without regard to budgetary constraints but then fail to require the taxes and appropriations necessary to finance them,[48] this tendency is strengthened. Low-level decisionmakers in private firms also confront resource needs and must often decide without adequate information. But if poorly informed or highly constrained decisions seem too risky to them, they can either

refuse to proceed or seek additional compensation to cover those risks
without violating any legal duty. Public officials, of course, also have
alternatives. They can act anyway, quit, or attempt to eliminate the risk
to themselves. In the remainder of this chapter I explore the plausibil-
ity of this last option.

## The Official's Decisional Calculus

How do these conditions affect street-level officials when they come
to choose whether, when, and how to act? To answer this question,
we must consider one more distinctive feature of their work context:
officials cannot retain any of the benefits that flow from their
decisions.[49] Private actors may willingly incur risks they think are
necessary to obtain desired benefits. Their public counterparts, however, cannot in any conventional sense reap the fruits of their official
actions. Even attempting to appropriate them might well subject
officials to criminal sanctions.[50] Officials, of course, may derive personal satisfaction (and possibly even advance their status and income)
from having performed decisively and well. Differential risks may be
reflected in civil service pay schedules to a limited degree. Nevertheless, the returns for accepting risk are far more intangible and remote
than the potential rewards that motivate private risk-taking.[51]

This nonappropriability of benefits flowing from official choices is
central to evaluating public tort remedies. Under the most plausible
assumptions about official motivation, it implies a strategy of personal
risk minimization. Most private actors would decide to incur any cost if
the expected value of the correlative benefit were great enough, but
officials tend to reject any course of action that would drive their
personal costs above some minimum level, what I call a "duty
threshold." The duty threshold, of course, varies from official to
official, for it is defined by one's idiosyncratic attitudes toward (and
trade-offs among) certain values and interests, some altruistic, some
more narrowly self-interested, that economic models of choice cannot
readily take into account[52]—feelings of professionalism; moral duty;
programmatic mission; fear of criticism, discipline, or reprisals for
self-protective behavior; concern for professional reputation; habitua-
tion to routine; personal convenience; and the like. Officials tend to
orient their decisions about whether, when, and how to act less toward
maximizing (or even "satisficing") net benefits, which they cannot appropriate, than toward minimizing (subject to their duty threshold)
those costs that they would incur personally. Costs take many forms.

Even perfectly proper conduct may generate some burdens, and many officials are routinely exposed to physical danger, repellent conditions, or deep anxiety. If officials violate agency rules or citizens' rights, either inadvertently or otherwise, they may suffer disciplinary sanctions, harm to professional reputation, reduced promotion opportunities, and litigation. These risks, we have seen, are endemic to street-level officials' life.

Here, we are concerned with officials' risks of being personally sued for damages. The precise magnitude of their (negative) expected value from litigation, of course, depends upon two analytically distinct factors. The first is the expected pecuniary and nonpecuniary cost of having to defend an action, quite apart from its outcome. This category includes the costs of uncertainty itself—uncertainty about contingencies such as the outcome of the case; its duration; its effect upon the official's creditworthiness; the circumstances under which the official may receive (or lose) free counsel and indemnification of any settlement or adverse judgment; the quality of legal representation that the defending agency will provide; and potential conflicts of interest on the part of the defending agency or assigned counsel. Some of these contingencies are discussed in chapter 4. The second is the expected frequency and pecuniary cost of an array of possible outcomes, ranging from dismissal at an early state of the case to a final judgment for compensatory and punitive damages.

Appraising remedies' behavioral effects demands that we consider several difficult empirical questions. The first relates to risk assessment: How do public officials in fact perceive and evaluate the risk of being sued and the costs associated with that risk? Despite the obvious public policy importance of this question, no answer—indeed, no systematic evidence bearing on the question—yet exists. One can easily understand why. Officials have only recently had any reason to think about the matter at all. Section 1983 and *Bivens* actions have assumed their contemporary significance only during the last decade or so, and personal liability for officials first became a real possibility several years ago with the narrowing of personal immunities in *Scheuer* v. *Rhodes* and *Butz* v. *Economou*.[53] But even if officials thought about the question, no consistent pattern of responses could be expected. The objective probability of being sued depends upon the official function being performed; policemen and FBI agents, for example, are sued more often than inspectors or social workers. Subjective probability assessments also vary,[54] and any methodology for eliciting them could suffer from a kind of "Hawthorne effect," in which merely calling attention to the risk might exaggerate its perceived magnitude.[55] Without a reliable measure (even one as controversial as "profit maximization"), moreover, subjective risk assessments cannot be rigorously tested or verified.

Even if we assume what is surely true—that any particular official is very unlikely to be held personally liable—there are still reasons to believe that they take the prospect of being sued seriously. First, although the risk of an official losing a case is extremely small (approximately 10,000 *Bivens* actions have reportedly produced only thirteen judgments for plaintiffs[56]), the risk of being sued is far greater, and even successful defenses can exact heavy personal costs from officials.[57] Testimony at recent congressional hearings on the subject confirms that when litigation lightning does indeed strike, the consequences can be personally devastating.[58] Second, we have seen that officials may be especially risk-averse with respect to personal litigation. Finally, for whatever it is worth, officials and those who speak for them *say* that they worry a good deal about being sued. It is reported, for example, that "caseworker concern over civil and criminal liability . . . has become the most popular topic at professional conferences on child maltreatment";[59] teachers and school board members are said to be similarly preoccupied.[60] Public employees appear to be purchasing liability insurance more frequently.[61]

If officials indeed worry about litigation, then a second empirical question, relating to official behavior, arises: How do officials actually respond to the risks associated with being sued? This question is perhaps even more difficult to answer than the first. Officials, like the rest of us, do not like to believe, much less publicly acknowledge, that they shirk their legal duty. And it is not obvious how one can distinguish (except analytically) between cognate motives or between their similar behavioral effects. The risk of litigation, after all, is only one risk that officials face, and fear of liability is but one incentive to minimize risk; concern for personal safety and sheer indolence are others. There is no reason, moreover, to expect all officials to respond alike. Nevertheless, certain general patterns of response to risk perceptions can be predicted with some confidence on the basis of what we know about officials' incentives and opportunities. Officials, I have maintained, are strongly motivated to minimize the personal costs of particular courses of action, and once their duty thresholds are met, they have little reason to advert to how that strategy might affect others. In the extreme case, they will be prepared to sacrifice all social benefits in order to reduce even slightly the personal costs that a decision entails.

To the extent they behave rationally, officials are tempted to shift as many decision-related costs as possible from themselves to others.

Street-level officials, moreover, are well positioned to pursue this strategy. They have ample opportunity to shift costs to members of the public in ways that elude detection or effective control. Neither legislative oversight, judicial review of administration, nor conventional bureaucratic controls can effectively monitor official decisions that are irreducibly discretionary, low-visibility, and rule-resistant.[62] Endowed with this freedom of action, officials can exploit it by drawing upon a repertoire of defensive, self-protective tactics often associated, none too charitably, with "the bureaucratic mind." These tactics, though protean in form, may usefully be classified into four general and somewhat overlapping categories: inaction, delay, formalism, and a change in the character of decisions. They are not so much predictable outcomes as general tendencies, less inescapable imperatives than inclinations encouraged by incentives.

INACTION

If officials perceive that performing their legal duty may generate personal costs that exceed their duty thresholds, they may simply refrain from acting. The Supreme Court has acknowledged the skewed incentives noted earlier[63]—the asymmetric litigation risks that officials face:

> While there is not likely to be anyone willing and legally able to seek damages from the officials if they do not authorize the administrative proceeding . . . , there is a serious danger that the decision to authorize proceedings will provoke a retaliatory response. An individual targeted by an administrative proceeding will react angrily and may seek vengeance in the courts. A corporation will muster all of its financial and legal resources in an effort to prevent administrative sanctions. "When millions may turn on regulatory decisions, there is a strong incentive to counterattack."[64]

This asymmetry encourages official inaction whenever that is a viable alternative, and either of two conditions will suffice to make it so. First, superiors or others may not notice the failure to act either because the choice of whether to act is so discretionary or because the structure of the situation conceals it. Narcotics agents' treatment of informers on the street not only is difficult to monitor but is largely intuitive and situation-specific.[65] No one is likely to know when police officers decline to follow up on suspicious behavior observed in a hostile or dangerous neighborhood. Inspectors who fail to enforce clearly applicable statutes against pugnacious or litigious violators are unlikely to be sued by the consumers whom they did not protect, whereas inspectors who *do* enforce vigorously may now be subject to suit under § 1983.[66] In such situations, any official duty to act affirmatively is as a practical matter unenforceable, and existing incentives favoring inaction are reinforced. Second, quite apart from officials' visibility or discretion, their inaction may primarily harm people who are likely to remain passive or silent. A schoolteacher's failure to discipline disruptive students may sacrifice the interests of their classmates, but these victims, even if they recognize themselves as such, will be reluctant to challenge the decision of one with authority over them.

Both of these conditions are common features of street-level official life. One authority on law and education, for example, suggests that as a result of the Supreme Court's decision in *Wood* v. *Strickland*,[67] which made it more difficult for school personnel to invoke a "good faith" immunity,[68] teachers

> may be less likely to make controversial decisions, such as suspending rowdy students or affording special treatment to children with unusual talents or disabilities. With the current distaste for any form of differentiation, equality of treatment may appear to be the safest, if not necessarily the soundest, course. Alternatively, school people may delegate to parents and students decisions which they previously took upon themselves.[69]

At least one college professor has maintained publicly that his fear of being sued, coupled with his employer's refusal to provide legal counsel, caused him to refuse to evaluate the work of candidates for tenured positions.[70] A recent study of inspectors also found inaction to be a common technique for minimizing personal risks:

> When he "writes up" a violation, an inspector's work is carefully reviewed by superiors; he may have to go back to the site to gather additional, more formal evidence; he may incur the anger and hostility of personnel in this regulated enterprise who berate him for being unreasonable. Thus it is certainly *easier* for field inspectors to overlook violations or to rely on informal prodding than to initiate formal prosecution, even when prosecution is clearly warranted.[71]

That discretion often encourages inaction is also suggested by Lipsky's finding that policemen "probably would not go out on the street if [detailed] instructions were promulgated, or they would refuse to intervene in potentially dangerous situations."[72]

## DELAY

Officials, despite incentives favoring passivity, may nevertheless wish to act. They may want to minimize further the small risk of being criticized or sanctioned for inaction, or they may feel that duty dictates that something affirmative be done. Under these circumstances, delayed action rather than total passivity may well serve their purposes.

Delay can assume many forms. Subordinate officials can insist upon receiving approval from their superiors before taking action. Agents of the FBI, for example, who jealously guard their pristine work records, often demand "written instructions from the highest level in order to protect themselves from the possibility of subsequent criticism."[73] Officials may decide to consult with legal counsel or even require formal legal opinions before acting. Thus, because litigation against child protection workers has increased,[74] Massachusetts has abandoned its long-standing practice of allowing caseworkers to make placement recommendations directly to the court; instead, departmental attorneys must now review placement plans in advance.[75] Delay may also take the form of additional perfunctory factual investigations prior to decisions. Whether or not more data, more committee meetings, and more reviews of documents improve the accuracy of predictions and decisions, they will surely fortify officials against subsequent criticism for having acted hastily or arbitrarily.

Decisions and actions delayed can mean opportunities forever foreclosed—a criminal who can no longer be apprehended, parental child abuse that can never be wholly remedied, a disrupted learning environment that cannot be restored. At the very least, delay threatens the same public interests as inaction and often increases the costs of even those actions that are ultimately taken.[76]

## FORMALISM

Officials who overcome the temptation to desist or delay and instead decide to act enjoy numerous opportunities to "build a record" with which subsequently to defend their actions, should that become necessary. These fortifications may readily be built by preceding and surrounding decisions with formal procedures. This strategy is closely related to delay, and officials have strong incentives to employ it even when the additional procedures generate costs out of all proportion to any likely benefits.

A close and revealing analogy may be discerned in a well-documented practice, "defensive medicine," in which physicians order additional laboratory tests and other diagnostic procedures with little or no regard to their cost.[77] Because the costs will be borne by a diffuse public and the procedures support a record of painstaking, conservative treatment, the risk to the physician of malpractice liability and other personal costs associated with the ultimate treatment decision is reduced.[78] In fact, officials' incentives to practice "defensive decision-making" are even more powerful than those of physicians. Profligate medical care occurs in large part because under present financing arrangements, providers and patients neither bear the marginal costs of these benefits nor otherwise attend closely to those costs.[79] Ethical, professional, and perhaps legal norms encourage physicians to authorize additional procedures and expenditures whenever the marginal benefit is even slightly positive, however high the marginal cost.[80] Officials, however, are not subject to even this minimal constraint; they need not justify a costly but liability-reducing expenditure by the prospect of even a slight marginal benefit to the public.

Manifestations of formalism are all too familiar. Officials maintain elaborate records and require that those whom they regulate do so as well. Flexible procedures are formalized and reduced to writing. A study of a new special education program, for example, found that partly in order to avoid costly recriminations from parents, teachers routinized and bureaucratized the student evaluation process by substituting formal procedures for the individual assessments and parental involvement that the statute had envisioned.[81] Ironically, perhaps, similar considerations may induce officials to avoid committing certain matters to writing at all, with perverse results.[82] Officials may also preoccupy themselves with what is measurable and objective—with processes and techniques, rather than with the more elusive but important ends and outcomes of public policies. Blau's study of state employment service workers, for example, found that when performance indicators were used to evaluate front-line officials' work, the officials responded with paper routines, legalism, and "ritualism," a hollow and subversive parody of the reform's purpose. This led to what sociologist Robert Merton has called a "displacement of goals whereby 'an instrumental value becomes a terminal value.' "[83] Mashaw's study of disability determinations reveals similar distortions resulting from efforts to formalize the assessment process and subject it to hierarchical control.[84]

Formalism of this kind leads almost ineluctably to legalism. As officials learn to find comfort—and a secure haven from liability—in what Blau calls "ritualistic conformity"[85] to bureaucratic rules and procedures, these rules and procedures assume ever more importance and prominence in the bureaucratic scheme of things. Officials come to regard the public not merely as clients or citizens but as potential adversaries and litigants. "Legalization [of public schools]," one commentator observed, "may result in formally correct decisions which nonetheless ignore the real interests at stake. It may impose inflexibility which makes adjustments to changing conditions more difficult. It certainly may impose substantial transaction costs."[86]

Bardach and Kagan's study of inspectors seems to confirm this melancholy prediction. Fear of criticism and sanctions encourages inspectors to approach their tasks rigidly. They insist upon excessive documentation, eschew qualitative judgments, avoid using discretion, resist negotiation and flexibility, and adopt a "checklist" mode of enforcement that emphasizes "violations" rather than "problems." They tend to perceive regulatory situations as static conditions rather than as dynamic and contextual. They become preoccupied with possibilities rather than with concrete experiences. This approach, according to the authors, causes inspectors to neglect important levers for securing compliance, to divert scarce regulatory resources to trivial problems, and to nourish an adversarial "culture of resistance" that elicits only minimal, technical, or grudging compliance—and virtually automatic court challenges.[87]

CHANGES IN THE CHARACTER OF DECISIONS

Instead of inaction, delay, or self-conscious formalism, officials wishing to avoid litigation may attempt to substitute one kind of action for another. In particular, they may substitute relatively riskless acts for relatively risky ones. Social workers, for example, may more quickly—but prematurely—remove children from troubled families rather than risk being sued on behalf of an abused child.[88] Parole officers may refrain from recommending release in order to minimize the risk of being sued by potential victims.[89] Supervisors may promote or give glowing recommendations to malingering or disruptive employees in order to be free of them rather than invite a suit for wrongful dismissal.[90]

This type of decisional transformation is accelerated in a political and bureaucratic culture that penalizes risky actions when they fail (as they sometimes must) but seldom even acknowledges, much less rewards, those same actions when they manage to succeed (as they occasionally

will). Society tends not to think about risk in relative terms and often
ignores the concealed costs of reducing it. Failure is usually more
visible and "newsworthy" than success, which is somehow taken for
granted. In our fragmented political system, credit for success can be
widely claimed and therefore diffused; blame for failure, however,
tends to be concentrated in a desperate search for scapegoats. The
prospect of success thus constitutes a less powerful motive for action
than the specter of failure. Most individuals probably begin by being
risk-averse when the possibility of catastrophic outcomes is perceived;[91] the conditions of public life systematically aggravate that
tendency.[92]

Consider an official who is willing to accept some risk that potentially
dangerous drugs will be erroneously approved in order to maximize
the probability that no therapeutically valuable drugs will be erroneously rejected. If he approves a drug that turns out to be a thalidomide,
he can expect to be hauled before congressional committees, disgraced
professionally, and perhaps even cashiered. Yet when the identical
strategy leads him to approve an important antibiotic, Congress will
probably not take notice of the official's work, much less applaud him.
Instead, his beneficial action will simply blend into the "background
noise" of administrative life. A former FDA commissioner has testified:
"In all the agency's history, we are unable to find one instance where a
Congressional hearing investigated the failure of the FDA to approve a
new drug . . . [T]he message conveyed by this situation could not be
clearer."[93] Blau makes a somewhat related point: "If insecurity per-
vades the work situation, risks must be avoided at all cost, and, since
endeavors to find the best means for the achievement of given objectives always involve an element of risk, such endeavors will be
abandoned."[94]

From society's perspective, the tactics of personal risk minimization
that I have discussed—inaction, delay, formalism, and decisional
transformation—are certainly not unmitigated evils. They may eliminate some imprudent conduct altogether, and they may also yield
decisions that, because they are more carefully considered, are also
more accurate, enjoy wider support, and tend to be perceived as
fairer.[95] From society's perspective, these advantages may sometimes
even outweigh the costs of official self-protection. The significant point,
however, is that street-level officials have both the incentives and the
opportunities to employ these tactics *without regard to where the balance of social costs and benefits lies*. It is in this sense that the problem
of controlling public torts presents special difficulties for a theory of

deterrence directed at private torts, such as Calabresi's approach for minimizing the costs of accidents. As Calabresi's own work on medical malpractice suggests, his prescriptions can produce very different results in different contexts. If a rule of official liability has been adopted following his criteria for general deterrence,[96] officials could avoid the full costs of their misconduct through these self-protection techniques. By shifting such costs to the public in low-visibility ways, they may overwhelm the cost-minimizing capability of the general deterrence approach. Similarly, officials can disarm a specific deterrence approach[97] by substituting for the prohibited act conduct that generates even fewer social benefits and greater social costs but happens to minimize officials' liability risks. Thus, official self-protection does not necessarily ensure or even encourage decisions that reflect a socially favorable balance. Indeed, desirable outcomes may be essentially adventitious rather than the consequence of sound remedial policy.

## The Possibility of Countervailing Incentive Systems

One can easily imagine political structures or legal regimes that might create a more socially benign set of incentives—that might encourage official risk-taking and decisiveness while discouraging self-protection. Political forces sometimes impel even risk-averse officials to act more audaciously. A police department criticized for failing to solve a well-publicized crime, NASA operating under a strict deadline to land an astronaut on the moon, New York City under irresistible fiscal pressures to trim municipal employment—these are political climates conducive to official risk-taking. Merely to mention them, of course, is to suggest how unusual they are and how critically they depend upon the ability of agency leadership, which receives political signals and incentives directly, to transmit those signals and incentives downward to their front-line personnel. This problem is discussed in part III.

In the more conventional bureaucratic realm, official audacity might be encouraged by creating a legal remedy in favor of victims of official self-protection. This remedy would complement the more familiar ones available to victims of affirmative official misconduct, such as § 1983, and to victims of official inaction where a mandatory duty to act exists, such as the writ of *mandamus*.[98] It would be designed to internalize the social costs of official passivity. Students whose education is impaired because teachers fail to eject unruly classmates, citizens harmed by criminals that more enterprising police might have apprehended, prisoners not recommended for parole by overcautious parole officers, workers injured by conditions that inspectors ought to have detected—these individuals and others harmed by official self- protection would be entitled to seek recoveries.

A remedy for bureaucratic passivity, however, would entail awesome difficulties. If the law would hold officials liable when they do not act at all or act only belatedly, it must first surmount several obstacles. It must define the individuals or classes of individuals to whom the official now owes a duty. At common law, as we saw earlier, the universe of potential plaintiffs was carefully circumscribed; where the defendant did not act ("nonfeasance"), it included only those to whom he owed a clearly defined duty of care, one usually based upon some actual or imputed preexisting relationship justifying an expectation of protection. He owed no duty to the public at large, and any duty that he did owe to others was limited to not harming them.[99] A remedy that relaxed these two restrictions would almost certainly expose officials to massive litigation and liability (albeit from different quarters), a result that would multiply further their incentives for self-protection.

A limiting principle might be sought, however, in the notion of causation; only those whose harm was "caused" by an official's inaction or delay would be permitted to sue. But this approach only reveals a second difficulty with the countervailing remedy. Legal scholars and philosophers have long wrestled with the problem of deciding which one or which few of the numerous acts preceding an injury are so causally linked to it that liability may be imposed without offending our notions of common sense, morality, and sound policy.[100] To implement the countervailing remedy, a literally infinite number of nonacts would have to be evaluated in the context of opaque means-end relationships and uncertain program technologies. If the policeman had responded to the call for help, would the crime have been averted or would it have occurred anyway?[101] If the teacher had conducted the class more energetically, would the student have learned more or not?[102] If the parole official had been less fearful of criticism about crimes committed by parolees, would he have recommended the prisoner's release?[103] In the realm of official inaction, at least, causation is not merely an unserviceable limiting principle; it simply poses the central question anew: What ought the official to have done?

A countervailing remedy would also have to be processed by an institution capable of *evaluating* ostensible self-protection. Such evaluations would require nothing less than social cost-benefit analyses of what the official did, did not do, and might have done. They would have to distinguish official risk minimization that was on balance socially justified from mere self-protection, and self-protection that produced incidental public benefits from that which did not. To avoid arbitrary second-guessing of highly specialized, context-sensitive official decisions, the law would have to confer immunities at least as generous as the "good faith" immunity to which administrative officials are ordinarily entitled. As chapter 4 suggests, it is highly doubtful that conventional triers of fact could sensibly apply these standards. It may be argued, of course, that none of these difficulties with a countervailing remedy for bureaucratic self-protection would be insuperable and that such an expansion is but a small step beyond the point to which tort law has already evolved. Perhaps judges and juries are no less capable of making the necessary judgments in these cases than they are in other kinds of cases, such as complex antitrust litigation.

Nevertheless, there can be no question that such a remedy would radically transform the working conditions of public officials by significantly increasing their exposure to suit and potential liability and by placing them in a perennial "damned-if-you-do, damned-if-you-don't" situation. The effects of such a change upon official recruitment, vigorous decisionmaking, civil service morale, and the visible and hidden costs of government are simply impossible to predict.

It would be rather surprising, however, if expanding the risk of litigation, a partial cause of official self-protection, also turned out to be an effective remedy for that pathology. A general deterrence remedy—liability for damages—aimed at the individual street-level official may simply be too crude to strike the delicate balance that the competing public values demand. General deterrence directed at higher levels of government, augmented by carefully designed specific deterrence measures, would appear to hold far greater promise. This is the subject of chapters 5 through 8.

## Conclusion

We do not know, and we are unlikely ever to learn, how often officials engage in self-protection and how much of this risk-minimizing behavior can fairly be attributed to fear of litigation. We also cannot calculate the social cost of such tactics or the extent to which any benefits that they produce inure solely to the official or instead (or in addition) advance broader public purposes. Nevertheless, there are strong reasons to regard official self-protection as a significant and growing problem. First, the fundamental remedial asymmetry discussed earlier prevents society from learning about the full costs that this tactic imposes. Identifiable victims of affirmative official wrongdoing are far more likely to seek and to obtain remedies for their harms, inadequate as those remedies often are, than the invisible victims of official self-protection, who suffer in silence, unaware that they have been injured or ignorant that their injury is the consequence of some official's self-regard. This asymmetry distorts the signals that litigation transmits to courts and that courts in turn transmit to society. Society systematically undervalues vigorous decisionmaking to the extent that the costs associated with its diminution are concealed. The distortions generated by this asymmetry inevitably affect the types of substantive claim asserted against officials, the mix of incentives that animate their behavior, the nature of the legal rules that courts formulate, and the kinds of social pressure for change that are exerted. A tort remedy against official self-protection, we may predict, would not cure this asymmetry but would instead engender significant, perhaps insuperable, difficulties of its own.

Second, the individuals most likely to be victimized by official self-protection are precisely those most dependent upon public services to ensure their safety and well-being, a fact that further distorts these social and evaluation processes. Disproportionately poor and vulnerable, these persons can least afford to bear the costs of official self-protection and are least likely to learn of their victimization and articulate their grievances. They are precisely the individuals whom a just society would least wish to burden. Because their stakes in decisive law enforcement, selfless social work, and a responsive civil service are especially high, a policy that threatens the energy with which those activities are conducted may well make the worst off even worse off.

Third, the fact that victims of official self-protection seldom sue successfully means that such behavior is a "free good" to officials (and perhaps to their agencies as well). Since they have no self-interested reason to advert to the social benefits forgone by their behavior, this strategy may appear quite rational to officials even if it imposes very high social costs, and they will engage in as much of it as their duty thresholds and organizational latitude allow. To adapt Calabresi's formulation, officials will seldom be the cheapest social cost avoiders precisely because they will almost always be the cheapest personal risk avoiders.

Finally, the Supreme Court's recent liability- and remedy-expanding decisions[104] have unquestionably strengthened the already powerful incentives for official self-protection. Not only have the risks of being sued and incurring costs increased markedly, but the subjectively perceived risks of litigation loom far greater than the objective probability of liability alone would suggest. When a Washington, D.C., jury renders a verdict for more than $700,000 against individual FBI agents and police officers after years of turbulent litigation, the officials' counterparts throughout the nation are sure to hear about and be affected by it—for better, for worse, or both.[105]

The powerful motives and opportunities of officials to conflate their duties to the public with their obligations to themselves are fundamental facts of our collective life. The remedy of individual official liability for damages throws these facts into bold relief. We ignore them at our peril. In the chapters that follow, I hope to show that a different remedial system, one more attentive to these realities, would better serve the public interest.

# 4: DISTRIBUTING THE COSTS OF OFFICIAL MISCONDUCT

By concentrating the costs of litigation and liability upon individual, risk-averse officials rather than spreading those costs through a public sector version of *respondeat superior*, public tort law exacts a high price. In chapter 3, I showed how official liability undermines vigorous decisionmaking. Most legal policymakers, of course, appreciate the importance of this value and the threat that official liability poses to it. By building incrementally upon the remedial system that they inherited, they have devised institutional and doctrinal adjustments calculated to preserve both the value and the remedy intact.

Two types of adjustments have been employed, each of which frees officials from misconduct-related costs and allocates those costs elsewhere. One, consisting of rules providing officials with a free legal defense and indemnifying or insuring settlements or judgments against them, *shifts* the costs of misconduct from officials to the government as a whole. The other, consisting of official immunity doctrines and the "American rule" (requiring parties to bear their own litigation expenses), *leaves* the costs of official misconduct and of challenging it on the victim. In this chapter I consider whether these structures in fact succeed in harmonizing the value and the remedy. I conclude that they do not, that the first leaves vigorous decisionmaking in jeopardy whereas the second intolerably frustrates compensation and other remedial values. In chapter 5 I propose a reformed system in which official liability would have little or no place.

*Shifting the Costs of Official Misconduct to Government*

In the private sector, individuals or firms exposed to the risk of litigation and liability can usually protect themselves by redistributing these risks and the attendant costs through contract, insurance, or additional compensation. But apart from the forms of self-protection discussed in chapter 3, what recourse is available to officials? Remarkably, no Supreme Court majority has ever so much as mentioned this question; only three minority opinions have even raised it in passing.[1] This silence is all the more astonishing because the issue has actually received some detailed empirical investigation.[2] These studies indicate that in practice, officials can usually shift these costs to the government. They cannot always do so, however, and they cannot shift the costs associated with certain risks at all in certain situations in which compensation appears to be most justified and vigorous decisionmaking most threatened by uncertainty.

Most liability-related cost-shifting in the private sector occurs through contractual arrangements. In a seminal article, Ronald Coase argued that disregarding the costs of transacting an agreement, a tort liability rule's initial allocation of injury costs—leaving them on the victim or shifting them to the injurer, imposing them upon an employee or instead upon the employer—does not affect how the costs of injury and injury prevention are ultimately distributed. Instead, those costs simply become items in the continual bargaining between affected interests, as each strives to improve his own net outcome.[3] The "Coase theorem" presupposes a private law regime in which benefits can be privately appropriated. Although its theoretical and empirical validity are controversial,[4] its central insight—that in tort law liability is constantly distributed, redistributed, and perhaps even neutralized through contract—is relevant to the design of public tort remedies.

In the public sector, where politics supplants markets as the principal mechanism for allocating resources[5] and *respondeat superior* is not generally accepted, officials' ability to shift costs to governmental employers depends less upon contract (though it continues to play a role, especially in collective bargaining) than upon whether and to what extent the government is legally authorized to defend and insure or indemnify these individuals. In each case, a cost that would otherwise fall on individual officials is assumed by government (with risk-sharing by a third party if the liability is insured). Whether particular officials can count on these protections depends chiefly upon the specific language of the statutory or (with insurance) contractual provisions applicable to their cases.

## LEGAL DEFENSE

Federal employees who are sued for actions taken in the scope of employment have no legal entitlement to government representation.

Nevertheless, the United States ordinarily defends them at public expense. When an official is under criminal investigation but no decision to indict has been made, or when several official defendants have conflicting interests, the United States may pay for private counsel. Counsel must be approved by the Department of Justice, funding is contingent upon appropriations, and the attorneys are paid at the government's ceiling rate, often well below prevailing market levels.[6]

Private counsel, however, apparently may not be retained at government expense in other situations where conflicts of interest between the government and officials may arise—for example, when the government wishes for political, policy, or other reasons to make legal or factual arguments contrary to an official's self-interest.[7] Indeed, when the Justice Department represents officials, they are subject to certain limitations that may place them at a serious disadvantage. Such officials, for example, may not assert any claim against the United States or against another federal official; the government will not waive certain privileges, such as those relating to confidential informants, even if the clients' interests demand a waiver; and the government may decline to appeal adverse judgments against their officials-clients. In most cases, officials apparently agree to these conditions at the outset, preferring to run the risk that conflicts of interest will develop between them and their Justice Department lawyer that will be resolved against them, rather than having to hire private lawyers at their own expense.[8]

Finally, the government will neither represent nor retain counsel for federal officials in three types of cases: where an official is a target of a federal criminal investigation or proceeding and will be indicted; where the government believes the acts sued upon were not within the scope of federal employment; and where the government determines that representation "is not in the interests of the United States."[9] No written guidelines flesh out these ambiguous standards.

In view of the potential for exploiting conflicts of interest between officials and the government, and for making officials anxious about the conduct and cost of their cases, it is not surprising that plaintiffs often name officials as additional defendants even when the United States can be sued under the FTCA. Other tactical considerations also encourage this practice.[10]

For state and local officials sued under § 1983, the availability of a publicly subsidized defense depends upon local law. Most jurisdictions apparently provide it for employees who acted within the scope of employment. Officials assured of representation by government counsel, however, may still be apprehensive, for they neither select, pay, nor directly control the lawyers assigned to their case; counsel may be incompetent, unresponsive, or subject to conflicts of interest that become apparent only after the case is well under way.[11]

### INSURANCE

Federal law does not provide for the purchase of insurance against the personal liability of officials, except for certain medical personnel.[12] Some state laws do authorize official liability insurance, but the scope of authority and coverage vary among jurisdictions and policies and no overview analysis exists. States and localities sometimes purchase insurance against their own liabilities or indemnification costs, but self-insurance is probably more common; even before *Monell*, *Owen*, and *Thiboutot*, carriers were apparently reluctant to insure against governmental liability.[13] Self-insurance by officials is surely quite limited.[14] In addition, officials' liability for some public torts, especially intentional ones, may be uninsurable;[15] as with analogous private law torts, insurance may be deemed contrary to public policy, as it tends to reduce deterrence.[16]

### INDEMNIFICATION

To shift the burden of liability to government, officials must be fully indemnified for any adverse settlements or judgments. Such indemnification, however, is neither certain nor universal. No general statutory authority exists for indemnifying federal employees, even for conduct clearly within the scope of their employment.[17] Nevertheless, claims against federal officials for actions that constitute torts under state law may be brought against the United States under the FTCA; the availability of this "deep pocket" presumably diverts most of these claims away from individual officials.[18] In a minority of these cases, the government's liability is exclusive and officials are absolutely immune from suit.[19] And where both the United States and an official are named defendants and liability under the FTCA is adjudicated, the government will satisfy the judgment in its entirety, thereby barring any further litigation against the official.[20] But many substantial claims of federal wrongdoing are not covered by the FTCA; in such cases, federal officials remain personally vulnerable.[21] According to Justice Department testimony, "If an employee suffers an adverse judgment, with very few exceptions, it is he or she who must pay it."[22]

Indemnification under state and local law, a matter of great significance in cases brought under § 1983 (or under state law), varies widely among jurisdictions; many of these laws protect officials even less than the FTCA does. Most states provide some form of indemnification or other protection against adverse judgments or settlements,[23] but some apparently provide it only in narrowly circumscribed situations.[24] Indemnification laws differ with respect to local autonomy, coverage, and other features. Some state laws provide for mandatory (or permissive) indemnification by any governmental entity,[25] whereas others cover only state employees, leaving municipal employees to local discretion.[26] To complicate matters further, protection may be obtained not only through law but under collective bargaining agreements.[27] Most states now mandate indemnification and defense of most state and local employees, either by making the governmental entity liable for official torts[28] or by retaining officials as nominal defendants and requiring the entity to pay their costs.[29] In some cases, blanket statutes cover all employees;[30] in others, categories of officials are addressed by individual statutes. Significantly, most laws preclude government liability for "bad faith" conduct, and some condition indemnification on good faith cooperation by the official in the defense of the case.[31]

Not all statutes follow this general pattern, and even within it there are many variations. Specific categories of employees and specific types of liability are often excluded. In particular, many state statutes do not specifically cover liability under federal laws but are geared to state tort claims and may even be limited to negligent torts.[32] Unless courts interpret the statute to encompass federal claims, this omission may be critical. In 1976, for example, the New York legislature retroactively amended its indemnification statute for New York City employees after learning that § 1983 claims were not covered.[33] The omission was discovered when two city policemen were held liable under § 1983 for a total of $102,400 for severely beating a man taken into custody for a minor crime. Because the previous law referred only to negligent acts, the city refused to indemnify. In successfully seeking corrective legislation, the Patrolmen's Benevolent Association said the officers would "be in hock for the rest of their lives" if the law were not amended.[34] Even the current law precludes indemnification if disciplinary action is taken in connection with the action sued upon.[35] Such a statute, of course, not only clouds the prospect of indemnification but discourages administrative efforts to correct errant behavior.

Some states limit the amount of the indemnity, leaving officials to satisfy excess claims.[36] Conversely, some states limit the size of claims (although they cannot limit claims under federal law).[37] Many states have their own tort claims laws, sometimes modeled on the FTCA;[38]

these often contain the same exclusions as the federal act. State laws also vary in the procedures by which protection is obtained. In some, the government becomes exclusively liable for officials' torts and acts as the defendant throughout. Other states require officials to request defense and indemnification at the outset of the litigation. Some states provide for a threshold determination by a legal officer as to whether the action sued upon is one for which protection may be provided. If the determination is negative, the official must conduct his own defense, subject to subsequent reimbursement if the ultimate judicial decision indicates that a public defense would have been appropriate (as where the court rules that the official acted in good faith). Other states reverse the burden in such cases, allowing the government to recover defense and judgment costs from the official after the fact if the court finds that the tort occurred outside the scope of employment or was committed in bad faith.[39]

Virtually every indemnity statute precludes reimbursement for actions committed in bad faith, variously defined by statutes and variously construed by courts. Depending upon the state, indemnification may be denied in cases of "actual fraud, corruption, or malice";[40] "willful or wanton acts or omissions";[41] "willful misconduct";[42] "malice or criminal intent";[43] "malicious or fraudulent" acts;[44] "gross negligence, fraud or malice";[45] or some other variation. As previously noted, at least one state (New York) denies reimbursement if the official is subjected to disciplinary action. These exclusions, of course, are a source of great uncertainty for officials who face litigation, as they create potentially large lacunae in indemnification schemes. If denial of indemnification could be surgically limited to truly _malicious_ officials held liable under § 1983 (or under state law), wrongdoing could be deterred with little or no cost to vigorous decisionmaking. But where bad faith is not restricted to actual malice but can be based upon other factors about which officials may bear the burden of proof under a decidedly amorphous judicial standard,[46] the threat to vigorous decisionmaking may be great.

Federal, state, and local laws, then, restrict indemnification in many ways. In the aggregate, these restrictions encourage confusion and uncertainty, especially as new areas of personal liability that may not be covered by existing indemnification laws, such as statutory torts and negligence torts,[47] are opened up to litigation. Street-level officials are unlikely to be familiar with the nuances of indemnity law in their jurisdiction; indeed, the complexities of indemnification apparently even confuse some triers of fact and courts, whose decisions may be affected by their beliefs about who will ultimately bear the cost.[48] In addition, these gaps in coverage probably deny adequate compensation to some innocent victims of official misconduct. Without governmental liability—for example, where state officials misbehave but their employers enjoy sovereign or Eleventh Amendment immunity—victims unfortunate enough to have been injured by officials whose liabilities are not indemnified (due to bad faith or for some other reason) may be unable to satisfy their judgments. Compensation may thus elude those citizens who have been most egregiously wronged.[49]

## Leaving the Costs of Official Misconduct on the Victim

In chapter 3, I suggested that the incentive system that surrounds officials' tasks encourages self-protection, regardless of that strategy's effects upon social welfare. Here, I have maintained that although enterprise liability could meet this difficulty (albeit not without creating others, as will be explained), neither contract, free legal defense, nor indemnification/insurance wholly succeeds in bringing that regime about. Immunity rules obviously impede this cost-shifting, leaving victims rather than officials or government to bear the burden of official misconduct. We shall see that these rules also fail to restore vigorous decisionmaking, their purported justification.

At first glance, the Supreme Court appears to have fashioned a clear, comprehensive scheme for allocating official immunity. Bifurcating immunity for discretionary acts into "absolute" and "qualified" and then assigning a particular level of immunity to each type of official,[50] the Court has sought to impart precision and predictability to the process of adjusting the competing goals of public tort law. This appearance, however, is somewhat illusory; in application, immunity rules are neither as precise nor as predictable as the theory suggests. This uncertainty does not necessarily indict the rules. Legal categories, after all, seldom can capture or anticipate the rich complexity of the phenomena they regulate. The reality of official life is to some degree ineffable; legal language cannot fully subdue or re-create it. Controls that would be flexible cannot be wholly determinate. Nevertheless, if immunity rules are to promote vigorous decisionmaking, they must be capable of putting officials on notice concerning what behavior will and will not subject them to potential liability and litigation, and of minimizing the costs to officials of vindicating valid claims to immunity.

To evaluate immunity doctrine, three questions must be addressed: (1) Is the allocation of absolute and qualified immunity to certain kinds of decisions in certain types of cases a coherent one? (2) At what stage in a litigation can "good faith"—and thus the availability of qualified immunity—be determined? (3) What are the likely behavioral effects of the good faith standard as applied to street-level decisions? These are complex questions, rendered even more difficult by a 1982 Supreme Court decision, *Harlow and Butterfield* v. *Fitzgerald*, whose implications for these questions remain unclear. I will take them up in turn.

### THE ALLOCATION OF ABSOLUTE AND QUALIFIED IMMUNITY

To officials at risk of being sued, the difference between absolute and qualified immunity is crucial. As we shall see, this is not simply a matter of the probability of an ultimately favorable verdict; it amounts to the difference between being able to obtain a dismissal at the outset of the case and having to go to trial with a substantial defense.[51] Despite the high stakes, however, the courts have allocated the two types of immunity on the basis of distinctions that bear little relationship to protecting vigorous decisionmaking, the avowed purpose of immunity.

Officials' ability to invoke absolute or only qualified immunity has been made to depend upon (1) the type of governmental function implicit in particular acts or decisions, and (2) the source of the law that has allegedly been violated. The first, functional criterion confers absolute immunity upon acts of a "judicial," "legislative," or "prosecutorial" nature.[52] The Court, however, has never indicated precisely what scope of immunity applies to the great bulk of conduct by executive officials, conduct that cannot be characterized as quasi-judicial, quasi-legislative, or quasi-prosecutorial. The questions of what constitutes an "executive act" and whether different features of an act performed by an executive official might justify different levels of immunity remain unanswered, for example.[53] In *Scheuer* v. *Rhodes*, the Court seemed to hold that the scope of executives' immunity varies depending upon their discretion, responsibility, and "all the circumstances,"[54] but it has never clarified either this ambiguous formulation or its suggestion that even executive officials might enjoy absolute immunity even for constitutional torts "where . . . absolute immunity is essential for the conduct of public business."[55] The Court has imposed different immunity rules for common law and constitutional torts without even attempting to explicate or justify the distinction.[56] Finally, the Court seems prepared to confer absolute immunity upon officials engaged in rulemaking,[57] a ubiquitous form of executive decisionmaking. Despite the potential sweep of this principle, however, its meaning remains unclear.

The question of why and under what conditions some executive activities can claim absolute immunity whereas others receive only a qualified immunity is crucial, yet the Court's major decisions concerning the immunity of nonprosecutorial executive officials have failed to shed much light on it. In *Pierson* v. *Ray*, involving local police officers (and a judge), the Court simply noted that judges had enjoyed an absolute immunity at common law while policemen had received a qualified immunity, without explaining or attempting to justify the difference.[58] In *Scheuer*, in which a governor, some national guard officials, and a university president were sued, the Court's reasoning in fact appeared to justify absolute immunity. Thus, after pointing out that police officers enjoyed only a qualified immunity at common law, the Court stated that the question was "far more complex" as to high-level officials because their discretion "is virtually infinite" and noted "the similarity in the controlling policy considerations in the case of high-echelon executive officers and judges," who enjoy absolute immunity.[59] Yet they received only a qualified immunity. In *Butz* v. *Economou*, which gave only qualified immunity to the secretary of agriculture, the Court did little more than cite to *Scheuer*.[60] And in the brace of 1982 decisions concerning suits against President Nixon and his aides, the Court added to these confusions in two ways. First, it failed adequately to explain why the president needs absolute immunity but the chief executive of a state does not.[61] Second, it failed to provide a convincing justification, especially in light of its rulings on legislative immunity, for conferring a lesser immunity upon the president's "alter ego" aides than upon the president himself.[62]

In fact, if we go back a step and closely examine the Court's rationale for its long-standing rule of *absolute* immunity for *judges*,[63] the case for granting a lesser immunity to executive officials, especially those at street level, appears quite weak. The Court has emphasized five justifications for absolute judicial immunity: (1) the need for a judge to "be free to act upon his own conviction, without apprehension of personal consequences to himself"; (2) the controversiality and importance of the competing interests adjudicated by judges and the likelihood that the loser, feeling aggrieved, would wish to retaliate; (3) the record-keeping to which self-protective judges would be driven in the absence of immunity; (4) the availability of alternative remedies, such as appeal and impeachment, for judicial wrongdoing; and (5) the ease with which bad faith can be alleged and made the basis for "vexatious litigation."[64]

But these are not convincing reasons for the judiciary's privileged status. Bureaucrats, no less than judges, are expected and required to act objectively and without regard to personal considerations. Those disadvantaged by executive decisions are as likely to be aggrieved and litigious as those who lose in judicial forums. The interests at stake in the one are not obviously or importantly different from those at issue in the other. The propensity to "build a record" in response to fear of liability is not limited to judges; indeed, we have seen that it is a tempting strategy for most street-level officials.[65] Alternative remedies for controlling executive misconduct are far more numerous than those available against judges.[66] Finally, as I discuss in the next section, plaintiffs can allege bad faith—and force a trial on those allegations—quite as easily against executive officials. Indeed, when one contrasts the circumstances under which street-level officials must often act (momentarily; with broad discretion and little guidance; with little information; under great stress and with uncertainty; in unfriendly surroundings; under severe resource constraints) with the conditions under which judges typically decide (at their own speed; with discretion narrowed and guidance provided by precedent and the wording of statutes, as well as by voluminous records and briefs; enjoying great deference; in friendly surroundings; able to treat time and information as "free goods"), one must conclude that street-level officials would be far more vulnerable to litigation liability than judges, immunity rules being equal.[67] If the slightest risk of suits against judges suffices to justify absolute immunity, a higher risk to street-level officials would seem to justify no less.

The Court's second test for allocating immunity seeks to determine whether the alleged misconduct is merely tortious (and thus entitled to absolute immunity) or unconstitutional (and thus only immune if done in good faith).[68] This doctrinal criterion seems no more relevant to the scope of immunity than the functional one just discussed. When the Court adopted this test in *Economou*, it did not attempt to justify it but simply cited *Scheuer*, in which it was not even discussed.[69] Indeed, as the dissenting opinion in *Economou* demonstrates, the fact that some torts are constitutional has little to do with the purposes of immunity; constitutional torts are not necessarily more damaging than common law torts, and many state law claims can easily be framed in constitutional terms, a characterization that cannot be confirmed or refuted until after trial, at which point the value of the immunity is considerably reduced.[70] If anything, this discussion underestimates the ease with which plaintiffs can strip away the protection of absolute immunity simply by alleging constitutional claims. In public employment litiga-

tion, for example, plaintiffs now commonly allege that their discharge
or other form of discipline was politically motivated and without constitutionally required procedures, allegations that ordinarily suffice to
force the superior officials to go to trial without assurance of any
immunity.[71]

The point of this analysis is not to criticize the Court's use of crude
analytical categories for allocating immunity. Indeed, simple categories
are essential if we wish to have more than one level of immunity and to
have the issue of its availability resolved very early in the litigation
rather than being made to turn upon factual questions whose resolution
requires extended discovery or trial. Instead, my point is that we
cannot have immunity rules that satisfy these desiderata without
thereby ensuring that the rules will also be simplistic, suppressing
important aspects of the decisionmaking context. We must pay that
price at a minimum if we insist upon retaining an official liability
remedy but are unwilling to write off vigorous decisionmaking. As we
shall see, however, the remedy's full social cost is in fact far higher than
this.

## THE STAGE AT WHICH THE QUALIFIED IMMUNITY IS CONFERRED

In remanding the case to the trial judge, the Court in *Scheuer*
observed that the immunity question would not necessarily be decided
at the threshold; a full trial on the merits might well be required to
resolve it.[72] Subsequent cases have confirmed that in fact a threshold
determination of good faith often cannot be made;[73] indeed, even the
right to *absolute* immunity may take years to establish due to the
complex factual issues involved.[74] The Court has even suggested that a
trial may be required to determine not only whether an official enjoys
qualified immunity but also how broad the immunity will be: ". . . in
varying scope, a qualified immunity is available to officers of the executive branch of government, the variation being dependent upon the
scope of discretion and responsibilities of the office and all the circumstances as they reasonably appeared at the time of the action on which
liability is sought to be based."[75]

Thus, officials who know that others in their job category can usually
claim a qualified immunity still face important uncertainties. These
include the case's duration; its effects, while pending, upon the
officials' creditworthiness;[76] the unpredictability of outcome when a
jury or judge must apply a general standard to particular facts; the
possibility that courts may choose to decide the merits (i.e., the legal
validity of defendants' conduct) before resolving the immunity

question,[77] that defendants' attorneys may decide not to raise the immunity question until late in the case,[78] or that conflicts of interest with the officials' government attorneys will develop;[79] and the uncertainty concerning the "varying scope" of the immunity itself, which is to depend, according to the Court, upon "all the circumstances."[80]

Procedural aspects of the immunity defense also contribute to the uncertainties surrounding its application. Because many official liability cases are tried before a jury, the good faith determination depends upon the vagaries of a deliberately ad hoc and unaccountable decision process.[81] Although it seems obvious that only judges can decide whether the substantive law was so clear and settled that officials ought to have apprehended it—a crucial element, as we shall see, of good faith—the Supreme Court has held that the jury must pass on all aspects of officials' good faith;[82] lower courts have dutifully followed this practice.[83] The burden of proving the prerequisites for the qualified immunity almost certainly rests upon the official;[84] although the location of this burden does not always decide the outcome of the immunity issue,[85] it sometimes has been determinative.[86] Extensive discovery is often necessary to resolve the good faith question in both its subjective and objective aspects.[87] This, too, entails time, money, anxiety, and uncertainty.

Finally, the immunity rules' ability to shield officials from the pecuniary and nonpecuniary costs of litigation and liability inescapably depends, as we have seen, upon the point in the litigation at which the immunity issue is resolved. If a trial is necessary to establish that an official should not have had to stand trial, then the immunity is largely ineffective even if it is ultimately conferred (or is denied but the official prevails on the merits).[88] Indeed, merely the direct, out-of-pocket cost of obtaining even a prompt dismissal of a case today amounts to thousands of dollars.[89] These realities belie the Court's bland assurances that "[i]nsubstantial lawsuits . . . should not survive" the earliest pretrial stages of litigation.[90] Officials who act in good faith may be reasonably confident that they will ultimately escape personal liability but they must prudently assume that their victory will nevertheless be a protracted and painful affair.

## APPLICATION OF THE "GOOD FAITH" STANDARD

Like the procedural context in which the good faith standard is administered, its substantive content intensifies officials' uncertainty. The doctrinal evolution of the standard has been described elsewhere.[91] My purpose here is to isolate several aspects of the standard, as judicially elaborated, that discourage vigorous decisionmaking. (That the standard defeats compensation as well is more obvious, if not necessarily less troubling, and is discussed in chapter 5.)

Until the Supreme Court's 1982 decision in *Harlow and Butterfield* v. *Fitzgerald*, the good faith standard both examined officials' subjective states of mind and included an objective test; officials who failed either examination were denied immunity.[92] Even though subjective bad faith or improper motivation was apparently seldom found,[93] the Court had insisted that this question could not ordinarily be resolved in advance of trial.[94] The "objective" prong of the good faith test required that the circumstances surrounding the disputed action be assessed, particularly whether defendant knew or reasonably should have known that the action violated "settled, indisputable law," "basic, unquestioned constitutional rights," or "clearly established constitutional rights"—depending upon which of the Court's formulations in *Wood* v. *Strickland* one prefers.[95] (Indeed, shortly after these were announced, the Court added yet another—the foreseeability of constitutional developments.[96]) And to complicate matters further, the lower courts sometimes denied good faith immunity to officials who, although acting in subjective good faith, were ignorant of "clearly established" *state* law (including regulations) underlying a § 1983 claim.[97]

The Court predicted in *Wood* that the qualified immunity standard would not encourage judges and juries to second-guess official decisions from the privileged vantage point of hindsight. This assertion, like the Court's earlier assurance that qualified immunity could be determined before trial, was quite implausible, as later cases were quickly to confirm.[98] The Court's good faith standard, after all, demands more than the absence of actual malice. If the standard's "objective" element means anything, it must require an inquiry into whether officials' actions were illegal and if so, whether the officials had reason to know this. Knowledge of law, then, must be directly relevant to good faith, yet a legal knowledge standard seems problematic. After all, many constitutional rights and duties, especially those within the expansive contours of the due process, equal protection, and cruel and unusual punishment clauses, are indeterminate and in constant flux.

Consider the facts in *Wood* itself. A school board had expelled several girls who had spiked sixty ounces of soft drinks with twenty-four ounces of malt liquor, for violating a school regulation that prohibited any "intoxicating beverage" at school-sponsored activities. Plaintiffs (the girls), defendant school board members, the district court, the court of appeals, and the Supreme Court each managed to interpret this regulation differently,[99] and after three pages of analysis and nine footnotes, the Court reached an inconclusive result as to its meaning. Interpretations differed on such questions as whether "intoxicating beverage" was linked to another term in a state statute, whether it included beer, and what events had led to the regulation's adoption. Yet this dispute revolved around the meaning of a simple regulation about school parties, not the ever-evolving, endlessly controversial meaning of the due process clause.

A recent lower court decision, although perhaps unusual, suggests that even a lawyer's opinion on the question, a luxury that street-level officials are not afforded, might not have established defendants' good faith to the satisfaction of a judge or jury.[100] A teacher was discharged for criticizing the school administration (so the court found) in violation of the teacher's First Amendment rights. When the matter came before the school board for review, it consulted an attorney. Asked if the discharge "would stand up in Federal Court," the attorney responded (albeit not with great lucidity) that liability was quite unlikely. Relying upon this advice of counsel, the board discharged the teacher. Despite the board's reliance upon counsel, however, the court refused to find objective good faith (defendants carried the burden of proof) and proceeded to impose liability against the individual board members.*[101]

As noted in chapter 1, many constitutional law norms elaborated by courts are difficult for street-level officials to predict, understand, and apply. Courts typically use the open-ended clauses of the Constitution to fashion broad doctrines whose precise contours can only be discerned after many specific adjudications. One example is the line of "procedural due process" cases decided after *Goldberg* v. *Kelly*[102] established the right of welfare recipients to a pretermination hearing.[103] Another example is the group of cases, now beginning to accumulate, concerning the "right to minimally adequate or reasonable training" in state institutions for the mentally ill and mentally retarded.[104] In part, this result reflects the fact that sharply divided courts tend to draw extraordinarily fine (not to say arbitrary) factual distinctions between apparently similar cases.[105] The practice often precipitates a corpus of

---

*Specifically, the attorney told the board that the legality of the firing "would depend upon a lot of factors that I could not and would not assume responsibility for" and "I didn't think it should be a major consideration in their deliberations." Reliance on counsel was held not to demonstrate defendants' good faith because they had not specifically inquired about constitutional rights, and because individuals "ought not [to be able to] avoid the responsibilities of public office by the simple act of consulting a lawyer."[101]

law that is complex, technical, and isolated from the training, common sense, and intuitions of ordinary street-level officials.

Supreme Court decisions concerning the power to make warrantless searches of "closed containers" illustrate this problem. On the same day in 1981, the Court invalidated the search of a recessed luggage compartment of a station wagon[106] and upheld the search of a zippered pocket of a jacket lying on the back seat of a car.[107] (The hairsplitting that enabled the Court majority to distinguish these cases led one wag to speculate about marketing a "Fourth Amendment protection hatchback," which would enable the driver to circumvent the latter decision by sealing off the luggage area of the vehicle as a police car approached.[108] It also led the Court, less than a year later, to overrule the first of these decisions.[109]) Other recent criminal procedure decisions have sown so much confusion that even academic experts in their libraries, not to say police officers on the street and those who train them, apparently do not know what to make of them.[110]

Whether such rulings are based upon "settled," "clearly established" principles of constitutional law (as the Court majority typically claims) or instead amount to novel departures from existing law (as the dissenters usually believe) may be a matter for scholarly debate. But when this question arises in the context of a claim of qualified official immunity, a trial judge or jury must resolve it, and how this is to be done is not at all clear. How similar must case *A*'s facts be to those in precedent *X* before the "rule" in *X* may be said to be settled or clearly established for purposes of case *A*? Was precedent *X* settled when a district court or court of appeals rendered it, or does "settledness" require the Supreme Court's imprimatur?[111] What if the precedent emerged from a closely divided court, or what if the Court's reasoning was criticized by leading commentators? And even if we can determine what qualifies as "law," how much of it should a police officer, prison guard, schoolteacher, or hospital administrator be expected to know? What if following a more or less "settled" rule would sacrifice other compelling interests that the official is also bound to protect? These and other questions that cannot really be answered or even formulated with much precision become relevant to "good faith" under the *Wood* standard.

In response, it might be argued that it is no more difficult for triers of fact to apply the good faith standard than to perform the task, routine in tort cases, of applying a "reasonableness" negligence standard to a defendant's conduct. The two standards, however, are not equivalent, nor are they equally comprehensible or readily applied by jurors. Deciding good faith requires a judgment about reasonableness, to be sure, but in a context in which an official's experience, discretion, and responsibility to act are centrally relevant, a world that has few if any parallels in a juror's own experience. Patrolling a high-crime area is not analogous to protecting one's own property, nor is administering a troubled inner city school like caring for the neighbor's children. A simple reasonableness test, sometimes advocated to replace the good faith standard,[112] would probably exacerbate the uncertainty and unpredictability inherent in the traditional test.

In 1982, a unanimous Court (at least on this point) acknowledged that the *Wood* v. *Strickland* standard had failed to prevent allegations of bad faith from forcing officials to go to trial. To alter this pattern, it decided to abandon the "subjective" prong of the standard and to rely entirely upon the "objective reasonableness of an official's conduct, as measured by reference to clearly established law."[113] As we have just seen, however, the "objective" test is not without its problems. Most questions of what the law was and whether it was clearly established can presumably be disposed of by judges without the need for discovery, as the Court hopes. But some probably cannot, for the applicable legal principles may not become apparent until after the facts are fleshed out by the evidence. Moreover, as three concurring justices noted, what the official *knew* at the time is often a factual question of considerable difficulty. In libel cases, the Court has warned against resolving such questions on the basis of summary judgment,[114] and in institutional cases concerning the issue of professional standards of treatment, it has invited expert testimony at trial.[115]

It would be extremely valuable to know how well any good faith standard actually distinguishes between honest, reasonable errors and egregious, malicious misconduct. Some commentators, correctly observing that § 1983 plaintiffs face many litigation obstacles and usually lose, maintain that application of the standard systematically favors officials.[116] This may well be true, but without knowledge of the actual incidence of official good faith, that inference cannot necessarily be drawn. More likely, the balance of advantage shifts in different cases. It probably favors the official when an individual with a criminal record sues an apparently overzealous policeman but favors the victim when an ex-mental patient sues a hospital administrator for refusal to discharge[117] or to treat.[118] Moreover, if officials are risk-averse,[119] and if even nonmalicious defendants must usually endure a full-dress trial in order to establish the immunity's scope and availability, they are likely to advert less to the average case that in fact vindicates them than to the occasional aberrant one that does them in. Sensitive to that prospect, many officials can be expected to subordinate their duty to the public to their concern for themselves.

## Conclusion: A Trial Balance

If the analysis in this chapter and the preceding one is correct, the damage remedy against individual officials chills vigorous decisionmaking, and none of the incremental compensating adjustments of that remedy—contract, free legal defense, indemnification, insurance, or "good faith" immunity—can restore that vigor entirely. None of these adjustments wholly eliminates the risks and uncertainties that spawn official self-protection, and some even create new anxieties for risk-averse officials, such as apprehension about being represented by government counsel.

If, despite this defect, the remedy-*cum*-adjustments at least ensured that innocent victims of harm at the hands of government would be compensated, there might be much to be said for it. In fact, however, empirical studies and informed commentary leave little doubt that the remedy defeats compensation of many valid claims.[120] The reasons are not difficult to imagine. Plaintiffs tend to be poor and ill-equipped to maintain a protracted lawsuit, typically against the litigation resources of the government. They often cannot even readily identify the person who injured them. Plaintiffs, who are often inmates or persons accused of crimes, are far less likely to elicit sympathy from, or be credible to, a jury than defendants, who are officials trained to convey an image of legitimacy and moral authority. Immunity defenses defeat many valid claims before they can be proved. Because damages for violations of many constitutional rights are only nominal,[121] litigation to vindicate them is discouraged. Individual defendants are often unable to pay judgments rendered against them.[122]

But vigorous decisionmaking and compensation are not the only casualties of the official liability remedy. To the apparently considerable extent that it fails to compensate legitimate complainants, it obviously also fails *pro tanto* to deter official misconduct. Its deterrence potential is also limited because much official wrongdoing is ultimately rooted in organizational conditions and can only be organizationally deterred. This reality in turn dims the remedy's moral luster, its capacity to project and affirm the values that justify our legal order.[123] Finally, the systemic costs of administering the remedy appear to be high, especially in view of the relative infrequency of recoveries. *Bivens* and § 1983 actions, for example, are complicated by, among other things, the necessity to litigate the issue of good faith and by the common practice of naming multiple defendants, who may then need separate legal representation to avoid conflicts of interest *inter se* and with the government. Moreover, the United States is not legally authorized to settle suits against individual officials unilaterally or to pay any judgments or settlements on their behalf; similar restrictions under state and local laws may also impede settlement of § 1983 actions against individuals. Doubtless, this protracts litigation and creates tensions between the government, which ordinarily bears litigation expenses and thus may favor early settlements, and defendants-officials, who will have to pay any adverse judgment or settlement personally.[124] It also precludes some settlement options entirely in certain kinds of cases.[125]

The critique of the damage remedy against individual officials is on its face quite damning, yet it might seem to suffer from a weakness that afflicts many public policy analyses—namely, it often seems to take a "first best" perspective, evaluating the remedy against standards that are seldom approximated in the real world. A legitimate challenge to my critique, then, would ask the question: "Compared with what?" In the next chapter, I propose an analytically compelling and institutionally realistic answer to that question, one centering upon the construction of a governmental liability remedy that would virtually supplant official liability. But desirable as it may be, such a reform by itself would leave several important problems unresolved while engendering some new ones. These difficulties are discussed in part III.

# 5: TOWARD REMEDIAL JUSTICE: EXPANDING THE DAMAGE REMEDY AGAINST GOVERNMENT

The most far-reaching defects of official liability—its propensity to chill vigorous decisionmaking; to leave deserving victims uncompensated and losses concentrated; to weaken deterrence; to obscure the morality of law; and to generate high system costs—can be traced to a single cause: public tort law's ancient refusal to incorporate fully the remedial principle of enterprise (governmental) liability, a concept that private tort law assimilated nearly three centuries ago. In this chapter, I hope to show that if enterprise liability for official misconduct is substantially expanded, society can enjoy significant and unambiguous gains. This argument is developed in five steps. First, I discuss the *consequences* that might be expected to flow from a regime of thoroughgoing governmental liability, especially compared with the current remedial system. Second, I explore the special problem of *deterrence*. Third, I analyze alternative *structural models* for achieving it. Fourth, I consider the appropriate *extent* of governmental liability. Finally, I discuss *implementation* of this reform and propose specific changes in § 1983, the Federal Tort Claims Act (FTCA) and *Bivens* rules.

## The Consequences of Governmental Liability

A remedial system built upon governmental liability would utterly dominate the status quo with respect to compensation, vigorous decisionmaking, and moral exemplification goals. In conjunction with other remedies of a "specific deterrence" kind, explored here and in part III, it would strengthen deterrence. It would probably not impair system efficiency and might even improve it. If this prediction is correct, the changes that I shall propose may constitute a frequently sought but seldom-achieved policy phenomenon—a reform that makes some of us better off without making any of us worse off (or what welfare economists refer to as a "Pareto-superior" change[1]).

Governmental liability would clearly maximize the probability that officially inflicted harms would be adequately compensated. Victims could more readily identify an appropriate defendant against whom suit might be brought, would receive a more sympathetic hearing from juries unconcerned about imposing liability upon officials of modest means, could obtain judgments that better reflected the significance of the rights infringed, and would be able to satisfy those judgments fully. As a result, significant gains in loss-spreading would be achieved, as the costs of misconduct were shifted from an individual (the victim or, if official liability had been imposed, the employee) to a far larger group of taxpayers. Vigorous decisionmaking would also be enhanced by a remedy that reduced or eliminated officials' personal exposure to litigation and liability. (The possibility that that threat might be restored through other sanctioning systems cannot, of course, be dismissed and is discussed in chapter 6.)

The moral basis of public tort law would also be reinforced by governmental liability. Imposing liability upon individual officials, whose "objective bad faith" may consist of little more than being an instrument of impersonal bureaucratic, political, and social processes over which they have little or no effective control, cruelly mocks that morality. When a prison guard says "I'm just doing my job" while he places a dangerous prisoner in solitary confinement, he is correct in an important (although perhaps legally irrelevant) sense. Personal liability serves no purpose if his organizational context and task structure constrain him from altering his behavior while still performing his job effectively within that same, unyielding reality.[2] Indeed, changing his conduct may be unavailing or even socially perverse if the larger machine of which he is merely a small cog grinds on in the customary way, or if behavior that seems rational to him nevertheless imposes large costs upon others. Thomas Schelling has observed:

> The fact that people voluntarily do something, or acquiesce in the consequences, does not mean that they like the results. Often the individual is not free to change the result; he can only change his own position within it, and that does him no good. We might all be better off speaking Latin or using a different calendar, but nobody can do much about it by learning Latin or hanging a thirteen-month calendar on his wall.[3]

Thus, the values that underlie substantive rules of conduct are more strongly affirmed when the costs of wrongdoing are imposed upon the entity responsible for recruiting, training, guiding, constraining, managing, and disciplining the actual violators, than when they are imposed upon individuals with little leverage upon reform, people who are probably more anvil than hammer. Enterprise liability would also reduce the randomness with which particular officials are now sued and held liable. In principle, official liability might frequently be imposed; in practice, however, officials seldom pay judgments personally.[4] Thus, being sued and, *a fortiori*, being held liable are not unlike being struck by lightning, an event whose adventitious quality makes it seem morally irrelevant and arbitrary when it does occur.[5]

Governmental liability would garner these advantages, moreover, while improving, or at least not impairing, the remedial system's operating efficiency. It would greatly simplify public tort litigation by reducing the number of issues requiring pretrial discovery, by avoiding multiple defendants and counsel, and by permitting government settlements and other economies that are not possible when, as in *Bivens* actions, the government is not a defendant and thus is not permitted to pay adverse judgments.[6] Moreover, it would probably do so without significantly increasing unjustified or erroneous awards. Because governmental liability only expands the application of an existing remedy and does not itself alter the legal standards governing officials' primary conduct, it simply increases the probability that those injured by wrongful conduct will be compensated. A risk remains that substituting a "deep pocket" defendant and removing obstacles to recovery might encourage more marginal claims of official misconduct to be filed.[7] If a small percentage of these penetrated the screen, more unjustified awards could result. Substantive liability rules might also be stretched under the gradual pressure of more close cases, novel fact situations, and compelling circumstances. Judges could minimize these risks by scrutinizing cases more closely before sending them to a jury and by reducing excessive awards. Even if some unwarranted compensation occurred, it seems unlikely that system efficiency would be significantly reduced on balance.

## Governmental Liability and Deterrence

Predicting the effects of broad governmental liability upon deterrence of official misconduct, however, is more difficult. To the extent that the remedy eliminates officials' risk of personal exposure, it reduces the price of violating the law, other things remaining equal. But in at least two crucial respects, governmental liability would not leave things equal. First, it would in most cases strengthen general deterrence by focusing at a better location the incentives that the substantive behavioral rule mobilizes. Second, it would still permit selective interventions relying upon specific deterrence measures to augment the general deterrence. In this section I discuss the locational advantage of governmental liability. The remedy's limitations and the need for specific deterrence adjustments are analyzed in part III.

Because the sources of official misconduct are diverse and complex, as we saw in chapter 1, the strategies for deterring it can be no less so.[8] Deterrence is a highly specialized, problem-specific, context-sensitive business; those who design public tort remedies—principally, legislatures and courts—are for the most part singularly ill-equipped to master its intricate and decidedly particularized technologies. Legislatures tend to frame rules categorically, not contextually. Courts must cast their judgments in principled, not technocratic, form. Neither legislators nor judges are likely to acquire a "feel" for the particular ingredients of effective police work, classroom teaching, prison administration, or treatment of the mentally ill. They cannot readily identify the precise variables that encourage deterrence in each of these very different decision contexts, encapsulate them in institutionally appropriate prescriptions, or manipulate them at street level. (Indeed, as suggested in chapter 4, the mere possibility that such matters might be decided in a courtroom aggravates the problem of remedial design.)

There will be situations, of course, in which specific deterrence will be called for and in which only legislatures or courts can be counted upon to provide it. In part III I consider when those situations are likely to occur and how they can best be handled when they do. The most important point, however, is that they are exceptions. Ordinarily, legislatures and courts are (and must be) architects of general deterrence. For them, the critical remedial design question cannot be the technocratic one of how this or that official practice or behavior can best be deterred. Instead, the question that they alone can answer, the one to which their competence is most germane, is the question of the appropriate locus of general deterrence: For deterrence to be effective, upon whom should liability be imposed in the first instance? More specifically (and borrowing from the somewhat analogous Calabresi-Hirschoff test for locating strict liability[9]), the question is: Who— the street-level agency, some other bureaucratic unit, the individual official whose behavior we want to deter, or the court itself—is in the best position to know (1) how that behavior can best be deterred, (2) how deterrence can best be traded off against vigorous decisionmaking, and (3) how to implement that knowledge?

None of these candidates is ideal for these purposes, of course, but some are clearly superior to others. In chapters 3 and 4, we saw that solitary officials are poor loci for generating deterrence, except perhaps in instances of purely willful, impetuous wrongdoing—the "frolic of his own" that has always constituted an exception to the common law rule of *respondeat superior*.[10] Such instances are surely quite atypical of official illegality. Christopher Stone, in discussing remedies for corporate misconduct, makes a similar point. He finds that even in the private context, "the bulk of harm-causing corporate conduct [finds its] source . . . in bureaucratic shortcomings—flaws in the organization's formal and informal authority structure, or in its information pathways—rather than in the deliberate action of any particular employee."[11]

The agency is relatively well equipped to deter. The ideal locus of liability, the Archimedean point of maximum leverage over deterrence, is at that level of the governmental apparatus at which a number of crucial ingredients converge: a comprehension of the full range of social values affected by the misconduct and by efforts to control it; an understanding of the technology of how particular misconduct can be deterred; the incentive to optimize not only deterrence but also competing values, notably vigorous decisionmaking; and the resources to ensure that this knowledge and incentive is used at street level. Although the precise location of this point is often uncertain, it is probably closer to the agency head than to the individual street-level official. Police departments, for example, can better identify and evaluate different strategies for deterring illegal arrests and can also better predict the likely effects of alternative deployments of police officers, training methods, or arrest guidelines upon both deterrence and vigorous decisionmaking.[12] A school administrator is more likely to discern precisely how student discipline and high teacher morale affect classroom learning and the best ways to attain these educational goals.

Even more important than their superior knowledge, perhaps, is agencies' superior influence over implementation of whatever deterrence strategies are selected. Unlike individual low-level officials, agencies control most of the resources, constraints, incentives, and conditions that actually influence officials' behavior toward the public. They can recruit different types of personnel and train and retrain them to perform their duties in particular ways. They can reward and punish officials for conforming to and departing from those norms, and they can develop new modes of supervision and control. They can provide a different mix of rules and discretion and experiment with different managerial strategies and incentive systems. They can seek changes in the substantive rules that govern official behavior and improve the quality and quantity of information and other resources that officials need. More generally, they can deploy organizational resources and incentives from a broad perspective and thus can take into account and shape a relatively comprehensive array of social costs and benefits. Because agencies are better risk spreaders, they are probably less risk-averse than individual officials. They will, in short, almost always be the cheapest social cost avoiders.[13]

Even if imposing liability upon agencies rather than officials would improve both the technology of deterrence and its implementation, however, two crucial questions remain. Might not agencies' parochial, mission-oriented perspectives, like officials' personal risk aversion, often diverge from the broader interests of society?[14] What is to prevent agencies from tolerating official misconduct out of narrow bureaucratic self-interest? These problems, of course, are not confined to the public sector. When private incentives and public interest diverge, as they frequently do, private tort liability rules can frequently bring them into a rough equivalence. Can a governmental liability remedy do the same in public law?

The answer is that it can—within limits, limits that I shall explore in chapters 6, 7, and 8. The political environment significantly constrains, without wholly eliminating, an agency's freedom to countenance wrongdoing. Politicians and public opinion, after all, expect agencies to control crime without trampling upon constitutional rights, to educate students without oppressing them, and to protect the community from mental patients that need hospitalization without confining those that do not. An array of legal, fiscal, political, and professional sanctions and controls enforce these expectations with varying degrees of success.[15] Some, such as criminal proceedings, do not operate against agencies, cannot compensate victims, and are difficult to mobilize. Others, such as administrative penalties, can only be initiated by high-level officials who may, along with the political culture of which they are part, tolerate (or even encourage) misconduct.

Although a remedy of agency liability would have none of these shortcomings, it would have two problems of its own. I shall call them the problems of *suboptimization* and *enforceability*. Together, they suggest that even if agency liability is superior to official liability, some governmental locus other than the agency may be better still.

SUBOPTIMIZATION

Earlier, I described the ideal locus of liability. But locating that point more precisely in bureaucratic space is no simple matter, for Leviathan is complex. Certain locations seem clearly inappropriate. The United States Treasury, the liability point in the current system, is too remote from officials' operating conditions in the field; it neither understands particular programmatic functions and techniques nor possesses the administrative resources necessary to implement such knowledge at street level. The opposite end of the administrative spectrum—the police squad, the cell block unit in which a prison guard works, the bureaucratic subunit to which a caseworker is assigned, the curricular department in which a schoolteacher teaches— displays contrary defects; it identifies too closely with street-level officials, is too parochial in its view of relevant interests, and lacks the varied administrative resources (e.g., training programs, disciplinary power, authority to obtain and shift funds) necessary to shape ultimate behavior.

The optimal location for liability, then, is ordinarily found somewhere in the vast bureaucratic continuum between the work detail and the government as a whole. But precisely where? As we move up the formal governmental hierarchy, away from the world of the street in which the misconduct occurs, we acquire a more cosmopolitan perspective of the interests at stake, more diverse instruments for shaping official behavior, and greater responsiveness to the larger political culture. At the same time, we sacrifice technical knowledge about street-level operations, as well as certain resources that can help to influence official behavior, including the intense esprit, loyalty, and respect that can only be engendered between colleagues who are engaged at close range in a common venture and undergoing common experiences. As we accumulate bureaucratic layers, we attenuate responsibility and fray the lines of effective administrative control.[16] As the liability point moves down through the hierarchy toward the street, of course, we generate an opposite pattern of benefits and costs, gaining in administrative responsiveness and technical expertise while paying a price in terms of greater insularity and fewer levers of influence.

The risk that particular liability points will produce unsatisfactory value trade-offs is one dimension of the suboptimization problem. Another is incentives. In practice, public agencies usually cannot retain the fruits of whatever efficiencies they manage to generate; any savings return to the Treasury, where agencies have no special claim on them. Similarly, the litigation, liability, and settlement costs resulting from misconduct by agency employees are in practice borne by the Treasury, not by the agency's own budget. Thus, agencies do not bear the full cost of their wrongdoing but enjoy whatever benefits flow from it. Under the current system, then, the incentives are perverse, at least from the public's point of view.

Neither aspect of suboptimization is peculiar to the public sector. Large private organizations also face value trade-offs at different hierarchical levels; similarly, costly low-level behavior within a private firm is insulated unless the firm manages to transmit altered incentives to whatever unit is best positioned to influence that behavior.[17] Nevertheless, the suboptimization problem is especially acute for public agencies, for they possess fewer, weaker, and less flexible tools for inducing field employees to adopt the agencies' more encompassing goals as their own.

ENFORCEABILITY

Now suppose that the suboptimization problem has been solved, or at least minimized; the optimal bureaucratic leverage point (say, the subagency program level) has been identified and the costs of lower-level misconduct can be imposed upon appropriate subordinate units by charging their budgets. At this point, another problem arises—how can we make that budgetary debit "stick"? Like suboptimization, this problem occurs in private organizations as well but is especially intractable for public enterprises. There, budgets are determined not by a careful balancing of programmatic costs and benefits but by a combination of crude rules of thumb, political influence, strategic behavior, and happenstance.[18] A decision to charge a public program's budget with the costs of defending claims and satisfying adverse judgments arising out of employees' misconduct is probably easier to evade and more difficult to enforce. Unless the liability-related charge were large enough to be budgetarily visible and politically salient, influential legislators or administrators sympathetic to the program's mission or to the plight of its needy and innocent beneficiaries might well restore that amount to its budget without calling public attention to the sanction-blunting effect of the restoration.

Suboptimization and enforceability are difficult problems but not, I think, insuperable. Certainly, the public tort law of the future must grapple with them. Fortunately, creative experimentation is eminently feasible. Congress, for example, could require that whatever liability costs are imposed upon the United States under the FTCA must be charged to the budgets of the agencies whose employees' conduct occasioned them[19] and that those agencies transmit the costs downward to the budgets of the smallest subunits capable of deterring the conduct in question. At that disaggregated budgetary level, the costs of liability might well loom large enough to create effective incentives for the subunit to control employee misconduct. Over time, as budgetary stringencies increase and the opportunity costs of employee misconduct become more palpable to administrators, the deterrent effects of this remedy should grow. And if, as I urge later in this chapter, public tort remedies are changed to permit recovery in appropriate cases of liquidated minimum damages, punitive damages, attorney's fees, and other litigation costs, the costs of misconduct should be high enough to make even the most callous bureaucrat sit up and take notice.

Because of the fluid, political nature of the budgetary process, however, this scheme must be augmented by other behavior-shaping incentives and tools that are not directly budgetary in nature. Congress might revise the civil service laws, for example, to authorize monetary fines or delayed promotion for officials who are truly individually responsible for torts that result in governmental liability. These penalties will have to be limited to cases of actual malicious intent, gross incompetence, and violations of crystal-clear legal standards; they must be both modest in amount (so vigorous decisionmaking is not chilled) and more or less automatic (so the deterrent is credible). One model might be the Clayton Act provision making an antitrust violation in a government-initiated proceeding prima facie evidence of liability in a private action against the defendant.[20] Congress might also require any agency suffering an adverse tort judgment to prepare a report to the appropriate committee of Congress, to convene a public hearing at which it must detail the measures it is taking to deter future misconduct of that type, and to monitor its own performance in implementing those measures. Alternative systems of administrative discipline, discussed in chapter 6, might also be established.

Our political institutions and system of public finance, of course, impose great obstacles to such reforms. There is no assurance that they would succeed in strengthening deterrence. One may well ask, then, what reasons there are to believe that expanding governmental liability would deter illegality more than the status quo. First, as noted earlier in this chapter and as detailed in chapter 6, governmental liability should induce agencies to supplant employees' fears of personal liability with other, more carefully targeted and effective means of deterrence; better training, more careful supervision, clearer guidelines, and stronger administrative sanctions can be credible deterrents and are likely to be more adaptable to the street-level context and compatible with vigorous decisionmaking than a damage action in court. Second, if governmental liability fails to induce agency self-policing sufficient to generate the levels of deterrence that society demands, resort to "specific deterrence" interventions by courts is still possible. These interventions are the subject of part III. Thus, governmental liability would be an improved remedy in all but the most exceptional cases, and the exceptional cases would be subjected, as they should be, to exceptional remedies. This would still leave us with the problem of drawing lines, of course, but that task, as Holmes once observed, is what civilization is all about.

## Structural Models of Governmental Liability

Suppose that we decided to broaden the governmental liability remedy. How should we proceed? Generally speaking (discussion of specific proposals is deferred until the last section), two remedial structures or models (and numerous variants) might be employed. Each relies primarily upon a particular mechanism for allocating costs.* Model 1 (indemnification/insurance) would require the government to indemnify to insure† officials for liability-related costs incurred by

---

*A third model is represented by the status quo. It relies upon contractual bargains and ad hoc statutory provisions to generate a pattern of cost-shifting arrangements that includes some, but not comprehensive, governmental liability. Its characteristic advantage (if advantage it be) is that it produces a highly diverse set of arrangements that might be thought to reflect different types of risks, preferences, and bargaining power associated with different working milieus—in brief, a market in risk-sharing. Even if one accepts this market analogy (which I do not), it clearly exhibits several marked imperfections, including externalities (the preferences of potential victims for remedies are unlikely to be fully reflected in the bargains struck between officials and government) and high information and bargaining costs. Even if the market analogy were persuasive, however, the outcome would still be objectionable, for it would destroy the fundamental value of uniformity of federal tort remedies across bureaucracies and jurisdictions. Even in a federal system, local variation in this respect is a great vice.

†Christopher Stone has pointed to an important difference between the two: "Unlike insurance . . . indemnification does not provide a superior compensation fund: indemnification only repays the [official] what the plaintiff was able to extract from him, which would be limited by the [official's] wealth. Indeed, if there is a tradeoff of indemnification for wages . . . then the effect, in terms of compensating victims, may be perverse. An increased indemnification right will imply lower wealth for the [official], thereby reducing his ability to compensate."[21]

them. Model 2 (governmental liability per se) would explicitly provide for direct governmental liability. Although both models would in effect produce the remedial outcomes and advantages that I have imputed to governmental liability, there are grounds on which to prefer model 2.

Model 1 is problematic for several reasons. First, a congressional requirement that state and local governments indemnify or insure their officials might raise constitutional issues under the Tenth Amendment.[22] Moreover, insurance contracts and indemnification laws would, unless proscribed by statute, inevitably contain certain limitations upon coverage. Like the "good faith" test for qualified immunity and similar tests under federal, state, and local indemnification arrangements, such provisions create new boundary problems, uncertainties about coverage, and a possible "action over" by the government against the official.[23] These gaps not only resurrect the very incentives for official self-protection that these reforms are designed to obviate but also frustrate compensation (and thus deterrence) by forcing victims to proceed against individuals who may be judgment-proof. Second, municipalities apparently experienced serious difficulties in obtaining insurance coverage for official liability even before the recent expansion of liability. Requiring insurance or indemnification, then, may amount to requiring governments to self-insure. Either is a rather indirect and cumbersome way to effect government liability.[24] Finally, insurers that underwrite risks of liability for official misconduct would presumably insist upon some influence over the agency policy and personnel decisions that affect the magnitude of those risks, a private interference with public administration that would surely be politically and morally, even if not legally, objectionable.

Some, but not all, of these objections would be met by model 2, which would expand governmental liability directly. Congress could impose direct governmental liability under its Fourteenth Amendment enforcement powers, as discussed below. Compensation of victims would be secured, enhancing both deterrence and loss-spreading. The agency would be well situated to tailor its internal controls to the different risks of misconduct and the need for vigorous decisionmaking posed by different types of official activities. The morality of public tort law would also be more strongly affirmed.

Model 2, to be sure, has shortcomings of its own. Its more impersonal, bureaucratic system of liability, for example, would probably frustrate victims' desire for personalized retribution more than model 1. And government purchases of private insurance for their risks would create similar opportunities for interference. Nevertheless, model 2 seems preferable to model 1 in all other respects. If we want victims to have recourse to a "deep pocket" defendant, it makes little sense to retain (even if only de jure) an official liability remedy that is not necessary to compensate, will cost something to insure against, will (because of continuing uncertainties about coverage) discourage vigorous decisionmaking somewhat, and will achieve no greater deterrence (and perhaps less) than model 2.*

Model 2 could be made more flexible by redesigning it to accommodate several cost-allocation schemes rather than only one. Details of the remedy for misconduct by police officers, for example, might vary from those applicable to social workers or inspectors. A statute might permit negotiation of different arrangements under certain conditions. Such official-specific or "opt-out" provisions, however, must ensure that any departures from the basic remedial structure would fully protect society's interests in adequate deterrence, sufficient compensation, vigorous decisionmaking, and basic remedial uniformity.

## The Extent of Governmental Liability

If governmental liability is expanded, just what should its parameters be? To answer this question, we must address a more general one: What losses should the government bear?

I propose that government be obliged to compensate for every harmful act or omission committed by its agents within the scope of their employment that is tortious under applicable law. Allowing for the differences between the substantive legal norms applicable to public officials and private actors, government ought to occupy no better position vis-à-vis its citizens than its citizens do vis-à-vis one another. This compensation principle derives from the nature of the contemporary activist state described in the introduction, a state conceived of not as an autonomous sovereign overarching civil society but as an accountable instrument of collective will. When the collectivity seeks to fulfill

---

*One largely theoretical difficulty with model 2 (and perhaps with model 1 as well) deserves brief mention. The governmental enterprise, having borne the costs of litigation and liability, might then seek indemnification for those costs from the wrongdoing official, in effect restoring official liability and negating governmental liability. This possibility seems remote for several reasons. The Supreme Court has already barred the United States from seeking indemnification from its own officials for its liability under the FTCA.[25] In addition, corporate employers apparently seldom seek indemnification[26] and it is even more doubtful that public employers would, given the likely effects upon employee morale, the poor prospects of obtaining and collecting an indemnity judgment, and agencies' frequent responsibility for, if not complicity with, the violation.

benign aspirations but errs and injures, as it often will, it must—like anyone else—repair its damage and compensate its victims.

This compensation principle seems to the classical and contemporary mind alike so manifestly fair, so palpably just that it borders on the self-evident and axiomatic. Corrective justice, as Aristotle put it, is indifferent to "whether a good man has defrauded a bad man, or a bad man a good one . . . ; the law looks only to the distinctive character of the injury, and treats the parties as equal . . . . Therefore, this kind of injustice being an inequality, the judge tries to equalize it . . . by means of the penalty, taking away from the gain of the assailant."[27] To say that government should pay its way and bear the costs of its transgressions is like saying that people should tell the truth, earn their keep, and pay their debts. We can imagine exceptions to each of these maxims, circumstances under which we might be prepared to suspend their force, but they remain foundation stones of our moral order. It is all the more disturbing, then, that the activist state flagrantly flouts the compensation principle in important respects. These include Eleventh Amendment limitations on federal court damage actions against states; a niggardly waiver of federal governmental immunity under the FTCA; common law immunities and exceptions to state and local governmental liability under § 1983; and procedural and practical impediments to the effectiveness of even these truncated remedies against government.[28] How to fill these and other remedial gaps is a question addressed in the next section.

To propose the compensation principle as the measure of governmental liability is not to advocate a system of strict liability (or "liability without fault") for officially caused harm. Strict liability concerns the nature of the *substantive* standards for liability; it would require the government to compensate victims without regard to the "fault" of the officials whose conduct occasioned the harm. Mere officially caused harm, without a showing that the harm was intentional or caused by officials' failure to exercise the degree of care required by the substantive law, would suffice for liability. The appropriate substantive standards can only be defined by closely analyzing the social contexts in which particular liability rules operate—for example, the distribution of opportunities for minimizing the costs of harm and harm prevention; the relative costs of administering different liability rules; the equity effects of competing liability rules; and the moral consequences of different standards. Strict liability, for example, may be a sound rule when government operates a mandatory immunization program and a poor rule for most law enforcement activities. The design of substantive liability rules, then, is a complex and important activity; it is also a different subject.[29] The only point being emphasized here is that the compensation principle as a measure of the extent of governmental liability is a *remedial* norm only, one that takes existing substantive liability rules as given. It does not logically imply any change in those rules but instead can coexist with a strict, "fault"-based, intention-based, or other liability standard.

By the same token, the compensation principle does not imply a system of social insurance for officially caused harms. The decision rule that prescribes the range of harms that government is obliged to remedy is logically distinct from the mechanism that is selected for compensating victims. The compensation principle could be implemented in a variety of ways. The payment may come from any number of government budget categories, as we have seen. The payment fund may be financed by general tax revenues (for example, the United States Treasury or the state treasuries, under the current system) or by special taxes imposed upon particular entities or activities. Again, the merit of social insurance financing and administration of compensation compared with that of the current system is a complex, but for present purposes tangential, question.[30] The compensation principle is consistent with both.

## Implementing Expanded Governmental Liability

What specific changes should be made in the existing remedial system in order to expand governmental liability in accordance with the compensation principle? I answer this question by discussing, first, claims against the United States, and second, those against state and local governments.

### CLAIMS AGAINST THE UNITED STATES

As I noted in chapter 2, the FTCA's waiver of sovereign immunity is highly qualified; the statute retains many exceptions to governmental liability, some broad and others quite specific. I consider only the broad ones here.

1. *The "Discretionary Function" Exception.* The FTCA does not apply to "any claim . . . based upon the exercise or performance or the failure to exercise a discretionary function or duty . . . whether or not the discretion involved be abused."[31] Although the legislative history reveals no rationale for the exception (the history simply provides examples of how it might be applied),[32] it presumably seeks to encourage

vigorous decisionmaking by agencies and to limit judicial second-guessing of policy judgments entrusted to those with programmatic and administrative responsibility for the outcomes. These are valid, indeed essential purposes; truly discretionary decisions, after all, are decisions that are not constrained by any legal standards. Nevertheless, the FTCA exception is broader than necessary to secure these purposes.

First, it explicitly retains immunity for abuses of discretion even though the courts can review agency decisions for such abuses and routinely do so when substantive or procedural decision criteria exist.[33] Although there is always some danger that courts will seize upon this standard to interfere excessively with administrative judgment, that risk has not yet materialized in federal cases; it should be accepted as the price of confining the exception to its proper sphere. Second, some lower courts, no doubt encouraged by an early Supreme Court decision interpreting the exception to immunize routine low-level implementation of high-level policy decisions,[34] have construed it more broadly than is justified.[35] Precisely because virtually all actions are "discretionary" in some sense, the term should be restricted to non-routine, essentially judgmental, policy-type decisions. (Recent administrations seem to have conceded as much by sponsoring legislation to waive this exception *altogether* in constitutional tort cases.[36] As suggested in chapter 4, however, this change should not be limited to constitutional torts but should extend to all official wrongs.)

2. *The State Tort Requirement.* The FTCA has been interpreted to provide a remedy only against acts or omissions that are tortious under the law of the state in which they occurred. The United States, then, is liable only in circumstances in which a private individual under like circumstances would be liable under state law.[37]

This limitation creates at least two anomalies. First, most federal statutes and regulations create legal duties that state law does not impose upon private citizens; thus, they cannot trigger liability under the FTCA. This reasoning, has, for example, resulted in denial of a remedy for harm caused by an official's failure to require a bond mandated by statute and for injuries caused by an Occupational Safety and Health Administration (OSHA) inspector's wrongful failure to follow up on a citation for a safety violation.[38] Second, the state tort requirement renders even federal constitutional torts immune from liability unless they can somehow be framed as state law torts. Because federal constitutional prohibitions do not ordinarily apply to private individuals, however, this condition is difficult to meet.[39] And because federal law violations do not always violate state law, violations of the Constitution may not support FTCA coverage.[40] Even if the state law requirement was warranted in 1946 when the FTCA was enacted (despite the absence in the legislative history of any rationale for it), it is no longer defensible. The number of federal laws lacking any counterpart in the private tort law of the states has grown enormously since then. This growth, coupled with the expansion of federal constitutional rights for which direct tort remedies have been recognized,[41] argues strongly that this requirement should be repealed and that the newer, distinctively federal law torts should be integrated into the remedial structure of the FTCA.

3. *The Strict Liability Exclusion.* A related restriction is the FTCA's limitation to acts or omissions that are "negligent or wrongful."[42] The Supreme Court, reading this phrase literally, held that it does not cover governmental conduct that would only be tortious under state law under principles of strict liability.[43] The fundamental transformation of state tort law since 1946—specifically the recognition of strict liability for manufacturing defective products, for engaging in abnormally dangerous activities, and for evincing certain other forms of conduct—makes examination of the question of strict liability under the FTCA long overdue.[44] It is difficult to imagine, however, why a remedial scheme like the FTCA, especially one grounded upon state tort law, should be allowed to immunize the relatively well-defined categories of activity that now generate strict liability under that law.

4. *The Intentional Torts Restriction.* Before 1974, the FTCA excepted from its coverage most intentional torts, including those most likely to be committed by federal officials. After the *Bivens* decision,[45] the act was amended to permit claims "arising . . . out of assault, battery, false imprisonment, false arrest, abuse of process, or malicious prosecution . . . [by federal] investigative or law enforcement officers."[46] Thus, immunity continues to extend to these intentional torts if committed by other types of federal officials, and to intentional torts such as libel, slander, misrepresentation, deceit, or interference with contract rights, when committed by any federal official. Indeed, the exception has been consistently interpreted as extending far beyond intentional torts to include the vast and rapidly growing category of *negligent* misrepresentations by officials, many of which would not be immunized by the "discretionary function" exception.[47] The legislative history of the FTCA leaves this exception both unexplained and inexplicable,[48] and it flies in the face of strong trends in public tort law at the state level.[49] This anomalous immunity has occasioned many apparent injustices[50] and should be repealed.

5. *The "Good Faith" Defense*. It has traditionally been assumed that in view of the FTCA's explicit exceptions, no additional good faith defense against liability was warranted or intended. But when intentional torts of law enforcement officers became actionable under the FTCA in 1974, the United States began asserting such a defense. At least one appellate court has upheld the defense in a case concerning an alleged constitutional tort.[51] My proposed expansion of governmental liability would reduce the threat to vigorous decisionmaking and obviate the need to rely upon official liability for deterrence and compensation. Coupled with the existing exception for discretionary functions, it would thus eliminate any justification for such a defense under the FTCA.[52]

The FTCA not only preserves unjustified substantive exceptions to governmental liability but countenances three important procedural obstacles to a governmental liability regime consistent with the compensation principle.

1. *Nonmonetizable Rights*. Compensation of victims implies not merely that liability should be imposed but that the resulting judgment should make the victim whole. Effective deterrence requires that damages be substantial, not merely nominal. Many constitutional and other legal rights, however, cannot readily be converted into monetary terms, and the nominal damages often awarded for their violation are inadequate.[53] If a police officer lacking a valid warrant or probable cause kicks down a citizen's door and invades his home, the citizen is hardly compensated when the government replaces the door.

Subjecting an interest to constitutional protection sometimes is a way of saying that it ought to be treated as if it were priceless—that we do not wish to allow government to take it, or compel citizens to relinquish it, at *any* price. We afford less constitutional protection to traditional property interests, which are bought and sold in markets and can be taken by government for public use for "just compensation," than we do to certain other interests, such as fair procedures, freedom from unwarranted intrusions into homes or personal effects, freedom of speech and religion, and freedom from being subjected to arbitrary classifications. These are not traded and are not subject even to compensated takings for public uses. We protect these nonmonetizable rights not simply through liability rules secured by damage remedies but also through injunctive relief and rules against alienation of such rights.[54] True, these rights may be subject to reasonable restrictions and they are often abridged in practice. But this does not imply that society is willing to price them explicitly, only that it sometimes acts as if it were. Even if they have been priced implicitly, doing so openly would entail what Calabresi and Bobbitt have appropriately called "the cost of costing"—the cost of denying our most fundamental social values and myths.[55]

This problem has a relatively straightforward solution, one that has been used successfully in other areas of public law. When Congress has created remedies for legal rights, constitutional or otherwise, that cannot readily be monetized or whose infringement would not occasion substantial damages, it has sometimes provided a schedule of minimum liquidated damages that are automatically assessed.[56] There is no pretense that these damages constitute an actual monetary equivalent of the rights that have been abridged; rather, they are justified as assuring some compensation and deterrence. The same reasoning should apply *a fortiori* to federal rights for which the FTCA and *Bivens* provide remedies. Minimum damages should be provided for all public torts. Congress, if it wishes to proceed incrementally, might begin with the category of constitutional torts.[57]

2. *Attorney's Fees.* Even a schedule of minimum or presumed damages for nonmonetizable rights will not fully compensate victims so long as they must bear their own attorney's fees and other litigation costs. Although there are powerful arguments for maintaining the "American rule," which generally bars the shifting of fees and costs in most private law disputes,[58] the rule has little justification in cases in which citizens successfully demonstrate that their government has wronged them, thereby vindicating social as well as private interests. The public interest demands both that such suits be brought and that such victims be made whole. Nevertheless, the FTCA expressly prohibits awards of attorneys' fees.[59] The incoherence of this prohibition is suggested by the fact that successful plaintiffs[60] may now recover counsel fees and other litigation costs in § 1983 cases,[61] in proceedings brought under many federal regulatory statutes,[62] and (under a 1980 statute) in many judicial and administrative proceedings brought by or against the federal government.[63]

Also objectionable is the FTCA provision that makes it a crime for plaintiffs' attorneys to charge more than 25 percent of a judgment or more than 20 percent of a settlement.[64] This percentage, unchanged since 1966, is lower than the contingent fee charged by many attorneys in private tort cases and may effectively preclude some valid claimants from being represented, as the pre-1966 ceiling apparently did.[65] Since the United States employs salaried attorneys to defend such cases and is not liable for interest prior to judgment,[66] its incentives to settle are fewer, and the prospects for protracted litigation greater, than in most private tort cases. In addition, the government, as the preeminent institutional litigator, must be more concerned than most with securing favorable precedents and principles. This concern often induces it to litigate strenuously and at great length many cases in which trivial sums of money are at issue, cases that few private citizens could afford to litigate without the prospect of a fee award.[67] To encourage lawyers to accept cases against the government, contingent fees must be high enough to compensate them for services rendered not only in the cases they win but also in those they lose (for which they receive nothing).[68] For government to injure citizens and then, in the name of consumer protection, to deny them access to lawyers who can remedy those injuries is doubly ironic—and doubly unjust.

3. *Punitive Damages*. Although other federal statutes authorize punitive damage awards in appropriate cases,[69] the FTCA prohibits them entirely.[70] If FTCA cases were tried before a jury, there might be some legitimate concern about the possibility that juries sympathetic to innocent victims might too casually award punitive damages against the United States, the quintessential "deep pocket" defendant. But since judges assess damages in FTCA cases, this concern is simply irrelevant. Especially in view of the absence of any minimum damages provision and the bar on attorney's fee awards, a blanket prohibition of punitive damages practically guarantees that even successful plaintiffs will often not be made whole and hence that many meritorious claims will not even be litigated. At the very least, such awards should be authorized under certain conditions specified by statute.

CLAIMS AGAINST STATE AND LOCAL GOVERNMENTS

We saw in chapter 2 that some of the Supreme Court's recent decisions have significantly enlarged the potential scope of governmental liability under § 1983. These decisions, by reducing reliance upon the damage remedy against individual officials, generally conform to my analysis and prescriptions. But in two major respects, the contemporary Court has displayed excessive timidity. First, it has continued to recognize absolute, Eleventh Amendment immunity from damage liability when states violate federal rights. Second, it has continued to reject *respondeat superior* principles under § 1983.

1. *Eleventh Amendment Immunity*. In *Quern* v. *Jordan*,[71] the Court declined to interpret § 1983 as having repealed Eleventh Amendment immunity. It did so even though the statute was enacted under the enforcement authority of the Fourteenth Amendment, which was

clearly intended to transform the relationship between federal and state law insofar as federally secured rights were concerned.[72] An interpretation of *pro tanto* repeal would have been a straightforward and defensible, if controversial, adoption of governmental liability,[73] but the Court has instead confined itself to observing that Congress can constitutionally limit, or even eliminate, Eleventh Amendment immunity by statute (for example, by amending § 1983) whenever it wishes, so long as it makes its intent to do so clear.[74]

In fact, powerful policy arguments favor such a change. For reasons discussed earlier, governmental liability at the state level would advance public tort law goals. States are the ultimate sources of the authority and power of individual officials and local governments, and these are now subject to § 1983 liability. In addition, the states can already be sued for much declaratory and injunctive relief and indeed for certain kinds of monetary relief, and state and local officials are already vulnerable to personal suit under § 1983.[75] In fact, repealing Eleventh Amendment immunity would not so much weave a new remedial fabric as remove a discordant thread. Subjecting states to new damage liability would doubtless affect certain financial and legal relationships between state governments, local governments, and their employees, but to the extent that states already indemnify or insure officials against their violations of federal law,[76] this change would not significantly affect those relationships. In any event, far greater intergovernmental adjustments have been necessitated by many previous judicial and legislative innovations, most notably by the Fourteenth Amendment itself; if the proposed change were thought burdensome to the states, it could easily be facilitated by transitional subsidies or other arrangements.

We live in a world in which the corpus of federal law is enormous and steadily growing, and in which state officials are the principal executors, and hence potential violators, of that law. It is also a world in which § 1983 is now the central legal mechanism for securing federal rights. It is almost inconceivable that constitutional architects designing a remedial structure to support today's system of federalism (not to say the "new federalism" envisioned by President Reagan) would continue to countenance a blanket immunity for the states that was established for a fundamentally different system almost two centuries ago.

2. *Respondeat Superior*. By persistently rejecting *respondeat superior* principles under § 1983,[77] the Court has made bad policy, as I argued earlier. It has also made bad law, however, as a brief review of the Court's reasoning demonstrates.

In its most recent reaffirmations of this position, the Court did not justify it but simply cited to its earlier opinion in *Monell*.[78] But its reasoning in *Monell* in fact undermines its position. There, the Court cited *Rizzo* v. *Goode*,[79] for the proposition that "the mere right to control or failure to supervise is not enough to support § 1983 liability."[80] But *Rizzo* had been decided at a time when governmental entities could not be sued *at all* under § 1983, a very different setting in which to analyze *respondeat superior* than one in which they were routinely subject to suit. Moreover, that quotation from *Rizzo* seemed to imply that either the employer's exercise of control or its failure to supervise *would* suffice for liability; both situations were clearly present in *Monell*. Indeed, the Court in *Monell* had no need to address the *respondeat superior* issue at all since it found that "unquestionably . . . official policy" was a "moving force" of the violation there.[81] When the Court imposed an "official policy" requirement for governmental liability in *Monell*, such a requirement had neither been raised nor briefed and had not been discussed by the courts below.[82] Finally, the Court in *Monell* seems to have implicitly embraced the rather surprising view that governmental entities do not in fact control or supervise their employees; else why eliminate *respondeat superior*, of which such control is a necessary prerequisite, as a basis of liability?

The Court in *Monell* also adverted to "constitutional" objections to *respondeat superior* liability under § 1983 but never really explained what those objections were.[83] It did note the difficulty of imposing an obligation to keep the peace on the states, but that is not at all the same thing as *respondeat superior* liability and raises very different questions. Finally, the Court in *Monell* overruled *Monroe* v. *Pape* for its error in having placed excessive weight upon Congress's rejection of the "Sherman Amendment" to the bill that ultimately became § 1983. Yet in *Monell*, the Court relied at least as heavily upon that same rejection (and with even less justification) to support the proposition that *respondeat superior* liability had not been intended by that Congress.[84]

In addition to rejecting the vicarious *respondeat superior* liability of governments under § 1983, the Court has confined municipalities' primary liability, as well as limiting elimination of their good faith immunity, to constitutional torts.[85] This approach is not only vulnerable to my earlier objection that this distinction is irrelevant to the liability issue but is particularly anomalous in view of the Court's subsequent decision extending § 1983 to nonconstitutional claims.[86] Instead, governmental liability under § 1983 should be as broad as the encompassing language of that remedy permits.

Finally, additional ways should be sought to strengthen § 1983 as a remedy for official misconduct. Punitive damages, now barred in actions against municipalities,[87] should be permitted. Higher levels of government could be authorized to seek damages under § 1983 as *parens patriae* against lower-level agencies that encourage or countenance official wrongdoing. By placing states' fiscal resources and moral legitimacy behind § 1983 claims, some practical obstacles to the remedy's effectiveness, so pronounced when individual citizens sue,[88] might be overcome.[89] Findings of liability in § 1983 actions might be made to trigger changes in the processes of internal administrative management and discipline. These processes, which must ultimately be the chief bulwarks against most official misconduct, are the subject of the final part.

# PART III

## INSIDE THE BUREAUCRATIC BLACK BOX

In part II, I demonstrated that a reformed system of governmental liability promises substantial gains in all areas of remedial policy. Of course, the ultimate distributional effects of legal changes are notoriously difficult to predict.[1] Nonetheless, one may plausibly anticipate that these gains, diffused throughout the population, would accrue disproportionately to relatively disadvantaged citizens: those most dependent upon public services, most likely to be injured by the officials who deliver them, and most desperately in need of effective compensatory remedies. But governmental liability is no panacea, and Pareto-superior outcomes are by no means inevitable. As we saw in chapter 5, success in deterring official misconduct depends upon how effectively the public agencies subjected to the risk and reality of damage liability mobilize the critical behavior-shaping incentives and resources and transmit them to where they count—the street. Governmental liability can create strong incentives for the agency to do so, but implementation is irreducibly a question of *organizational process*.

Earlier, I characterized a public tort law regime as a specialized form of communication in which messages to officials are transformed by the organizational media through which they must pass to their destinations. Two related kinds of transformation occur. First, the message's substantive, conduct-oriented norms affect, and in turn are affected by, the agency's goals (treating the agency for the moment as a unit). Official behavior not only regulates private activity but also implicates a quite independent set of public values, often of constitutional dimension. It is therefore a matter of supreme organizational significance, indeed of survival, for the agency to control how these norms—for example, those that prescribe how the police should investigate criminal activity—are elaborated, internalized, and enforced. Second, the elaborate bureaucratic filter that transmits messages to officials may amplify or muffle a norm, distort or clarify it, transmit it in isolation, or envelop it in other norms. But once the norm passes through this organizational screen, it acquires a new, organizationally conditioned existence.[2]

Each of these transformations may undermine the use of legal norms to control official misconduct. The norm may threaten, or at least be perceived to threaten, what the agency wishes to do or to be—its programmatic mission, professional values, political identity, social structure, or bureaucratic operating routines. In such a conflict, the norm may not survive. At a minimum, its bureaucratic journey and street-level reception will alter its meaning and significance.

In this part I consider the hard truth that general deterrence alone, even in the remedial form that I have proposed, will sometimes prove unequal to these organizational challenges. When that occurs, resort to specific deterrence measures may be necessary to exert the level of control over officials' behavior that society demands. Whether these measures are initiated in the first instance by agencies themselves, by legislatures, or by courts, these groups cannot succeed without mobilizing the process of organizational change. This process is exceedingly opaque; it is like a "black box" that receives discernible inputs (norms and resources) and generates palpable outputs (compliance and misconduct) but whose internal technologies are largely invisible. In chapter 6 I attempt to glimpse inside it and to analyze specific strategies that legislatures and change-oriented agency leaders might employ to encourage agency self-policing of official behavior on the street. But for a variety of reasons, legislatures may not act and agency self-policing will sometimes be doomed to failure. In that event, court interventions may seem appropriate. In chapter 7 I consider the propriety of deep judicial probes into the black box and ways in which judges ought to proceed when they are tempted to undertake them.

# 6: MOBILIZING ORGANIZATIONAL CHANGE: HOW WILL AGENCIES RESPOND TO GOVERNMENTAL LIABILITY?

Even if government were wholly immune from tort liability, administrators would have an enormous stake in how their employees perform their tasks. Administrators' political needs, professional and policy commitments, and desires for personal success constitute powerful motives to control the level of wrongdoing by subordinates. By levying a budgetary tax upon such wrongdoing, governmental liability reinforces and augments these motives.

But even when they face governmental liability for damages, administrators feel countervailing pressures to tolerate low-level misconduct. The political environment may countenance or even reward lawbreaking that appears to advance important programmatic or ideological goals such as crime control, intelligence-gathering, or preservation of neighborhood schools. Bureaucratic needs—for example, to preserve employee morale or to maintain order within a custodial institution—may induce agencies to wink at illegal behavior.[1] Administrative imperatives, such as the duty to process massive case loads, may encourage dubious procedures or shortcuts in the interests of "efficiency."[2] These organizational incentives may on balance outweigh the fiscal ones that governmental liability creates.

Unfortunately, our understanding of how bureaucracies behave is so rudimentary that one cannot predict how the balance will actually be struck in diverse situations. Administrators can distribute resources (e.g., information, equipment) to their personnel, as well as increase incentives (e.g., compensation, promotions, sanctions) and encourage positive values (e.g., goals, loyalty, a sense of fellowship),[3] but these tactics may simply be insufficient and leaders cannot always use them skillfully. Moreover, organizational influence is not like a mountain stream, flowing downward only. Subordinates can use strategies of their own to shape their superiors' behavior. In street-level agencies, it is in fact seldom clear who ultimately controls whom.[4] Organizational change, then, is irreducibly contingent. Indeed, when an administrator orders street-level officials to change the way in which they go about their work, the instruction must be viewed as little more than a commencement of hostilities (or at least negotiations), an opening gambit in a protracted and problematic struggle over policy implementation.

Yet agency leaders sometimes do succeed in reforming low-level conduct; occasionally, the change is quite dramatic.[5] Every organization, after all, enjoys some maneuvering room, some freedom to innovate. At a minimum, organizations can exploit individuals' "zones of indifference" (in Chester Barnard's phrase), psychological domains within which they are relatively vulnerable to inducements.[6] The question, then, is not whether agency leaders, spurred to reform by the burden or prospect of governmental liability, can work their will on their subordinates, but rather under what circumstances they are most likely to try and to succeed. In short, how confident can we be that governmental liability for damages will in fact produce the desired street-level behavior?

I explore that question in this chapter. The first section, drawing upon a small but growing literature about organizational change, identifies the processes and resources that seem essential to its success, the crucial ingredients of deterrence that either governmental liability or injunctive relief must somehow mobilize. The second section analyzes why even agencies burdened by those remedies may not be motivated to control low-level misconduct and considers how that motivation might be strengthened. The final section examines why even reform-minded agencies may lack the capacity to implement organizational change and how that capacity might be developed. This analysis will also be applied in chapter 7, where I consider the effects of *judicial* intervention on the process of bureaucratic reform.

*The Process of Organizational Change*

Richard Elmore has distilled four distinct processes of organizational change, which he calls "organizational models of social program implementation."[7] Like all models, these are artificial and incomplete representations of reality; like many, their conceptual organizing principles remain unclear. Nevertheless, Elmore's models, which apparently embrace all agency efforts to innovate, are useful for present purposes in helping to identify systemic obstacles to organizational change in street-level agencies and corresponding strategies for seeking to overcome them.

Elmore's first model stresses "systems management" impediments to change. Here, the organization is conceived of as a problem-solving system whose elements must be integrated and controlled in order to focus action on a common purpose. Its distinctive implementation problem is hierarchical control; failures to control result in poor planning, incoherent allocation of tasks, inadequate measurement of subunit performance, and ineffective sanctions.

The "bureaucratic process" model emphasizes the pervasiveness in some organizations of low-level discretion structured by bureaucratic routines. Here, implementation is stymied by fragmentation, by the dispersal of power to the lowest reaches of the organization where innovation is perceived as most threatening and is most fiercely resisted. This model, Elmore notes,

> forces us to contend with the mundane patterns of bureaucratic life and to think about how new policies affect the daily routines of people who deliver social services. Policy-makers, analysts, and administrators have a tendency to focus on variables that emphasize control and predictability, often overlooking the factors that undermine control and create anomalies in the implementation process. Bureaucratic routines operate against the grain of many policy changes because they are contrived as buffers against change and uncertainty; they continue to exist precisely because they have an immediate utility to the people who use them in reducing the stress and complexity of work. Failing to account for the force of routine in the implementation of policy leads to serious misperceptions.[8]

The "organizational development" model stresses individuals' social-psychological strivings in organizations, particularly their need for personal relationships, autonomy, trust, support, and involvement. Here, implementation critically depends upon interpersonal and emotional factors that cannot be readily supplied or manipulated by administrators but can only result from individuals' commitments to change. In that sense, Elmore observes, "the process of initiating and implementing new policy actually begins at the bottom and ends at the top."[9]

Finally, the "conflict and bargaining" model stresses that power within organizations depends upon the distribution of many resources, of which hierarchical position is only one. Here, implementation has little to do with central direction or the achievement of a common organizational purpose. Rather, it is constrained and defined by a series of conflicts and compromises at and between all levels of the agency.

The most striking fact about Elmore's models is that the impediments to organizational change that they highlight—ineffective hierarchical control, low-level discretion embedded in largely autonomous routines, personal commitments that discourage innovation, and internal conflict—seem to converge in one particular kind of organization: the direct service, street-level agency.[10] In addition to the task-related centrifugal forces discussed in chapter 3, power in such agencies is further dispersed by powerful public employee unions, civil service rules, isolation of front-office administrators from the front-line rank and file, and external political pressures. Low-level employees with little to say about the policies that are adopted tend to control how they are executed. Top-down change that strikes at what they view as their vital interests can thus be readily contained, if not aborted.

When significant organizational innovations occur—for example, the FBI's transformation since J. Edgar Hoover's death,[11] the Civil Aeronautics Board's rapid change from enthusiastic cartel manager to ardent deregulator,[12] the Army Corps of Engineers' *volte-face* on citizen participation and environmental values during the 1970s,[13] and the federal disability programs' apparent reversal of the Social Security Administration's earlier claims-granting policies[14]—they tend to do so in bureaucracies in which the "systems management" approach to implementation is possible. In these bureaucracies, one and usually more of the following conditions exists: Formal lines of authority roughly correspond to the distribution of actual influence within the organization; a strong programmatic mission or ideology serves to weld bureaucratic subunits into a common enterprise subject to centralized discipline; the nature of the tasks facilitates close supervision of and control over low-level officials.

Unfortunately, most street-level misconduct occurs in organizational settings not readily amenable to a "systems management" approach to control. There, weak management, fragmented authority, politically strong unions, broad low-level discretion, and internal conflicts are more the norm.[15] It is not that power diffusion makes street-level agencies resistant to change per se; indeed, innovative low-level officials can facilitate the changes they desire.[16] What is problematic is top-down change imposed upon recalcitrant subordinates.

For the leadership of a street-level agency to prevail in such an effort, four resources are especially important: information, communicative power, behavior-shaping incentives, and political support.[17] The first two resources are useful in dealing with the problems of comprehension-based, capacity-based, and (to a lesser extent) negligence-based illegality discussed in chapter 1. The last two are appropriate to the problem of motivation-based illegality. An important theme of part III is that agencies and courts have very different capacities to mobilize and deploy these resources to alter low-level behavior and that an understanding of these differences is crucial to designing sound remedial policy. Here, I emphasize the role of agencies (and to a lesser degree, legislatures), responding to tort liability signals, in effecting such change; in chapter 7, I stress the role of courts.

INFORMATION

To mandate and effectively implement social change, one must know a great deal about the world. One must be able to develop causal information that identifies the conditions and behaviors that produced the problem in question and the changes that can produce a desired end-state; technical information that generates remedial alternatives and reveals their costs, benefits, and other empirical dimensions; and political information that predicts how these alternatives will affect the way relevant actors respond.

In theory, and to some degree in practice, agencies are well situated to adduce these types of information. They can commission scientific research, hold hearings, order reports to be prepared, disseminate proposals, and analyze public opinion until they are satisfied that their data base is adequate. Even then, they are not obliged to make a decision or to justify their inaction in a principled fashion.[18] They can more or less set their own agendas, tailoring their decisions according to what they wish to do and think they know. As well-staffed, institutionalized policymaking organs with continuing oversight and programmatic responsibilities, they often acquire a "feel" for the contours of the problems within their jurisdictions—a sense of which alternatives might work and which cannot, of how and where changes in one part of the system are likely to reverberate, of the likely costs and benefits of different alternatives and how they will be distributed. Perhaps most important, agencies receive a constant stream of relevant political information about how the social interests implicated by a change believe it will affect them and about how they and their politically active representatives will react. Highly specialized to process this flow of information, they become adept at interpreting and evaluating its provenance, meaning, weight, intensity, and accuracy.[19]

Agencies, of course, do not fully exploit these formidable informational capacities. They sometimes adopt far-reaching policy changes on the basis of slender, nonexistent, or distorted factual records.[20] Hearings may be perfunctory or one-sided, studies and reports superficial or preconceived, decisional agendas set less by self-conscious priority-setting and instrumental rationality than as a result of narrow electoral ambitions and parochial political pressures. Functional specialization may produce not panoramic vistas but tunnel vision; it may generate narrowly conceived remedies, not broad-gauged ones.

Some problems that spawn official misconduct may be eliminated by advancing the state of the art. For others, however, better information is simply unavailable. Much more is known today than was known a generation ago about how to teach certain kinds of children, but we are probably no better at training teachers for the "typical" child than we were a century ago. If officials confine too many patients in mental hospitals who might manage tolerably well in the community, it may be because psychosocial diagnostic theory is not sufficiently well developed to enable risk-averse hospital staff members to identify with confidence who those patients are. More generally, our inability to measure how particular changes affect social problems encourages clumsy, almost random interventions in which officials are obliged to use indirect input or process measures that often yield inaccurate predictions.

COMMUNICATIVE POWER

To implement change, one must communicate one's demands clearly and effectively to those who must execute them. (Of course, one must also be able to receive incoming information and feed it back into one's decision processes, a problem discussed in the preceding subsection.) In chapter 1, we saw that street-level bureaucracies experience systematic difficulties in communicating with low-level operatives. In theory, at least, several strategies might succeed in reducing this problem. Managers could attempt to monitor, clarify, and then reinforce what their subordinates understand the demands from above to be. In a number of ways, higher-ups may be able to boost the "power" of norms as they are transmitted to the lower levels. For example, they might dramatize the norms' content, augment training to enhance agents' receptivity to them, refine the organization's hierarchical controls, and reduce the number of bureaucratic layers through which messages must pass.

Because of its control over the formal organizational structure and the formal channels of communication, agency management is well positioned to design and implement these strategies and to test their effectiveness. Although informal networks of communication and values can pose serious obstacles to this approach, as we saw in chapter 1, those networks can at least in principle be influenced, and perhaps even dragooned into affirmative service, by adroit agency management. In any event, it is difficult to imagine that a court or legislature could succeed in this effort where the agency has failed.

### INCENTIVES

Like the rest of us, street-level officials settle into routine ways of thinking and doing, habitual behavior that roughly accommodates their duties, desires, and constraints. They invest in these "coping strategies" (as Lipsky calls them)[21] over time in the hopes of attaining technical job skills; social, ideological, and emotional satisfactions; a sense of purpose; and material benefits. The prospect of change jeopardizes both the investment and the rewards. Costs of transition to new routines, and costs of uncertainty as to outcomes, must be incurred. Fears about the magnitude and distribution of these costs plague efforts to alter official behavior. Reforms that fail to address these fears seem doomed to failure.

Even in street-level agencies, however, change is the only constant. Usually incremental but occasionally rapid, even convulsive, change presses relentlessly against entrenched habit and routine and sometimes triumphs. Thousands of handicapped children have been "mainstreamed" into conventional classrooms, and hundreds of formerly segregated school systems are now integrated. Law enforcement agencies perform some tasks very differently today than they did prior to the Warren Court's criminal justice rulings. Many state mental hospitals have been closed and their patients and employees have been moved to community settings; others treat patients in ways that depart dramatically from earlier clinical practice. Other examples were mentioned earlier in this chapter.

When such transformations of street-level agencies occur, as they often do, what accounts for them? The answer is elusive, for causal patterns are usually a Gordian knot of technological, ideological, social, political, legal, bureaucratic, and economic influences. Deinstitutionalization of the mentally ill, for example, a change that reduced the patient population in state mental hospitals from 559,000 to 150,000 between 1955 and 1980,[22] reflected many factors: the marketing of new psychotropic drugs, the ideological dominance of a new community model of treatment among leading mental health professionals, changes in federal and state legislation and program structures, fiscal pressures on state mental health systems, and court decisions. (It was also a reform the success of which could be monitored and measured by "the numbers"—though imperfectly, of course—far more readily than most.) These factors surely increased the probability of change, but successful implementation ultimately depends upon the ability of those who administer a change to secure acceptance, or at least acquiescence, by those at the bottom who must carry it out. Mental health workers and their unions (in this case) had to at least be persuaded that deinstitutionalization was not inconsistent with their own interests as they defined them. For many of them, professional and ideological values favored the change.

Incentives can be used to influence low-level behavior in a number of ways. An agency can select personnel who are already more or less sympathetic to the change and competent to carry it forward, or who can be induced to become so. The character, motivation, and competence of the individuals charged with executing a program of social change are crucial to its success. They can commit their energies and talents to its realization, or they can become its implacable foes. Agencies, of course, are not altogether free to select their low-level agents, but their discretion, influence, and margin for individuation in personnel decisions remain considerable. Even under normal personnel restrictions, agency administrators reserve some appointing discretion.[23] Moreover, legislation sometimes exempts innovation-oriented agencies from civil service merit or pay restrictions altogether; it can also reorganize into impotence those who resist change.

Most important, agencies control an extraordinarily diverse array of resources and sanctions that can be manipulated to induce behavioral change in indifferent, reluctant, or even hostile officials. They may increase the expected benefits of compliance and the expected costs of noncompliance in numerous ways. In addition to exerting some power over personnel selection, agencies can tax, subsidize, combine substantive and procedural rules in many different ways, reorganize existing programs and structures or create new ones, impose criminal and civil sanctions and informal sanctions such as adverse publicity or political reprisal, and manipulate budget. These inducements are both positive and negative, carrots as well as sticks, and they can be aimed at whichever social actors seem relevant to resolving the particular problem at hand, be they private citizens or public officials.

If the problem, for example, is that compliance with a rule or policy seems too costly to those subject to it, its content may be altered so that it imposes fewer costs or distributes the same costs differently. Even without changing it, an agency may manage to subsidize its costs or confer compensating benefits. Perceptions about the magnitude or the acceptability of the costs may be changed. Leadership and statecraft, after all, consist of precisely this ability to persuade and to teach—what Walter Lippmann described as "giving the people not what they want but what they will learn to want."[24]

If instead the problem is that low-level officials view the rule or policy as poorly conceived and probably ineffective (or worse), agency management may try to change the reality (either the rule itself or the environment in which it is to be implemented) or the perception. It may be true that if the reality could be changed the rule would have been unnecessary, but this is not invariably so. Field operatives know many things that their superiors do not about how changes in policy are likely to work out. The rulemaker may simply have failed to consider superior alternatives; an integration-minded public housing authority, for example, may have neglected scattered-site housing in its fascination with large projects. Even if the rule cannot be changed, altering the environment in which it will operate may enhance its perceived effectiveness. Additional resources may be used to mollify those who might otherwise resist the change. The Emergency School Assistance Act,[25] which provides federal funds to localities to assist them in the implementation of school desegregation orders, is a notable instance of this tactic.

Even if the reality cannot be altered, the official's perception of ineffectiveness can perhaps be. Persuasion can take many forms. New theories or data may be adduced to justify and reinforce the change. Legitimating symbols may be mobilized to buttress its acceptability and therefore its perceived efficacy. President Eisenhower's dispatch of troops to Little Rock and President Reagan's personal and dramatic imposition of statutory sanctions against striking air traffic controllers demonstrate the potential viability of this approach. Public discussion, unforeseen events, and the passage of time often alter attitudes.

If the rule is perceived as illegitimate, however, the problem may be serious, even insoluble. Legitimacy cannot be generated at will but accrues gradually, if at all. "Legitimacy," Alexander Bickel wrote, "comes to a regime that is felt to be good and to have proven itself as such to generations past as well as in the present."[26] Yet even a failure of legitimacy is not always fatal to compliance. Bickel notes that another institution may be able to bestow the legitimacy that the rule's issuer could not confer:

Not only is the Supreme Court capable of generating consent for hotly controverted legislative or executive measures; it has the subtler power of adding a certain impetus to measures that the majority enacts rather tentatively. There are times when the majority might, because of strong minority feelings, be inclined in the end to deny itself, but when it comes to embrace a measure more firmly, and the minority comes to accept it, because the Court—intending perhaps no such consequence—has declared it consistent with constitutional principle.[27]

The legitimacy-granting and legitimacy-receiving roles, of course, may be reversed. Through confirmatory legislation, Congress has occasionally conferred acceptability upon a controversial Court decision that for some reason—perhaps a closely divided vote or unprincipled, unpersuasive reasoning—seemed to lack it.[28] The president may also confer and receive legitimacy. When President Nixon reluctantly acquiesced in the Court's ruling upholding the subpoena of the Watergate tapes,[29] he transformed an extraordinarily controversial decision that might have precipitated a constitutional crisis into one carrying undoubted moral authority and force. In a reversal of these roles, the Court legitimated President Carter's hotly disputed transfer of assets to Iran.[30]

POLITICAL SUPPORT

Implementation of a significant change in official policy and behavior requires that the change enjoy the support, or at least the acquiescence, of politicians, organized constituencies, political institutions, and the public at large (which does not always amount to the same thing), especially those citizens or groups directly affected by it.

Political and public support is a special kind of resource; it has the distinctive capacity to generate other resources and to multiply itself. An agency that can mobilize support for a change, for example, may be able to transmute that support into an addition to its budget, media attention, or other resources that can be used to influence low-level officials and others who might have opposed it, thereby attracting further support. Obviously, political and public support varies, depending on many factors. Some of the most important are: the magnitude and distribution of costs and benefits across the population; prevailing ideological currents; the attitude and behavior of "opinion leaders"; media coverage; and the entreprenurial and leadership skills of strategically placed individuals and groups.[31]

Legislatures are designed in ways that are quite clearly calculated to generate support for their innovations. The publicity apparatus, the opportunities for casework on behalf of constituents, and coalition-building through logrolling are examples.[32] Regulatory agencies, with their ability to allocate benefits and costs through the elaboration of legal rules, are likewise capable of attracting support for their policies.[33] Direct service, street-level agencies like police departments and public schools must often rely upon different sources of support—principally the sheer number (and thus political weight) of their employees and unions and the indispensability of the services they deliver.

These, then, are the crucial ingredients of organizational change, the resources that must be brought to bear upon street-level misconduct if it is to be reduced. Elmore's models suggest that street-level agencies face structural obstacles in doing so. Agencies' effectiveness with regard to reform ultimately depends upon both their *motivation* to alter employees' behavior and their *capacity* to succeed. In the final two sections of this chapter, I consider how each might be strengthened. I do not suggest that these approaches are either novel or certain to succeed, but only that success demands recourse to at least some of them.

## *Improving Agency Motivation to Control Official Misconduct*

The balance of political and bureaucratic incentives that has produced an agency's present posture toward low-level misconduct is neither sacrosanct nor immutable; it is simply an adaptation to current conditions that, if changed, might well generate different adaptations. Governmental liability, especially as proposed in chapter 5, should encourage agencies to value proper behavior more highly. *Constituency-building for deterrence* is potentially the most effective way to respond to and reinforce this new incentive.

The necessary constituencies must be created—or more accurately, empowered—both inside and outside the agency. The call for an expanded commitment to lawfulness by agency officials should not be taken either as a denigration of existing official morality or as a pious and naive appeal for "better" men and women to staff our public agencies. To the contrary, it acknowledges that administrative remedies for official misconduct must use for the most part the organizational materials already in place and that efforts to deter must engage the commitment of existing officials. Still, officials' beliefs about what behavior is appropriate do not grow in a vacuum. They are influenced, as we have seen, by external institutions and expectations. These outside forces can be used to supply motives otherwise lacking or to reinforce existing inclinations, encouraging them to ripen into lawful behavior. I shall discuss four constituency-building techniques: professionalization, building of political alliances, reform of disciplinary procedures, and enforcement by higher levels of government.

PROFESSIONALIZATION

Constituency-building within agencies can begin with attempts to increase professional and political incentives. Professionalization—as measured by general education, specialization, salaries, training, merit promotion, and its close cousin, bureaucratization—has been shown to improve official evaluation of, and behavioral response to, legal and policy innovations.[34] Professionalization is marked, indeed defined, by basic attitudinal changes that reflect increased education and training in the application of universalistic, cosmopolitan norms, including what might be called "legalism," and attentiveness to the values and opinions of persons *outside* officials' particular bureaucratic and political contexts. Thus, professionalism broadens officials' perspectives and is generally conducive to compliance with the law. Wilson's studies of police behavior, for example, have found that more professionalized departments tend to have more "legalistic" styles of law enforcement, stressing the importance of "going by the book" and placing a higher value upon compliance with norms by themselves and by others.[35]

Professionalization, of course, is only one factor affecting officials' inclination to comply, especially in street-level agencies. In his study of police departments' responses to the *Miranda* decision, Milner found that more professionalized departments were more likely to support *Miranda* (though only weakly) and to create formal procedures consistent with it. Instead of threatening outright noncompliance, however, they used low-level techniques to counteract these changes; "in their informal procedures they were much like their less professionalized counterparts."[36] Moreover, just as low-level professionalization can fragment and weaken informal organizational allegiances, encouraging officials to seek legitimation from realms beyond the parochial and political frontiers of the agency, it may hobble managerial authority by making competing sources of authority more salient. In extreme cases, such as a work stoppage by hospital workers protesting the conditions to which their clients are subjected, professional values may even encourage disobedience that amounts to a violation of the law.[37]

Empirical evidence suggests that agency management's refusal to tolerate low-level misconduct, an attitude closely related to professional values, increases the effectiveness of other control techniques. Several recent studies have found that the critical factor in apparently successful policy changes aimed at restricting police use of deadly force is the willingness of the chief to make it clear that unwarranted shootings will be severely disciplined. Indeed, after the chief who adopted the policy in Kansas City left the force, the policy remained unchanged but the number of police shootings returned to the same level as before the policy was instituted.[38] Adding lawyers to an agency's staff may also encourage compliance.[39] That professional (and hence legalistic) attitudes can counteract even the most powerful peer subcultures of street-level official life is further suggested by recent evidence indicating a marked increase in the proportion of complaints about police misconduct in New York City that come from the police officers themselves.[40]

BUILDING POLITICAL ALLIANCES

Outside the agency, constituencies to support greater deterrence can sometimes be created among politicians, groups that represent potential victims, and their quondam allies, including the media. There are almost always some politicians and journalists with political or professional incentives to expose wrongdoing. Legislative oversight hearings, broad "freedom of information" guarantees, demands for criminal sanctions or new statutory controls, threats of reduced appropriations, close scrutiny of personnel appointments—these and many other formal and informal instruments of reward and punishment can be used to encourage compliance and build public support. A political climate congenial to continued illegality may of course undercut their effectiveness; indeed, some researchers have suggested that official practices, including police misconduct, closely mirror prevailing community attitudes.[41] Still, potential victims' groups, led by a political entrepreneur or crusading reformer, may be able to muster a level of public backing or moral force that will persuade even reluctant politicians to move against errant agencies.[42]

REFORMING ADMINISTRATIVE DISCIPLINARY SYSTEMS

When a street-level agency feels the bite of a liability judgment, its internal disciplinary machinery can be an important lever for securing low-level compliance, as well as for building constituencies for deterrence among outsiders. In fact, control of the disciplinary machinery involves such high stakes for all concerned that it can become a political lightning rod, distorting rather than rationalizing an agency's incentive structure.

For internal discipline to deter illegality without unduly stifling vigorous decisionmaking, a number of conditions seem essential. First, the system must be flexible and must control an array of inducements, sanctions, and dispute-resolution techniques, rather than limiting choices to "nuclear bombs" or "slaps on the wrist." Second, it must be widely perceived as just and impartial. It must therefore enjoy the confidence of potential victims as well as potential offenders, and it must be sensitive both to the operating realities and constraints of officials on the street and to the legal norms and expectations of the larger community. This delicate balance requires a varied, carefully selected administrative membership—constituencies, one might say, chosen not only for deterrence but also for vigorous decisionmaking. Finally, the system must be linked to the tort adjudication process. When an agency has been held liable for an employee's misconduct, there must be some assurance that the disciplinary process will be activated and that some remedial action (in addition to the government's payment of damages) will be taken.

It is not possible here to essay a general evaluation of the different mechanisms of administrative discipline now in use. (It is of interest, however, that an attorney general of the United States recently expressed public doubts about their adequacy, at least in the federal service.[43]) Rather, I shall confine myself to discussing the most important conflicts that must be addressed if nontort, nonbudgetary control mechanisms are to meet the demands that a regime of expanded governmental liability would place upon them. Perhaps the most difficult of these is the conflict between the powerful desire of a street-level agency to control its own disciplinary processes and the public's need for confidence in the credibility and effectiveness of those processes. At its highest levels, where external constraints upon the agency are most keenly felt and public criticism and political sanctions are most deeply feared, powerful motives exist to maximize agency autonomy in dealing with employee misconduct. Low-level officials regard agency control over discipline as essential to prevent outsiders, whose motives and knowledge about conditions on the street are suspect, from judging officials unjustly.[44] This is especially true of agencies, like the police, in which administrators feel embattled by hostile and implacable forces on the street; misunderstood by politicians, judges, or prosecutors; unappreciated by the public; and chronically concerned about their employees' morale and sense of mission.

Victims, for their part, may tend to view a self-contained, autonomous disciplinary process as illegitimate and to view its outcomes as so much whitewash.[45] If they belong to ethnic or other groups deeply suspicious of the fairness of the agency, this belief may be virtually unshakable; they will demand participation in, if not control over, the process. In general, several forms of "lay" involvement are possible. First, citizen complaints of official misconduct can be reviewed by external bodies. Second, a position or unit can be created within the government to represent alleged victims. Third, aggrieved individuals can be authorized to activate and participate in the disciplinary process beyond merely filing a complaint. Each of these has its advantages, but none is fully satisfactory.

The classic example of external review is the civilian complaint review board. A number were created at the local level during the 1960s in an effort to reduce tensions between the police and the public, especially minority groups; some had been established much earlier.[46] These boards have generally been designed to work independently of the judicial system; a citizen's complaints are unrelated to, and have no effect upon, his right to bring a tort action. If internal action were linked to tort liability, however, agency compliance might be strengthened. The unlawfulness of the activity having been established in court, agencies could not as easily resist the disciplinary recommendations of a review board.

The effectiveness of such boards has been hampered by the strong opposition of the police, and many have been abolished. Law enforcement agents' antipathy toward civilian review has led one commentator to conclude that "the ill feeling the institution provokes may not be worth the benefit it confers."[47] New York's citizen board, established in July 1966, lasted only four months until it was abolished by a referendum; a modified version continued under internal agency control. Philadelphia's, which was established in 1958, was hampered by limited staff and restricted enforcement powers and was crippled in 1967 when the local policemen's association obtained a court injunction against it. In December 1980, a civilian complaint review panel created by the mayor of Chicago was dissolved after only three months.[48]

Clearly, the particular auspices under which the review board operates critically affect both its perceived usefulness to complainants and officials' sense of autonomy. Injured citizens may be skeptical about lodging a complaint with the very agencies that have caused their grievances. An external review board, in contrast, provides a more impartial forum and seems to encourage the filing of complaints. The New York citizen board, during its four-month life, received more complaints than the predecessor departmental board had received in a year.[49]

The need for an external review agency depends, of course, upon the particular behavior under attack. The police may be an extreme case because of their potential to inflict physical harm and the mistrust with which they are regarded by some segments of the community. The problem of accountability may not be as great for other officials and internal review of complaints concerning them may be more satisfactory. But other things being equal, the mutual acceptability—and thus effectiveness— of civilian complaint review boards is probably least in precisely those situations in which the need is greatest, and vice versa. For this reason, more limited variants of the idea, such as including a minority of civilians in a disciplinary body (composed largely of officials) or providing arbitration by a mutually agreeable panel, may be more promising.

The second form of lay influence is achieved by locating various kinds of "advocates" within the governmental structure (though not necessarily within the particular agency). These advocates, who enjoy some degree of independence from the agency in question, may be prosecutorial or may exercise only advisory, ombudsmanlike powers. An example of the first type is the Office of Special Counsel, created under the Civil Service Reform Act of 1978 to investigate and administratively prosecute specified categories of alleged misconduct by federal supervisory employees.[50] Another kind of prosecutorial "advocacy" unit, entirely internal to the agency, is employed by the New York City police. Allegations concerning an officer may be brought before the department either by the Community Complaint Review Board, a branch of the police department that receives complaints of brutality and other wrongdoing, or by the Internal Affairs Division, which independently investigates police corruption. When prosecution is recommended, it is handled by an advocate's staff of police attorneys. A trial-type administrative hearing is held and penalties can be assessed ranging from short suspensions to dismissal. Those within the department reportedly view the process as effective; 600 to 700 officers are tried annually. Accountability remains a problem, however, for a citizen cannot compel action on a complaint that internal review has not found to be meritorious. Also, this system apparently is used to deal primarily with allegations of brutality and corruption, not with alleged Fourth Amendment violations or other actions more typical of § 1983 claims.[51]

An example of an ombudsman-type advocate is the Office of Advocacy within the Small Business Administration. It lacks the power to prosecute or initiate proceedings against individuals but has filed *amicus* briefs in selected cases. Generally, it serves as a go-between for small businesses dealing with federal agencies, and it makes policy recommendations to other agencies on behalf of small business interests. The office usually becomes involved in a specific dispute prior to litigation; its role is often to help both parties reach a satisfactory compromise, reducing the need for litigation. It therefore supplements rather than supplants tort litigation.[52]

In the third form of lay involvement, individuals are empowered to pursue complaints even after the entity authorized to prosecute violators has rejected them. The underlying rationale, of course, is that deterrence is weakened so long as agencies retain control of the process and can refuse to prosecute meritorious complaints. Victim-centered disciplinary processes are exceedingly controversial; indeed, they have been a chief stumbling block to passage of legislation to substitute governmental liability under the FTCA for official liability in *Bivens* actions.[53] Law enforcement officials fear that such a process could be used for harassment purposes and maintain that it impugns their integrity. Victims' groups, however, justify this approach by pointing to instances in which agencies failed to discipline employees whose misconduct had been the subject of adjudication by a court.[54]

Especially in a public tort law system that substitutes governmental for official liability, thereby bureaucratizing responsibility for deterrence and moral affirmation, internal disciplinary procedures must be credible, effective, and fair. So important to the integrity of the remedial system is this goal that we should be prepared to run some risks and incur some additional overhead costs in order to seek improved procedures. Tort plaintiffs who have already prevailed, for example, have strong incentives to keep the system honest. They could be permitted to request that a disciplinary inquiry be undertaken against officials whose misconduct led to governmental liability, to participate in any subsequent proceedings (as by presenting evidence, submitting statements, and perhaps cross-examining witnesses), to receive a written statement of reasons for the decision to take or not take disciplinary action, and to appeal that decision to a superior administrative tribunal and perhaps ultimately to a court.[55] Such a scheme leaves many technical questions to be answered—for example, whether, according to what standards, and at whose initiative judicial review of disciplinary decisions should be permitted; whether requests should be acted upon before the tort claim is resolved; and whether the initial inquiry should be conducted and decided by the employing agency or by an independent entity. The basic principles, however, seem just and feasible.

Other variants, combining elements of the three types of lay involvement—external review, ombudsmen, and victim participation—can be devised. Victims could be permitted, for example, to initiate agency disciplinary proceedings with appeals permitted only if recommended by an "advocate" inside or outside the agency. This would limit the role of advocate to a manageable function and assure agencies that they would not be harassed by frivolous claims, while still allowing citizens some meaningful role in the disciplinary process. Complaint review boards might be structured to include an internal or external advocate either as a member or in some other role. Victim-centered disciplinary processes could perhaps be confined to particular categories of official misconduct, such as behavior that has already been found to have been malicious or that has resulted in the imposition of punitive damages against the government.[56] Agency discretion with regard to discipline could be constrained somewhat by creating statutory presumptions (rebuttable by the employee) in favor of prescribed penalties upon certain finding of fact in the tort action or disciplinary proceeding.

### ENFORCEMENT BY HIGHER LEVELS OF GOVERNMENT

Under the supremacy clause of the Constitution,[57] rights created under federal law are binding upon all levels of government and are enforceable by and against them. This constitutes both a crucial safeguard for our rights and a potentially rich and largely untapped source of public tort remedies. The federal government could be mobilized as a potent vindicator of citizens' rights in situations in which state or local governments, despite having sustained governmental liability for damages, refuse to control their errant officials. State governments could perform the same role vis-à-vis local government agencies that consistently countenance employee misconduct. One possible reform would be to authorize higher-level governments to sue lower-level ones on behalf of their citizens as *parens patriae* not only for violations of substantive rights, a remedy discussed in chapter 5, but for systematic refusals by lawbreaking governments to discipline responsible employees.

## Increasing Agency Capacity to Control Misconduct

If, because of governmental liability, an agency wishes to obtain low-level compliance, the motivation-enhancing strategies just discussed can also increase the likelihood that it will realize that goal. I have been at pains to show, however, that actual control is a formidable problem even for the most compliance-minded agency. Nevertheless, two strategies for strengthening control seem especially promising: expanding officials' duty thresholds and confining low-level discretion.

## EXPANDING OFFICIALS' "DUTY THRESHOLDS"

The tendency of officials to gravitate toward personal risk minimization does not simply depend upon their perception of the costs and benefits to them of particular behavior. It also depends upon what I have called their "duty threshold," the level of personal risk that they are willing to accept out of feelings of moral or professional obligation, simply because that is part of their "job." Within this range, officials will act without regard to the risk that they may be sued, for here deterrence does not compete with official self-protection.

The magnitude and intensity of officials' duty thresholds are not unalterable facts. Within limits, both can be shaped and influenced by the organizations of which these officials are a part. The FBI and the Marine Corps, for example, are especially skillful at creating an esprit de corps, an overriding sense of mission, an atmosphere in which unusual bravery, selflessness, audacity, and industry are rewarded. And this value indoctrination need not be confined to military or paramilitary organizations, as Herbert Kaufman's study of the forest rangers demonstrates.[58]

The unusual tensions surrounding the work of their low-level employees make it especially difficult for street-level agencies to raise their duty thresholds. Increased professionalism and improved recruitment and training can help, but conveying a sense of organizational support and loyalty for those on the front lines is even more significant. Whether agencies can foster these values while also developing more effective disciplinary controls is a difficult question, particularly if those controls are influenced by "outsiders." What does seem clear is that additional efforts along these lines could yield high dividends.

### CONFINING LOW-LEVEL DISCRETION

At bottom, the problem of street-level illegality reflects an inescapable reality: official discretion. But though it is ineradicable, it is not irreducible. There is no reason to assume that the existing mix between agency rule and low-level discretion is socially or even administratively optimal.[59] Intelligent and effectively implemented rulemaking can generate many social benefits: increased agency control over low-level behavior; higher-quality policy choices; a more visible policy-making process; greater guidance for officials; protection of citizens against arbitrary decisions; improved administrative efficiency; and less second-guessing of street-level decisions by the courts and other monitoring agencies. Nevertheless, in the areas of official activity that generate most § 1983 and *Bivens* claims—law enforcement, running of institutions, and public employment—that discretion is not always optimally confined by substantive rules of conduct.

More rulemaking is hardly a novel suggestion. For many years, presidential commissions, prominent scholars of administrative and criminal procedure, the organized bar, and thoughtful judges have urged it, especially with respect to police agencies.[60] These arguments have had some results. The Justice Department, for example, recently issued rules restricting the use of entrapment by the FBI and rules restricting the use of search warrants aimed at obtaining materials in the hands of journalists, lawyers, physicians, and clergymen not suspected of any crime.[61] The New York City police department issued rules in 1979 establishing special procedures for dealing with mentally ill or temporarily deranged individuals; a high-ranking departmental commander was severely disciplined when several subordinates violated those procedures.[62] A rigorous empirical study of the effect of a New York City police department rule restricting officers' use of weapons found a decline in the use of deadly force without any effect on the incidence of crime, injuries to officers, or arrest activity.[63]

Doubtless, other street-level agencies could also use new or existing rules to more closely confine their agents' discretion. Recently, for example, Connecticut's Department of Children and Youth Services issued standards for the first time to guide removal decisions by social workers.[64] Most agencies are authorized to engage in "management rulemaking" as part of their conventional administrative responsibilities. If they fail to issue rules, legislatures can compel them to do so informally or by statute. Indeed, liability for harm resulting from failure to issue clear rules might flow from constitutional or common law principles,[65] and an obligation to issue them might even be enforceable by injunction.[66] It is true that political and bureaucratic opposition to rulemaking will often be heard, enforcement of the rules may be problematic,[67] and rulemaking may in some cases increase the risk of governmental liability.[68] Nevertheless, a powerful case can be made that soundly developed rules will on balance *protect* street-level officials—by reducing uncertainty, discouraging ill-founded citizen complaints, focusing the attention of higher-ups upon critical policy and resource allocation issues, and ensuring that such choices are made (at least in the first instance) by agency officials rather than by judges deciding in a policy vacuum. Creative administrators should be able to make that case.

Rules and guidelines are probably the most important ways to confine low-level discretion but they are not the only ones. Structural and operational changes can sometimes strengthen the agency's communications process, increasing the strength, salience, and clarity of administrators' directives. More refined standards for evaluating officials' performance can often be devised; if met, they could improve compliance and if violated, they could trigger agency discipline. Information and reporting systems can be developed to assist higher-ups in understanding, monitoring, and influencing low-level behavior. Separate staff units can be established inside or outside the agency structure to monitor and inspect the activities of street-level agents.[69]

None of these reforms can fully solve the problems of agency motivation and capacity to control low-level wrongdoing. Each implicates fundamentally conflicting values and each therefore entails some risks; we saw, for example, that professionalism in the rank and file can threaten managerial control. Each reform also unsettles existing organizational routines and vested interests; it thus invites opposition, as the experience of civilian complaint review boards suggests. Finally, because each affects only one or a few elements of a complex administrative-social system, it is susceptible to evasion. Blau, for example, shows how new reporting requirements in the employment service were quickly subverted by adaptive employee behavior.[70] Some skepticism is therefore clearly warranted.

Recent developments, however, provide grounds for cautious optimism that agencies can muster both the will and the ability to see that their officials observe legal norms. Recent court decisions, by dramatically expanding public tort liability, have already significantly increased the fiscal and programmatic incentives for agencies to control street-level behavior more effectively. Public attitudes toward official misconduct also seem to have hardened considerably, especially in the post-Watergate years. The political incentives for agencies to maintain a credible system of control and discipline may thus be greater than before. In addition, a formidable legal and organizational apparatus now exists whose principal purpose is to bring official misconduct to light and to heel. "Public interest" groups and law firms of all ideological persuasions, united by a common distrust of governmental officialdom and armed with new and more effective remedies, have proliferated. Reimbursement of certain costs and counsel fees in both court litigation and administrative proceedings are now widely available. An adversarial media, growing in influence and assisted by the freedom of information laws, thrives on the exposure of official misconduct.[71] Persistent budgetary pressures have necessitated freezes and cutbacks in government employment at all levels, and this may weaken the ability of employee groups to resist effective disciplinary measures. Finally, certain institutional innovations under the federal Civil Service Reform Act, such as establishment of the Office of Special Counsel and the individualized performance appraisal system, as well as politically ambitious and activist attorneys general and public advocates at the state level, may begin to alter the balance of incentives that influence much official misconduct.[72]

When all is said and done, however, the remedial efforts of agencies, citizen watchdog groups, and litigious victims cannot eliminate all street-level misconduct, especially low-visibility wrongdoing committed against helpless and particularly vulnerable members of society. Nor is society always content with after-the-fact remedies for certain kinds of legal wrongs. Instead, effective justice may sometimes demand remedies that can prevent harm from ever occurring or continuing, remedies that can act directly upon offending conditions rather than through the indirect medium of a bureaucracy's budget. These remedies are the subject of the remaining chapters.

# 7: THE COURTS AND SPECIFIC DETERRENCE: THE JUDGE AS BUREAUCRATIC REFORMER

In chapter 5, I sketched the centerpiece of a remedial system for the future: expanded governmental liability for damages imposed on the appropriate bureaucratic unit. I argued that this system, premised upon general deterrence, was likely to be superior to the status quo in all relevant respects. In chapter 6, I showed that although this remedy would in principle create fiscal incentives for agencies to improve their control over misconduct, it would not always generate socially desired levels of deterrence, even in agencies bent upon compliance. Where it did not, I argued, specific deterrence remedies, such as rules and value indoctrination, might seem desirable or necessary to alter low-level official behavior. Here, I explore the special problems that arise when courts attempt to fashion more intrusive forms of specific deterrence.

This chapter consists of four sections. First, I consider when specific, rather than general, deterrence remedies may be called for. Second, I distinguish the structural injunction—a broad order seeking to transform the behavior of public bureaucracies—from other forms of judicially designed specific deterrence. Third, I explore the special obstacles to formulating and implementing this remedy. Fourth, I analyze the problem of legitimating judicial interventions of this kind. In chapter 8, I suggest how courts faced with requests for such relief ought to respond.

## The Occasions for Specific Deterrence Remedies

In at least four situations, even the broad governmental liability system that I have proposed may fail to deter and remedy official wrongs, and more particularized and intrusive interventions may be justified: Society's valuations of the consequences of official behavior may be preferred to defendants'; the costs of official misconduct may be significantly nonmonetizable; certain misconduct may remain immune from damage remedies; and the interest in preventing harm directly may be especially great.

### THE SUPERIORITY OF SOCIAL VALUATIONS

General deterrence presupposes that those upon whom liability is imposed are best situated—by virtue of self-interest, access to information, or otherwise—to make and implement the appropriate balancing judgments that motivate conduct. They are presumed, in one classic formulation, to be in the best position both to make the appropriate cost-benefit analysis and to act upon it.[1] These assumptions are valid for most human behavior, including most activities that can harm others. Even when individuals' information is imperfect, it is usually better than that available to collective decisionmakers. Whether the activity is driving an automobile, selecting a college, or purchasing a used television set, the assumptions underlying general deterrence seem solidly rooted in the reality of comparative informational advantage.

When the actors are street-level officials whose behavior chiefly affects the *public*, these assumptions become quite heroic, as chapter 3 revealed. In such circumstances, the costs of misconduct are often displaced onto citizens and therefore neglected by officials, whereas the benefits of misconduct (say, a police department's pursuit of order at the expense of law) may easily be exaggerated. But even a regime of governmental liability that charges agencies' budgets with the full costs of their employees' misconduct cannot possibly eliminate all misconduct "worth" rooting out. In chapters 5 and 6, we explored the problem of suboptimal deterrence—as the locus of liability moves upward within and beyond the agency, the motivation and capacity to control low-level misconduct may decrease. If the governmental damage liability cannot reduce misconduct to socially acceptable levels, other remedies that place a higher value upon deterrence may seem necessary.

### NONMONETIZABLE COSTS

We saw in chapter 5 that many harms created by official wrongdoing cannot readily be monetized and that the very effort to do so can impose additional "costs of costing" upon society. Damage remedies, then, not only cannot internalize these costs, but may actually magnify them. But even if these rights could somehow be monetized and compensation assured, limiting citizens to damages—permitting the government in effect to compel citizens to exchange their rights for a sum of money—would deny the autonomous moral claims that these legally protected interests represent.[2] Of course, although certain rights can never be satisfactorily monetized and doing so may actually depreciate their value, we should nonetheless seek to assess monetary damages when the rights are violated.[3] Compensation and deterrence goals demand that damages be assessed, and in chapter 5 I proposed how this might be accomplished. But even this remedy may sometimes be inadequate to compensate for or deter certain misconduct. In that event, specific deterrence may commend itself.

## ENCLAVES OF IMMUNITY

Even in a system of expanded governmental liability, certain enclaves of immunity would remain; within them, misconduct would not be constrained by fear of damage liability. In order to encourage vigorous decisionmaking, for example, most judicial and prosecutorial decisions would continue to be categorically immune even if their outcomes or procedures were egregiously improper.[4] Violations, however, might be systematic yet be spread so "thin" that no victim has standing to challenge them.[5] If we conclude that such decisions must be protected from challenge or restraint in litigation but that they must nevertheless be subjected to some control, specific deterrence may be necessary.

We may believe, for example, that because "judicially manageable standards" for locating or allocating scarce public housing units cannot be devised, these substantive choices should generally be exempted from judicial review. But we may also believe that requiring the housing agency to issue its own standards or at least maintain a list of applicants is essential to procedural fairness.[6] In the extreme case (say, a claim of racial discrimination), we may even conclude that an injunction prescribing where units must be located is necessary.[7] Similarly, a state mental hospital's choices concerning the nutritional content of food served to patients may be considered irreducibly discretionary and thus immunized from damage liability. But if the outcome of those choices (say, widespread malnutrition) is socially intolerable, a requirement that particular dietary standards be observed may seem appropriate.[8] In such a case, decreeing carefully tailored specific requirements may actually be less intrusive than judicial second-guessing of discretionary decisions in damage actions.

## THE DESIRE TO PREVENT HARM

Damage remedies are primarily compensatory in purpose, for they are aimed at restoring one who has sustained harm. But their purpose is also to prevent future misconduct by giving notice to others that they too can expect to be charged for similar transgressions. Prevention, however, only works if this signaling process effectively activates the defendant's incentives and controls. We saw that the organizational media can both strengthen and weaken the capacity of damage remedies to transmit effective signals. Even a strong liability signal, however, may penetrate the system too slowly, leaving uncertainty about precisely how the agency and specifically its low-level employees will respond behaviorally to the signal. If official misconduct threatens life or threatens to inflict serious harm and if we think we understand its specific causal pathways, we may not be prepared to tolerate this risk of delay, indirection, and imprecision in inducing behavioral change. If police officers' excessive use of firearms is killing or maiming citizens, we may feel obliged to move prospectively and directly against that specific practice rather than watching the body count rise while waiting for damage liability signals to have their intended effect. Forestalling future harm before it occurs, rather than hoping that compensation will prevent it in the future, may seem a compelling strategy, and a remedy that immediately proscribes specified activities may satisfy that desire for prevention in a way that a damage remedy cannot.

In the remainder of this chapter, I shall consider the conditions under which specific deterrence remedies can fulfill these beguiling promises. I shall show that these remedies, when designed and administered by courts, may be relatively crude instruments for regulating official behavior that is deeply embedded within a structure of bureaucratic incentives and relationships. In chapter 8, I shall argue that when specific deterrence is properly viewed as merely one arrow in the judicial quiver and when courts attend fully to the implementation problems it may engender, such remedies can be refined and rendered more effective.

## The Problematics of the Structural Injunction

The injunction can be a powerful instrument of specific deterrence.[9] By ordering officials to do, or to refrain from doing, particular things and by placing the court's coercive power behind that order, this remedy may achieve a more specific, predictable, and rapid change in official behavior than damage remedies can accomplish. In chapter 1, I distinguished analytically between three types of injunctions on the basis of their intrusiveness into the defendant's decisionmaking processes. I noted that the prohibitory form tends to be the least intrusive and that the mandatory injunction, especially in its most detailed and expansive "structural" form, typically effects a far broader judicial displacement of defendant's decisional initiative, autonomy, and programmatic expertise.

The prominence and significance that the structural injunction has acquired in public tort law during the last decade can hardly be exaggerated; it therefore will occupy center stage for the remainder of this chapter. Throughout the discussion, I shall refer to it as if it were a discrete, well-defined phenomenon in comparison with other, less intrusive judicial interventions. In truth, of course, it is simply an analytical category, an ideal type that calls to our attention particular abstract features of certain recurring patterns of judicial behavior. Owing to the remedy's increasing importance, a sizable literature has accumulated that enables one to isolate its essential features.[10]

The remedy's purpose is to alter broad social conditions by reforming the internal structural relationships of government agencies or public institutions. Instrumentally, it operates through the forward-looking, mandatory injunction but assumes a relatively intrusive form, a more or less detailed order whose prescriptions displace significant areas of defendants' discretion. It relies upon a rather fluid, group-oriented party structure and often demands an active, administrative role for the judge. It usually finds its justification in the more open-ended constitutional provisions, such as the equal protection or due process clauses. Its issuance often precipitates an extremely protracted process typically including judicial wheedling, spasmodic negotiation, and bureaucratic resistance. In this section I lay the groundwork for an evaluation of the structural injunction by identifying how this remedy differs from earlier judicial interventions and thus, *a fortiori*, from more conventional injunctive relief.

Recently some scholars, notably Eisenberg and Yeazell,[11] have maintained that the structural injunction is not a novel form of judicial intervention but in fact rests quite comfortably within a centuries-old common law remedial tradition in which courts occasionally coerced intransigent debtors and supervised complex enterprises and activities, including corporate reorganizations, probate work, and trust administration. This analysis has been echoed by some others closer to the action.[12] In my view, however, it invokes fundamentally mistaken analogies; in a number of crucial respects, these earlier judicial interventions, complex though they were, are not really comparable with today's most far-reaching structural decrees.

First, the structural injunction is directed at a *public* agency or institution, not at a private business corporation or estate. Individuals apppointed by courts to administer a decedent's estate, liquidate a bankrupt company, or operate a receivership or reorganized company can look—indeed, courts compel them to look—to prudent business judgment as measured by profit maximization, and to the testator's (or, in bankruptcy proceedings, Congress's) intent. These guidelines, of course, do not necessarily yield clear answers. Intent is often opaque, long-term and short-term profit opportunities may differ, nonmarket factors are sometimes relevant, and in unusual cases, such as the Penn Central reorganization, political considerations cannot be avoided. Still, the maximizing criterion does provide a benchmark of technical and economic rationality against which the court and its agents can evaluate proposed courses of action. For courts that must supervise the operations of prisons, mental hospitals, or school districts, however, implementation questions are highly controversial public issues, engendering an intensely political process in which many organized interests contend for influence. Courts have no coherent guidelines for resolving the bitter and protracted conflicts that frequently ensue. They cannot look to anyone else's intent (unless it be the Founders'), and the rights in question—say, to an equal educational opportunity—are extremely difficult for anyone, especially a judge, to reduce to operational terms,[13] for the controlling considerations are not economic efficiency or prudent business judgment but distributive justice, administrative feasibility, and acceptability to politically relevant institutions and interests.[14]

A second difference concerns the pool of resources and the claimants.[15] In the kinds of judicial interventions to which Eisenberg and Yeazell refer, the dispute consists essentially of relatively finite claims to a relatively fixed corpus of assets. In such cases, the problem usually is not how to conserve this static fund or whether to use it as productively as possible—all parties share an interest in assisting the court and its agent to do so—but how to accord priorities to the claims. Even in corporate reorganizations, where future rehabilitation is the goal, the court is seldom obliged to grapple with entrenched political, economic, ideological, or institutional commitments to the status quo, for virtually all claimants benefit from changing the entity's operations. And any resistance that courts encounter, as in intransigent debtor cases, is unlikely to have widespread political or moral support in the community. In contrast, structural injunctions seek not to preserve a fixed fund for a limited group of claimants but instead to assert new, different, and expanding claims (that is, institutional reforms) against a relatively fixed stream of future income (that is, budget). Here, the problem is how to change the fundamental mission and service patterns of the bureaucracy in politically controversial ways, often without any significant change in revenue. In such cases, resistance is (by definition) systemic and structural, legitimated by widely shared (albeit not judicially sanctioned) norms and buttressed by powerful forces in the community. The court must expect to contend with a different kind of adversary who is armed and motivated in different ways. A somewhat related difference is that in the earlier judicial interventions, the courts were dealing with actors who, by reason of their financial condition, could not be deterred by the prospect of damage liability; thus, only injunctive relief could control their behavior. In structural cases, however, that threat may constitute a powerful, indeed overpowerful, deterrent to misconduct, as chapter 3 revealed.

Third, unlike more traditional interventions, structural decrees against federal agencies approach, even if they do not cross, the constitutional boundaries defined by separation of powers principles;[16] the decrees issued under § 1983 implicate, even when they do not transgress, federalism values.[17] This is not the place to analyze the constitutional limitations on the power of federal courts to order structural relief. Able scholars of all philosophical persuasions have entered the lists on the subject.[18] No consensus or resolution is in sight; the question of constitutional limits is an open one and will remain so at least until the Court manages (if it can) to close it, an effort that the Court has so far assiduously avoided.[19] It suffices for present purposes to note that the persistence of these concerns among courts and scholars underscores another dimension of the structural injunction's distinctiveness.

The most important difference between the structural injunction and the earlier judicial interventions stressed by Eisenberg and Yeazell has been noted by Owen Fiss. "What is extraordinary about the structural injunction," Fiss observes, "is the nature of the enterprise and what that does to the judicial office."[20] In the rest of this chapter I attempt to demonstrate the problematic relationship between "the nature of the enterprise" to which the structural injunction is committed and the nature of "the judicial office." To do so, I focus upon the following questions: What capacities and resources are required if courts are to implement structural injunctions effectively in the real world? To what extent can courts, compared with other institutions and reform processes, actually meet those demands? Once these practical questions are explored, we can turn to the more abstract, and necessarily speculative, issue of the relationship between the structural injunction remedy and judicial legitimacy.

This emphasis upon implementation is essential, for it is not obvious how questions of relative institutional competence and legitimacy can otherwise be addressed. If historical and logical-deductive arguments cannot satisfactorily resolve those questions,[21] a coherent answer demands at the very least an understanding of what structural reform actually requires a court to know and do. Judges who are asked to grant structural relief are well advised, as we shall see, to take matters of implementation very seriously, for their conceptions of the problems that await them can and should influence whether, when, and how they respond. Finally, judicial efficacy and legitimacy are continuous standards of evaluation, not binary ones. Courts are neither "good" nor "bad" at structural reform, nor are they either legitimate or illegitimate. Instead, they are likely to be more or less effective or legitimate, depending upon the context. Whatever use committed defenders or opponents of structural decrees may make of implementation analysis, it may encourage agnostic observers (of which I count myself one) to take a more discriminating, case-by-case approach to evaluating the remedy. Where more conventional remedies seem inadequate (for one or more of the reasons discussed earlier), courts can choose to proceed in many different ways. A sophisticated conception of judicial role ought to take account of this range of choice.

## Formulating and Implementing the Structural Injunction

The stakes in successful implementation could hardly be higher. Aborted implementation not only jeopardizes plaintiffs' interests and impairs judicial credibility but may also depreciate plaintiffs' substantive claims and their underlying values. On the other hand, a sensitivity to implementation-relevant factors, a willingness to take them seriously, can help courts to decide whether, when, and how to proceed with structural relief.

Few systematic evaluations of structural decrees' actual effects outside the school busing area have been undertaken.[22] Commentators willing to hazard a judgment usually conclude that in general, structural orders have been largely, though not wholly, ineffective;[23] few claim that they have been a thoroughgoing success.[24] A review of mental hospital reform litigation, for example, reveals that the implementation record "has not been impressive,"[25] and a review of prison reform decrees shows mixed results.[26] Even sympathetic observers have stressed the failure and even disastrous effects of school desegregation decrees.[27] In truth, however, the success of structural injunctions in implementing substantive rights probably cannot accurately be assessed, even in principle. It is not merely that "the returns are not all in," as Abram Chayes reminds us.[28] More fundamentally, structural decrees are so much at the confluences of large social forces, so concerned with values that cannot be reduced to operational terms, and so resistant to controlled experimentation that neither their short-term nor their long-term impacts can be rigorously evaluated. We simply cannot know what would have occurred if the court had acted differently, or not at all.

It is striking that some leading commentators on the remedy have avoided the subject of implementation—or quickly change the subject when it is raised. Eisenberg and Yeazell, for example, casually dismiss implementation as a question of "technique and administration."[29] Fiss, who plainly takes the problematics of implementation seriously, takes comfort in the observations that judges are "shrewd" and that other institutions have also failed instrumentally. To him, the problem is not implementation per se but the possibility that its practical imperatives will affect the judge's conception of rights, remedies, and roles,[30] a prospect that he evidently finds repellent.[31] Indeed, Fiss suggests that the widespread concern about judicial efficacy betrays society's skepticism that "any public values" exist, its belief that "all is preference."[32] Chayes devotes but a single paragraph to the implementation question, raising but not bothering to explore it.[33] Judge Frank Johnson maintains (citing Eisenberg and Yeazell) that structural remedies are simply "conventional judicial tools . . . in an unconventional setting."[34] Moreover, when commentators do (however briefly) discuss the methodology of structural reform, as often as not they address the formal machinery of judicial administration—the special court-appointed master, broadened party structure, negotiated decrees, and expert testimony—and not the processes of implementation or bureaucratic change. It is rather like an orchestral conductor insisting that he can extract a splendid performance from his ensemble merely by flourishing a larger baton.

We saw in chapter 6 that some obstacles to implementation arise from the sheer difficulty of devising an intellectually coherent solution to certain social problems. Causes may be poorly understood; a technology for effectively dealing with them may not exist; progress may be inherently difficult to measure. Other obstacles, however, reflect the dense social environment in which even a promising solution must be worked out and institutionalized. In chapter 6, I identified four essential resources for surmounting these obstacles. In this section I examine how each of them affects courts' institutional capacity to regulate low-level misconduct in public bureaucracies.

INFORMATION

To formulate a sound structural remedy, a court must know enough both to adjudicate the substantive right and to implement the relief. These functions demand different kinds of information. Judges seem especially well suited—by reason of professional training, insulation from short-term political pressures, and the dialogic nature of their decisional processes—to discern when official practices violate constitutional norms.[35] A court must first find that the defendant has "caused" or is "responsible for" the segregated school system or other offending conditions. Determination of causality in this sense— who did what to whom, when, and with what effect—is a conventional form of judicial inquiry, yet structural litigation radically transforms even this familiar task. If the bureaucratic practice has evolved over a long period, has been shaped by numerous social forces, and is affected by the conduct of many actors, Chayes has noted, "notions of will, intention, or fault increasingly become only metaphors."[36] And when the court, having adjudicated the right, considers a structural remedy, the causal findings that supported that liability become largely irrelevant. In a structural case, liability and remedy are separated by a chasm that logic cannot bridge. To support such a remedy, the court's causal theory must derive from "facts" of a very different sort.

These distinctive types of causal data are exemplified by two paradigmatic conceptions of fact, which Donald Horowitz has termed "social" and "historical."[37] The historical fact paradigm conceives of reality as a set of quite specific, limited propositions about how particular antecedent behaviors influenced certain discrete, historical events. It seeks to freeze reality in space and time, asking who did what to whom, when, and with what effect. In the private tort, bipolar, nonstructural litigation context to which the paradigm is most relevant, it usually can answer those questions without great difficulty.[38] The social fact paradigm, in contrast, conceives of reality as a set of broad propositions about how large social forces and structures interact to influence the behavior of institutions, groups, and individuals. Here, causal inquiry does not ask "what happened" but instead asks more predictive and evaluative questions of the following form: If condition $X$ (e.g., racially segregated housing patterns) offends fundamental value Y (e.g., equal protection of the laws), would changes in institution Z (the public housing authority) in ways 1, 2, . . . , n (e.g., to require building of scattered-site projects, addition of new public transit services, institution of racial preferences in allowing access to certain projects) reduce X to a constitutionally tolerable level?

Doubtless, social and historical facts are more analytically than empirically distinct. Through the use of presumptions and by shifting evidentiary burdens, for example, legal doctrine often simplifies causal inquiry by converting social facts issues into historical ones.[39] Even so, courts remain seriously handicapped in their attempts to develop rigorous factual support for structural injunctions.[40] Deciding questions of broad social policy on the basis of whatever fact-gathering, alternative-generating, and outcome-monitoring abilities the adversary process in a particular case brings to the court can leave the judge hostage to happenstance.[41] The process of case selection in much "public interest" litigation, for example, increases the risk that the record before the court will be unrepresentative of the broader social reality.[42] Social science data tend to reflect conditions in individual schools or institutions, yet this situation-specific evidence supports decrees that apply, as a matter of precedent or practice, to entire school systems or even to a nation of such systems.[43] The sheer number and importance of social facts relevant to structural relief exacerbates this tension between particularized fact-finding and individualized justice, on the one hand, and social fact-finding and social policy, on the other.

In addition, social facts are dynamic, constantly evolving conditions, not static data. In protracted, complex, structural litigation, the facts in the court record upon which both liability determination and decree formulation are based can quickly become stale. By the time implementation is at hand, these transitory data may bear little resemblance to reality. Moreover, structural remedies must often rest upon social science findings that are tentative and fragmentary; at best, they negate conclusions but cannot affirmatively prove them. And as Donald Horowitz has shown, courts are easily misled when complex social science materials are translated into simplified form; these dangers are heightened by the distortions of the adversary process and by the susceptibility of generalist judges in the presence of a "soft" record to being influenced by the pronouncements of ostensibly neutral official bodies and by their own preconceptions.[44] Indeed, judicial independence, a great virtue in conventional adjudication, can be problematic in structural litigation, where it isolates the judge from important sources of causal and other implementation-relevant information that does not appear of record. Paul Mishkin reminds us that judges, as successful lawyers, are an elite within an already rarefied elite; their views are unlikely to be representative or to be free of systematic class or professional bias.[45]

These limitations also constrain courts' ability to generate technical information about the costs, benefits, and other features of alternative remedial strategies, as well as political information about the distribution of influence in the community and how that influence will be wielded. Judges cannot readily identify technologies of change that parties do not choose to bring to their attention. Because they lack any fund of experience in operating or administering complex institutions or social programs on which to draw, their means-ends judgments will often be poorly informed or naive. Judges are primarily in the business of articulating what the law requires to be done, of discerning and evaluating the means and ends selected by others. Seldom are they called upon explicitly or systematically to reduce broad social values to operational or programmatic terms, to devise measures of effectiveness, or to analyze and balance costs and benefits.[46] Formulating and enforcing pollution abatement orders probably comes as close to this as anything courts do, yet even here society has increasingly transferred this activity to administrative agencies that are specialized to make such technical judgments.[47] And it is likely that judicially devised criteria for measuring polluters' performance, however arguable, are still more technically feasible and rationally defensible than the largely subjective criteria for evaluating the restructuring of a voting district or a school system.

Accurate political information is notoriously hard to come by; politicians literally spend their careers accumulating it. Although Chayes is no doubt correct that a judge "is likely to have some experience of the political process,"[48] that generalized experience is probably neither fresh nor especially relevant to the specialized politics of the particular social problem *sub judice*. Political prediction is an especially elusive art, one unlikely to be advanced by the techniques of legal briefs and courtroom argumentation. Intensity of preference, perhaps the most important political datum, is not illuminated by, and may easily be misrepresented by, the litigation process. But the problem goes far beyond political naiveté or ignorance. Judicial legitimacy, as Fiss emphasizes, demands the court's insulation from politics as conventionally understood. It requires that decisions be perceived as principled, transcending considerations of political expediency.[49] A court that openly investigated the political impacts and acceptability of proposed decisions would surely undermine a crucial source of its authority.

At this point, an important qualification of the analysis must be emphasized. The institutional choice in developing specific deterrence is not between fully competent, efficacious legislatures and agencies on the one hand, and hapless, ignorant courts on the other.[50] I noted in chapter 6 that the former usually fail to exploit fully their informational capacities. By the same token courts, recognizing that the kinds of rights and remedies at issue in structural cases create unusual informational demands, sometimes manage to enlarge their own capacities. They do this chiefly by appointing special master or other adjunct institutions (e.g., ombudsmen, implementation committees, receivers), encouraging negotiated decrees, and expanding participation in the litigation. Because evidence concerning the effectiveness of these innovations has begun to appear,[51] I shall consider their bearing upon an evaluation of the judicial role in structural cases.

Masters, negotiated decrees, and participation can be structured in many different ways, and these differences may matter a great deal. The court, for example, may devolve to a master merely fact-gathering and advisory responsibilities or may grant it the far broader authority to resolve disputes. The judge may simply ratify the decree agreed upon by the parties or may play an active role in its negotiations. Broader participation may be limited to the filing of *amicus* briefs or extended to the making of full evidentiary presentations. Even when the importance of specific context and form are acknowledged, however, some common shortcomings emerge.

These techniques appear to have conflicting and inconclusive effects upon the court's informational capacities. To be sure, a court-appointed master can sometimes generate technical information that the parties might neglect.[52] Masters can generate political information by holding public hearings on proposed remedies, talking to community leaders, and helping to resolve disputes. They may have (or be able to develop) expertise in the substantive problem areas and consequently can usually advise the court as to causes and cures. Masters can encourage the parties to negotiate with one another directly, rather than talking past each other to the judge, thus eliciting information about the parties' true preferences and practical concerns that more formal adversary processes might conceal.[53] (Expanded participation can also develop implementation-relevant information that the parties themselves would not adduce.)

In practice, however, these advantages are only incompletely realized; more important, they appear to entail substantial countervailing risks. Masters cannot avoid serious role conflicts and limitations. If a master's fact-gathering is to enlarge the corpus of social data available to the court, he must immerse himself in the specific institutional and behavioral milieu out of which the litigation arises. Yet this immersion compromises the very detachment that judicial independence and impartiality require. He cannot gather information for the judge informally without engaging in *ex parte* communications, sacrificing the values that formal norms of procedure, such as the right of cross-examination, are meant to protect.[54] He cannot develop and advocate his own remedial approaches without forsaking objectivity and acquiring the stigmata of the special pleader.[55] He cannot act as the judge's surrogate without the risk of jeopardizing the judge's prestige and autonomy.[56]

Inevitably, then, an effective master distances the court from the facts, creating additional risks of unintended misunderstandings and distortion. Masters seldom have access to significant staff or other resources, a deficiency that limits their influence.[57] Yet staff members could replicate or even aggravate many of these problems. Indeed, even under existing staffing arrangements, the bureaucratization of the judiciary is cause for serious concern.[58] It could destroy (in Fiss's words) "the distinctive character of the dialogue that has long been central to the judicial function: it will be difficult to believe that a judge is truly listening or responding to the grievances or is assuming individual responsibility for the response."[59]

Finally, masters cannot perform effectively without the confidence of the court and the parties, yet that confidence must be earned and can quickly be lost.[60] Success in mastering, as in so much else, appears to depend largely upon personal attributes and situational factors that cannot be improvised, presumed, or formalized.

The negotiated decree, too, is fraught with dangers. First, the consensus it manifests may in fact be deceptive, hollow, or coerced. In the landmark *Wyatt* case, for example, where the issue was the reform of Alabama's state mental hospitals, defendants' "consent" to over 90 percent of the requirements in the final decree was obtained only under the threat of judicial sanction.[61] Rather than being the product of a vigorous adversary process, a decree may be a welcome signal to defendants who can promote their personal, bureaucratic, or professional ends by extracting additional appropriations from the legislature under cover of court order.[62] Second, a negotiated decree may actually exacerbate the court's information problem. The fact that a consent order has been negotiated by the parties, after all, does not indicate to the judge whether he should accept, reject, or modify it. To make that decision intelligently, judges need much the same information that they would need in the absence of consent, as the problem of the all-too-willing defendants suggests. The negotiated decree that sought to restructure the United States Employment Service concealed from the court its own ignorance concerning what implementation would require, and by foreclosing appeal it inhibited modification of the decree when implementation problems later arose.[63] Finally, consensus on a decree may be reached by displacing its costs onto those who are not a party to it, as when a legislative reapportionment formula is agreed upon at the expense of absent minority parties.

Participation-expanding techniques entail chiefly the risks of protracting the litigation, making it more costly and cumbersome, and of diffusing the issues. The court, however, can contain these risks by imposing conditions on the new participants. Although *amicus* briefs are clumsy media for conveying the kinds of implementation analysis the court needs most, additional evidentiary presentations can somewhat ameliorate the court's information problem, especially if the existing parties do not represent the full range of interests affected or if they fail, by design or inadvertently, to explore all relevant issues.[64] Special periodic reporting requirements may also help to fill the informational void.

But inadequate information plagues even those courts resourceful enough to overhaul their fact-finding machinery. The problem reflects the importance of social facts in structural cases and the limitations of the adversary process in illuminating those facts. Procedural innovations, although probably essential in such cases, can attempt to eliminate these difficulties only by risking the creation of new ones of significant, and perhaps even greater, concern.

COMMUNICATIVE POWER

We saw earlier that when a legislature or agency head transmits a directive downward through the ranks of a street-level agency, communication becomes problematic in several respects.[65] A structural injunction adds the court to that hierarchy, making it yet another medium through which the directive must pass; if a master is appointed, it adds still another. The remedy thus exacerbates the message's loss of strength and clarity, its "leakage of authority."[66]

The nature and context of judicial pronouncements, especially structural decrees, actually multiply this loss of communicative power. Federal courts, for example, usually must transmit their messages across the vast chasm we call the federal system, for structural orders are typically directed to state or local agencies operating in alien political cultures. Even when the defendant is a federal agency, its programs are probably carried out by state and local governments.[67] The federal system, of course, was designed to frustrate the ambitions of efficient governance, and it advances this goal in part by fragmenting and distorting communications between governments.[68] In fact, communications *within* federal agencies are weakest in precisely those units whose functions are primarily administered by other levels of government.[69]

Even apart from the remoteness of their audience, however, courts tend to be poor communicators. They control no systematic channels of communication to the outside world, much less to street-level officials. They must therefore rely upon their published opinions, media coverage of their decisions, dissemination of their orders by the very organizational defendants whose illegality prompted them, and special publication and notice requirements. In addition, they seldom specify the actions defendants must take. Prohibitory injunctions prescribe what may *not* be done, leaving defendants to figure out what affirmative courses of action may ultimately pass judicial muster.[70] Some decisions of a quasi-structural nature—for example, requiring police to give specified warnings to suspects[71]—are reasonably clear about what defendants must do,[72] and some structural decrees achieve truly stupefying levels of detail.[73] But most courts almost instinctively recoil from issuing orders that look like provisions of the Internal Revenue Code. They prefer to preserve flexibility to navigate what is predictably a long journey into the unknown and to avoid detailed regulatory requirements that seem legislative and administrative in character.

Finally, judicial norms in such cases are almost always communicated through a bureaucratic filter that tends to view the source as illegitimate (if not generally, then in this instance) and the instruction as intrusive, ill-informed, and unwarranted. Indeed, the farther down the message goes toward street level, where the dilemmas of service delivery are most keenly felt, the stronger these perceptions are likely to be. Nor must low-level resistance to judicial norms be universal to be effective, as the response to the decree in *Wyatt* suggests:

> The Superintendent's use of the court order to strengthen his hand in relation to the staff has had some detrimental effects. One of the major problems in implementation has been resistance to the decree by both professional and nonprofessional staff

members—especially those who have worked in the institution a long time. These staff members have been suffering an "extinction reaction," a perceived loss of control which they formerly exercised over the residents. By justifying his actions on the ground that they were compelled by the court decree, the Superintendent indirectly endorsed the staff's view that the decree was an intrusion upon the institution and an unjustified limitation on both the staff's and the administration's authority. As a result of this "extinction reaction," there have been reports of some personnel becoming more abusive to the patients since the issuance of the decree; moreover, the already strong solidarity among many staff members has increased, producing a "no-ratting" policy whereby many staff members do not report incidents that reflect poorly on others.[74]

Unfortunately, procedural innovations can no more eliminate these judicial communications barriers than can the informational ones, and they may even make matters worse. An appointed master, for example, can make the screen between judge and officials impermeable unless he can establish an unusual rapport with the latter without relinquishing the detachment and impartiality needed to protect the former's legitimacy. So long as the message is unwelcome to officials, of course, legislatures or agency heads will find them no less refractory. The important point, to which I now turn, is that a court is in a particularly poor position to do much about it.

INCENTIVES

Unlike legislatures and agencies, federal courts cannot ordinarily select those who are to implement their decrees.[75] A judge may attempt to influence this situation indirectly by mandating credentials, training, and even salary of personnel,[76] but this influence is at best categorical, not individualized. Courts' most serious weakness in securing implementation, however, lies in their extremely limited resources for inducing compliance. In stark contrast to the endlessly diverse and flexible means available to legislatures and agencies, courts control only two—the formal power to coerce, and the informal influence exerted by their moral legitimacy—and their effects are likely to be sporadic and limited.

Superficially, of course, the contempt power appears potent, but in reality it is seldom invoked. A review of prison reform cases, for example, found that the contempt sanction was never used.[77] And even when courts do resort to it, the penalty tends to be a contingent or nominal fine.[78] Indeed, "the only sanction used with any frequency in reported cases is the relatively mild and largely compensatory action of awarding plaintiffs their attorney's fees."[79] The reasons for this timidity are not difficult to imagine.[80] Contempt proceedings are a time-consuming process, diverting energy and attention from the substantive issues of structural reform. Responsibility for noncompliance is often difficult to locate in bureaucratic organizations.[81] Finally, sending people to jail can confer a kind of martyrdom, galvanizing otherwise disparate groups into opposition to the decree and hardening positions on all sides. The Boston school case, in which Judge Garrity used the contempt power, illustrates that this risk can be enormous. Ultimately, he was obliged to withdraw from the case with the school system far more segregated than it was when the case began.[82]

The mere availability of contempt, of course, may deter misconduct. The threat to employ it may render actual resort to it unnecessary; multistage contempt procedures are designed to induce compliance without a showdown. Indeed, its availability was probably indispensable to desegregating Southern schools in the years after the *Brown* decision.[83] But if contempt were a powerful deterrent in the generality of cases, one would expect compliance with structural decrees to be greater than it apparently is.

A court's moral persuasiveness—its power to inspire official obedience by inducing a sense of moral obligation or duty to comply without regard to personal consequences—is ultimately its chief weapon for mobilizing support for its decrees, and I shall discuss it at length in the next section. Here, I only wish to stress that it is a *generalized* resource, difficult to refine or tailor to particular situations or instances of noncompliance. Suppose, for example, that a court perceives that a hospital union's opposition is likely to be a significant obstacle to court-ordered deinstitutionalization. The court cannot wield a discrete quantum of legitimacy targeted at particular union leaders or employees in the same way that a legislature or agency might bestow, say, a subsidy or a job guarantee. Legitimacy is roughly analogous to what welfare economists call a "public good"[84] and to what organization theorists call an "indivisible benefit."[85] It is a resource, like clear air, national defense, or legal precedents, whose benefits cannot readily be conferred upon one person without thereby being extended to all. Just as these collective, indivisible resources cannot readily be sold in a market or traded for political support, so a court cannot manipulate or individuate its legitimacy in order to secure compliance with a particular structural order.

These judicially controlled incentives—contempt and legitimacy —are of limited value in shaping official behavior for another reason: they constitute what we might call "constraining" rather than "transforming" inducements. A behavior-transforming inducement provides affirmative reasons to act in particular ways. It mobilizes a broad range of human motivations—not merely fear of punishment but love of status or economic gain, not simply the desire to obey the law but the wish to be politically or bureaucratically efficacious. A behavior-constraining inducement, on the other hand, provides reasons *not* to do X but does not *encourage* one to do Y or Z. A grudging, formalistic kind of compliance may be better than nothing but it does not represent enduring structural reform. For that, courts must do more than merely induce officials to avoid behavior for which they fear they will be punished or inspire a minimal compliance with the letter of the decree. The essential nature of what defendants are being required to do—for example, provide more humane custody or fair treatment—and the realistic limits on the court's ability to monitor low-level compliance demand that officials also identify with the decree's spirit and pursue its objectives conscientiously.[86] A sympathetic warden or prison staff member will accomplish more meaningful reform than an official performing a checklist of mandated actions in a hostile or hollow spirit. A contempt sanction, unlike the transforming inducements that other governing institutions wield, cannot elicit such affirmative motives; instead, it is more likely to engender a perfunctory or "paper" compliance or stiffen resistance than to win loyal advocates. Judicial legitimacy also suffers from this limitation, albeit far less so than the contempt power. It can be viewed as a transforming inducement of sorts but differs from those available to legislatures and agencies in one crucial respect. At best, it can deprive certain arguments for opposing the decree (say, one's personal view of its merits) of moral sanction, and this can reduce opposition. But it cannot generate in the dubious or indifferent the personal identification or affirmative commitment that successful implementation of reform may require.

Finally, both the contempt power and the court's moral legitimacy rely for their effect upon a certain ethereal detachment and grandeur, an ineffable, almost mystical quality of sovereign power and disembodied justice that can attach to a court and its pronouncements. Yet when a court must resort to that power to compel obedience, justice loses its sublime dimension. Materialized as an individual—albeit one in black robes—struggling desperately to assert control over the uncontrollable, the judicial enterprise seems less awesome, and the symbolic force upon which its power ultimately rests may drain away.[87] To oblige judges to call upon these resources is, paradoxically, to call their reality and potency into question.

A familiar image, an artifact of popular culture, illuminates this point. In the film *The Wizard of Oz*, after Dorothy and her friends have performed the tasks necessary to receive the Wizard's justice, they enter his chamber to claim their due. Impressed and intimidated by the awesome trappings of his power, they respectfully submit themselves to his judgment. The Wizard begins to stall, however, and Dorothy senses impending injustice. She begins to protest but is terrified by the thundering majesty of the Wizard's disembodied voice. As Dorothy quakes and cowers, her dog trots over to the curtain and parts it, revealing the Wizard in all his humanity—a small, pitiful old man desperately pulling levers and pushing buttons in order to maintain the illusion of supernatural power and wisdom that his subjects demand and somehow find reassuring. Unmasked and exposed as a mere mortal of ordinary gifts, the Wizard can no longer command Dorothy's fearful reverence and submission; instead, he inspires in her only pity, scorn, and rage.

The scene suggests the dilemma of the reform-minded court confronted by opponents who must somehow be subdued. If the recalcitrant embroil the court in a pitched battle to vindicate its dignity and power, it may forfeit its detached majesty, becoming just another advocate of institutional self-interest. If opponents call the court's bluff and it cannot effectively fulfill its pretensions, it may appear as feckless and ordinary as the Wizard; indeed, the court may seem less powerful than it really is. The court's grandeur and legitimacy are venerated only so long as they are seen as attributes of an underlying reality rather than simply as tools manipulated instrumentally in the service of the judge's all-too-human will. When Dorothy becomes indignant at the Wizard's response even before learning of his deception, she affirms an important truth—that a court that tolerates injustice cannot long retain legitimacy. But her abrupt transformation in mien when the Wizard's ordinariness is revealed also reminds us that judicial legitimacy and influence depend upon an identification of judicial power with the mystique of the judicial office rather than with the personality of the individual judge.

Structural reform, it seems, requires a court to strike a precarious balance. It must acknowledge and struggle with reality; at the same time, it must continue to obscure the reality of what it is actually doing. When a court invokes the contempt power or invests its legitimacy in a particular structural remedy, it inevitably threatens that balance.

When it adjudicates rights and determines violations, its legitimacy-enhancing powers are at their zenith. Operating in the spacious realm of abstract justice and drawing upon the mystical, visionary powers of the Constitution and "the law," the judges can collectively speak rights-language in a majestic oracular voice. It is here that they can create, in Fiss's phrase, "the terms of their own legitimacy."[88] But remedy-language, as we saw in chapter 1, is very different. Mired in the humdrum vocabulary of instrumentalism and the technocratic grammar of bureaucratic policy, structural reform underscores the worldly, power-dependent quality of the court's enterprise. It belies the distinctive grandeur of judicial legitimacy even as it affirms the court's splendid aspiration to do justice.

POLITICAL AND PUBLIC SUPPORT

A court that would implement a structural decree cannot successfully go it alone; many other institutions and individuals must be mobilized to achieve reform. At the remedial stage, what the court says is far less important than what politicians, bureaucrats, and relevant groups actually do and the manner and spirit in which they do it. A consent that is passive, minimal, and grudging may be as fatal to success as implacable opposition. The active support of these groups for change, their willingness to incur some costs in its behalf, is essential. The commitment of politicians, community leaders, and the general public to court-ordered reform, of course, is itself a resource that can be transmuted into incentives and sanctions for influencing the behavior of those who might otherwise oppose it. But political support differs from the court's other behavior-shaping resources in important respects, and these differences warrant separate treatment.

Courts' contempt power and moral legitimacy attach by reason of the courts' special institutional role, but political support does not. A court's rulings need external support most when they overturn (as structural decisions almost invariably do) the manifest will, or at least acquiescence, of the majority. Occasionally, of course, a court decision may become a convulsive political event in its own right, capable of catalyzing widespread support. *Brown* v. *Board of Education* and the Reapportionment Cases[89] were preeminently decisions of this kind.[90] More generally, however, a court that orders structural change cannot count upon the decree itself to galvanize the political support necessary for effective implementation. Instead, the court must either self-consciously contrive to generate it or proceed in the hope that it will somehow materialize along the way.

Courts have pursued both of these courses. One analysis of eight

structural decrees in school cases concluded that the courts stepped out
of their normal roles in order to attract the support of political leaders,
generally without great success.[91] Some courts have managed to persuade community leaders representing important political constituencies to monitor compliance; the "human rights committee" established
by Judge Johnson in the *Wyatt* case was an example.[92] More commonly, courts have encouraged a kind of bargaining process that might
generate a political consensus to support implementation.[93] Occasionally, however, courts have pushed forward with the decree without
waiting to mobilize consensus, correctly assuming that it would even-
tually crystallize around an accomplished, judicially legitimated fact.
Again, *Brown* and the Reapportionment Cases exemplify this strategy.
Some courts, as in the Boston school and *Pennhurst* cases, have waited
for support to consolidate, only to see opposition harden and defiance
spread.[94]

Each of these approaches is perilous. The passive court runs the risk
of ineffectiveness, of seeing the decree flouted or ignored. The more
activist approach, on the other hand, transforms the judge into what
Colin Diver calls a "political powerbroker," presiding over or par-
ticipating in a series of intricate "bargaining games" in which the relevant interests will, it is hoped, be conciliated, accommodated, and won
over.[95] The difficulty, however, is that the same deficiencies that tend
to impede implementation of judicially ordered structural reform also
subvert the court's effectiveness in performing this most unfamiliar
managerial and political role. Reliable political information, we saw, is
elusive. A court's communication apparatus, even (or perhaps especially) when a special master is added, is decidedly ill-suited to the
rapid, fluid, multi-issue, often unprincipled bargaining processes in
which politicians characteristically engage.[96] Courts can marshal few
resources—and no behavior-transforming, divisible inducements—
with which to attract potential adherents. In short, unless judges' interventions carry overriding and universal moral legitimacy (which an-
timajoritarian structural orders seldom do) they can only mobilize those
resources in one way. They must "play politics."

The felt need to play politics is sometimes a motive in appointing a
special master or accepting a negotiated decree. The theory is that the
master, by operating at one remove from the judge, can somehow
unite the virtues of court, politician, and bureaucrat, while preserving
unimpaired the judge's image of detachment, objectivity, and principled decisionmaking. But such a ruse—for ruse it must be unless the
master, whose authority comes entirely from the judge, in fact acts on

his own—cannot succeed very often. Even a gifted master cannot conjure up political resources that the court does not possess. This arrangement may instead politicize and personify the judicial office while leaving the master politically impotent.[97] Similarly, when defendants accept or help draft a decree, that no more implies a commitment to shoulder the political costs of implementation than a criminal defendant's acceptance of a bargained guilty plea implies remorse or a commitment to mend his ways. If anything, the history of court-ordered reforms suggests that the process of implementation soon exhausts whatever good will defendants originally possessed.[98]

The reality is that with rare exceptions, even the most resourceful court cannot readily elicit political consent for a structural decree that otherwise lacks it. Indeed, the dilemma is more poignant than that, for by attempting to play politics effectively—and there is no point in playing it any other way—the judge almost inevitably compromises his principal claims to moral legitimacy. "The role of powerbroker," as Diver puts it, "implies a degree of partisanship, manipulation, and guesswork offensive to accepted judicial virtues of neutrality, passivity, and objectivity."[99] That the court's moral capital is spent for a good cause may make the expenditure more palatable, perhaps even compelling. But if the court would use this precious but limited endowment wisely, it must attend not merely to the beguiling vision of a New Jerusalem but also to the costs of the long, perilous journey necessary to reach it, and to the real possibility that those costs will turn out to have been incurred in vain.

## The Problematics of Legitimation

What, then, is to be done? When a court determines that constitutional rights have been systematically violated and that structural relief is appropriate, how can it integrate its constitutional obligation to do justice with its recognition that the remedy may be beyond its powers or prudence to implement? In short, how is the structural decree to be legitimated?

At the outset, the true dimensions of the legitimacy issue must be isolated. The problem of judicial legitimacy is not endemic to constitutional cases, injunction cases, or novel cases of far-reaching significance. When courts adjudicate constitutional or other claims and grant damage remedies or prohibitory or most mandatory injunctions, their judgments almost always exact deference and at least substantial compliance. In such cases, the political branches may contest a decision's wisdom or legal support but seldom dispute its legitimacy and binding quality. Grudgingly or not, they presume the decision to be valid and for all practical purposes take it to represent a true instantiation of the constitutional value.

Moreover, in the relatively few cases in which conflicting constitutional meanings rendered by different governing institutions persist beyond the final judicial decision, those differences only rarely acquire significance. Even if another institution extracts from a constitutional value some meaning contrary to that found by a court and refuses to concede the latter's legitimacy, it will seldom resist the court outright. The potential costs of such a confrontation are a powerful deterrent, and opportunities to stymie the court's judgment are in reality quite limited due to the nature of the remedies typically provided. If a damage award is not paid, execution can be levied to satisfy it. A preventive injunction can be enforced by employing the contempt sanction or by voiding actions that violate its terms. A mandatory injunction can be subverted by inaction or foot-dragging, but so long as the order does not impose extensive affirmative duties and so long as the duties are well specified, the potential scope of subversion is narrow. Affirmative obligations being few and clearly defined, they can readily be enforced. Minimalism in such cases provides defendants with no secure haven.

Mandatory injunctions seeking broad structural change, however, are decidedly different. Here, the enforcement problem may reach acute proportions. Although the other governing institutions sometimes accept the court's decision, at other times and in other cases they may view the decision—the finding of liability, the selection of remedy, or both—as so illegitimate that they are prepared to resist its implementation. Many strategies of resistance can be deployed, ranging from outright, nose-thumbing defiance of the court to a long war of attrition in which the most perfunctory compliance may be forthcoming, and then only when the court is about to invoke sanctions. Certain unique features of the structural decree—its extensive affirmative duties, the difficulty of measuring compliance, the extraordinary obstacles to its implementation posed by uncooperative institutions, its lack of positive incentives and the crudeness of its negative ones—make such foot-dragging and minimalism particularly promising responses for recalcitrant defendants. Not surprisingly, then, these responses are more common than either outright defiance[100] or substantial compliance.[101]

Thus, only in a subset of structural cases, few in number though large in potential impact, do other governing institutions seriously resist the court's decree. It is these cases that ineluctably raise the question of how, if at all, structural injunctions are to be legitimated. To this question, a variety of answers may be (and have been) given. Each is based upon a distinctive conception of constitutional meaning—or more precisely, of the relationship of governing institutions to that meaning. In the remainder of this chapter I will discuss three abstract representations of these conceptions—what I shall call the "pure rights," "judicial interpretivist," and "institutional competition" conceptions.

## THE "PURE RIGHTS" CONCEPTION

The "pure rights" view of constitutional meaning is preoccupied with the teleology, the vision of ends, that animates the decree; it regards other values, when it considers them at all, as essentially instrumental and subsidiary. The structural decree is fully legitimated, in this view, because a court issued it as a necessary adjunct to its indisputably appropriate function: adjudicating and vindicating constitutional rights. The view postulates that the political branches, having caused the violation, will not remedy it _ex proprio vigore_ and that judicial coercion is essential if constitutional rights are to be more than hollow sentiments. The differences between courts and other governing institutions, in this view, are irrelevant to the legitimacy of structural decrees, and a remedial jurisprudence that takes these differences into account will devalue and ultimately subvert the substantive rights-ends at stake. If protecting those rights and instantiating those ends is a legitimate judicial enterprise, then the structural decree that seeks to serve that end is, ipso facto, legitimate as well.[102]

The pure rights conception is a decidedly unsatisfactory response to the question of how to legitimate structural decrees. First, it utterly misconceives the nature of that inquiry. It is not simply a controversy about substantive values—not merely a dispute over how many prisoners should be confined in a single cell, whether racial integration of urban public schools is a good thing, whether police should be free to violate the rights of poor people, or even what resources we should devote to realizing public ends. Concerns about substantive values certainly surround the legitimacy question; they raise the stakes, as it were, in its correct resolution. But it is also a controversy about the role of courts in our society, their relationship to other sources of power and other articulators of values, and the processes by which power and values ought to be fused into public policy. A liberal society like ours characteristically takes these questions of institutional relationship and process seriously; it affirms that how those questions are resolved affects the quality of social justice. Such a society would not exalt form over substance or process over outcome. It would acknowledge that if the results of particular institutional arrangements and processes systematically offend public values, they are to be viewed as hollow and unworthy of veneration or continuation. A liberal society believes that how and by whom public decisions are made are first-order questions, morally anterior to the second-order question of what the outcomes of those public decisions ought to be. Thus, the question of legitimacy is properly directed to premises about institutional role and process, and not simply or even primarily to the analyses of the substantive merits of one dispute or another.[103]

Second, the pure rights response fails to acknowledge either the extent to which the structural injunction differs from other judicial remedies or the implications of these differences for its legitimacy. In this chapter I have already discussed the first of these questions—the distinctive, problematic character of the remedy. But the second question, how these differences are relevant to its legitimacy, requires elaboration. The legitimacy of any governing institution—its moral claim to obedience, its ability to elicit genuine consent to its decisions—neither depends upon a single attribute nor is revealed by any particular litmus test. It depends instead upon a combination of factors. The institution must demonstrate a certain stability and longevity.[104] The general run of its decisions must seem not only minimally rational but just, and its symbolic force must also be sufficient to invest its decisions with an authority that does not rest wholly upon rational appeals.[105] Finally, the processes and forms by which it decides must possess what I shall call "functional integrity"; they must be adequate for deciding the kinds of questions that society puts to the institution, and the values they exemplify must be consistent with those the institution is supposed to pursue.

Historically, the courts—especially the federal courts—have met these conditions of legitimation. Their continuity of membership and tradition; the perceived rationality and justice of the generality of their decisions; the successful nesting of their authority in the charisma and majesty of the law; their functional integrity as evidenced by their decisions in the vast majority of cases; and their exemplification of the virtues of detachment, independence, neutrality, and principled elaboration of rules[106] have, together, vindicated the courts' claims to obedience.

Several points about these sources of judicial legitimacy must be stressed. First, they are quite distinct from the ways in which the decisions of other governing institutions are legitimated. The legislative process, for example, derives legitimacy from its consensual nature, its accountability to relatively contemporaneous expressions of public values as revealed and transformed through intensities of preference, deliberative processes, concrete policy choices, and negotiated decisions. Political rationality, not principled elaboration, is the value that legislative choice purports to exemplify. Legitimating the administrative process is more problematic precisely because that process's major premise—the agency's subordination to the legitimating processes of courts and legislatures—has increasingly been called into question.[107]

Second, it is not a fatal flaw that neither the judicial process nor those of legislatures or agencies perfectly embodies its particular theory of legitimation. Irrational, unprincipled judicial decisions are the stuff of which law school curricula and some academic careers are made. The representational distortions of legislatures and agencies are equally well established.[108] These imperfections may in a given instance be so pronounced that they undermine the legitimacy of particular decisions rendered by particular institutions. But such decisions are exceptional. Usually, they are quickly denounced and the larger legal-governmental system of which their authors are merely a part manages to reverse them or limit their impact. That system's responses to the Supreme Court's substantive due process decisions of the 1930s, President Roosevelt's court-packing plan, and President Nixon's firing of the special Watergate prosecutor are familiar examples of this legitimacy-restoring dynamic.

The important point for present purposes is that the effort to formulate and implement many structural decrees threatens most sources of judicial legitimacy. As we have seen, the functional integrity of the judicial process may be seriously compromised when the court is called upon to accommodate broad social fact-finding to the processes of adjudication, to design rules of far-reaching public impact, and to coax a resistant political and institutional reality into submission. In such instances, judicial efficacy approaches its nadir: there, the judiciary's decision processes are least adequate to the demands placed upon them, the essentially political character of its remedial choices is most manifest, and its moral legitimacy is in greatest peril.

## THE "JUDICIAL INTERPRETIVIST" CONCEPTION

A second view, judicial interpretivism, holds that courts possess a special access to constitutional meaning denied to other governing institutions. Like the pure rights view, it regards relative institutional competence as a useless criterion of role in structural cases, a blind alley leading to a dead end. Owen Fiss, an eloquent exponent of this approach, puts it this way:

> Courts may have their difficulties in giving a constitutional value its correct meaning, but so would the other branches. History is as filled with legislative and executive mistakes as it is filled with judicial ones. Admittedly, adjudication will have its class and professional biases, because so much power is entrusted to lawyers, but the legislative and executive processes will have their own biases—wealth, dynasty, charisma. It is not clear which set of biases will cause the greatest departure from the truth.[109]

What chiefly distinguishes judicial interpretivism from the pure rights view is the former's recognition that structural remedies are not simply logical or moral derivations from adjudicated violations of constitutional rights but are instead autonomous constructions of a decidedly different sort. Fiss remarks that

> the judge has no special claim of competency on instrumental judgments, on means-end rationality, whether it be in the bureaucratic context or elsewhere; he may be no worse than others, and now and then be even better, but there is no general or systematic reason for believing he will be better. There is no likely connection between the core processes of adjudication, those that give the judge the special claim to competence, and the instrumental judgments necessarily entailed in fashioning the remedy.[110]

In view of this observation, Fiss's conclusion is all the more stunning and, for the judicial interpretivist, revealing: the judge, armed with the structural injunction, should "assume responsibility for practical reality and its consonance with the Constitution."[111]

To understand judicial interpretivism, we must examine two premises that support this conception and consider how they are linked. One relates to the nature of the judicial institution; the other relates to the rights-remedy distinction. The first premise, the very foundation stone of Fiss's argument, is that the judge "among all the agencies of government is in the best position to discover the true meaning of our constitutional values."[112] This conclusion follows, Fiss believes, from the impressive and unique institutional strengths that courts bring to the interpretive enterprise—chiefly, their relative independence from vested interests, openness to the claims of politically vulnerable minorities, legitimacy-conferring ethos, capacity for principled decisionmaking, and duty to decide and to justify.[113]

This claim is generally valid; judges doubtless are superior expositors of certain constitutional values, especially those that protect minority rights and individual freedoms against a heedless majoritarianism. But, just as surely, there are constitutional values that only the "political" branches can adequately express. This seems especially true of values that reflect our affirmative will and solidarity as a nation, our willingness to impose burdens upon ourselves to serve the greater public good, as in time of war or national crisis. The Gettysburg Address was an epiphany of constitutional meaning, yet a president, not a court, was required to articulate it.

But even when thus limited, Fiss's descriptive insights about judicial capacities cannot sustain the elaborate normative superstructure that he erects upon them, especially his expansive prescription that judges should reconstruct social reality to comport with their conceptions of constitutional meaning. This brings us to Fiss's second and related premise—that by treating substantive rights and structural remedies as mutually dependent rather than as distinct and autonomous, courts "distort" or "compromise" both right and remedy and threaten the integrity of the judicial enterprise itself.[114] But what can distortion mean in this context? We have seen that legal rights and structural remedies are very distinct phenomena; they operate in different spheres, are animated by different motives and considerations, implicate different conceptions of justice, and require different evaluative criteria.[115] If one takes these differences seriously, as Fiss clearly does, then courts are not necessarily, or even plausibly, entitled to the same deference, autonomy, and legitimacy when they formulate and implement structural remedies as when they declare rights (or award damages or issue prohibitory injunctions). Competency and legitimacy, after all, are closely related to functional integrity. A court's strengths when it expounds constitutional norms often are distinct weaknesses when the task is to actualize abstract rights in a complex, intransigent reality.

Only in the structural case do the differences between right and remedy become truly salient and consequential. There, a finding of liability, as we saw, simply commences a long and uncertain process of implementation. There, the declaration of right does not imply any particular decree but leaves the court adrift without a compass on a sea of remedial discretion. There are countless ways, after all, to try to desegregate a school system—reconfiguring district boundaries, designing magnet schools, and altering housing and transportation patterns are only some of them—yet all are logically consistent with the right to a desegregated education.

In the special context of the structural case, then, it is wrong to speak of judges "distorting" a right or compromising "the true meaning" of a constitutional value when they recognize and act upon what Fiss concedes to be a "tight connection" between the reality of a right's meaning and the possibility and form of its implementation.[116] One should applaud this integration in that context rather than lament it and should affirm (as Fiss did only a few years before making these observations) that in the structural case "[a] judgment about violation *should* reflect, and in fact *does* reflect, a judgment about remedy."[117] Building a Chinese wall between rights declaration and remedy formulation might actually weaken structural decrees rather than strengthen them.

Fiss's two premises converge in a decidedly parochial, "juridico-centric" conception of constitutional meaning and of the meaning-giving enterprise. "The true meaning of our constitutional values" is no more to be found *solely* in a court's pronouncements than the true meaning of love is encapsulated in the protestations of an ardent suitor. Constitutional meaning is *also* to be found in the process by which those values are actualized, in the extent to which those values, once authoritatively declared and disseminated, are in fact absorbed into the life and practice of the society. The truest measure of constitutional meaning lies in the magnitude of the gap that we are prepared to tolerate between our ideals and our reality. The former are mediated, articulated, and legitimated principally by courts, the latter chiefly by our political agents. When principle and practice, conscience and consensus, aspiration and actuality clash, then and only then is our willingness to act upon our ideals fully tested and our collective morality made truly manifest. It is there, and not in the rights-language of courts, that this truer and more vital definition of constitutional meaning is most nakedly and vividly revealed.

Fiss acknowledges this duality but maintains that a "unity of functions" is nevertheless required: "[b]oth sources of meaning must be entrusted to the [courts] to preserve the integrity of the meaning-giving enterprise itself."[118] He does not say why the discovery of this richer vein of constitutional meaning should be vouchsafed to the courts alone, or indeed to any single institution. Courts are not the sole custodians of our constitutional values or destiny. It is true that they are uniquely fitted to expound authoritatively one aspect of those values—the principled, aspirational dimension of constitutional meaning. But there are other meanings as well, expounded by other governing institutions otherwise constituted and validated by other justifications. What we say we wish to be is a crucial element of what we are. But it is not the whole truth, either of what we wish to be or of what we are.

Fiss offers only one reason for his normative leap from a description of functional division to a prescription that these functions must be unified in a single meaning-giving institution: "A division of functions, a delegation of the task of actualization to another agency, necessarily creates the risk that the remedy may distort the right, and leave us with something less than the true meaning of the constitutional value."[119] But this reason is wholly unconvincing. First, as we just saw, it begs two central questions. It fails to explain how and under what circumstances a remedy "distorts" a right. And it fails to explain why or to what extent the claims of the reality in which a remedy must be implemented should not be considered part of a value's "true meaning."

Second, Fiss's argument betrays a Platonic, absolutist view of rights and values, a view curiously inconsistent with his recognition earlier (indeed, in the very same paragraph) that "[a] constitutional value . . . derives its meaning from both spheres, declaration and actualization," and that a "tight connection [exists] between meaning and remedy."[120] Society might well wish to treat certain fundamental rights *as if* they were absolute, exempting them from utilitarian, implementation-sensitive considerations.[121] But even a cluster of "natural rights" would have little application to structural cases, for most claims that structural decrees seek to secure, compelling as they may be, simply cannot be shoehorned into the "natural rights" category. Conditions in some prisons, mental hospitals, and schools may be socially intolerable and their reform eminently desirable—as I so believe. But if legal rights to such changes were as "natural" as all that, one is hard put to explain why they have managed to elude recognition during the almost two centuries of the Republic and why, even today, they remain novel and highly controversial. One might argue that the right is natural and fundamental and that only its application to new conditions is novel. But surely any right fundamental enough in a particular application to trump all contrary considerations must be so self-evident, so deeply rooted in common morality, that it could galvanize a political constituency more widespread and representative than plaintiffs and this or that lower-court judge.[122] In truth, the rights secured by structural decrees are seldom fundamental in that sense but usually demand (in Bickel's phrase) "principled flexibility." When courts seek to accommodate such rights to the claims of reality, they neither distort the rights nor impugn their value.[123]

Finally, even if "the risk that the remedy may distort the right" could be rendered intelligible, Fiss does not say why this risk is socially unacceptable or why we must simply "live with" the far more palpable and predictable hazards associated with relinquishing to life-tenured judges the responsibility for conforming "practical reality" to open-ended constitutional principles.[124] When a particular institution purports to discover, expound, and legitimate a constitutional meaning, our acceptance of that version demands, at a minimum, that it have emerged from a process with functional integrity, exemplifying that institution's distinctive values, competencies, and essential role. As Fiss puts it, "We impute function largely on the basis of process and at the same time function shapes process."[125] What a court can legitimately and effectively do in reforming social structure is limited by the same functional attributes of the judicial process that legitimate the judicial derivation of substantive rights.

## THE "INSTITUTIONAL COMPETITION" CONCEPTION

A third conception of constitutional meaning, richer and more encompassing than the others, emerges from the integration of partial, institution-specific meanings. This integration is achieved through a collective, competitive, dynamic process in which the perspectives, strengths, and weaknesses of one institution are pitted against those of others. The conception is legitimated not by a substantive teleology or by "juridico-centric" criteria but by its capacity to establish itself in a world in which conflicting goals, limited resources, political and ideological struggle, and human and institutional imperfections transform partial meanings into social reality. Consider, for example, the great chasm that separates the requirement of minimally acceptable physical and psychosocial conditions in prisons, which some courts have derived from the Eighth Amendment's "cruel and unusual punishment" clause,[126] from the appalling prison conditions that society has sometimes tolerated.[127] Does the reality demonstrate that the judicially discovered meaning is false or insignificant? Does the coexistence of the courts' meaning and the reality demonstrate that the society is schizophrenic, that the rule of law is a mere illusion?[128]

I reject these inferences. However one views the legal merits of these decisions, the fact is that the substantive meaning that the courts

have articulated is both valid and significant—valid because it is derived by constitutionally sanctioned institutional decision processes,
significant because courts speak to us with both moral and legal authority about constitutional values and because we listen intently and
accept their teaching almost automatically when they do. The political meaning is also valid and significant—valid because it has been
reached by a process that reveals the actual terms of trade between our
values and measures our current willingness to realize them when talk
is no longer cheap, significant because society inevitably has the last
word. The triumph of political meaning, however, is inherently transitory and unstable. Constantly in tension with the courts' meaning,
which contradicts and rebukes it, political meaning is transformed by
the very processes of conflict, persuasion, and preference-formation
that legitimate it. Society is not schizophrenic, nor is the rule of law
illusory simply because their abstract aspirations outstrip their actual
achievements. Both society and law know, with Shakespeare, that to
do is not "as easy as to know what were good to do."[129] Both have
ordained that courts are there to speak principle to power, to hold a
mirror up to social reality,[130] to remind society of what we are all
inclined to forget—that one cannot derive what ought to be from
what is.

The Constitution is the apotheosis of this larger conception of constitutional meaning, for it raises it to a first principle of our public life.
Mr. Justice Jackson, speaking in the context of a confrontation between
Congress and the president, captured the subtle dynamic between the
supremacy of law and competing versions of constitutional truth. He
stressed that the rule of law transcends and survives this struggle
between particular institutional notions of constitutional meaning:

> The actual art of governing under our Constitution does not and
> cannot conform to judicial definitions of the power of any of its
> branches based on isolated clauses or even single Articles torn
> from context. While the Constitution diffuses power the better to
> secure liberty, it also contemplates that practice will integrate the
> dispersed powers into a workable government. It enjoins upon its
> branches separateness but interdependence, autonomy but reci-
> procity. Presidential powers are not fixed but fluctuate, depend-
> ing upon their disjunction or conjunction with those of
> Congress.[131]

The Framers of the Constitution, then, contrived institutional competition and interdependence, which, in a polity as in a family, imply

tension and conflict over meanings and values. Congress and the president (and, *mutatis mutandis*, their state counterparts) can stymie the effectiveness of judicial power in many ways that the Constitution sanctions, explicitly or implicitly. The president can suspend the writ of habeas corpus,[132] decline to nominate persons to fill judicial vacancies, veto appropriations for judicial branch operations or for implementing court decrees, refuse to appoint enforcement personnel, and otherwise fail to enforce judicial orders vigorously. Congress can hobble judicial power or punish particular courts even more readily and has done so throughout our history.[133] Congress too can suspend habeas corpus. It can also enact legislation to limit the jurisdiction of courts, impose onerous duties upon them, refuse to appropriate funds for the judicial branch, refuse to confirm new judicial nominations or to raise judges' salaries,[134] impeach incumbent judges, enlarge the number of judges on federal courts, withhold the personnel or other resources necessary to enforce decrees, and enact legislation or propose constitutional amendments to overrule or emasculate certain decisions. Indeed, some authorities maintain, albeit controversially, that Congress may abolish the inferior federal courts altogether, withdraw jurisdiction from them in narrow classes of cases, and enact substantive limitations on the appellate jurisdiction of the Supreme Court.[135] The Constitution immunizes Congress from judicial process to enforce court orders,[136] and no less a constitutional authority than Abraham Lincoln claimed a right in the president to resist Supreme Court decisions he thinks are profoundly wrong unless he is a party to the judgment.[137]

I certainly do not suggest, nor does the institutional competition conception of constitutional meaning imply, that structural decrees are significant only insofar as the political branches are willing to cooperate in their implementation. The institutional competition conception is not a positivistic, Panglossian celebration of whatever social equilibrium this competition happens to produce.[138] In fact, almost all judicial decrees are enforced and accepted without question.[139] Even in those rare instances of institutional stalemate, courts are powerfully armed. Judicial sanctions—the possibility of monetary damages, fines, or contempt, and the courts' power to invalidate actions, stigmatize lawlessness, and withhold legitimacy—invite compliance. But like papal maledictions hurled at medieval potentates, judicial decrees carry considerable temporal force independent of such sanctions. Courts' powerful hold on public affection assures their version of constitutional meaning a full, presumptively persuasive, hearing. Were all of this not true, our collective reality would be very different and so, probably, would my theory.

The point, then, is not that broad structural decrees are empty gestures or are necessarily misconceived. Rather, it is that the judicial interpretivist and pure rights conceptions, no less than the reflexive majoritarianism that they eschew, suffer from a kind of institutional myopia that obscures the full subtlety of constitutional meaning, a parochialism that imputes to structural decrees an autonomy and a legitimacy that cannot simply be self-conferred by courts. As Alexander Bickel put it, "the Court's principles are required to *gain* assent, not necessarily to have it."[140] A court is an important, indeed typically decisive, part of the institutional system for deriving constitutional meaning. But when it issues a structural decree, it inescapably makes itself radically dependent upon the rest of that system to legitimate and actualize the meanings that it articulates. To ignore the dependence that the court has precipitated is to create an illusion of judicial autonomy that at best may encourage arrogance or folly and that at worst may transform the very act of judging, thereby compromising what has earned it a precious and hard-won legitimacy.

There is no simple or entirely satisfactory solution to these difficulties, certainly none that can fully harmonize a court's version of constitutional meaning with the versions that other governing institutions and the larger society are sometimes prepared to reify. The Constitution is neither an algorithm nor a Delphic oracle; it does not provide a single "correct" answer to all questions put to it. Thus, to criticize the institutional competition conception because it reposes ultimate constitutional authority in an open-ended, indeterminate process rather than in the single determinate voice of the judge misses Justice Jackson's essential point: the Constitution envisions, indeed demands, some indeterminacy, some "play in the joints."

This indeterminacy, so pronounced in the structural case, creates risks to all concerned. It means that some small portion of citizens' constitutional endowment may not be implemented in the end. For political institutions, it means that the Constitution and the courts, two of our most venerated institutions, may sometimes seem to be ranged in costly struggles against them. For a court, indeterminacy poses special difficulties. Yielding to another institution's competing version of constitutional truth hazards that the integrity of its own will perish in the hothouse environment of actuality. But if the court does not yield, it risks a protracted struggle with other institutions in which it is unlikely (if history is any guide) to vindicate its position fully. Its authority then becomes hostage to forces that it cannot control. It may prevail in the end but at Pyrrhic cost. In the concluding chapter I suggest how courts might go about resolving this dilemma.

# 8: CONCLUSION:
# A REMEDIAL SYSTEM
# FOR THE FUTURE

The importance of a legal right, we now know, tells us nothing about how it can best be secured to citizens. Officials violate rights in different ways, and each may require a different kind of remedy. Because each remedy, in turn, creates a distinctive structure of incentives, set of institutional relationships, and capacity to regulate official behavior, each achieves remedial goals (themselves multiple and conflicting) to a different degree. Securing justice in and against the activist state, then, demands not only that the basic legal entitlements be established but also that this complexity be reduced and integrated into a sound remedial design.

This remedial challenge has become evident only in the wake of recent large-scale governmental activity and changing views about how the benefits and burdens of that activity should be distributed. During the 1970s, the federal courts responded in two quite distinct ways by overhauling the remedial structure that Congress had fashioned in earlier, simpler days. First, they enlarged the familiar judicial terrain of general deterrence, by expanding damage remedies against both individual officials and governments. Second, they entered the relatively unexplored realm of specific deterrence, issuing detailed mandatory and structural injunctions designed to restructure public bureaucracies in far-reaching ways. Both responses have advanced important social goals, but both are also problematic.

By expanding general deterrence, the federal courts sought to constrict the large enclaves of sovereign immunity—principally, the Eleventh Amendment immunity of states and the broad exceptions to the FTCA—that public tort law preserved when it repudiated enterprise liability as a general remedial principle. To circumvent these remnants of an essentially feudal notion of the relationship of the state to law and to citizens, judges fashioned alternative remedies. Drawing upon an English common law tradition, they diverted their aborted remedial energy to the one readily available compensatory channel: the remedy of official liability for damages. This remedy has serious infirmities, however, in a world of far-flung, affirmative governmental responsibilities. In order to encourage vigorous decisionmaking and official initiative, legislatures and agencies permitted officials to slough off the costs of their misconduct to their employers and victims through broad immunity defenses, free legal representation, and indemnification/insurance. These adjustments, however, produced unsatisfactory results: uncompensated victims, inadequate deterrence, incentives for official self-protection rather than vigorous decisionmaking, moral incongruity, and systemic inefficiency. Governmental liability for damages, another general deterrence remedy, had few of official liability's defects, and the courts ardently embraced it, especially the Supreme Court in its decisions since 1978. But broad governmental immunities under the Eleventh Amendment and FTCA exceptions continue to bar the way. Full consummation has not been possible.

The courts' other response to the remedial challenge was to explore the use of specific deterrence designed and sometimes administered by judges. This approach managed to avoid not only governmental immunity but also certain other shortcomings of general deterrence—agencies' unwillingness or inability to control low-level misconduct, their "incorrect" valuation of important social interests, and damages' more indirect effect upon low-level behavior. But these more intrusive judicial interventions, we have seen, raise fundamental questions of both efficacy and legitimacy.

Today, then, our system of public tort remedies stands at a crossroads. Along one path lies a confusing tangle of incremental remedial adjustments, straining to achieve greater compensatory and deterrent power but shackled by anachronistic doctrines and incoherent policies. Along another path lies an array of spasmodic judicial probes into the bureaucratic unknown, interventions contrived in desperation and holding out little prospect for success. In this final chapter, I draw upon the earlier analysis and attempt to map a third, somewhat different route to the remedial destination toward which these other paths tend but will never reach.

## The Elements of Reform

In a just, effective remedial system, each remedy discussed in this book—official liability for damages, governmental liability for damages, injunctive relief in various forms and with varying degrees of intrusiveness, declaratory relief, judicial remands to agencies, and a vast range of possible legislative and administrative interventions—would have some role to play in the campaign against official misconduct. Nevertheless, the forms that these remedies would take and the precise nature of their relationships to one another would be very, very different than they are today.

The remedial system of the future should look to an expanded governmental liability for damages as its first and basic line of defense against public torts. The burden of chapters 3, 4, and 5 was to demonstrate that a properly reformed governmental liability remedy would dominate official liability over the full range of public tort goals and constraints. Its scope would be greatly extended, covering all officially caused wrongs. It would be buttressed by ancillary supports, such as counsel fee awards and minimum damages, necessary to render the system practically as well as theoretically effective. Internal control procedures within individual agencies and the civil service apparatus as a whole would be strengthened, linked more closely to the tort process and influenced more systematically by those outsiders, principally victims, with a stake in increased deterrence. Administrators would thereby be pressed to anticipate and respond to low-level misconduct by deploying their stock of behavior-shaping resources—rules, training, discipline, incentives, information, organization support, and the like—in more imaginative and powerful ways.

Even as reconstructed, however, governmental liability for damages would still be systematically inadequate to deter some kinds of official misconduct and situationally inadequate to deter others. In both circumstances, therefore, specific deterrence must continue to play an essential remedial role. Courts should place initial emphasis upon legislative and adminstrative interventions, reflecting the relative versatility of resources, strategies, and leverage available to those institutions for influencing low-level behavior. But legislatures may fail to act, or their actions may not succeed in deterring or eliminating official wrongdoing that threatens clearly established legal rights. Administrators may likewise fail to control low-level misconduct; they may even be accomplices in it. In such cases, citizens must look to the courts to fashion relief. Ordering minimally intrusive relief in the form of a narrowly targeted prohibitory injunction normally presents no unusual difficulties either of design or of implementation. Even when official misconduct of an apparently systemic or "structural" nature is proved, courts will be tempted to swallow hard and proceed to intervene, utilizing whatever leeways they can find.

When and how should courts undertake this task? There is, first of all, the question of intellectual temperament and spirit, the professional predisposition that courts should bring to the remedial enterprise. The analysis in chapters 6 and 7 suggests that courts must proceed with a full awareness of the implementation problems they may encounter, the importance of social and institutional context in resolving those problems, the rich diversity of remedial weapons available, and the competing strengths and weaknesses of each, including the different demands each places upon judicial capacities.

Exhorting courts to think this way may seem unnecessary and uncontroversial, but it is neither. Although most judges appear to be quite cautious when formulating equitable relief, some are evidently more impetuous and impatient[1] and all act under the strong compulsion of a constitutional obligation to do justice without delay. Like all of us, judges' perceptions can become the prisoners of their hopes. But even a cautious, strategic approach to structural relief must leave us uneasy. For when judges begin to think opportunistically, as bureaucrats and politicians do as a matter of course, they may abandon the very qualities of mind, character, and temperament that distinguish their institutional enterprise and lay moral claim to our obedience. If we really want the bureaucratic or political mind to govern a social decision, after all, why turn to the erstwhile imitator, whose life tenure and institutional isolation would disable a politician or bureaucrat? Why not rely instead upon the genuine article? Would it really serve society's interests to encourage judges to substitute the prognosticator's crystal ball for the blindfold of Justice?

Owen Fiss believes that this judicial "desire to be efficacious" is the "core dilemma" presented by the structural injunction, one that will incline judges to "tailor the right to fit the remedy."[2] To a judicial interpretivist, this is an unacceptable perversion of justice. Courts, in this view, should instead get on with the business of decreeing structural reform that instantiates their conceptions of constitutional meaning; society, for its part, should be prepared to "live with" the consequences.[3] But another conception of judicial role and constitutional meaning, the "institutional competition" view developed in chapter 7, implies more qualified responses. They do not oblige courts to choose between undertaking structural reform and abandoning victims' rights to the vicissitudes of practical politics, between doing everything that vindicating rights requires and doing nothing. The real risk in urging courts to think strategically about the more intrusive remedies is that they will be poor at it, not that they will be forced to abandon their constitutional role.

In reality, the choice between remedies belongs to the courts, and it is largely unconstrained by law. Their equitable power is not only exceedingly broad but has been essentially self-defined.[4] Congress's constitutional power directly to limit judicial remedies for constitutional violations, either by regulating the courts' jurisdiction or under section 5 of the Fourteenth Amendment, remains uncertain.[5] Appellate control of lower court choices of remedy is quite limited; it is essentially confined to the so-called tailoring principle, which requires trial courts to demonstrate some organic linkage between the violation and the remedy selected.[6] Only in extreme cases—for example, a decree that contravenes explicit constitutional provisions or one that orders a legislature to appropriate funds[7]—does the Constitution significantly inhibit judicial choice of remedy. Neither familiar incantations that courts' equitable powers are only as broad as necessary to remedy underlying violations,[8] nor efforts to deduce remedies from the nature of violations, provides much useful guidance as to how remedies should actually be formulated to contend with the entrenched sources of official misconduct.

The earlier analysis suggests several guidelines or implications for developing judicial answers to this question in hard cases. These include procedurally integrating right-adjudication and remedy-formulation, using decree implementation analysis, and imposing the "least restrictive remedy."

## PROCEDURAL INTEGRATION OF RIGHTS-REMEDY ISSUES

In chapter 1, I drew a sharp distinction between the concepts of right and remedy. In chapter 7, I emphasized the difficulties in implementing rights through structural remedies and I concluded that courts should take account of these difficulties when they define rights and design remedies. It is in that sense and in that context that right and remedy, so different in fundamental respects, should nonetheless be thought of as highly interdependent.

For this reason, the common practice in structural litigation of bifurcating trials into separate liability and remedy stages[9] needs to be reexamined. Although it is intended to avoid the time and expense of a hearing unless plaintiff actually prevails on the merits, bifurcation may also have the unfortunate effect of undermining this interdependence. By inviting judges to think about and confer rights in the abstract, it encourages them to neglect implementation problems and cost questions until they have already committed themselves to a decision on the merits. Yet it is precisely in those cases in which right and remedy are most interdependent that disciplined consideration of costs and constraints is most urgently needed.

The administrative character of structural remedies suggests how this technique might be altered without sacrificing its efficiencies. Administrative agencies often adjudicate by issuing "tentative decisions" that speak to the merits or remedy, or both. This decision may later be modified or even withdrawn in the light of subsequent information and public comments. Thus, agencies can tentatively commit themselves to a substantive position while inviting pointed evidence bearing upon its wisdom, legality, or feasibility. After considering this additional evidence, agencies may confirm the original position or modify it.[10] Courts, however, typically adjudicate rights once and for all; only when rights have been established but the remedy is problematic do they then move on to consider the latter in a systematic way. (Judges presumably *think* about remedy during the liability phase, of course, and some evidence introduced at that stage is also relevant to remedy.) Courts thus relinquish their flexibility and capacity to learn, painting themselves into a corner. Having defined the rights with finality, they cannot later redefine them in the light of what they may learn without appearing to repudiate their own handiwork. Yet the true costs will surface later when implementation is undertaken, and then the rights will be redefined de facto through aborted implementation, mocking the courts' pretensions to efficacy and legitimacy.

In remedially difficult cases, courts should adjudicate rights while retaining the capacity to tailor them. They can do so by issuing decisions on liability in a tentative, declaratory form much as administrative law judges now do.[11] Consideration of appropriate remedy would then proceed as under current practice. In appropriate cases, courts could give decisions interim effect by issuing what would amount to temporary injunctions. Oral testimony and written comments relating to the cost, feasibility, effects on nonparties, and other aspects of remedy would be solicited from the public, as in many agency rulemaking proceedings. If appropriate, courts could then modify their decisions on the merits on the basis of this evidence.

Several objections to this procedure may be anticipated. One criticism—that a right is not merely the bottom line of an elaborate social benefit-cost analysis but is absolute, trumping instrumental considerations—has already been shown to have relatively little force where broad, structural relief is concerned. A related but more troublesome objection concerns the effect of such a procedure upon judicial role and legitimacy. This objection stresses that courts differ importantly from administrative agencies and that policy flexibility in response to complaints by defendants and other affected interests is not a virtue in a judge. If rights are conditional, tentative, only presumptively effective, if they can be altered or nullified whenever an entrenched status quo prevents them from being readily implemented, then courts no longer possess independent moral force; they are merely barometers that measure and legitimate prevailing pressures and conditions.

This objection, however, ignores the fact that court-ordered structural reform *inescapably* entails this kind of instrumentalism if it is to have a chance to be effective. The constitutional system *as a whole* can at once be principled and instrumental, detached and embroiled. A court itself, however, cannot. It cannot enter a wholly new and different game and expect to be governed by the same rules. It cannot seek to exercise political or administrative power without being evaluated by the criteria appropriate to those ambitions. It cannot cry "foul" when others hold a mirror up to its new face and it does not like what it sees.

DECREE IMPLEMENTATION ANALYSIS

I stressed in chapter 7 that the implementation of structural relief is perhaps its most problematic feature and that abortive implementation may jeopardize both plaintiffs' rights and courts' legitimacy. The court might reduce these risks by requiring that any such decree be preceded by an "implementation analysis" prepared by independent analysts under the court's direction and that this analysis be subjected to adversary proceedings before any remedial order is issued. The analysis would seek, among other things, to identify the fiscal, bureaucratic, political, informational, and other barriers that the proposed decree, if adopted, would have to overcome; the steps that would be necessary to surmount them; the magnitude and distribution of the costs of doing so; and the effects of alternative, less intrusive remedies.

It must be acknowledged that policy implementation analysis as a discrete field of study is in its infancy (important work in the field began only a decade ago) and the analytical process is thus likely to be difficult.[12] As a "soft" specialty in a "soft" discipline ("policy sciences"), the methodology of implementation analysis is rudimentary and its findings are sure to be imprecise. The cost of producing such analyses would probably not be trivial. Nevertheless, the alternative—judicial decisions that systematically obscure or neglect such crucial questions until it is too late—seems unacceptable.

Precedents and analogies for such an analytical requirement exist. The best known are the environmental impact studies that must be prepared before environmentally significant decisions may be made;[13]

the benefit-cost or cost-effectiveness analyses that must precede certain governmental decisions;[14] and the competitive impact analyses required before certain regulations may be issued.[15] The effectiveness of these analytical efforts, of course, is necessarily quite difficult to evaluate, and they have often been criticized.[16] Most of these objections can be met, however, if the court retains control over whether, under what circumstances, and in what form to require an implementation analysis and remains free to use the analysis as it sees fit. In addition, the courts should be authorized to impose the costs of preparing the analysis upon the defendant agency or institution, which will already have been held liable for the misconduct that necessitated the analysis.

## THE LEAST RESTRICTIVE REMEDY

We have seen that the functional integrity of courts is greatest when they are applying general norms to particular facts but is most threatened when they must decide which of the many possible technologies of reform is likely to be best in terms of cost, ease of implementation, and overall effect upon official misconduct. Thus, a court that leaves the terra firma of rights and ventures into the uncharted, treacherous waters of structural remedy should attend to the limitations of its craft and respect the elements. Like all mariners, it should select a tack that accommodates to and exploits the wind, rather than one that faces it head-on. This suggests an important criterion for deciding whether, when, and in what form courts should grant intrusive or structural relief: The relief should take the form of the "least restrictive remedy" consistent with the level of judicial intrusiveness needed to actualize the right.

In First Amendment, antitrust, and deinstitutionalization cases, where somewhat analogous criteria have been developed, the least restrictive remedy test emphasizes that those who exercise decisional initiative ought not to be unduly constrained. It holds that society benefits when decisionmakers (in those cases, speakers, business firms, and the mentally disabled; here, public officials responsible for running complex programs and organizations) enjoy the maximum freedom of action consistent with other, overriding values.[17] In this context, the criterion recognizes courts' comparative disadvantage in the realm of instrumental rationality and the extraordinary character of such relief. Indeed, it reflects the same cautious spirit with which equity doctrine approaches injunctions generally—only more so.[18]

The least restrictive remedy criterion implies several guidelines for courts considering intrusive relief.[19] The first is *remedial cost internalization*. The remedy should limit the autonomy and choices of as few innocent individuals and institutions as possible. (For present purposes, it is not necessary to address the thorny question of precisely what "innocent" means in this context.) Their losses of freedom are external costs of the remedy that must be counted against any benefits; such losses also raise difficult moral questions of interpersonal comparisons among plaintiffs and affected nonparties. Broad deinstitutionalization orders that throw the burdens of patient care onto families unable or unwilling to provide it,[20] for example, might well be condemned by this principle.

The second guideline is *instrumental freedom*. The remedy should allow defendants latitude to employ as many possible implementation strategies as may, in the light of operating realities, seem prudent. Only if a court were confident that only one or another method of compliance could adequately secure the right and that defendants would not adopt it without judicial coercion could the level of specificity embodied in some institutional decrees possibly be justified. Even imperfect outcome measures of the quality of institutional care, for example, are likely to be preferable to standards that prescribe the credentials of institutional staff or the duration and types of therapies to be administered.[21] It is a matter of some interest that courts have gravitated toward more detailed, intrusive input or design standards in structural decrees at a time when regulatory policymakers and commentators increasingly denounce "command-and-control" regulation of this type and advocate incentive-oriented, general deterrence remedies.[22] My point is not that the administrative and structural injunction contexts demand identical remedial systems; indeed, I argued earlier that incentives often play different roles when directed at public and private organizational behavior. My claim instead is that many considerations that counsel against command-and-control regulation condemn detailed, discretion-supplanting judicial interventions at least as strongly.

These two guidelines suggest a third: *graduated and diversified response*. Judges formulating relief, like military strategists assessing battlefield conditions, should seek to multiply and diversify the weapons and tactics that they can deploy. Here as in war, graduated interventions carefully calibrated to the level of opportunities and constraints can improve effectiveness. Other things being equal, a court should select that remedy that (1) minimizes and internalizes the total

costs of misconduct and of implementing the remedy, and (2) max-
imizes defendants' freedom to decide precisely how to comply.

A strategy of graduated and diversified response implies a hierarchy
of remedies, the ordering of which should reflect their relative abilities
to render complete and effective relief while minimizing the risks of
judicial intrusiveness. Under those critiera, as I have emphasized,
governmental liability for damages should enjoy remedial primacy. But
where that remedy is insufficient for any of the reasons discussed
earlier, the court should *add* to it a second remedy, a conditional
declaratory judgment.[23] Here, the court would not only pronounce
that defendant has violated plaintiff's rights in particular respects and
grant damages, but it would state its willingness to consider more
intrusive relief if the political branches, after being given a full opportunity to consider the implications of the court's findings, fail to design
a legislative or administrative remedy for it. The Supreme Court did
essentially this in its first decision in *Brown* v. *Board of Education*,[24]
and many lower courts have done so since.[25]

Conditional declaratory relief presumes that when a court determines that officials have violated the law, that ruling can itself
significantly alter the status quo because of the unquestioned legitimacy that almost all judicial decisions enjoy. Rather than assuming that
agencies whose practices have been authoritatively condemned will sit
in stony silence, unchanged and unregenerate, this remedy presumes
that they will respond by seeking to reform themselves, relieving
courts of the necessity to intervene. It also recognizes that compliance
may be more effective if the agency has genuinely committed itself to a
remedy that it has devised itself than if one is imposed upon it from
without. The tactic is frequently effective; indeed, the mere intimation
that liability will probably be found often goads the government into
adopting preemptive reforms.[26]

Even conditional declaratory judgments combined, as I propose,
with a substantial damage award may be ineffective. By returning
the initiative to the very officials whose misconduct made a remedy
necessary in the first place, such an order provides defendants with
additional opportunities to temporize in order to forestall judicial intervention. Indeed, even structural decrees, especially those that stress
negotiation, would not eliminate this possibility. If the court finds that
defendants are not responding to the damages-*cum*-conditional declaratory order in good faith and wishes to increase the pressure, it
should take a third step—remanding the case to the agency for reme-

dial action within a prescribed time. Remand is probably the most common judicial remedy in proceedings under the Administrative Procedure Act, and it ordinarily brings agencies into at least "paper" compliance. By retaining jurisdiction, the court can evaluate agencies' remedial responses; unless and until it is satisfied with the result (or becomes exhausted), it can simply continue to remand.

If remand is unavailing, the court might move to the next more intrusive remedy, a prohibitory injunction. This is certainly the most common injunctive remedy and thus needs little elaboration. It precludes the agency from subjecting plaintiff to particular conduct or conditions but does not otherwise limit the agency's freedom of action. A prohibitory decree might simply bar a state from placing prisoners in particular facilities found to be unconstitutionally crowded; it would not specify either what conditions would satisfy the court or how they must be achieved. This remedy, of course, may be quite intrusive in practice; it may in effect leave the state with no choice but to close the prison, at least in the short term.[27] But even a nonintrusive prohibition can stimulate broader reform by encouraging legislative and bureaucratic reappraisals of policies and priorities. States whose prisons are barred by court order from accepting any more prisoners due to overcrowding, for example, are likely to turn to construction of new facilities or revision of parole and diversion procedures, or they may make other, more systemic changes.

The court may conclude that a narrow-gauged prohibition is inadequate to remedy the violation. In that event, a more intrusive prohibitory injunction, one that bars the agency from engaging in a broad practice or policy (such as educational "tracking"), may be necessary. Failing that, the court may be driven to issue a mandatory injunction requiring the agency to adopt specified reforms (such as training programs or staffing patterns). At that point, of course, the road to a full-blown structural injunction is short. But even there, the least restrictive remedy criterion can affect how the court proceeds. The court might issue the injunction in conditional form, for example, permitting defendants to *purchase* the injunction under terms and at a price acceptable to plaintiffs, thus converting the structural decree into a property right in plaintiffs, monetizable at their option.[28] The injunction's price would then reflect plaintiffs' valuation of the rights in question and defendants' preferences for their own methods of compliance. Alternatively, the court might set the purchase price, as it does in ordinary tort cases, thus converting the decree into a form of governmental liability for damages and allowing the agency to substitute for compliance with the court's decree other methods that it deems more efficient. In either form of purchasable injunction, of course, the court would need to protect interests not immediately before it.

Short of using these more novel strategies, courts can draft even mandatory decrees in ways that are less, rather than more, intrusive. They can attempt to preserve defendants' decisional initiative and discretion, emphasize outcomes rather than technical means, encourage flexible processes of accommodation between the parties (and with nonparties), and strengthen bureaucratic incentives for compliance.

But even a court that follows these prescriptions may sometimes confront yet another dilemma: under what circumstances should the court move up the remedial hierarchy to a more intrusive intervention, even to structural relief? We saw that the court's choice of whether and in what form to grant a remedy is dictated less by law than by prudence. But what does prudence dictate? The answer, of course, is that "it depends"—or at least it ought to. In the hard cases, where implementing and legitimating relief are highly problematic, no single aspect of the situation can dictate the appropriate choice. The earlier analysis, however, permits us to enumerate some of the important questions that courts should ask themselves (and the parties) before deciding the "when" and "how" questions.

1. *Substantial Adequacy of Relief.* Are damages or other less intrusive remedies likely to afford these plaintiffs substantial, even if not complete, relief from the particular violation? Are those remedies likely to deter future violations of this kind? These questions, similar to those that courts now ask before granting injunctive relief, focus attention upon both the type of harm suffered by plaintiffs and the agency's propensity for wrongdoing. By the end of a trial, the court may be in a good position to predict whether the shock of a substantial damage judgment will alter the agency's modus operandi or will simply be absorbed by a recidivistic institution as a cost of doing business.

2. *Responsiveness to Centralized Controls.* Is the kind of official misconduct and the nature of the defendant organization in question more or less amenable to control by central decisionmakers, such as judges and agency managers? Here, the court should consider the likely feasibility and effectiveness—in *this* agency and regarding *this* conduct—of setting goals, monitoring low-level behavior, devising performance measures, issuing rules, and deploying other hierarchical controls. Of course, no organization, least of all a public street-level agency, perfectly exemplifies Elmore's "systems management" model.[29] But as suggested by Wilson's comparisons of the FBI and

drug enforcement organizations,[30] and by his comparisons of police departments in different communities,[31] some agencies come much closer than others engaged in the same kind of work. Other things being equal, those that come closest can be expected to respond better either to a damage judgment or to a more intrusive remedy. The choice between these remedies can then be made on other grounds.

3. *Alternative Technologies of Compliance.* How many possible plausible solutions to the misconduct problem are likely to exist? Other things being equal, if the court can imagine many competing technologies of compliance and if the agency seems best situated to identify and operationalize the most efficient and effective of them, the court should rely upon general deterrence remedies instead of more intrusive interventions. If it can imagine only one plausible solution and believes that even a damage judgment would not induce the agency to adopt and implement that solution on its own, the court should be less hesitant to intrude.

4. *The Costs of Uncertainty.* When there are many technologies of compliance, what are the likely effects of continuing uncertainty concerning which of them the courts will ultimately find acceptable? Less intrusive remedies afford defendants the flexibility to select the best way to eliminate the misconduct, but this feature, a virtue in many ways, may create problems because it leaves the legitimacy of defendants' responses to liability unsettled until they can be tested in court. In contrast, detailed structural decrees, whatever their other vices, at least dispel any uncertainty about what will ultimately pass muster with the court. In some cases, such as reapportionment disputes in which the continuing legitimacy of legislative decisions may be thrown into doubt by delay, the social costs of that uncertainty may be very high, perhaps outweighing other factors. But in others, such as cases that concern staffing and treatment patterns in institutions, those costs may on balance be acceptable.

5. *The Importance of Substantive Rights.* How important are the underlying substantive rights at stake? All rights seem precious when threatened, but some are more fundamental than others. Most people would affirm that the right of black children to attend nonsegregated schools stands on a higher moral footing than that of prisoners to receive nutritious food or sanitary conditions, although both rights are equally protected by law. In remedially hard cases, in which the choice among remedies affects important values quite independently of its effect upon the substantive violation, these differences ought to be relevant to which remedy is selected. Other things being equal, the

more fundamental the right, the greater the risks we ought to accept in seeking to vindicate it.

Many other relevant factors, of course, could be mentioned. Some, like the nature of the political environment, are likely to be somewhat speculative and perhaps even inappropriate for a court to consider explicitly. Others, like the pervasiveness of the violation or the necessity for a protracted judicial administration of the remedy, may well become apparent to the judge by the conclusion of the trial. The point here is not to urge that the remedial analysis be comprehensive or systematic, for the subject admits of neither comprehensiveness nor system. It is merely to suggest that courts faced with the questions of when and how to intervene enjoy several degrees of freedom and some reasoned bases for exercising it.

In the remedial system of the future, even more than that of today, sound choice of remedy in the difficult case will depend not upon checklists or logical deduction but upon what Cardozo called "the creative element in the judicial process."[32] No remedy discussed earlier, not even the structural injunction, can ensure that bureaucracies will not continue to subvert the rights that courts declare. Remedies must be evaluated and compared, with all of their warts. All things considered, even a structural injunction that qualifies under the least restrictive criterion may actually pose greater threats—to defendants' ability to carry out crucial public functions, to plaintiffs' prospect for actually improving their situation, to the interests of nonparties, to the court's legitimacy and efficacy—than even a damage remedy that does not fully compensate, a declaratory judgment that may conceivably be ignored, a prohibitory injunction that does not impose affirmative duties, a mandatory injunction that imposes only a few of them, or some combination of these remedies. A court that conscientiously rejects structural relief in favor of less intrusive remedies neither abdicates its responsibility to do justice nor relinquishes its version of constitutional meaning; instead, it accepts the pronounced interdependence of our governing institutions and intentionally fragmented public authority. Even if we wished "the judge to take responsibility for practical reality and its consonance with the Constitution,"[33] as Fiss urges, the judge could not do so. We have linked our collective destiny to a system of institutionally competitive constitutional meanings that reposes the principal responsibility for governance, for the practical reality of our public values, elsewhere. In such a system, the risk that political institutions will occasionally fail to implement the courts' versions of meaning is one that can never be wholly avoided, *regardless*

of what courts do. In the end, that risk is one for which no democratic polity can, or should, attempt to provide a truly perfect judicial
remedy.

## Reform and the Problem of Institutional Choice

The remedial system of today is, as we have seen, markedly incoherent. Fragmented by its diverse constitutional, institutional, doctrinal,
and behavioral elements, it distorts incentives and works at cross-
purposes. The changes that I have proposed have the potential to
overcome this incoherence only if the *systematic* nature of the problem
is acknowledged and addressed. If approached in a piecemeal, ad hoc
fashion insensitive to the interrelationships of these elements, reform
may succeed only in pulling the system in conflicting directions,
perhaps exacerbating its most problematic features. Our social land-
scape is littered with failed reforms that had just this effect.

The analysis and prescriptions advanced in this book raise one final
question, a question of what might be called the institutional technology of law reform: Assuming the wisdom of these innovations, *which*
institution or combination of institutions—the Congress, the Supreme
Court, the state legislatures and courts, or the service bureaucracies at
each level of government—ought to design the legal and institutional
changes necessary to implement and legitimate them?

It is a striking fact that almost every important recent development
in the law of public tort remedies has been a product of judicial rather
than legislative innovation. Congress enacted § 1983 more than 110
years ago and passed the FTCA just after World War II. Except for
amending the FTCA in 1974 (to ratify the *Bivens* decision) and authorizing attorney's fee awards in § 1983 actions four years later (to
ratify lower court decisions), Congress has failed to conduct any systematic review of the FTCA or the Eleventh Amendment despite the
enormous social, political, and legal changes that have occurred since
their adoption. A thorough review of § 1983 has only begun within the
last year.[34] Congress has held hearings during which it has occasionally
considered amending one feature or another of the remedial system,
but with the two exceptions just noted, no amendment has ever come
close to enactment. Instead, the federal courts have been the dominant
force in remedial reform. As we saw in chapter 2, the Eleventh
Amendment was itself the direct consequence of an early Supreme
Court decision, and its contours have been shaped and reshaped by the
courts alone. The federal courts also created the *Bivens*-type remedy

and then extended it to claims under a variety of constitutional provisions. They rehabilitated the § 1983 remedy after almost a century of obscurity, interpreted it to extend its reach, and created (or re-created) a set of common law immunity rules. The rather skeletal structure of the FTCA has also been fleshed out by the courts.

On the basis of this history, one might suppose that judicial initiation of the proposed remedial changes would be quite consistent with the courts' leading role, especially in recent years. Several considerations, however, argue strongly—indeed in my view, compellingly—that Congress be the chief architect for the remedial system of the future. First, public expectations and institutional arrangements have, with the Court's blessings, settled around earlier judicial pronouncements in this area.[35] The kinds of incremental changes courts are best suited to make, and with which they are most comfortable, would probably fail to break the present system's hold over these expectations and arrangements; they would tend to reaffirm the status quo rather than signal a fundamental departure. Only clearly announced legislated action is likely to break that cycle.

Second, the courts cannot effectively integrate the components of a reformed system through their traditional case-by-case adjudicative method. A decision that contracts official liability for concededly illegal conduct, for example, may be desirable if accompanied by expanded governmental liability; taken together, these changes would advance remedial goals. But if official liability were contracted in isolation, compensation and deterrence would be frustrated. A legislature can more easily impose change in a comprehensive and coordinated fashion and can withhold action until it is prepared to do so.

Finally, an equitable transition to the remedial system of the future may well require exceptions, trade-offs, recognition of special needs, temporary subsidies, side payments, or other arrangements that lend themselves to political compromise and ad hoc adjustment rather than principled elaboration. In addition, an expansion of governmental liability, for reasons explored in chapter 5, may well encourage some increase in ill-founded claims, and a phased approach or administrative screening of claims[36] may be needed. The legislative process is clearly superior to adjudication in meeting these kinds of needs.[37]

If Congress is better situated than the federal judiciary to undertake remedial reform, its comparative advantage over state legislatures and state courts is even more pronounced. This is most obvious with respect to changes affecting *Bivens* and FTCA claims, in which the conduct of federal officials is at issue, but it is also true for changes affecting the § 1983 remedy. Federally created rights, after all, are at stake. Most of those rights were established as part of a fundamental post–Civil War settlement (or more properly, resettlement) in which the states were obliged to cede part of their sovereignty to Congress in order that those rights might be enforceable against them and their officials. Indeed, § 1983 was necessary precisely because the states were thought to threaten those rights. Congress therefore has unique policymaking responsibilities in this area. States cannot be allowed to define the scope of their own obligations to remedy their agents' violations of federally created rights. Nor can the scope of federally created rights and the nature of remedies for their protection be permitted to depend upon the vagaries of state legislation and case law;[38] instead, they should be uniform for all citizens.

The administrators of street-level agencies must also play an important role in reforming public tort remedies. Although they cannot much alter the form and application of those remedies or modify risk-shifting arrangements between officials and government, they can exercise whatever latitude the remedial system permits them to advance that system's goals—for example, in the decision about whether and how to discipline their employees. Perhaps their chief importance lies in their capacity to educate legislators and courts concerning how particular remedial changes will affect their particular programmatic missions and organizational behavior, to devise the substantive standards of conduct to which their officials ought to be held, and to influence their actual behavior. The nature and scope of citizen remedies for official misconduct are and ought to be largely beyond agencies' control. But agencies can help to shape the behavioral and legal contexts in which those remedies will be applied, thereby guiding public tort law toward a fuller realization.

## APPENDIX 1: VOLUME OF
## FEDERAL COURT LITIGATION
## AGAINST GOVERNMENTS AND PUBLIC OFFICIALS

The following discussion is a summary of the currently available statistics on the volume and types of actions under § 1983, FTCA, and *Bivens*.

### § 1983 Cases

Only nineteen decisions were rendered under § 1983 in the first sixty-five years after its adoption in 1871. Today, however, § 1983 is the second most heavily litigated section of the United States Code; only federal habeas corpus claims are more numerous.[1] Unfortunately, § 1983 cases are not identified separately in the federal judicial work load statistics published by the Administrative Office of the United States Courts, the only continuous statistical series available on civil actions against public officials. The statistics do not permit one to isolate § 1983 suits from other cases (for example, those brought under the Constitution and other statutes) in the "civil rights" categories in the data base. Hence, the data on "civil rights" litigation must be the statistical proxy for the volume of § 1983 cases.

In the period 1960–81, the volume of civil litigation in federal courts increased steadily, from just under 60,000 cases commenced in 1960 to 175,694 cases commenced in the statistical year ending March 31, 1981—an increase of some 193 percent.[2] During the same period, however, the "civil rights statute" subcategory grew even more dramatically, from 280 filings in 1960 to just over 27,000 in 1980—*an increase of 9,578 percent*. In the decade 1970–80 alone, "federal question" civil rights cases (including prisoner civil rights petitions) rose by 350 percent.

The rate of increase during the last two decades has also grown. In the early 1960s, the number of civil cases in the district courts eased upward "on a modest scale of from 2 to 4% per year,"[3] but beginning in 1969 (when civil cases filed were up 8 percent), a sharp upturn occurred and has continued to the present. Thus, civil filings in 1970 rose 13 percent above 1969; the case load growth in 1969–70 exceeded the combined increase of the preceding

Civil Rights Cases Commenced in Federal Courts, 1960–81

| | 1960 | 1970 | 1975 | 1976 | 1977 | 1978 | 1979 | 1980 | 1981 |
|---|---|---|---|---|---|---|---|---|---|
| Total civil cases commenced in | | | | | | | | | |
| U.S. district courts | 59,284 | 87,321 | 117,320 | 130,597 | 130,567 | 138,770 | 154,666 | 168,789 | 175,694 |
| Federal question only | 13,175 | 34,846 | 52,688 | 56,822 | 57,011 | 45,028[a] | 63,221 | 68,299 | 69,659 |
| Total civil rights cases filed in U.S. District Courts, not | | | | | | | | | |
| including prisoner petitions | 280 | 3,985 | 10,392 | 12,329 | 13,113 | 12,829 | 13,168 | 14,101 | 14,741 |
| Prisoner petitions | — | 2,031 | — | 7,460 | 8,235 | 10,366 | 11,783 | 13,000 | 15,409 |
| Total civil rights cases | — | 6,016 | — | 19,789 | 21,348 | 23,195 | 24,941 | 27,101 | 30,150 |
| Percentage increase in civil rights cases over preceding year, | | | | | | | | | |
| not including prisoner cases | — | 1,323%[b] | 160.8%[c] | 18.6% | 6.3% | -2.2% | 2.6% | 7.0% | 4.5% |
| Civil rights cases as percentage of total civil cases filed, not | | | | | | | | | |
| including prisoner petitions | .47% | 4.56% | 8.85% | 9.44% | 10.04% | 9.24% | 8.51% | 8.35% | 8.39% |
| Including prisoner petitions | — | — | — | 15.15% | 16.33% | 16.71% | 16.12% | 16.05% | 17.16% |
| Total civil rights cases filed in courts of appeals, not | | | | | | | | | |
| including prisoner petitions | 44 | 668 | 1,168 | 1,341 | 1,389 | 1,989 | 2,276 | 2,661 | — |
| Prisoner petitions | — | 311 | 633 | 619 | 744 | 842 | 1,171 | 1,737 | — |
| Total civil rights appeals | — | — | 1,801 | 1,960 | 2,163 | 2,831 | 3,447 | 4,398 | — |

SOURCES: *Annual Report of the Director*, Administrative Office of the U.S. Courts, Washington, D.C.—statistics compiled as of June 30 (fiscal year); *Federal Judicial Workload Statistics*, 1979–80 and 1981. The administrative office reports various case load figures for the twelve months ending December 31, 1979, and December 31, 1980, and other figures for the twelve months ending March 31, 1981. I have used the fiscal year (June 30) data in this table for all years before 1981. In 1981 the fiscal year was changed to end September 30.

a. The decline in civil rights, securities, antitrust, and labor litigation in 1978–79 discussed in the 1979 *Annual Report of the Judicial Conference* at p. 107.

b. 10-year increase.

c. 5-year increase.

eight years. Similarly, appeals from the district courts in civil cases in 1970 were up 13 percent over 1969; in the subcategory of civil rights cases, the increase was 74 percent over 1969.[4] These trends have not abated in recent years. In 1981, the Administrative Office of the United States Courts reported that the 45,467 civil cases filed in the first quarter (July–September) represented "the largest influx . . . into the district courts during any comparable period" for which statistics were available: 5.5 percent over 1980, 14.2 percent over 1979, 19.8 percent over 1978, and 32.1 percent over 1977.[5] Since 1976, almost one of every three new private federal question suits filed in the district courts was a civil rights action against a state or federal official.[6]

As the table shows, civil rights suits continue to constitute a major proportion of the rising volume of cases in both federal district courts and the dockets of the courts of appeals. Unfortunately, the available data are aggregated. The only data subcategories are for general classes labeled "voting," "jobs," "accommodations," "welfare," and "other," for civil rights cases filed, pending, and terminated in each fiscal year. Only beginning in 1970 were prisoner civil rights petitions separately listed. (They were classified that year under "habeas corpus and other.") Nor do the data distinguish actions for damages from suits seeking injunctions or declaratory relief, or cases brought against named individual employees from those brought against governmental agencies.

As noted earlier, § 1983 cases cannot be isolated within the federal question–civil rights statute category for which data are collected. Nor do the data reflect § 1983 actions brought in state courts. Nevertheless, the statistics on both the volume of and rate of increase in civil rights suits brought since 1960 are revealing. The district court data have already been discussed. At the appellate level, the 44 civil rights appeals of 1960 are dwarfed by the 1980 total of 4,398 (including prisoner petitions). In recent years, there has been no leveling off but rather a further rise; the annual increment in the number of such appeals taken by the circuit courts between 1975 and 1980 totaled 159, 203, 668, 616, and 951. The table shows this increase as well as the increase in the civil rights component of the case load in the past two decades for both the federal district courts and the courts of appeals.

## Federal Tort Claims Act and Bivens cases

Civil actions brought under the FTCA were recorded separately until 1977; only estimates are available for subsequent years.[7] The FTCA case load experienced a modest growth after 1960, compared with the exponential surge in § 1983 litigation suggested by the table. The number of cases commenced in the district courts for the comparable years are as follows:

| 1960 | 1970 | 1975 | 1976 | 1977 |
|------|------|------|------|------|
| 1,261 | 1,571 | 2,054 | 2,002 | 2,050 |

In part, at least, this difference may reflect the stability in federal employment relative to nonfederal public employment. In 1960, there were 2,421,000 federal civilian employees; in 1979, the total was 2,869,000. During the same period, however, state and local government employment rose—from

6,387,000 (72.5 percent of the total government work force of 8,808,000) in 1960 to 13,102,000 (82 percent of the total government work force of 15,971,000) in 1979.[8]

Tort claims against individual federal employees continue to be brought under the FTCA despite the availability since 1971 of the *Bivens* remedy for constitutional torts. Justice Department officials estimate there were "in excess of 2,000 lawsuits" concerning federal tort claims pending in November 1981, the majority of which involved "multiple defendants, some as many as thirty to forty-five" individual government officials.[9] Estimates of the total expenditures since 1976 on private attorneys in cases in which the Justice Department itself does not defend government officials being sued but retains private counsel, range between $2 million and $3 million.[10] No figures are available for similar suits against federal officials at common law, or under non–civil rights statutes.

Approximately 75 percent of *Bivens* actions involve multiple defendants.[11] Although no governmentwide statistics document the incidence of filings of *Bivens* suits, the available data indicate a steady increase. Between 7,500 and 10,000 *Bivens* suits against government employees have been brought since 1971;[12] at least 600 individual FBI agents have named defendants in these cases.[13] The Torts Branch of the Department of Justice's Civil Division records filings of *Bivens* cases against individual employees for the three years 1979–81 as follows: 1979, 535; 1980, 547; 1981, 601. The percentage of *Bivens* cases within the overall Torts Branch case load increased to 9 percent of the total in 1979, to 16 percent in 1980, and to 18 percent in 1981.[14] These percentages, obtained from only one branch of the Civil Division, do not include actions that other Justice Department units, such as the Civil Rights Division, handle, nor do they include similar cases litigated by independent agencies that defend their own *Bivens* defendants, such as the Securities and Exchange Commission. The Justice Department estimates that approximately 2,200 *Bivens* suits, against an average of 3–5 federal employees, were pending as of March 31, 1981.[15] According to testimony given in March 1982, the "annualized cost" of the present case load is running at $15,821,000, plus payment to private counsel by the department of about $500,000 per year.[16]

Whereas the *Bivens* case itself arose in a law enforcement context, those cases are now a declining percentage of the total filings against federal official defendants.[17] Of the three main categories of *Bivens* actions (excluding cases filed by prison inmates), law enforcement cases appear to comprise less than one-third; two-thirds consist of nonpersonnel cases and personnel cases against federal supervisors.[18]

# APPENDIX 2: GOVERNMENTAL AND OFFICIAL LIABILITY-IMMUNITY DOCTRINE IN THE FEDERAL COURTS

A. *The Current State of Liability-Immunity Doctrine in § 1983 Actions*

Although the current rules governing the liability of state and local officials and governmental entities under § 1983 are complex and to some degree unsettled, the following summary, simplified and divested of unnecessary refinements, may be gleaned from the case law.

1. If a state official violates federal constitutional or statutory law (and perhaps regulations and common law as well),[1] the victim may sue the official in his individual capacity for monetary damages under § 1983. Under the Eleventh Amendment, however, such an action may not be brought against a state agency or the state itself unless the relief requested is "prospective"[2] or merely "ancillary" to prospective relief,[3] in contrast to a "retroactive award" requiring payment of funds from the state treasury.[4] Section 1983 also authorizes actions for injunctive or declaratory relief against either the official or the government; these actions are also barred by the Eleventh Amendment if they are in effect suits against the state.[5]

2. If a municipal or other local official violates federal law, the victim may sue the appropriate local agency for monetary damages or injunctive or declaratory relief under § 1983 if, but only if, an "official policy" or a governmentally legitimated "custom or usage" is "the moving force" of the violation.[6] Moreover, the agency may not be held liable solely on the basis of *respondeat superior* principles (that is, simply because the employee was acting within the scope of his employment), or on the basis of a general allegation of administrative negligence.[7] The victim may sue the offending local official in his individual capacity without regard to these limitations.

3. Damage remedies under § 1983 are subject to whatever official or governmental immunities the defendant is entitled to invoke. The immunities are wholly creatures of federal common law; their availability in a given case depends upon a two-part inquiry that analyzes both historical and

policy considerations. First, if an immunity was established at common law in 1871 (when § 1983 was enacted), did the enacting Congress intend to preserve or abrogate it? Second, if an immunity was not so established, would the purposes of § 1983 be advanced by recognizing it?[8]

"Absolute" immunity, where applicable, extends to all acts performed "within the outer perimeter of [the official's] line of duty," however malicious the motivation.[9] The "outer perimeter" is viewed as being quite capacious; in *Stump* v. *Sparkman*,[10] for example, the judge met this test despite taking action (i.e., ordering the sterilization of a young girl) under circumstances that rendered it clearly illegal. The availability of absolute immunity can readily be determined at the outset of the litigation (i.e., on a motion to dismiss). A "qualified" immunity, in contrast, extends only to acts performed in "good faith." Until very recently, this standard contained both subjective and objective elements,[11] and its availability ordinarily could not be established on a pretrial motion but only by evidence presented at trial, a problem discussed in chapter 4. In a 1982 decision involving close presidential aides, however, the Court sought to eliminate this problem by dropping "subjective" good faith as a prerequisite of immunity.[12] Although that case was brought as a *Bivens* action rather than under § 1983, the Court noted that immunity claims should be treated according to the same standards in both types of cases.[13]

The following immunity rules may be distilled from the Court's § 1983 decisions. For acts performed pursuant to nondiscretionary duties, no immunity is available to either an official or a government entity,[14] unless the Eleventh Amendment applies. A state or state agency may claim absolute immunity from suits for retrospective monetary damages under the Eleventh Amendment; a local government entity, however, enjoys none. For acts performed pursuant to discretionary duties, officials may, depending upon their functions, invoke either an absolute immunity or a qualified, "good faith" immunity. The Court has extended absolute immunity from damage actions to acts of judicial, legislative, and prosecutorial nature,[15] even if performed by executive branch officials.[16] For acts that allegedly violate the Constitution, however, executive officials enjoy only a "good faith" immunity.[17] The scope of immunity for nonconstitutional torts committed by state and local officials is not yet clear.

The Court has preserved several areas of flexibility in applying immunity rules. First, the rules may vary depending upon whether the relief sought is prospective or retrospective. In suits seeking only prospective relief, for example, immunity has been denied even for judicial or prosecutorial acts.[18] Second, "exceptional situations" might justify absolute immunity if they are "essential for the conduct of public business,"[19] but neither a governor's efforts to deal with "mob rule,"[20] a cabinet secretary's law enforcement activities,[21] nor any other conduct has yet managed to qualify for this exception. Finally, the Court has only recently recognized a remedy under § 1983 for nonconstitutional violations;[22] thus, it has not yet clarified the scope of immunity for executive acts that allegedly violate a statute, regulation, or common law rule.

4. Punitive damages may, "in appropriate circumstances," be recovered against individual defendant officials,[23] but "absent a compelling reason," not against governmental entities.[24] Attorney's fees and litigation costs may be awarded to "substantially prevailing plaintiffs" in § 1983 actions, regardless of the defendant.[25]

## B. *The Current State of Liability-Immunity Doctrine in Actions against the United States or Federal Officials*

As in section A, which concerned the liability and immunity of state and local governmental entities and officials, the summary presented here is simplified.

1. If a federal official violates the Fourth, Fifth, or Eighth Amendments (and perhaps other provisions of the Constitution as well),[26] the victim may sue the official in his individual capacity for monetary damages or injunctive or declaratory relief, even if an action (for damages) might have been maintained under the FTCA. In this *Bivens*-type action (and in the absence of contrary congressional direction), the federal official enjoys the same immunity that the analogous state official would enjoy in a § 1983 action,[27] with one exception: the president may claim an absolute immunity from *damage* actions despite the fact that state governors may not.[28] It appears that punitive damages may be awarded in such actions,[29] but attorney's fees ordinarily may not.[30]

2. If a federal official engaged in (*a*) a "negligent or wrongful" act or omission, or (*b*) certain intentional torts of "investigative or law enforcement officers," the victim may maintain an action for damages against the United States under the FTCA.[31] No immunities may be claimed in an FTCA action, but a number of exceptions apply.[32] If the illegal conduct supports both a *Bivens*-type claim and an FTCA claim (for example, an unconstitutional search by an FBI agent), the victim may pursue either (or both),[33] although double recovery is not permitted.

3. If a federal official engages in conduct for which no damage remedy has been provided under the *Bivens* line of cases (because it does not violate a constitutional provision under which such a direct action may be maintained) or under the FTCA (because one of the exceptions to coverage applies), he presumably remains subject to suit under common law principles.

# APPENDIX 3: SOVEREIGN IMMUNITY
## IN THE STATES

In *Russell* v. *Men of Devon*, a seminal English case decided in the very year President Washington took office, an unincorporated county was sued for injuries caused by a bridge that it had negligently maintained. The court held the county immune, asserting that no corporate fund was available for paying a judgment and that a contrary rule would encourage an avalanche of actions. "It is better that an individual should sustain an injury," the court observed, "than that the public should suffer an inconvenience."[1] An early Massachusetts decision relied upon *Russell* although the defendant town was incorporated, had a fund, and violated a statutory duty to maintain the highway that occasioned plaintiff's injury,[2] and the Massachusetts rule was almost universally adopted in American jurisdictions well into the twentieth century.[3]

The state courts, however, managed to relieve the growing pressures for public tort liability somewhat in several ways. First, many state courts imposed personal liability upon officials, even those who exceeded their jurisdiction in good faith. This "jurisdictional fact" doctrine swept more broadly than the "manifestly or palpably" *ultra vires* test that was applied to federal officials. In perhaps the most notorious case, *Miller* v. *Horton*, the Massachusetts high court, per Oliver Wendell Holmes, held members of a board of health personally liable for the destruction of a horse that they erroneously believed had contracted glanders, a condition that would condemn it under a local ordinance. To Holmes, whose defense of absolute governmental immunity was thoroughgoing but oddly unpersuasive,[4] the erroneous condemnation entitled the owner to compensation despite the board's good faith. Fear of contagion required the board to proceed without a prior hearing; this, coupled with the government's immunity and the owner's right to compensation for his healthy horse, justified recovery against the officials.[5] In Holmes's view, officials must be held strictly liable for good faith errors about facts upon which their jurisdiction is premised; only errors as to nonjurisdictional facts ought to be immune.

Not all state courts accepted Holmes's approach. In immunizing public health officials who had erroneously destroyed plaintiff's property as a nuisance, for example, the Connecticut court stressed the chilling effect of liability upon officials' initiative regardless of whether the error was "jurisdictional" or not:

> The statute does not mean to destroy property which is not in fact a nuisance, but who shall decide whether it is so? . . . If the board of health are to decide at their peril, they will not decide at all. They have no greater interest in the matter than others, further than to do their duty; but duty, hampered by a liability for damages for errors committed in its discharge, would become a motive of very little power.[6]

Many state courts also restricted governmental immunity through a classic judicial move—the elaboration of distinctions giving rise to fluid, easily manipulated analytical categories. Most courts distinguished "discretionary" and "governmental" functions, both of which were absolutely immune, from "ministerial" and "proprietary" functions, which were not.[7] Another distinction, between incorporated entities such as municipalities (liable) and unincorporated entities such as counties (immune), cut across each of the other two and added to the confusing pattern of decisions produced by these elastic categories.[8] Torts arising out of the maintenance of public parks and highways, for example, were immune in some jurisdictions and not immune in others.[9]

The persistence of governmental immunity was perhaps most evident in the narrow constructions accorded to statutory waivers of immunity. Courts commonly distinguished between statutes that created a new governmental liability and those that merely created a new remedy for an existing liability. As the New York court put it, "immunity from action is one thing. Immunity from liability for the torts of . . . officers and agents is something else."[10] Where the government's immunity was based solely upon its status as sovereign, a statutory waiver could lead to liability. But where the immunity rested instead (or in addition) upon policy considerations, as in *United States v. Kirkpatrick*[11] and analogous state cases,[12] it survived despite the enactment of statutes subjecting the government to suit. In such cases, the government was obliged to respond to the complaint but could successfully defeat the suit on a preliminary motion to dismiss. Today, judicial and statutory recognition of some governmental immunity under state law persists in most localities. Indeed, in 1980 when the Court eliminated it in § 1983 actions, Justice Powell could identify only five states that imposed broad liability upon their local governments.[13]

# NOTES

## Introduction

1. *The Federalist* No. 51, at 337 (A. Hamilton or J. Madison) (Modern Library ed., 1937).

2. Olmstead v. United States, 277 U.S. 438, 485 (1928) (Brandeis, J., dissenting).

3. *See Report to Congress on the Activities and Operations of the Public Integrity Section,* Criminal Division, U.S. Dept. of Justice, April 1982, table II.

4. *See infra,* appendix 1 and note 8. Even at the federal level, where growth has been slowest, civilian employment grew over 20 percent between 1955 and 1979. U.S., Bureau of the Census, *Statistical Abstract of the United States: 1980,* 279, 318 (101st ed., 1980).

5. *See generally,* e.g., Schuck, "The Politics of Regulation," 90 *Yale L. J.* 702 (1981).

6. For a systematic exploration of the implications of these conflicting values in an administrative context, *see* J. Mashaw, *Bureaucratic Justice* (1983).

7. Reich, "The New Property," 73 *Yale L. J.* 733 (1964).

8. Goldberg v. Kelly, 397 U.S. 254 (1970).

9. E.g., Logan v. Zimmerman Brush Co., 102 S. Ct. 1148, 1153–59 (1982).

10. E.g., Clean Air Act of 1970, 42 U.S.C. § 7604 (civil action against United States or any other government agency to the extent permitted by the Eleventh Amendment).

11. W. Prosser, *Handbook of the Law of Torts* (4th ed., 1971).

12. 5 U.S.C. §§ 551–59.

13. There are some notable exceptions. *See,* e.g., O. Fiss, *The Civil Rights Injunction* (1978); Fiss, "Foreword: The Forms of Justice," 93 *Harv. L. Rev.* 1

(1979); Stewart and Sunstein, "Public Programs and Private Rights," 95 *Harv. L. Rev.* 1195 (1982).

14. J. Thibaut and L. Walker, *Procedural Justice: A Psychological Analysis* (1975); Shapiro, "Decentralized Decision-Making in the Law of Torts," in S. Ulmer, ed., *Political Decision-Making* (1970).

15. M. Lipsky, *Street-Level Bureaucracy: The Dilemmas of the Individual in Public Services* (1980).

16. E.g., A. Neiderhoffer, *Behind the Shield* (1969) (police); J. Q. Wilson, *Varieties of Police Behavior* (1968); J. Q. Wilson, *The Investigators: Managing the FBI and Narcotics Agents* (1978); H. Kaufman, *The Forest Ranger* (1960); P. Blau, *The Dynamics of Bureaucracy* (2d ed., 1963) (state employment service); G. Sykes, *The Society of Captives* (1958) (prison guards); E. Bardach and R. Kagan, *Going by the Book* (1982) (inspectors); Schuck, "The Curious Case of the Indicted Meat Inspectors," *Harper's* 245 (September 1972): 81. For studies of high-level administrators, *see*, e.g., H. Kaufman, *The Administrative Behavior of Federal Bureau Chiefs* (1981); H. Heclo, *A Government of Strangers* (1977); M. Bernstein, *The Job of the Federal Executive* (1958).

17. Butz v. Economou, 438 U.S. 478, 506 (1978).

18. Rizzo v. Goode, 423 U.S. 362, 375–80 (1976).

19. E.g., Nixon v. Fitzgerald, 102 S. Ct. 2690 (1982); Scheuer v. Rhodes, 416 U.S. 232, 247 (1974).

20. E.g., Polk County v. Dodson, 453 U.S. 925, 102 S. Ct. 445, 453 (1981).

21. *Infra*, chap. 2.

22. E.g., Weinberger v. Salfi, 422 U.S. 749, 781–85 (1974).

23. Monroe v. Pape, 365 U.S. 167 (1961).

24. *See*, e.g., testimony of William L. Gardner, Chief of Criminal Section, Civil Rights Division, U.S. Dept. of Justice, before State, Justice, Commerce, the Judiciary, and Related Agencies Subcommittee, FY 79 Budget, H.R. 12934, pt. 5, p. 1807.

25. E.g., Proclamation 4311, 39 Fed. Reg. 32,601 (1974) (President Ford's pardon of Richard Nixon); 17 Weekly Compil. of Pres. Docs. 437, April 15, 1981 (President Reagan's pardon of high-ranking FBI officials).

## Part I Introduction

1. Quoted in C. Jacobs, *The Eleventh Amendment and Sovereign Immunity* (1972), at vii.

## Chapter 1

1. The conceptualization of official misconduct developed in this section draws upon, but departs significantly from, a variety of sources. E.g., Coombs, "The Bases of Noncompliance with a Policy," 8 *Policy Studies Journal* 885 (1980); Sabatier and Mazmanian, "The Implementation of Public Policy: A Framework of Analysis," 8 *Policy Studies Journal* 538 (1980); Baum, "The Influence of Legislatures and Appellate Courts over the Policy Implementation Process," 8 *Policy Studies Journal* 560 (1978); Van Meter and Van Horn, "The Policy Implementation Process: A Conceptual Framework," 6

*Administration and Society* 445 (1975); Johnson, "The Implementation and Impact of Judicial Policies: A Heuristic Model," in J. Gardiner, ed., *Public Law and Public Policy* (1977); Baum, "Judicial Impact as a Form of Policy Implementation," in *id.*; Carter, "When Courts Should Make Policy: An Institutional Approach," in *id.*; Elmore, "Organization Models of Social Program Implementation," 26 *Public Policy* 185 (1978).

2. K. Dolbeare and P. Hammond, *The School Prayer Decisions: From Court Policy to Local Practice* 7 (1971). For explicit applications of dissonance theory to legal phenomena, *see*, e.g., W. Muir, *Prayer in the Public Schools: Law and Attitude Change*, chap. 1 (1967); R. Cover, *Justice Accused: Antislavery and the Judicial Process*, chap. 13 (1975).

3. *See* S. Rose-Ackerman, *Corruption: A Study in Political Economy* 168 (1978), and sources there cited.

4. M. Lipsky, *Street-Level Bureaucracy* 187 (1980).

5. Weatherley and Lipsky, "Street-Level Bureaucrats and Institutional Innovation: Implementing Special-Education Reform," 47 *Harv. Educ. Rev.* 171 (1977).

6. N. Milner, *The Court and Local Law Enforcement: The Impact of Miranda* (1971).

7. J. Pressman and A. Wildavsky, *Implementation* 69, 135, 143 (1973).

8. E.g., Schuck, "The Graying of Civil Rights Law: The Age Discrimination Act of 1975," 89 *Yale L. J.* 27 (1979).

9. Pressman and Wildavsky, *supra* note 7, at 143.

10. A. Downs, *Inside Bureaucracy* 134 (1967); *see also* P. Schuck, "The Policymaking Process at H.E.W." (unpublished manuscript).

11. Downs, *supra*, at 135–36.

12. *Infra*, chap. 4.

13. Wynne, "What Are the Courts Doing to Our Children?" 64 *The Public Interest* 7 (Summer 1981); Muller and Fix, "Federal Solicitude, Local Costs: The Impact of Federal Regulation on Municipal Finances," 4 *Regulation* 29 (July/August 1980).

14. Weatherley and Lipsky, *supra* note 5, at 190–93.

15. Rabkin, "The Office of Civil Rights," in J. Q. Wilson, ed., *The Politics of Regulation* (1980).

16. Phelps, "Syracuse Police Trial Has Better Finish," *New York Times*, May 21, 1981, at B2; "Directive on Deadly Force Angers Philadelphia Police," *New York Times*, October 12, 1980, at 61.

17. E.g., Wright v. Rusken, 642 F.2d 1129 (1981); Campbell v. Cauthron, 623 F.2d 503 (1980); Campbell v. McGruder, 580 F.2d 521 (1978).

18. Bird, "Wanderers Find Shelter and a New Life," *New York Times*, April 21, 1981, § 2 at 6; Rule, "Deadline Is Set on Plan to Aid Homeless Men," *New York Times*, November 28, 1980, at 25–26; Fowler, "Koch Pays Visit to New Shelter on Wards Island," *New York Times*, January 4, 1980, at B2.

19. *See generally*, H. Aaron, *Politics and the Professors: The Great Society in Perspective* (1978).

20. "Don't Build, Study Says," 15 *Crime Control Digest* (April 20, 1981), at 4–5.

21. Note, *White Flight as a Factor in Desegregation Remedies: A Judicial Recognition of Reality*, 66 *Va. L. Rev.* 961 (1980).

22. *See generally,* J. Q. Wilson, *Thinking about Crime* (1975).

23. Harris, "The Organization of Hospitals: Some Economic Implications," 8 *Bell J. Econ.* 467 (Autumn 1977); Calabresi, "The Problem of Malpractice: Trying to Round Out the Circle," 27 *U. Toronto L. J.* 131 (1977); Greenwald and Mueller, "Medical Malpractice and Medical Costs," in S. Rottenberg, ed., *The Economics of Medical Malpractice* (1978).

24. Rose-Ackerman, *supra* note 3, at 88.

25. Milner, *supra* note 6, at 219.

26. Weatherley and Lipsky, *supra* note 5, at 188–90.

27. *See* Ramos v. Lamm, 520 F. Supp. 1059 (1981); Dionne, "Judge Limits Ways to House Inmates," *New York Times,* December 25, 1981, at A1; "U.S. Appeals Court Blocks Release of 300 from Prisons in Alabama," *New York Times,* December 21, 1981, at A16.

28. E.g., Welfeld, "The Courts and Desegregated Housing: The Meaning (If Any) of the *Gautreaux* Case," 45 *The Public Interest* 123 (Fall 1976).

29. Milner, *supra* note 6, at chap. 9.

30. Kaufman, *The Forest Ranger* 75–77 (1960).

31. Schuck, "The Curious Case of the Indicted Meat Inspectors," *Harper's* 245 (September 1972): 81.

32. A. Neiderhoffer, *Behind the Shield* 69–75 (1969); Rose-Ackerman, *supra* note 3, at 168.

33. Sykes, *The Society of Captives* 54–58 (1958).

34. Schuck, *supra* note 31.

35. Muir, *supra* note 2, at 86.

36. Cover, *supra* note 2, at 159–74.

37. E.g., Ely, "The Wages of Crying Wolf: A Comment on *Roe* v. *Wade* (93 S. Ct. 705)," 82 *Yale L. J.* 920 (1973).

38. Milner, *supra* note 6, at 190–97.

39. E.g., 5 U.S.C. § 7311.

40. *Supra* note 16.

41. *Infra,* chap. 3; *see,* e.g., Rose-Ackerman, *supra* note 3, at 84–87.

42. D. Mazmanian and J. Neinaber, *Can Organizations Change? Environmental Protection, Citizen Participation, and the Corps of Engineers* 192 (1979).

43. C. Barnard, *The Functions of the Executive* (1946).

44. *Infra,* chap. 3.

45. *Infra,* chap. 2.

46. Canterbury v. Spence, 464 F.2d 772 (D.C. Cir.), *cert. denied,* 409 U.S. 1064 (1972).

47. Logan v. Zimmerman Brush Co., 102 S. Ct. 1148, 1152 (1982).

48. *But see* Owen Fiss's analysis of the civil rights injunction in an explicitly comparative and behavioral framework. Fiss, *The Civil Rights Injunction* (1978).

49. *See generally, id.* For an example, *see* Hobson v. Hansen, 265 F. Supp. 902 (D.D.C. 1967), *appeal dismissed,* 393 U.S. 801 (1968), 269 F. Supp. 401 (1967), *aff'd sub nom* Smuck v. Hobson, 408 F.2d 175 (D.C. Cir. 1969), *further relief ordered,* 320 F. Supp. 720, 327 F. Supp. 844 (1971), unreported opinion and order denying plaintiff's motion to hold defendants in contempt, Civ. No. 82-66, D.D.C., February 17, 1973.

50. E.g., Wyatt v. Stickney, 344 F. Supp. 373, 344 F. Supp. 387 (M.D. Ala. 1972), *enforcing* 325 F. Supp. 781, 344 F. Supp. 1341 (M.D. Ala. 1972), *aff'd in part, remanded in part, decision reserved in part sub nom.* Wyatt v. Aderholt, 503 F.2d 1305 (5th Cir. 1974); Pugh v. Locke, 406 F. Supp. 318 (M.D. Ala. 1976), *rev'd in part,* 559 F.2d 283 (5th Cir. 1977); Hills v. Gautreaux, 425 U.S. 284 (1976); NAACP v. Brennan, 360 F. Supp. 1006 (D.D.C. 1973) (United States Employment Service).

51. J. Q. Wilson, *Thinking about Crime* 179 (1975); J. Hanlon, "Deterring Police Abuse of Citizens through Administrative Measures" 12–13 (1982) (unpublished manuscript).

52. *Infra,* chap. 4.

53. G. Calabresi, *The Costs of Accidents: A Legal and Economic Analysis* (1970).

54. *See,* e.g., Supreme Court of Virginia v. Consumers Union of United States, 446 U.S. 719, 736 (1980). For discussion of a somewhat related question, see City of Kenosha v. Bruno, 412 U.S. 507 (1973).

55. This analysis, *mutatis mutandis,* draws upon the argument developed in Calabresi, *supra* note 53; and Calabresi, "Torts—The Law of the Mixed Society," 56 *Tex. L. Rev.* 519 (1978).

56. *Infra,* chap. 2.

57. The relationship of this formulation to Rawls's "difference principle" is obvious. J. Rawls, *A Theory of Justice* § 13 (1971).

58. For reviews of the literature on the impact of judicial rulings, *see,* e.g., Johnson, *supra* note 1, at 114; Baum, "Judicial-Impact as a Form of Policy Implementation," *supra* note 1, at 131.

59. Adamson v. California, 332 U.S. 46 (1947).

60. 49 C.F.R. §§ 571.209, 571.212.

61. *See generally,* Leff, "Injury, Ignorance, and Spite—The Dynamics of Coercive Collection," 80 *Yale L. J.* 1 (1970).

62. *Infra,* chaps. 2, 4–7.

63. *Infra,* chap. 7.

64. *See,* e.g., R. Posner, *An Economic Analysis of Law* (2d ed., 1977).

65. For other formulations of much the same point, *see* R. Dworkin, "Hard Cases," in his *Taking Rights Seriously* 98 (1977) (distinctions between "abstract" and "concrete" rights); and B. Ackerman, *Social Justice in the Liberal State* 231–34 (1980) (distinction between "ideal" and "second best" theory).

66. C. Black, *The Occasions of Justice* 96–102 (1963). *See also* G. Calabresi, *A Common Law for the Age of Statutes,* chaps. 14, 15 (1982).

67. For a criticism of this still-dominant approach, *see* Fiss, *supra* note 48.

68. E.g., Bounds v. Smith, 430 U.S. 817, 824 (1977); Wyatt v. Aderholt, 503 F.2d 1305, 1315 (5th Cir. 1974).

69. *See generally,* Frug, "The Judicial Power of the Purse," 126 *U. Pa. L. Rev.* 715, 773–84 (1978).

70. *See generally,* Chayes, "The Role of the Judge in Public Law Litigation," 89 *Harv. L. Rev.* 1281 (1976).

71. *Id.* at 1293–94,

72. *See* Fiss, "Foreword: The Forms of Justice," 93 *Harv. L. Rev.* 9–16 (1979).

## Chapter 2

1. A. Goldstein, "History of the American Public Prosecutor," in Kadish et al., eds., *Encyclopedia of Crime and Justice* (1982); E. T. Atkinson, "The Department of the Director of Public Prosecutions," 22 *Can. Bar. Rev.* 413 (1944).

2. *See generally*, J. Vining, *Legal Identity* (1978); Stewart, "The Transformation of American Administrative Law," 88 *Harv. L. Rev.* 1669 (1975).

3. *See* O. Fiss, *The Civil Rights Injunction* (1978).

4. Polk County v. Dodson, 102 S. Ct. 445, 453 (1981).

5. This trend has numerous doctrinal manifestations, such as the widespread adoption of strict liability for defective products [*see Restatement* (Second) *Torts* § 402A (1965)] and for certain other categories of injurious activity, e.g., Spano v. Perini Corp., 25 N.Y. 2d 11, 250 N.E. 2d 31 (1969). Other manifestations include the substitution of comparative for contributory negligence, e.g., Li v. Yellow Cab Co., 13 Cal. 3d 804, 532 P.2d 1226 (1975); the narrowing of other defenses to liability, e.g., Williamson v. Smith, 83 N.M. 336, 491 P.2d 1147 (1971); the abrogation of common law immunities, e.g., Muskopf v. Corning Hosp. Dist., 55 Cal. 2d 211, 359 P.2d 457 (1961); the expansion of old torts, e.g., Dillon v. Legg, 68 Cal. 2d 728, 441 P.2d 912 (1968); the recognition of new ones, e.g., Canterbury v. Spence, 464 F.2d 772 (D.C. Cir.), *cert. denied*, 409 U.S. 1064 (1972); the broadening of vicarious liability, e.g., Rodgers v. Kemper Constr. Co., 50 Cal. App. 3d 608 (Ct. App. 1975); the proliferation of new categories of compensable damages, e.g., Ferriter v. Daniel O'Connell's Sons, Inc., 413 N.E. 2d 690 (1980); and the facilitation of plaintiffs' proofs, e.g., Robbins v. Footer, 553 F.2d 123 (D.C. Cir. 1977).

6. *See generally*, G. Calabresi, *The Cost of Accidents* (1970); F. Harper and F. James, *The Law of Torts* (1956); W. Prosser, *Handbook of the Law of Torts* (4th ed., 1971).

7. The scant historical literature on the subject of vicarious liability casts very little light upon the reasons for failure of *respondeat superior* to take hold in the domain of public law. The most thorough historical treatment is found in Thomas Baty, *Vicarious Liability* (1916), but this work is somewhat flawed by the author's strong position in opposition to the concept of vicarious liability. By 1929, William O. Douglas could speak of the accumulated historical literature as "admittedly ineffectual" and express the hope that doctrinal analysis would clear the ground for future historical accounts. "Vicarious Liability and the Administration of Risk," 38 *Yale L. J.* 585 (1929). Harper and James, in 1956, had no more material available for their survey of the law of vicarious liability than that which Douglas had dismissed, nearly thirty years earlier. *Supra* note 6, at § 26.2. The most recent comprehensive study of the theory of vicarious liability has traced the issues no further back than the late nineteenth century. *See* P. Atiyah, *Vicarious Liability* 75–78, 391–97 (1967).

8. W. Blackstone, 1 *Commentaries on the Law of England*, *239, *241–42 (1765).

9. Maitland, ed., 3 *Bracton's Note Book*, case 1108 at 127–28 (1887). *See also* Henry de Bracton, *De Legibus et Consuetudinibus Angliae*, ed. Thorne (1968), at f. 107, f. 382b.

10. Y.B. 33–35 Edw. I (R.S.) 470.

11. Spedding, ed., 7 *Works* 694 (1858–74).

12. *See* Ludwik Ehrlich, *Proceedings against the Crown, 1216–1377,* in Vinogradoff, ed., 6 *Oxford Studies in Social and Legal History* (1921).

13. For a discussion of modern practice in the U.S. Congress, *see* P. Schuck, *The Judiciary Committees* 242–65 (1975).

14. Ehrlich, *supra* note 12, at 118–23; W. S. Holdsworth, 9 *A History of English Law* 14 (1944).

15. 1 R.P. 416–17 (18 Edw. II, no. 3) (1325).

16. *See,* e.g., Tobin v. Regina, 16 Com. B. (N.S.) 363–65 (1864).

17. These devices are described in 3 Holdsworth, *supra* note 14, at 126–27. For a discussion of the actions, see *id.* at 300.

18. 3 Holdsworth, *supra* note 14, at 1–21. Against a private party engaging in the activities complained of by Robert de Clifton, for instance, the remedy would have been the action of assize of nuisance.

19. These included the *monstrans de droit* and the traverse of office. The details of these actions may be found in Holdsworth, "History of Remedies against the Crown," 38 *L. Q. Rev.* 141, 156–61 (1922).

20. *Id.* at 141, 148.

21. As one sixteenth-century commentator put it, "Peticion is al the remedy the subject hath when the kyng seiseth his land or taketh away his goods from his havinge no title by order of his lawes so to do. . . . And therefore is his peticion called a peticion of right, because of the right the subject hath against the King by the order of his lawes to the thing he sueth for." Sir William Staunford, *Prerogative,* f. 72b (London, 1568).

22. Ehrlich, *supra* note 12, at 49. The precise extent to which the Crown remedied official torts through the petition of right remains uncertain. To Blackstone, the petition was "a matter of grace" not of "compulsion." *Supra* note 8, at 236. To Louis Jaffe, "consent apparently was given as of course." *Judicial Control of Administrative Action* 197 (student ed. 1965). *See* the opinion of the U.S. Supreme Court on this point in United States v. O'Keefe, 78 U.S. 178 (1870).

23. Pawlett v. Attorney-General, Hardres 465 (1668).

24. 3 Blackstone, *supra* note 8, at 428–29; Viscount Canterbury v. Attorney-General, 1 Phillips 306 (1842).

25. 14 State Trials 1 (1690–1700). The Crown's liability for breaches of contract producing unliquidated damages was not clearly settled until the late nineteenth century. Thomas v. Regina, L.R. 10 Q.B. 31 (1874).

26. O. Holmes, *The Common Law* 11–22, ed. Howe (1963); 2 Holdsworth, *supra* note 14, at 47.

27. F. Pollock and W. Maitland, 2 *The History of English Law* 528–30, ed. Milsom (1968).

28. 13 Edward I (Statute of Westminster II), c. 2 (1285).

29. 2 Pollock and Maitland, *supra* note 27, at 533; Y.B. 20–21 Edw. I (R.S.) 64 (1292).

30. 3 Holdsworth, *supra* note 14, at 382–87. *But see* Wigmore, "Responsibility for Tortious Acts," 7 *Harv. L. Rev.* 315, 383, 441 at 384 (1894) for the view that "an undercurrent of feeling" in favor of the master's broader liability existed through the beginning of the fifteenth century.

31. Statute of the Staple, 27 Edw. III, st. 2, c. 19 (1353), which codified mercantile law in the staple towns.

32. 3 Holdsworth, *supra* note 14, at 387 n.2.

33. *Id.* at 385–86; e.g., Y.B. 2 Hy. IV Pasch. pl. 6.

34. 8 Holdworth, *supra* note 14, at 250–52.

35. Kingston v. Booth, Skin. 228 (1682).

36. Boson v. Sandford, 2 Salk. 440 (1691); Turberville v. Stamp, Comb. 459, 1 Ld. Raym. 264 (1698) (the two reports differ significantly); Middleton v. Fowler, 1 Salk. 282 (1699). *See also* Ward v. Evans, 1 Salk. 442 (1704); Hern v. Nichols, 1 Salk. 289 (1709).

37. For example, *Boson* and *Turberville* could have been decided on the basis of traditional exceptions to the master's nonliability; *Hern* was actually a warranty action. *See* the opinion of Bramwell B. in Udell v. Atherton, 7 H. N. 192 (1861).

38. For a review of the eighteenth-century English cases, see Thomas Baty, *Vicarious Liability* 29–32 (1916). The early American cases are reviewed in *id.* at 184–93.

39. Philadelphia & Reading R̈.R. v. Derby, 55 U.S. 468, 485–86 (1852).

40. 1 Ld. Raym. 646, 652–53 (1701).

41. *Id.* at 657.

42. *See,* e.g., Ashby v. White, in which plaintiff alleged that an election official had maliciously refused to record his vote for the successful candidate. Although plaintiff had not suffered actual damage, Chief Justice Holt would have imposed liability, broadening the tort of misfeasance in public office. The existence of a right, Holt maintained, implied a remedy to vindicate it, and Holt's position was vindicated by the House of Lords. 6 Mod. 45, 87 E.R. 808 (Q.B. 1702), 14 State Trials 695 (1704). *See also* Entick v. Carrington, a 1765 trespass action against royal agents who had executed an invalid warrant, in which the court denied defendants the benefit of an immunity statute that protected sheriffs and bailiffs in similar circumstances. As individual lawbreakers, they could not look to it for any special protection. 2 Wils. 275 (1765). For the importance of official liability in sustaining sovereign immunity, *see* Rogers v. Ragendro Dutt, 13 Moore P.C. 207, 236 (1860).

43. A. Smith, *The Wealth of Nations* (1776).

44. *See* J. Goebel, *History of the Supreme Court of the United States,* vol. 1, *Antecedents and Beginnings to 1801* at chaps. 2–4 (1971). For the view that this tradition was a more ambivalent one, *see* G. Wood, *The Creation of the American Republic, 1776–1787,* at chap. 7 (1969).

45. For the most part, the issue is passed off in a footnote. *See* Jaffe, "Suits against Officers—Sovereign Immunity," 77 *Harv. L. Rev.* 1, 19 n.56 (1963). Certainly colonial assemblies appropriated monies for the relief of claims against the colony, but with what frequency and with what answering activity in the courts is unclear.

46. Nathan v. Virginia, 1 Dall. 77 (Court of Common Pleas, Philadelphia, 1784), discussed in C. Jacobs, *The Eleventh Amendment and Sovereign Immunity* 13 (1972).

47. Jacobs, *id.* at 8. The Constitution, however, later recognized this debt. U.S, *Constitution,* Article VI.

48. *Articles of Confederation,* Art. IX. National courts under the Articles were restricted to "piracies and felonies committed on the high seas and establishing courts for receiving . . . appeals in all cases of captures."

49. U.S., *Constitution,* Art. III, § 2.

50. 2 U.S. (Dall.) 419, 476–77 (1793).

51. *Id.* at 478. Justice Cushing also perceived a justification for different immunity rules for the states and for the federal government. 2 U.S. (Dall.) at 469.

52. 1 Cranch 137 (1803).

53. 418 U.S. 683 (1974).

54. Cohens v. Virginia, 6 Wheat. 264, 411–12 (1821).

55. United States v. McLemore, 4 How. 286 (1846).

56. United States v. Kirkpatrick, 22 U.S. 720, 735 (1824); *see also* United States v. Vanzandt, 24 U.S. 184 (1826).

57. J. Story, *Law of Agency* § 319 (1844 ed.). In the first edition of the treatise, published in 1839, Story had also rejected imposing *respondeat superior* liability upon supervisory officials, asserting that "it would operate as a serious discouragement to persons who perform public functions." *Id.* at § 321.

58. E.g., United States v. Buchanan, 49 U.S. 83, 106 (1850).

59. 6 Stat. 8 (1792).

60. For an example of legislative complaint as to the burden of claims settlement, see 8 *Memoirs of John Quincy Adams* 479–80 (1876). *See also* Schuck, *supra* note 13.

61. 12 Stat. 820 (1863) and 10 Stat. 612 (1855).

62. The Tucker Act, 24 Stat. 5051 (1887), limits the jurisdiction to "cases not sounding in tort." The earlier law, 10 Stat. 612 (1855), restricted the Court of Claims to "contracts express and implied." *See*, e.g., Gibbons v. United States, 75 U.S. 269 (1868).

63. Langford v. United States, 101 U.S. 341, 343–46 (1879).

64. See discussion in section on liability for state and local government torts, *infra; see also*, e.g., United States v. Lee, 106 U.S. 196 (1882).

65. Kendall v. Stokes, 44 U.S. 87, 98 (1845).

66. Spaulding v. Vilas, 161 U.S. 483, 498 (1896).

67. "Competent persons could not be found to fill position of the kind, if they knew they would be liable. . . ." Robertson v. Sichel, 127 U.S. 507, 515 (1888). For a similar result in a state case, *see* Keenan v. Southworth, 110 Mass. 474 (1872).

68. 36 Stat. 851 (1910), amended by 40 Stat. 705 (1918); *see* 28 U.S.C. § 1498.

69. *See* W. Wright, *The Federal Tort Claims Act* 4–5 (1957).

70. Borchard, "Government Liability in Tort," 34 *Yale L. J.* 1, 129, 229 (1924–25); 36 *Yale L. J.* 1, 757, 1039 (1926–27); 28 *Colum. L. Rev.* 577, 734 (1928).

71. One commentator has counted over 200 articles, notes, and comments on municipalities alone between 1924 and 1942. Repko, "American Legal Commentary on the Doctrines of Municipal Tort Liability," 9 *Law & Contemp. Probs.* 214 (1942).

72. Borchard, "The Federal Tort Claims Bill," 1 *U. Chi. L. Rev.* 1, 2 (1933).

73. 42 Stat. 1066 (1922 ). The various partial measures of the 1920s and 1930s are described in Holtzoff, "The Handling of Tort Claims against the Federal Government," 9 *Law & Contemp. Probs.* 311, 313–21 (1942). This article also includes a valuable recitation of the procedure followed in this period for the production of private legislation in the U.S. Congress.

74. Keifer & Keifer v. Reconstruction Finance Corp., 306 U.S. 381, 397

(1938) (Frankfurter, J.); Federal Housing Administration v. Burr, 309 U.S. 245 (1939).

75. *Report of the Attorney General* at 10 (1938).

76. 60 Stat. 842 (1946).

77. Yaselli v. Goff, 275 U.S. 503 (1927).

78. Class v. Ickes, 117 F.2d 273 (D.C. Cir. 1940), *cert. denied,* 311 U.S. 718 (1941); Standard Nut Margarine Co. v. Mellon, 72 F.2d 557 (D.C. Cir. 1934), *cert. denied,* 293 U.S. 605 (1934). Absolute immunity had earlier been conferred upon the postmaster general. Spaulding v. Vilas, 161 U.S. 483 (1896).

79. Jones v. Kennedy, 121 F.2d 40 (D.C. Cir. 1941), *cert. denied,* 314 U.S. 665 (1941) (SEC); Adair v. Bank of America Nat. Trust & Savings Assn., 303 U.S. 350 (1938).

80. Cooper v. O'Connor, 99 F.2d 135 (D.C. Cir. 1938).

81. 177 F.2d 579, 580 (2d Cir. 1949), *cert. denied,* 339 U.S. 949 (1950).

82. See appendix 3.

83. *See,* e.g., Jennings, "Tort Liability of Administrative Officers," 21 *Minn. L. Rev.* 263 (1936) (against absolute immunity); Davis, "Administrative Officers' Tort Liability," 55 *Mich. L. Rev.* 201 (1956) (in favor of absolute immunity).

84. 360 U.S. 564 (1959).

85. 28 U.S.C. § 2680(h).

86. 360 U.S. at 575–76.

87. *Id.* at 587 (Brennan, J., dissenting).

88. J. Lieberman, *The Litigious Society* 150 (1981).

89. Nixon v. Fitzgerald, 102 S. Ct. 2690 (1982), which conferred absolute immunity upon the president, does not contradict this assertion. There, the Court did not rely upon *Barr* at all, resting the decision instead upon the uniqueness of the presidential office.

90. 28 U.S.C. § 2672.

91. 28 U.S.C. § 2679.

92. Turner v. Ralston, 409 F. Supp. 1260 (W.D. Wisc. 1976).

93. United States v. Gilman, 347 U.S. 507 (1954). For a contemporary comment, *see* Davis, *supra* note 83, at 209–11.

94. Carlson v. Green, 446 U.S. 14, 28 n.1 (1980) (Powell and Stewart, J., concurring in judgment).

95. *See* Schuck, *supra* note 13.

96. 403 U.S. 388 (1971).

97. Bell v. Hood, 327 U.S. 678 (1946).

98. *See* 28 U.S.C. § 2680(h), prior to the 1974 amendments to the FTCA.

99. 403 U.S. at 422–23.

100. 88 Stat. 50, amending 28 U.S.C. § 2680(h).

101. Davis v. Passman, 442 U.S. 228 (1979).

102. Carlson v. Green, 446 U.S. 14 (1980).

103. *Id.* at 21–23.

104. 446 U.S. at 30 (Burger, C. J., dissenting).

105. 438 U.S. 478 (1978).

106. The earlier case was Scheuer v. Rhodes, 416 U.S. 232 (1974).

107. Harlow and Butterfield v. Fitzgerald, 102 S. Ct. 2727 (1982); Nixon v. Fitzgerald, 102 S. Ct. 2690 (1982).

108. See appendix 1.

109. See chap. 4.

110. 28 U.S.C. §§ 2402, 2674. *See also* discussion in Carlson v. Green, 446 U.S. 14, 21–23 (1980).

111. 28 U.S.C. § 2678.

112. See chap. 4.

113. Jacobs, *supra* note 46, at chap. 2.

114. *Id.* at 41–43.

115. Vanstophorst v. Maryland, 2 U.S. (Dall.) 401 (1791).

116. Jacobs, *supra* note 46, at 43–44.

117. *Id.* at 43–46.

118. 2 U.S. (Dall.) 419 (1793). For reviews of the opinions in *Chisholm, see* Jacobs, *supra* note 46, at 46–55; Currie, "The Constitution in the Supreme Court: 1789–1801," 48 *U. Chi. L. Rev.* 819, 831–39 (1981).

119. 2 U.S. (Dall.) at 429–30.

120. 2 U.S. (Dall.) at 450–53 (Blair, J.), 466–69 (Cushing, J.).

121. *Id.* at 472.

122. *Id.* at 457.

123. *Id.* at 460–62.

124. Formal certification of ratification took longer. *See* Jacobs, *supra* note 46, at 67–74.

125. For a detailed review of the cases, *see* Jacobs, *supra* note 46, at chap. 4. *See also* Ex parte Young, 209 U.S. 123, 150–55 (1908).

126. 209 U.S. 123 (1908).

127. 9 Wheat. 738 (1824).

128. 209 U.S. 123 at 159–60.

129. *See generally,* Jacobs, *supra* note 46, at chaps. 4–5.

130. *Id.* at 107–08.

131. Hans v. Louisiana, 134 U.S. 1, 9–10 (1890).

132. Lincoln County v. Luning, 133 U.S. 529 (1890).

133. *See* E. S. Corwin, *Twilight of the Supreme Court* 81–89, 99–101 (1937); Duker, "Mr. Justice Rufus W. Peckham and the Case of *Ex Parte Young:* Lochnerizing *Munn v. Illinois,*" 1980 *B.Y.U.L. Rev.* 539 (1980).

134. The most recent Eleventh Amendment decisions of importance have been Edelman v. Jordan, 415 U.S. 651 (1974); Milliken v. Bradley, 433 U.S. 267 (1977); and Quern v. Jordan, 440 U.S. 332 (1979). All dealt with the extent to which equitable relief against state officials in fact operates as a monetary award against the state that is barred by the amendment.

135. See appendix 2.

136. *See*, e.g., Cory v. White, 102 S. Ct. 2325, 2328–29; Florida Dept. of State v. Treasure Salvors, Inc., 102 S. Ct. 3304 (1982); Patsy v. Board of Regents of State of Florida, 102 S. Ct. 2557 n.19 (1982), remanding for consideration of whether the Eleventh Amendment bars the action. The issue had not even been briefed by the parties but was raised *sua sponte* by several members of the Court at oral argument. *Id.*

137. *See* Reich, "The New Property," 73 *Yale L. J.* 733 (1964); see also discussion in the introduction.

138. Shapo, "Constitutional Tort: *Monroe v. Pape* and Beyond," 60 *N.W. U.L. Rev.* 277, 281 n.21 (1965).

139. For a review of these decisions, see *id.* at 282–94.

140. 365 U.S. 167 (1961).

141. *Id.* at 203 (Frankfurter, J., dissenting), cited in Shapo, *supra* note 138, at 277–78 n.2.

142. 365 U.S. at 183–87.

143. *Id.* at 211.

144. *Id.* at 187–92.

145. Official court statistics cited by Shapo, *supra* note 138, at 326 n.249.

146. Scheuer v. Rhodes, 416 U.S. 232, 247–48 (1974). The 1959 decision was Barr v. Matteo, 360 U.S. 564.

147. Wood v. Strickland, 420 U.S. 308 (1975).

148. Monell v. Department of Social Services of the City of New York, 436 U.S. 658 (1978).

149. Lake County Estates v. Lake Tahoe Regional Planning Agency, 440 U.S. 391 (1979).

150. Owen v. City of Independence, 445 U.S. 622 (1980).

151. Gomez v. Toledo, 446 U.S. 635 (1980).

152. Supreme Court of Virginia v. Consumers Union, 446 U.S. 719 (1980).

153. Martinez v. California, 444 U.S. 277 (1980).

154. Maine v. Thiboutot, 448 U.S. 1 (1980).

155. Middlesex County Sewerage Authority v. National Sea Clammers Assn., 453 U.S. 1 (1981).

156. Fair Assessment in Real Estate Association v. McNary, 102 S. Ct. 177 (1981).

157. Parratt v. Taylor, 451 U.S. 527 (1981).

158. Patsy v. Florida Board of Regents, 102 S. Ct. 2557 (1982).

159. E.g., Baker v. McCollan, 443 U.S. 137 (1979); Procunier v. Navarette, 434 U.S. 555 (1978).

160. 451 U.S. at 544–45 (Stewart, J., concurring).

161. 451 U.S. at 543.

162. Carlson v. Green, 446 U.S. 14, 19–23 (1980).

163. 42 U.S.C. § 1988.

164. *See* Parratt v. Taylor, 451 U.S. at 550 (opinion of Powell, J., concurring in result).

165. Logan v. Zimmerman Brush Co., 102 S. Ct. 1148, 1158 (1982) (invalidating state's inadvertent failure to meet statutory deadline). For a recent lower court case that strengthens this prediction, *see* Watson v. McGee, 527 F. Supp. 234 (S.D. Ohio 1981) (upholding § 1983 claim by inmate who inhaled smoke from negligently caused fire in local jail).

166. Quern v. Jordan, 440 U.S. 332, 338–45 (1979).

167. Edelman v. Jordan, 415 U.S. 651 (1974); Cory v. White, 102 S. Ct. 2325 (1982).

168. E.g., Stump v. Sparkman, 435 U.S. 349 (1978) (judicial immunity); Imbler v. Pachtman, 424 U.S. 409 (1976) (prosecutorial immunity).

169. City of Newport v. Fact Concerts, Inc., 453 U.S. 247 101 S. Ct. 2748 (1981).

170. Parratt v. Taylor, 451 U.S. 527 (1981).

171. Martinez v. California, 444 U.S. 277 (1980).

172. City of Newport v. Fact Concerts, Inc., 101 S. Ct. 2748, 2761 (1981); *see also* Carey v. Piphus, 435 U.S. 247, 257 n.11 (1978).

173. City of Newport v. Fact Concerts, Inc., 453 U.S. at 259, 101 S. Ct. at 2761.

174. *Supra* note 5.

175. The classic formulation was Holmes's: "the public generally profits by individual activity. As action cannot be avoided, and tends to the public good, there is obviously no policy in throwing the hazard of what is at once desirable and inevitable upon the actor." *Supra* note 26, at 77.

176. E.g., cases cited in Harper and James, *supra* note 6, at 1370–74; M. Franklin, *Injuries and Remedies: Tort Law and Alternatives* 386–91 (2d ed., 1979); Calabresi, *supra* note 6, at 50–54.

177. *See generally,* Wilson, "The Politics of Regulation," in J. Q. Wilson, ed., *The Politics of Regulation* (1980); Schuck, "The Politics of Regulation," 90 *Yale L. J.* 702 (1981); sources cited at Schuck, "Suing Our Servants," 1980; *Sup. Ct. Rev.* 289 n.28 (1981).

178. E.g., J. Lieberman, *The Tyranny of the Experts* (1970). *See also* sources cited in Schuck, "Suing Our Servants," *supra* note 177.

179. *See generally,* Scalia, "Vermont Yankee: The APA, the D.C. Circuit, and the Supreme Court," 1979 *Sup. Ct. Rev.* 345, 388–400 (1980).

180. For a discussion of these phenomena in the context of the Clean Air Act, *see* B. Ackerman and W. Hassler, *Clean Coal/Dirty Air,* chaps. 1, 7 (1981).

181. *See generally,* Schuck, "Public Interest Groups and the Policy Process," 37 *Pub. Adm. Rev.* 132 (1977); A. McFarland, *Public Interest Lobbies: Decisionmaking on Energy* (1976).

182. Fair Assessment in Real Estate Assn. v. McNary, 102 S. Ct. 177 (1981).

183. *See* discussion of deterrence purpose of § 1983, e.g., City of Newport v. Fact Concerts, Inc., 453 U.S. 247, 259, 101 S. Ct. 2748, 2760–61 (1981); and of *Bivens* actions, e.g., Carlson v. Green, 446 U.S. 14, 21–22 (1980).

184. E.g., Toilet Goods Assn. v. Gardner, 387 U.S. 158 (1967).

185. Rizzo v. Goode, 423 U.S. 362, 378–80 (1976).

186. E.g., Hampton v. Mow Sun Wong, 426 U.S. 88 (1976).

187. E.g., A. Bickel, *The Supreme Court and the Idea of Progress* (1978); Glazer, "Towards an Imperial Judiciary," 41 *Pub. Int.* 104 (1975); Fuller, "The Forms and Limits of Adjudication," 92 *Harv. L. Rev.* 353 (1978).

188. Orrin Hatch introduced a bill to limit the applicability of § 1983 in S.584 and S.585, 97th Cong., 1st sess., 127 *Cong. Rec.* 31, 1626 (1981), and the Senate has voted to restrict the use of Dept. of Justice appropriations for the enforcement of busing orders. Amendment to A.951, 97th Cong., 2d sess., 128 *Cong. Rec.* 8, 414 (1982).

189. This point is noted in B. Bittker, *The Case for Black Reparations* (1973).

190. *See* O. Fiss, *The Civil Rights Injunction* (1978).

191. See chap. 8.

## Part II Introduction

1. Respublica v. Sparhawk, 1 U.S. (Dall.) 357, 363 (Pa. Sup. Ct. 1788).

2. Compare, e.g., O. Williamson, *Markets and Hierarchies* (1975); Coase, "The Nature of the Firm," in *Readings in Price Theory* 331–52 (1952);

and Stone, "The Place of Enterprise Liability in the Control of Corporate Conduct," 90 *Yale L. J.* 1 (1980); with H. Kaufman, *The Forest Ranger* (1960); and J. Q. Wilson, *The Investigators* (1978).

3. E.g., A. Downs, *Inside Bureaucracy* 29–31 (1967); M. Lipsky, *Street-Level Bureaucrats* 40–70 (1980).

4. Combs and Slovic, "Causes of Death: Biased Newspaper Coverage and Biased Judgments," *Decision Research Report* 78-8, Eugene, Oregon (December 1978); Kahneman and Tversky, "Prospect Theory: An Analysis of Decision under Risk," 47 *Econometrica* 263 (1979).

5. U.S., Congress, Senate, Judiciary Committee, Subcommittee on Agency Administration, *Federal Tort Claims Act: Hearings on S.1775*, 97th Cong., 2d sess., March 31, 1982 (statement of Donald J. Devine, director, U.S. Office of Personnel Management).

6. Bellante and Link, "Are Public Sector Workers More Risk Averse than Private Sector Workers?" 34 *Indus. & Lab. Rel. Rev.* 408 (1981).

## Chapter 3

1. E.g., W. Niskanen, *Bureaucracy and Representative Government* (1971); A. Downs, *Inside Bureaucracy* (1967); G. Tullock, *The Politics of Bureaucracy* (1965).

2. H. Simon, *Administrative Behavior* (3d ed., 1976).

3. C. Barnard, *The Functions of the Executive* (1946); Clark and Wilson, "Incentive Systems: A Theory of Organizations, 6 *Administrative Science Quarterly* 219 (September 1961).

4. Lindblom, "The Science of 'Muddling Through,' " 19 *Pub. Adm. Rev.* 79 (1959).

5. E.g., T. Schelling, *The Strategy of Conflict* (1960); H. Raiffa, *Decision Analysis: Introductory Lectures on Choice under Uncertainty* (1968); J. Steinbruner, *The Cybernetic Theory of Decisions* (1974).

6. J. Q. Wilson, *The Investigators* 8 (1978).

7. E.g., see sources cited in introduction, *supra* at note 16.

8. A. Hirschman, *Exit, Voice, and Loyalty* (1979). *But see* M. Lipsky, *Street-Level Bureaucrats* (1980), at 13–18.

9. For illuminating examples of the subtle psychological dynamics of some such relationships, *see* R. Burt, *Taking Care of Strangers* (1979), chaps. 2 and 3.

10. For a recent review, *see* Weinrib, "Case for a Duty to Rescue," 90 *Yale L. J.* 247 (December 1980). *See generally*, J. Ratcliffe, ed., *The Good Samaritan and the Law* (1981).

11. Hurley v. Eddingfield, 156 Ind. 416, 59 N.E. 1058 (1901).

12. E.g., Tarasoff v. Regents of University of California, 17 Cal. 3d 425, 551 P.2d 334 (1976); *see also* cases cited at Weinrib, *supra* note 10.

13. Landes and Posner, "Salvors, Finders, Good Samaritans, and Other Rescuers: An Economic Study of Law and Altruism," 7 *J Legal Stud.* 83 (1978).

14. Epstein, "A Theory of Strict Liability," 2 *J Legal Stud.* 151 (1973).

15. E.g., Ames, "Law and Morals," 22 *Harv. L. Rev.* 97 (1908); Weinrib, *supra* note 10.

16. *See*, e.g., 12 Vt. Stat. Ann. § 519 (Supp. 1971).

17. Besharov, "Civil Liability in Child Abuse Cases," 54 *Chi-Kent L. Rev.* 687 (1978); Stone, "Place of Enterprise Liability in the Control of Corporate Conduct," 90 *Yale L. J.* 1 (1980).

18. Youngberg v. Romeo, 102 S. Ct. 2452 (1982); Dixon v. Weinberger, 405 F. Supp. 974 (D.C. D.C. 1975).

19. *See* generally, Note, *A Damages Remedy for Abuses by Child Protection Workers*, 90 *Yale L. J.* 681 (1981).

20. *Infra*, chap. 4.

21. Scheuer v. Rhodes, 416 U.S. 232, 246 (1974).

22. "[T]he law . . . sometimes tells the official that a failure to injure—that is, to coerce compliance with a predetermined rule of conduct—is a dereliction of official duty." Mashaw, "Civil Liability of Government Officers: Property Rights and Official Liability," 42 *Law & Contemp. Probs.* 8 (1978).

23. Calabresi and Melamed, "Property Rules, Liability Rules, and Inalienability: One View of the Cathedral," 85 *Harv. L. Rev.* 1089 (1972).

24. "[T]he public generally profits by individual activity." O. Holmes, *The Common Law* 77, ed. Howe (1963).

25. 403 U.S. at 392; *see id.* at 394–95.

26. For examples, *see* R. Harris, *Freedom Spent* (1974); J. Lieberman, *How the Government Breaks the Law* (1972).

27. Burt, *supra* note 9, at 133–36.

28. E.g., J. Q. Wilson, *Varieties of Police Behavior* 206–12 (1968); Lipsky, *supra* note 8, at 18, 187, and chaps. 7–10; G. Sykes, *The Society of Captives*, chap. 3 (1958); P. Blau, *The Dynamics of Bureaucracy*, chaps. 2, 3 (2d ed., 1963); Schnapper, "Civil Rights Litigation after *Monell*," 79 *Colum. L. Rev.* 213, 253 (1979); N. Milner, *The Court and Local Law Enforcement*, chap. 10 (1971). See also *supra* chap. 1.

29. *See*, e.g., Lipsky, *supra* note 8, at 29–30; E. Bardach and R. Kagan, *Going by the Book*, chap. 2 (1982).

30. *See*, e.g., Lipsky, *supra* note 8, at 29–31, 85; Wilson, *supra* note 28, at 18. For a systematic effort to evaluate such an investment in the context of the Social Security disability program, *see* J. Mashaw, *Bureaucratic Justice*, chaps. 4, 6 (1983).

31. For one example, *see* Schuck, "The Graying of Civil Rights Law: The Age Discrimination Act of 1975," 89 *Yale L. J.* 27, 31–35 (1979); Schuck, "Age Discrimination Revisited," 57 *Chi-Kent L. Rev.* 1029, 1030–40 (1981).

32. *See*, e.g., O'Connor v. Donaldson, 422 U.S. 563 (1975); Cleveland v. La Fleur, 414 U.S. 632 (1974).

33. *See*, e.g., Lipsky, *supra* note 8, at 85.

34. *See* F. Harper and F. James, *The Law of Torts* § 16.6 (1956; 1968 Supp.).

35. *See*, e.g., Lipsky, *supra* note 8, at 14–16; Sykes, *supra* note 28, at 23; Blau, *supra* note 28, at 123.

36. E.g., Lipsky, *supra* note 8, at 14; Blau, *supra* note 28, at 124–26. Bardach and Kagan, *supra* note 29, at chap. 6, regard selective enforcement by police, parole officers, and inspectors as an important, flexible regulatory tool.

37. For example, see Wilson's comparison of patrolmen and investigators in this respect. *Supra* note 6, at 19–20.

38. *Id.* at 83.

39. Amsterdam, "Perspectives on the Fourth Amendment," 58 *Minn. L. Rev.* 349, 415 (1974).

40. *See,* e.g., Mashaw, *Bureaucratic Justice, supra* note 30, at chap. 2 (analyzing the importance of clinical judgments in evaluating disability claims); Wilson, *supra* note 28, at 65–66 (comparing police and psychiatric decision-making).

41. *See,* e.g., Wilson, *supra* note 6, at 161–62, 199; Blau, *supra* note 28, at 125–26; Wilson, *supra* note 28, at 65, 279–80.

42. *See,* e.g., Wilson, *supra* note 28, at 7–8; Blau, *supra* note 28, at 124–26; Bardach and Kagan, *supra* note 29; Sykes, *supra* note 28.

43. Weatherley and Lipsky, "Street-Level Bureaucrats and Institutional Innovation: Implementation of Special-Education Reform," 47 *Harv. Educ. Rev.* 172 (1977) (emphasis in original).

44. Wilson, *supra* note 6, at 198–99.

45. Wynne, "What Are the Courts Doing to Our Children?" 64 *The Public Interest* (Summer 1981).

46. *See,* e.g., Lipsky, *supra* note 8, at 31.

47. *Id.* at 33–39.

48. E.g., Bounds v. Smith, 430 U.S. 817, 825 (1977); Wyatt v. Aderholt, 503 F.2d 1305, 1307 (5th Cir. 1974); Finney v. Hutto, 410 F. Supp. 251 (F.D. Ark. 1976); Serrano v. Priest, 96 Cal. Rptr. 601 (1971). *See also* Gerald Frug, "The Judicial Power of the Purse," 126 *U. Pa. L. Rev.* 715, 773–84 (1978); Note, *Judicial Intervention and Organization Theory,* 89 *Yale L. J.* 513, 515 (1980).

49. This point has been mentioned by the Supreme Court only once, casually in a footnote and without apparent appreciation of its policy significance. Lake Country Estates, Inc. v. Lake Tahoe Regional Planning Agency, 440 U.S. 391, 405 n.29 (1979). There, the Court suggested that because plaintiffs had not alleged that the officials-defendants had profited personally from the acts in question, relief against the agency should suffice.

50. *See,* e.g., 18 U.S.C. §§ 201–24 (bribery, graft, and conflict of interest statutes); United States v. Manton, 107 F.2d 834 (1939).

51. *See* Mashaw, *supra* note 22, at 26–27.

52. For somewhat analogous concepts, *see* O. Williamson, *Markets and Hierarchies* (1975), at 37–39; Liebenstein, "Microeconomies and *X*-Efficiency Theory," special issue, *The Public Interest* 97 (1980).

53. See chap. 2.

54. Kahneman and Tversky, "Prospect Theory: An Analysis of Decision under Risk," 47 *Econometrica* 263 (1979).

55. Combs and Slovic, "Causes of Death: Biased Newspaper Coverage and Biased Judgments," *Decision Research Report* 78-8, Eugene, Oregon (December 1978).

56. U.S., Congress, Senate, Judiciary Committee, Subcommittee on Agency Administration, *Federal Tort Claims Act: Hearings on S.1775,* 97th Cong. 2d sess., March 31, 1982 (statement of Donald Devine, director, U.S. Office of Personnel Management).

57. Besharov, "Protecting Abused and Neglected Children: Can Law Help Social Work?" *Loy. L. Rev.* (in press); *infra,* chap. 4. *See also* U.S.,

Congress, Senate, Judiciary Committee, Subcommittee on Agency Administration, *Federal Tort Claims Act: Hearings on S.1775*, 96th Cong., 1st sess.,
November 16, 1981 (statement of William H. Taft IV, general counsel, Department of Defense).

58. U.S., Congress, Senate, Judiciary Committee, Subcommittee on
Agency Administration, *Federal Tort Claims Act: Hearings on S.1775*, 96th
Cong., 1st sess., November 13, 1981.

59. *Supra* note 57.

60. Telephone interview with Kelly Frels, Esq., counsel to many school
boards and public officials, January 11, 1982.

61. E.g., Besharov, *supra* note 57; Frels, *supra* note 60.

62. *See*, e.g., Lipsky, *supra* note 8, Blau, *supra* note 28, at chaps. 3, 11;
Wilson, *supra* note 28, at 64–78; Sykes, *supra* note 28, at 40–42; Bardach and
Kagan, *supra* note 29, at 152–54; H. Kaufman, *The Forest Ranger* (1960), at
66–67. Even key corporate employees are similarly resistant to bureaucratic
controls. C. Stone, *Where the Law Ends*, chaps. 6, 7 (1975).

63. *Supra* at 68–71.

64. Butz v. Economou, 438 U.S. 478, 515 (1978).

65. *See* Wilson, *supra* note 6, at 65–79. The film *Prince of the City* (S.
Lumet, dir., 1981) vividly dramatizes this particular behavior.

66. State of Maine v. Thiboutot, 448 U.S. 1, 4 (1981), discussed in chap. 2.

67. Wood v. Strickland, 420 U.S. 308 (1975). See discussion in chap. 4.

68. This question is discussed in chap. 4.

69. Yudof, "Liability for Constitutional Torts and the Risk-Averse Public
School Official," 49 *S. Cal. L. Rev.* 1322, 1397 (1976). *See also* Wilson, *supra*
note 6, at 181.

70. Freeman, "When a Professor Must Stand Alone in Court," *New York
Times*, September 23, 1980, at A22.

71. Bardach and Kagan, *supra* note 29, at 40.

72. Lipsky, *supra* note 8, at 15.

73. Wilson, *supra* note 6, at 181.

74. *See*, e.g., "News Note," 5 *Fam. L. Rptr.* 2100 (1978) (state health
department ordered to pay $60,000 to father of child beaten to death, for
inadequate investigation of reports of abuse by mother); 5 *Fam. L. Rptr.* 2437
(1979) (social worker made codefendant in $7 million suit arising out of child
abuse incident). To make things especially difficult, a social worker may also be
sued for investigating a complaint too vigorously. *See* Martin v. County of
Weld, 598 P.2d 532 (Colo. Ct. App. 1979).

75. Interview with John M. Connors, assistant general counsel, Massachusetts Department of Social Services, July 23, 1980. *See also* Yudof, *supra*
note 69, at 1397 (public schoolteachers and administrators). Similar behavior
has been observed in business executives. Interview with Professor James
March, Stanford University Graduate School of Business, July 1980.

76. E.g., Breyer, "Vermont Yankee and the Courts' Role in the Nuclear
Energy Controversy," 91 *Harv. L. Rev.* 1833 (1978) (costs of delaying power
plant construction).

77. E.g., Greenwald and Mueller, "Medical Malpractice and Medical
Costs," in S. Rottenberg, ed., *The Economics of Medical Malpractice* (1978).

78. Several other commentators have drawn upon this analogy in some-

what different connections. E.g., Bardach and Kagan, *supra* note 29, at 284–85; Yudof, *supra* note 69, at 1395–97; Calabresi, "The Problem of Malpractice: Trying to Round Out the Circle," 27 *U. Toronto L. J.* 131 (1977).

79. For one review of the argument, *see* Clark, "Does the Non-profit Form Fit the Hospital Industry?" 93 *Harv. L. Rev.* 1416 (May 1980).

80. *See*, e.g., V. Fuchs, *Who Shall Live?* chap. 3 (1974); Scheff, "Decision Rules, Types of Error, and Their Consequences in Medical Diagnosis," 8 *Behav. Sci.* 97 (1963); Harris, "The Internal Organization of Hospitals: Some Economic Implications," 8 *Bell J. Econ.* 467 (1977).

81. Weatherley and Lipsky, *supra* note 43.

82. *See*, e.g., Yudof, *supra* note 69, at 1397–98.

83. Blau, *supra* note 28, at 233–41.

84. Mashaw, *supra* note 30, at chap. 8.

85. Blau, *supra* note 28, at 235.

86. Yudof, *supra* note 69, at 1394–95. For amusing musings by one critic of legalization of the academy, *see* Stigler, "A Sketch in the History of Truth in Teaching," 81 *J. Pol. Econ.* 491 (1973).

87. Bardach and Kagan, *supra* note 29, at 36–39. Christopher Stone finds legalistic approaches to corporate misconduct to be similarly counterproductive. *Supra* note 62, at 104–05.

88. *Supra* note 74; *See also* Besharov, *supra* note 59 ("defensive social work" encourages unnecessary removals from home).

89. E.g., Martinez v. California, 444 U.S. 277 (1980). *See generally,* "Holding Governments Strictly Liable for the Release of Dangerous Parolees," 55 *N.Y.U.L. Rev.* 907 (1980).

90. The author's observations as a federal official suggest that this is a common strategy among supervisors in civil service systems. Newly designed legal remedies for sexual harassment of employees will probably encourage this strategy. 29 C.F.R. 1604 (1981).

91. *Supra* at 96.

92. *See* Wildavsky, "Richer Is Safer," 60 *The Public Interest* 23 (1980).

93. Dr. Alexander Schmidt, quoted in Quirk, "Food and Drug Administration," in J. Q. Wilson, ed., *The Politics of Regulation* 216 (1980). *See also* Peltzman, "An Evaluation of Consumer Protection Legislation: The 1962 Drug Amendments," 81 *J. Pol. Econ.* 1049 (1973).

94. Blau, *supra* note 28, at 247.

95. *See* Burt, *supra* note 9, at 166–67; Mashaw, "Supreme Court's Due Process Calculation for Administrative Adjudication in *Matthews v. Eldridge* [96 S. Ct. 893]," 44 *U. Chi. L. Rev.* 28 (Fall 1976).

96. *See supra*, chap. 1, and G. Calabresi, *Costs of Accidents*, chap. 5 (1976).

97. *See supra,* chap. 1, and Calabresi, *supra* note 96 at chap. 6.

98. *See generally,* "Judicial Control of Systemic Inadequacies in Federal Administrative Enforcement," 88 *Yale L. J.* 407 (1978).

99. *Supra* at 89.

100. E.g., H. L. A. Hart and A. M. Honore, *Causation in the Law* (1959); Calabresi, "Concerning Cause and the Law of Torts: An Essay for Harry Kalven, Jr.," 43 *U. Chi. L. Rev.* 69 (1975), and sources there cited.

101. For one foray into that nebulous realm, *see* decision in Weiser, "Citi-

zens Can Sue Police for Inaction," *Washington Post,* December 25, 1980, at A1. *See generally,* "Police Liability for Negligent Failure to Prevent Crime," 94 *Harv. L. Rev.* 821 (1981).

102. For a decision denying a remedy in such cases, *see* Donohue v. Copiague Union Free School District, 47 N.Y. 2d 440, 391 N.E. 2d 1352 (1979).

103. For a damage action brought by prisoners against parole officials, *see* Green v. McCall, Civ. no. N-78-23 (D. Conn.).

104. *Supra,* chap. 2.

105. Hobson v. Wilson, Civ. No. 76-1326 (D.D.C. December 23, 1981). *See also* Epps v. U.S., Civ. No. J-78-2373 (D. Md. 1981), in which a judgment for $200,000 was awarded against a federal branch chief of the IRS. Officials tend to be disproportionately aware of the "horror stories" in which plaintiffs recover large judgments. Interview with Harry Schnibbe, Executive Director, National Association of State Medical Health Directors, July 18, 1980.

## Chapter 4

1. Monell v. Department of Social Services of City of New York, 436 U.S. 658, 713 n.9 (1978) (Powell, J., dissenting); *Monell, id.* at 717 (Rehnquist, J., dissenting); Carlson v. Green, 446 U.S. 14, 46 n.13, 47 (1980) (Rehnquist, J., dissenting). At least two of these three comments—Powell's in *Monell* and Rehnquist's in *Carlson*—exaggerate the certainty of indemnification. See discussion in this chapter, *infra.*

2. E.g., Jaffe, "Suits against Governments and Officers: Damage Actions," 77 *Harv. L. Rev.* 209, 216–17 (1963); Bermann, "Integrating Governmental and Officer Tort Liability," 77 *Colum. L. Rev.* 1175, 1190–1202 (1977); Yudof, "Liability for Constitutional Torts and the Risk-Averse Public Official," 49 *S. Cal. L. Rev.* 1322, 1397 (1976); Newman, "Suing the Lawbreakers," 87 *Yale L. J.* 447, 456–57 (1978); Casto, "Innovations in the Defense of Immunity under Section 1983," 47 *Tenn. L. Rev.* 47, 118–19 (1979); Project, "Suing the Police in Federal Court," 88 *Yale L. J.* 781, 810–11 (1978). *See also* the results of the survey conducted by Richard G. Miller, University of Hawaii at Manoa, which have generously been provided to me.

3. Coase, "The Problem of Social Cost," 3 *J. Law & Econ.* 1 (1960).

4. For discussions and critiques, *see,* e.g., Calabresi, "Transaction Costs, Resource Allocation, and Liability Rules—A Comment," 11 *J. Law & Econ.* 67 (1968).

5. For systematic comparisons, *see,* e.g., C. Dahl and C. Lindblom, *Politics, Economics, and Welfare* (1953); C. Lindblom, *Politics and Markets* (1977).

6. 28 C.F.R. §§ 50.15–16 (1980). *See* U.S., Congress, Senate, Judiciary Committee, Subcommittee on Agency Administration, *Federal Tort Claims Act: Hearings on S.1775,* 97th Cong., 2d sess., March 31, 1982 (testimony of William H. Webster, director, FBI). *See also* Nelson, "Funding Cut for Defense of Officials in Tort Cases," *Legal Times,* June 14, 1982, p. 1.

7. *See,* e.g., Aetna Cas. & Surety Co. v. United States, 570 F.2d 1197 (4th Cir. 1978).

8. *See* Nelson, *supra* note 6. *See also* testimony of William H. Webster, *supra* note 6. The case referred to by Webster was Hampton v. Hanrahan, 600 F.2d (7th Cir. 1979).

9. 28 C.F.R. § 50.15(b) (1980). The Dept. of Justice sometimes invokes this last escape clause. Interview with Joseph Sher, U.S. Dept. of Justice, August 4, 1980.

10. Litigation reasons for doing so might include a desire to increase pressure for settlement and to invoke more permissive discovery rules applicable to parties. *See Fed. R. Civ. P.*, Rules 29–37.

11. Interview with Philip Michael, first deputy commissioner, New York City Dept. of Investigation, July 16, 1980.

12. *See* Dolan, "Constitutional Torts and the Federal Tort Claims Act," 14 *U. Rich. L. Rev.* 281, 296 n.98 (1980).

13. *See* National League of Cities, *The New World of Municipal Liability* 4 (1978).

14. Interviews with Kenneth Stroud and Ev Mann, Association of Federal Investigators, July 17, 1980; interview with John McNerney, Association of Federal Criminal Investigation, August 8, 1980.

15. E.g., Hartford Accident & Indemnity Co. v. Villiage of Hempstead, 48 N.Y. 2d 218, 228, 397 N.E. 2d 737, 744 (1979).

16. Insurability of a private defendant for liability under Title VII was upheld in Union Camp Corp. v. Continental Casualty Corp, 452 F. Supp. 565 (S.D. Ga. 1978), but only because no discriminatory intent had been found. The court there suggested that intentional violations should not be insurable. Under § 1983, individual liability would ordinarily entail a finding of intent to harm or unreasonable failure to know relevant legal norms. *But see* Parratt v. Taylor, discussed in chap. 2. In the corporate sector, the SEC has opposed indemnification of corporate directors and officials who violate the Securities Act of 1933 but curiously does not object to purchase of insurance on their behalf by the employer. With regard to other statutes whose purpose is chiefly compensatory, the SEC opposes neither insurance nor idemnification. J. Bishop, *Indemnifying and Insuring the Corporate Executive* (1981).

17. Dolan, *supra* note 12, at 296; Bermann, *supra* note 2, at 1191. There appear to be only two exceptions in which indemnification is specifically authorized by statute: for actions based on "anything done" in enforcement of the Internal Revenue Code (26 U.S.C. § 7423) and for malpractice suits against medical personnel of several named agencies [see 10 U.S.C. § 1089(f), 22 U.S.C. § 817(f), 38 U.S.C. § 4116(c), and 42 U.S.C. § 233(f)]. The latter provisions apply only to actions based on incidents occurring outside the United States. In domestic malpractice suits, the remedy against the United States under the FTCA is exclusive.

18. 28 U.S.C. § 1346(b), 28 U.S.C. §§ 2671–80. Other statutes authorizing suits against the United States are 5 U.S.C. § 552a(g) (for willful failure of an agency to respond to a request for correction of information on file), 26 U.S.C. § 6110(i) (for failure of the Dept. of the Treasury to release tax records to the public as provided by law, or to protect confidentiality of tax files when released), and 18 U.S.C. § 2520 (against any person who illegally intercepts private communications).

19. The United States is the exclusive defendant in cases brought for

negligent operation of a vehicle [28 U.S.C. § 2679(b)]; patent infringement (28 U.S.C. § 1498); improper levying on property to collect taxes, where the suit is brought by someone other than the taxpayer levied upon [26 U.S.C. § 7426(d)]; medical malpractice by Veterans Administration staff members (38 U.S.C. § 4116); and unlawful seizure of seagoing vessels (46 U.S.C. § 745).

20. 28 U.S.C. § 2676. Interview with Justice Dept. officials James Steinberg, Michael Dolan, Jack Farley, and John Euler, July 17, 1980. Bermann, *supra* note 2, at 1192. The United States is barred from seeking a contribution from the offical. United States v. Gilman, 347 U.S. 507 (1954). *See* L. Jayson, *Handling Tort Claims: Administrative and Judicial Remedies* 3–55, § 88 (1964; 1980 Supp.).

21. See discussion in chaps. 2 and 5.

22. *Hearings, supra* note 6 (testimony of J. Paul McGrath, assistant attorney general, U.S. Dept. of Justice).

23. This analysis applies in general to settlements as well as judgments. Like judgments, settlements are indemnifiable or otherwise protected against in most states. By the same token, for federal employees, settlements, like judgments, are not indemnifiable, although the government will pay any settlement where it is named as a codefendant. In those states that immunize officials and impose liability directly on public employers, the employers naturally bear the cost of any settlement. Of those states that retain official defendants but provide indemnification, some provide explicitly for payment of settlements. *See*, e.g., Cal. Govt. Code § 825. Other states use a general term that appears to include settlement. *See*, e.g., N.Y. Publ. Off. Law § 17. Some states allow reimbursement of a settlement only if it has received prior approval from a government legal officer. Cal. Govt. Code § 825. Thus, reimbursement might not be made if the official is for some reason more anxious to settle than the agency. Conversely, the government may settle more readily than the officials. Provisions protecting officials in such instances may sometimes be required. *See* N.C. Gen. Stat. §§ 143–300.6, requiring employee's approval of settlement if it exceeds state's statutory ceiling on liability. Another possible loophole arises in the laws of states that provide insurance rather than, or in addition to, indemnification. Such laws typically allow insurance against "tort liability" (Nev. Rev. Stat. § 41.038; S.C. Gen. Stats. § 1-11-140), which may or may not include settlement costs. *See* Yudof, *supra* chap. 3 note 69, at 1387–88.

24. For example, the only activity for which employees appear to be explicitly protected in Alabama is civil defense. Ala. Code § 31-9-(6). In Kentucky, there is a general provision for the defense of state employees but apparently not for their indemnification, except that they are immune from claims for pain and suffering. Ky. Rev. Stat. §§ 12.211, 44.070. The only actions for which South Carolina state employees appear to be held harmless by statute are those relating to removal or disposal of feral dogs (Code of Laws of S.C. § 47-3-320), although the state has general authority to purchase insurance against its own liability and that of its employees, *id.* at § 1-11-140. New Hampshire has a general provision for indemnification of local employees (N.H. Rev. Stat. Ann. § 31:104–07) but does not appear to have such a provision for state employees.

25. For example, Cal. Govt. Code § 825 provides for defense and

indemnification for employees of any "public entity." *See also* Kansas Stat. Ann. §§ 75–6109. More commonly, state and local employees are treated separately and coverage may or may not be equal in scope. *See*, e.g., N.Y. Publ. Off. Law § 17 (state employees) and N.Y. Gen. Munic. Law §§ 50-a to 50-k (municipal employees).

26. Louisiana provides for defense and indemnification of state employees (La. Rev. Stat. § 13:5108.1) but appears to have no similar provision for local employees. Missouri provides a tort defense fund for certain identified categories of state employees only (Mo. Ann. Stat. §§ 105–710 [Vernon]); provisions for local employees appear to be highly selective. *See id.* at § 537.165 (duty to defend, but not to indemnify, tort actions against firemen violating the use of motor vehicles). Other states provide for defense and indemnification but only at local option. *See*, e.g., N.C. Gen. Stat. §§ 160A–167.

27. Telephone conversations with Janet Kail, Research Department, American Federation of State, County and Municipal Employees, July 15, 1980. Cal. Govt. Code § 825 provides that statutory defense and indemnification provisions may be supplemented by contract provisions for employees of the higher education system.

28. *See*, e.g., Conn. Gen. Stat. Ann. §§ 4–165.

29. *See*, e.g., Cal. Govt. Code § 824.

30. Compare Cal. Govt. Code § 825 (applying to any "employee or former employee of a public entity") with N.Y. Gen. Munic. Law §§ 50-a to 50-k and 52 (treating separately claims against police, corrections officers, physicians, etc., and claims based on negligent operation of a vehicle and permitting but not requiring purchase of insurance for employees generally).

31. *See*, e.g., Ariz. Rev. Stat. §§ 41–621.

32. E.g., Conn. Gen. Stat. Ann. §§ 7–465; Del. Code Ann. § 4001; Ind. Code Ann., chap. 16.7; Iowa Code Ann., chap. 25A.21; La. Rev. Stat. Ann. § 13:5108.1; N.M. Stat. Ann. § 41-4-4-C; N.H. Rev. Stat. Ann. § 81:106; and Tex. Civ. Stat. Ann. § 6252-26(1)(a)(2) (Vernon).

33. New York L. 1976, c. 832. (This provision was later repealed and replaced by a more comprehensive law covering all New York City employees, New York L. 1979, c. 673 (codified as N.Y. Gen. Munic. Law § 50-k).

34. *See New York Times*, December 21, 1975, at 25; *id.*, July 29, 1976, at 37.

35. N.Y. Gen. Munic. Law §§ 8-50-k(5).

36. South Dakota permits but does not require indemnity up to $10,000. S.D. Comp. Laws Ann. chap. 3-19-2. South Carolina has limits on the state's liability under its Motor Vehicle Tort Claims Act of $5,000 for property damage and $30,000 for injury [S.C. Code § 15-77-230(d)], although the state has authority to purchase liability insurance for its employees under a separate provision (*id.* at § 1-11-140).

37. *See*, e.g., Cal. Govt. Code § 825. Wisconsin allows a maximum recovery of $100,000 in tort actions against local governments and their employees and provides that employees be indemnified for any defense or liability costs. Wis. Stat. Ann. § 895.46. The claim limit presumably would not be applicable to a § 1983 claim.

38. *See*, e.g., Ann. Code of Md., Article 32A, § 12B. Some of the states

that have complete tort claims acts are: Oregon, Ore. Rev. Stat. §§ 30.260–300; Iowa, Ia. Code Ann., chap. 25A; and Kansas, Kan. Stat. Ann. §§ 75–6101 to 6116. Although these acts do not all follow the FTCA closely, they do have similar provisions. *See*, e.g., Ore. Rev. Stats. § 20.265(c); Kan. Stat. Ann. § 75-6104(d), providing "discretionary function" exceptions; and Ia. Code Ann. §§ 25A.14(1) and (4), which are almost identical in wording to 28 U.S.C. §§ 2680(a) and (h), respectively.

39. *See*, e.g., Cal. Govt. Code § 825.6.

40. E.g., Colo. Rev. Stat. § 24-10-110(1).

41. E.g., Idaho Code §§ 6–903(b) and (c).

42. E.g., Utah Code Ann. § 60-30-4.

43. E.g., *id.*

44. E.g., Ill. Rev. Stat., chap. 24, § 1-4-5.

45. E.g., N.M. Stat. Ann. § 41-44-B.

46. See discussion *infra* at 130.

47. Concerning statutory and negligent torts, see discussion of State of Maine v. Thiboutot and Parratt v. Taylor, respectively, in chap. 2.

48. Some state statutes prohibit revealing the availability of indemnity to the jury. *See*, e.g., Idaho Code, § 6-903(f). On the other hand, there are (necessarily anecdotal) accounts of judges who awarded sizable damages against federal employees under a mistaken impression that they would be reimbursed by their agencies. Interview with Dept. of Justice officials, *supra* note 20. As already noted, the Supreme Court's few remarks on the subject may have exaggerated the certainty of indemnification. *Supra* note 1.

49. *See* Bermann, *supra* note 2, at 1194.

50. See appendixes 1 and 2.

51. *See* discussion in Nixon v. Fitzgerald, 102 S. Ct. 2690 (1982). *But see* Eide v. Timberlake, 497 F. Supp. 1272 (D. Kans. 1981), in which even the availability of *absolute* immunity was the subject of an extensive evidentiary hearing and some four years of litigation.

52. *See* appendix 2. In Nixon v. Fitzgerald, *supra* note 51, the Court also conferred it on actions of the president.

53. In some cases, the line separating judicial or prosecutorial from executive activity is fine indeed. *See*, e.g., Safeguard Mutual Ins. Co. v. Miller, 456 F. Supp. 682 (E.D. Pa. 1978); Rheuark v. Shaw, 477 F. Supp. 897 (N.D. Tex. 1979).

54. 416 U.S. at 247 (1974).

55. Butz v. Economou, 438 U.S. 507 (1978).

56. *See*, e.g., *id.* at 494–95, 507–08.

57. Supreme Court of Virginia v. Consumers Union, 446 U.S. 719, 733 (1980). The rulemaker in that case was a court, but it might as easily have been an agency or executive official. The Court mentioned only two factors unique to the Viriginia case: the court's claim to "inherent" rulemaking authority, and its having exercised "the State's entire legislative power" as to the subject matter in question. *Id.* It is difficult to see why either factor should be relevant to the scope of immunity. *Cf.* Duchesne v. Sugarman, 566 F.2d 817 (2d Cir. 1977).

58. 386 U.S. at 553–55. The Court noted that the police officers in this case had not claimed an absolute immunity. *Id.* at 555.

59. 416 U.S. 245–46, 246 n.8. Moreover, in reviewing what it regarded as the immunity-relevant considerations—e.g., the need for prompt actions, the need to rely on factual information supplied by others, the situational ambiguity and complexity in which decisions must often be made—the Court implied that such officials require no less and usually greater protection than police officers. *Id.* at 245–47. Of course, it is possible that the Court had in mind a more flexible, multitiered system of immunity rules. No such system has been developed, however, and the uncertainty costs of one would surely be great.

60. 438 U.S. at 506–17, especially 511–12.

61. Nixon v. Fitzgerald, 102 S. Ct. 2690 (1982).

62. Harlow and Butterfield v. Fitzgerald, 102 S. Ct. 2727 (1982).

63. The Court's treatment of prosecutorial immunity adds little to the analysis, for its focuses almost entirely on the effect of the fear of "harassment by unfounded litigation." 438 U.S. at 512.

64. Bradley v. Fisher, 13 Wall, 335, 347–54 (1872). *See also* Stump v. Sparkman, 435 U.S. 349, 355, 364 (1978). Another possible argument not mentioned by the Court is the importance of finality in judicial decisions. But even if that interest were more significant for judicial than for executive decisionmaking, damage actions against judges could not affect the finality of any underlying decisions already rendered.

65. See chap. 3.

66. See part III.

67. Ironically, the Court notes, as an argument favoring absolute immunity for officials who initiate or adjudicate administrative actions against private parties, that when "millions may turn on regulatory decisions, there is a strong incentive to counter-attack." Butz v. Economou, 438 U.S. at 514–15. Yet this observation is at least as pertinent to executive immunity as to quasi-judicial immunity.

68. *Id.*, 438 U.S. at 495, 497 n.24, 507. By distinguishing Barr v. Matteo, 360 U.S. 564 (1959), on precisely this ground, the Court may have breathed new life into that much-criticized decision.

69. *Id.* at 503–04, 506–08.

70. *Id.* at 522–24 (Rehnquist, J., dissenting).

71. *See*, e.g., Burns v. Rovaldi, 477 F. Supp. 270 (D. Conn. 1979); Atcherson v. Siebenmann, 605 F.2d 1058 (8th Cir. 1979); Buckley v. City of Omaha, 605 F.2d 1078 (8th Cir. 1979); Fujiwara v. Clark, 477 F. Supp. 822 (D. Hawaii 1979); Harper v. Blumenthal, 478 F. Supp. 176 (D.D.C. 1979). In the context of an employment relationship in which improper political motivation is easy to allege and the interests of the public in an efficient governmental apparatus are significantly implicated, the weapon of a damage action against a supervisor who enjoys only a qualified immunity may further rigidify an already unresponsive system of public management. Other remedies for employer misconduct are not lacking. A somewhat novel approach was taken in the Civil Service Reform Act of 1978 (Pub. L. 95-454), which established the Office of Special Counsel to investigate and prosecute allegations of supervisory abuses within the civil service disciplinary structure. *See Hearings, supra* note 6 (testimony of Donald J. Devine, director, U.S. Office of Personnel Management).

72. 416 U.S. at 250.

73. For cases in which qualified immunity was granted only after trial, *see*, e.g., Ohland v. City of Montpelier, 467 F. Supp. 324 (D. Vt. 1979); Knell v. Bensinger, 522 F.2d 720 (7th Cir. 1975). The difficulty of obtaining a finding of good faith is illustrated by Paton v. Laprade, 471 F. Supp. 166 (D. N.J. 1979).

74. *See*, e.g., Eide v. Timberlake, 497 F. Supp. 1272 (D. Kans. 1981).

75. Scheuer v. Rhodes, 416 U.S. at 247. If by "varying scope" the Court meant that levels of immunity might be recognized in addition to those of "absolute" and "qualified," no court has explicitly taken that approach yet. But if the Court meant simply that the determination of whether the official acted in "good faith" would depend upon "all the circumstances," then its reference to "varying scope" was either redundant or infelicitous.

76. According to testimony by the chief federal personnel officer, *Bivens* actions often last five or six years, during which officials may be "unable to obtain an automobile loan or a home mortgage merely because of their status as defendants." Testimony of Donald J. Devine, *supra* part II, introduction, note 5 at 6. *See also Hearings, supra* note 6 (testimony of Robert Lehman, district ranger, Forest Service, U.S. Dept. of Argriculture); and U.S., Congress, House, Judiciary Committee, Subcommittee on Administrative Law and Governmental Relations, *Federal Tort Claims Act: Hearings on H.R. 24*, 97th Cong., 1st sess., November 5, 1981 (testimony of Peter H. Wallison, general counsel, U.S. Dept. of the Treasury).

77. E.g., Fujiwara v. Clark, 477 F. Supp. 794 (D. Hawaii 1978) and 477 F. Supp. 822 (D. Hawaii 1979).

78. Attorneys familiar with such litigation assert that "if you start with the good faith defense, you've lost." Interview with Paul Trause, deputy general counsel, and Lydia Parnes, attorney, Office of Personnel Management, July 17, 1980.

79. See subsection on indemnification, *supra*.

80. Scheuer v. Rhodes, 416 U.S. at 247.

81. *See* G. Calabresi and P. Bobbitt, *Tragic Choices* 57–64 (1978).

82. *See* O'Connor v. Donaldson, 422 U.S. 563, 577 (1975).

83. E.g., Duchesne v. Sugarman, 566 F.2d 817 (2d Cir. 1977); Negron v. Ward, 458 F. Supp. 748 (S.D.N.Y. 1978); Dellums v. Powell, 566 F.2d 167 (D.C. Cir. 1977).

84. The Supreme Court has not definitively settled the question (Harlow and Butterfield v. Fitzgerald, 102 S. Ct. 2727 (1982) at n. 24, but lower courts have so held. E.g., Tyrrell v. Speaker, 535 F.2d 823, 828 (3d Cir. 1976); United States v. Sieloff, 564 F.2d 153, 155 n.2 (3d Cir. 1977); McCray v. Burrell, 516 F.2d 357, 370 (4th Cir. 1975); Dellums v. Powell, 566 F.2d 167, 176 (D.C. Cir. 1977). *But see*, e.g., Cruz v. Beto, 603 F.2d 1178 (5th Cir. 1979); Kostka v. Hogg, 560 F.2d 37 (1st Cir. 1977). The factors mentioned by the Court in Gomez v. Toledo, 446 U.S. 635 (1980), that led to imposing the burden of pleading upon defendant (especially plaintiff's relative ignorance of the pertinent facts) are also relevant to the location of the burden of persuasion and suggest that the Court will ultimately resolve the latter question in the same way.

85. E.g., Cruz v. Beto, 603 F.2d 1178; United States v. Sieloff, 564 F.2d 153.

86. E.g., Eckerd v. Indian River School District, 475 F. Supp. 1350, 1368 (D. Del. 1979).

87. E.g., Fujiwara v. Clark, 477 F. Supp. 822, 837 (D. Hawaii 1979). *See* discussion in Harlow and Butterfield v. Fitzgerald, 102 S. Ct. 2727 (1982).

88. See discussion of Barr v. Matteo in chap. 2.

89. *See, e.g.,* Brill, "You Win but You Lose," *New York Times,* July 2, 1980, at A27, describing the writer's expenditure of $5,134.80 to obtain a threshold dismissal of a libel suit brought in the wrong jurisdiction and after the statute of limitations had expired.

90. Butz v. Economou, 438 U.S. at 507–08. Here as elsewhere in its descent down the slippery slope, the Court was forewarned. *Id.* at 527 (Rehnquist, J., concurring in part and dissenting in part).

91. E.g., Cass, "Damage Suits against Public Officers," 129 *U. Pa. L. Rev.* 1110, 1119–33 (1981); Casto, *supra* note 2, at 85–102; Note, "Developments in the Law: Section 1983 and Federalism," 90 *Harv. L. Rev.* 1133, 1211–17 (1977); Newman, *supra* note 2, at 459–62.

92. 102 S. Ct. 2727 (1982).

93. *But see* Crowe v. Lucas, 595 F.2d 985 (5th Cir. 1979), in which defendant, defeated by plaintiff in a contested election, ordered plaintiff's arrest in retaliation. Punitive damages were upheld. *See also* Dellums v. Powell, 566 F.2d 167; Redmond v. Baxley, 475 F. Supp. 1111 (E.D. Mich. 1979); Negron v. Ward, 458 F. Supp. 748.

94. Hutchinson v. Proxmire, 443 U.S. 111, 120 n.9 (1979).

95. 420 U.S. at 321, 322. *See also* Procunier v. Navarette, 434 U.S. 555, 562 (1978).

96. O'Connor v. Donaldson, 422 U.S. at 577.

97. E.g., Williams v. Treen, 671 F.2d 892 (5th Cir. 1982).

98. 420 U.S. at 321–22, 326. Here again, the Court had been forewarned. Four dissenting justices had predicted some of the difficulties that lay ahead, especially that of denying immunity for what would appear to be good faith ignorance of the law. *Id.* at 327–31 (Powell, J., concurring in part and dissenting in part).

99. *Id.* at 322–26.

100. Eckerd v. Indian River School District, 475 F. Supp. 1350, 1369–70 (D. Del. 1979).

101. *Id.* at 1369–70.

102. 397 U.S. 254 (1969).

103. *See, e.g.,* Mashaw, "Supreme Court's Due Process Calculation for Administrative Adjudication in *Matthews v. Eldridge* [96 S. Ct. 893]," 44 *U. Chi. L. Rev.* 28 (Fall 1976).

104. Youngsberg v. Romeo, 102 S. Ct. 2452 (1982).

105. For one formulation of this problem, *see* Malone, "Ruminations on Cause-in-Fact," 9 *Stan. L. Rev.* 60, 99 (1956).

106. Robbins v. California, 453 U.S. 420 (1981).

107. New York v. Belton, 453 U.S. 454, 101 S. Ct. 2860 (1981).

108. Kamisar, "Fourth Amendment Hatchback," *Washington Post,* October 15, 1981, at A29.

109. United States v. Ross, 102 S. Ct. 2157 (1982).

110. E.g., Greenhouse, "On Balance Defendants Still Gain New Rights,"

*New York Times,* June 22, 1980, at 8E; Barbash, "Police Confusion: Supreme Court Decisions Grow Harder to Interpret," *Washington Post,* July 21, 1980, at A1.

111. The recent dispute over the Reagan administration's response to lower court decisions (and a summary affirmance by the Supreme Court) upholding the denial by the IRS of tax-exempt status to segregationist private schools raises this question dramatically. *See* Greenhouse, "High Court to Rule on Tax Status of Racially Biased Schools," *New York Times,* April 20, 1982, at A1.

112. E.g., Freed, "Executive Official Immunity for Constitutional Violations: An Analysis and a Critique," 72 *N.W. U. L. Rev.* 526, 557 (1977); Casto, *supra* note 2, at 116–18; Schnapper, "Civil Rights Litigation after Monell," 79 *Colum. L. Rev.* 213, 247 (1979).

113. Harlow and Butterfield v. Fitzgerald, 102 S. Ct. 2727 (1982).

114. *Id.* at 2740 (Brennan, J., concurring). *See also* Hutchinson v. Proxmire, 443 U.S. 111 (1979).

115. Youngsberg v. Romeo, 102 S. Ct. 2452 at n.31 (1982).

116. See chap. 5.

117. E.g., O'Connor v. Donaldson, 422 U.S. 563 (1975).

118. E.g., Youngsberg v. Romeo, 102 S. Ct. 2452 (1982).

119. See introduction to part II, *supra.*

120. One study of a federal district court in California found that of 236 *Bivens* or § 1983 actions filed in 1975–76, plaintiffs obtained some success (which was defined to include nonmonetary relief) in fewer than 50. Eisenberg, "On Section 1983: Theoretical Foundations and an Empirical Study," 67 *Cornell L. Rev.* 483 (1982). In another study of a sample of § 1983 actions against police in the federal trial court in Connecticut, "serious doubts [were expressed] . . . about the efficacy of § 1983 suits against the police." Project, *supra* note 2 at 781, 782. This view is shared by other observers. E.g., Newman, *supra* note 2; Foote, "Tort Remedies for Police Violations of Individual Rights," 39 *Minn. L. Rev.* 293 (1955); Note, *"Damages Nothing"—The Efficacy of the Bivens-Type Remedy,* 64 *Cornell L. Rev.* 667, 694–95 (1979). Obviously, such studies cannot conclusively establish the extent to which valid claims were actually asserted by losing plaintiffs. Even if immunity is ultimately conferred, officials may remain liable for plaintiffs' attorney's fees. E.g., Entertainment Concepts, Inc. v. Maciejewski, 631 F.2d 497 (7th Cir. 1980), *cert. denied,* 450 U.S. 919 (1981).

121. E.g., Carey v. Piphus, 435 U.S. 247 (1978).

122. E.g., Newman, *supra* note 2.

123. See chap. 5.

124. *See Hearings, supra* note 6 (testimony of Donald J. Devine).

125. *See Hearings, supra* note 6 (testimony of William H. Webster) (cases involving informants).

## Chapter 5

1. For a lucid explanation of this concept in a legal setting, *see* Ackerman, "Introduction: On the Role of Economic Analysis of Property Law," in B. Ackerman, ed., *Economic Foundations of Property Law* (1975), at xi.

2. *See*, e.g., M. Lipsky, *Street-Level Bureaucrats* 184 (1980); G. Sykes, *Society of Captives* 61 (1958).

3. Schelling, "On the Ecology of Micromotives," 25 *The Public Interest* 61, 89 (1971).

4. See chap. 3, text at note 56.

5. *See* Furman v. Georgia, 408 U.S. 238, 249 (1972); *see also* Jaffe, "Suits against Governments and Officers: Damage Actions," 77 *Harv. L. Rev.* 209, 212 (1963), discussing Muskopf v. Corning Hospital District, 55 Cal. 2d 211, 216 (1961), in which Judge Traynor noted that with its many exceptions to liability, immunity "operates so illogically as to cause serious inequality."

6. *See* U.S., Congress, Senate, Judiciary Committee, Subcommittee on Agency Administration, *Federal Tort Claims Act: Hearings on S. 1775*, 97th Cong., 2d sess., March 31, 1982 (testimony of Donald J. Devine, director, U.S. Office of Personnel).

7. *But see id.*

8. For a discussion of the problems of analyzing the deterrent effects of public tort rules, *see* Schuck, "Suing Our Servants: The Court, Congress, and the Liability of Public Officials for Damages," 1980 *Sup. Ct. Rev.* 341–44 (1981).

9. Calabresi and Hirschoff, "Toward a Test for Strict Liability in Tort," 81 *Yale L. J.* 1055, 1060 (1972).

10. W. Prosser, *Handbook on the Law of Torts* 461–62 (1971). But note that even this is changing. *See*, e.g., Rodgers v. Kemper Construction Co., 50 Cal. App. 3d 608 (1975); Ira S. Bushey & Sons, Inc. v. U.S., 398 F.2d 167 (2d Cir. 1968).

11. *See* Stone, "The Place of Enterprise Liability in the Control of Corporate Conduct," 90 *Yale L. J.* 1, 2 n.8, 31 (1980).

12. *See*, e.g., McGowan, "Rule-Making and the Police," 70 *Mich. L. Rev.* 659 (1972); Amsterdam, "Perspectives on the Fourth Amendment," 58 *Minn. L. Rev.* 349 (1974).

13. See chaps. 3 and 4. A comparison between agencies and *courts* in this regard is made in chap. 7.

14. For case studies illustrating the point, *see*, e.g., J. Q. Wilson, ed., *The Politics of Regulation* (1980). See also sources cited in chap. 3, note 1.

15. For a partial list, *see* Schuck, "Suing Our Servants," *supra* note 8, at 281, 348, n.230. Oddly enough, the Supreme Court has seemed to regard the existence of these other sanctions as irrelevant to its remedial design specifications [*see*, e.g., Bevins v. Six Unknown Named Agents of the Federal Bureau of Narcotics, 403 U.S. 388, 397 (1961); Jaffe, *supra* note 5, at 209, 214], sometimes reasoning as if deterrence depended upon the damage remedy against individual officials. *See*, e.g., Carlson v. Green, 446 U.S. 14, 18–22 (1980).

16. See chap. 1.

17. *See*, e.g., Stone, *supra* note 11.

18. *See generally*, e.g., A. Wildavsky, *The Politics of the Budgetary Process* (1964).

19. *See* the Equal Access to Justice Act of 1980, 28 U.S.C. § 2412(c)(2), which provides that in cases of official bad faith, fee awards shall be paid by the agency itself.

20. 15 U.S.C. § 16.

21. Stone, *supra* note 11, at 48 n.180.

22. Compare National League of Cities v. Usery, 426 U.S. 833 (1976); and Federal Energy Regulatory Commission v. Mississippi, 102 S. Ct. 2126 (1982). *Usery*, of course, dealt with an exercise of the commerce power, whereas the measures discussed here, aimed at furthering the aims of § 1983, would allow Congress to exercise powers granted to it under § 5 of the Fourteenth Amendment, which provides a different basis for expanding the federal role relative to that of the states. Tenth Amendment concerns could possibly be allayed as well by making adoption of an indemnity scheme a condition for receipt of federal grants, rather than a direct requirement imposed on the states. Whether this would constitute sound policy is a different question.

23. See chap. 4.

24 The reluctance of carriers even before the *Monell* decision to offer such insurance was attributed to factors ranging from poor data on exposures and increased uncertainty because of changing legal doctrines to alleged manipulation of the market. In response, some cities had to adopt self-insurance plans or form risk-sharing pools. *See* National League of Cities, *The New World of Liability* (1978). This situation will surely be exacerbated as a result of *Thiboutot, Owen,* and *Parratt.* See chap. 2.

25. United States v. Gilman, 347 U.S. 507 (1954). But *Gilman* did not prevent the United States from recovering as an "insured" under its employee's own auto liability insurance policy; the Court stressed that it was simply interpreting the policy, not ordering indemnity. Government Employers Ins. Co. v. United States, 349 F.2d 83 (10th Cir.), *cert. denied,* 382 U.S. 1026 (1966).

26. *See* Stone, *supra* note 11, at 57.

27. *The Nichomachean Ethics* (trans. W. D. Ross, 1915) at 1132a. At least one modern scholar, pressing the private law analogy to its (illogical) extreme and grounding it in the just compensation clause, would regard this principle as *constitutionally required,* at least prima facie. Richard Epstein, "Eminent Domain: An Interpretivist Approach," lecture delivered at Yale Law School, April 9, 1982.

28 See chap. 2 and appendix 2.

29. *See,* e.g., G. Calabresi, *The Costs of Accidents* (1970); Calabresi and Hirschoff, *supra* note 9.

30. *See* Calabresi, *supra* note 29, at 43–47.

31. 28 U.S.C. § 2680(a).

32. H.R. Rep. No. 1278, 79th Cong. 1st sess. 5–6 (1945).

33. *See,* e.g., the Administrative Procedure Act, 5 U.S.C. § 706(2)(A); Citizens to Preserve Overton Park, Inc. v. Volpe, 401 U.S. 402 (1971); First Girl, Inc. v. Regional Manpower Adm., 499 F.2d 122 (7th Cir. 1974); Overseas Media Corp. v. McNamara, 385 F.2d 308 (D.C. Cir. 1967).

34. Dalehite v. United States, 346 U.S. 15 (1953).

35. *See,* e.g., American Assn. of Commodity Traders v. Dept. of Treasury, 598 F.2d 1233, 1235 (1st Cir. 1979); Wright v. United States, 568 F.2d 53 (10th Cir., 1977).

36. *See,* e.g., *Hearings, supra* note 6; Bell, "Proposed Amendments to the

Federal Tort Claims Act," 16 *Harv. J. on Legis.* 1 (1978).

37. *See* 28 U.S.C. §§ 2674 and 1346(b). E.g., United States v. Muniz, 374 U.S. 150, 153 (1963).

38. Derbin Lumber & Supply Corp. v. United States, 488 F.2d 88 (4th Cir. 1973); Davis v. United States, 395 F. Supp. 793 (D. Neb.), *aff'd*, 536 F.2d 758 (5th Cir. 1976).

39. Some courts, in order to preserve constitutional tort claims, have felt obliged to contrive tortuous state tort law analogies. *See,* e.g., Birnbaum v. United States, 588 F.2d 319, 329 (2d Cir. 1978); Myers & Myers, Inc. v. U.S. Postal Service, 527 F.2d 1252 (2d Cir. 1975).

40. *See,* e.g., Carlson v. Green, 446 U.S. 14, 23 (1980).

41. *See* discussion of *Bivens* and its progeny in chap. 2.

42. 28 U.S.C. §§ 1346(b) and 2672.

43. Laird v. Nelms, 406 U.S. 797 (1972).

44. For earlier discussions of this question, *see* Peck, "Absolute Liability and the Federal Tort Claims Act," 9 *Stan. L. Rev.* 433 (1957); Jacoby, "Absolute Liability under the Federal Tort Claims Act," 24 *Fed. B. J.* 139 (1964); Abend, "Federal Liability for Takings and Torts," 31 *Fordham L. Rev.* 481 (1963). For post-*Nelms* criticism, see Note, *Utility, Fairness, and the Takings Clause: Three Perspectives on* Laird v. Nelms, 59 *Va. L. Rev.* 1034 (1973); Peck, "*Laird* v. *Nelms:* A Call for Review and Revision of the Federal Tort Claims Act," 48 *Wash. L. Rev.* 391 (1973); Reynolds, "Strict Liability under the Federal Tort Claims Act: Does "Wrongful" Cover a Few Sins, No Sins, or Non-Sins?" *Am. U.L. Rev.* 813 (1974).

45. See discussion in chap. 2.

46. 28 U.S.C. § 2680(h); Pub. L. 93-253, § 2;88 Stat. 50, March 16, 1974.

47. *See,* e.g., Reynolds v. United States, 643 F.2d 707, 711–13 (10th Cir.), *cert. denied,* 102 S. Ct. 94 (1981), and cases there cited.

48. *See,* e.g., Boger, Gitenstein, and Verkuil, "The Federal Tort Claims Act Intentional Torts Amendment: An Interpretative Analysis," 54 *N.C.L. Rev.* 497 (1976).

49. E.g., Herrera v. Valentine, 653 F.2d 1220 (8th Cir. 1981); Thompson v. New York, 487 F. Supp. 212 (N.D.N.Y. 1979).

50. E.g., Fitch v. United States, 513 F.2d 1013 (6th Cir. 1975); Rey v. United States, 484 F.2d 45 (5th Cir. 1973).

51. Norton v. United States, 581 F.2d 390 (4th Cir. 1978).

52. For criticism of *Norton, see* Comment, *FTCA: Liability of U.S. for Torts Committed in Good Faith by Federal Law Enforcement Officers,* 63 *Minn. L. Rev.* 1293 (1979).

53. *See,* e.g., Carey v. Piphus, 435 U.S. 247 (1978).

54. *See* Calabresi and Melamed, "Property Rules, Liability Rules, and Inalienability: One View of the Cathedral," 85 *Harv. L. Rev.* 1089 (1972).

55. G. Calabresi and P. Bobbitt, *Tragic Choices* 32 (1978). For another discussion of this issue, *see* O. Fiss, *The Civil Rights Injunctions* 75–76 (1978).

56. E.g., 18 U.S.C. § 2520, 15 U.S.C. § 1640(a). For one proposal along these lines, see Comment, *Presumed Damages for Fourth Amendment Violations,* 129 *U. Pa. L. Rev.* 192 (1980).

57. Congress has considered such a reform in the past but has not enacted it. E.g., S.1775, 97th Cong., § 3 (1981); H.R. 2659, 96th Cong. (1980); S.2117, 95th Cong. (1978).

58. *See* Wilderness Society v. Morton, 495 F.2d 1026, 1031–32 (D.C. Cir. 1974), *rev'd* in Alyeska Pipeline Co. v. Wilderness Society, 421 U.S. 240 (1975).

59. 28 U.S.C. § 2678.

60. There are several different formulations of this category of litigants in attorney's fee provisions. *See* discussion in Alyeska Pipeline Co. v. Wilderness Society, 421 U.S. 240, 261–62 (1975); Grumman Corp. v. LTV Corp., 533 F. Supp. 1385, 1387 (E.D.N.Y. 1982).

61. 42 U.S.C. § 1988.

62. For a partial listing as of 1975, *see* Alyeska Pipeline Co. v. Wilderness Society, 421 U.S. 240, 260 n.33 (1975).

63. *See* Equal Access to Justice Act of 1980, 28 U.S.C. § 2412(b)(d), Pub. L. 96-481, 94 Stat. 2327, October 21, 1980. The act precludes such awards if the government's position was "substantially justified or . . . special circumstances make an award unjust." It also contains yet another express prohibition against such awards in tort cases against the United States. The first case under the 1980 law denied an award to a taxpayer even though he had prevailed against the IRS. Alspach v. Div. of Internal Revenue, 527 F. Supp. 225 (D. Md. 1981). The Dept. of Justice takes the position that this prohibition applies to *Bivens*-type actions as well. Telephone interview with Barbara O'Malley, special counsel, March 26, 1982. In such actions, however, the United States apparently may recover *its* costs of representing the defendant-official where the plaintiff sued in bad faith. Moon v. Smith, 523 F. Supp. 1332 (E.D. Va. 1981).

64. 28 U.S.C. § 2678.

65. *See* empirical study described in W. Wright, *The Federal Tort Claims Act* 138 (1957).

66. 28 U.S.C. § 2674. *See* Note, *Interest in Judgments against the Federal Government: The Need for Full Compensation,"* 91 *Yale L. J.* 297 (1981).

67. *See*, e.g., Holly v. Chasen, in which the government took a case to the D.C. Circuit twice: first, on the issue of whether a *pro se* litigant under the Freedom of Information Act is entitled to attorney's fees, 71 F.R.D. 115 (D.D.C. 1976), *aff'd*, 569 F.2d 160 (D.C. Cir. 1977); and second, when those attorney's fees were allowed but were not paid for more than a year and a half, on the issue of whether the litigant was entitled to interest on them for the intervening period. The amounts in controversy on those appeals were, respectively, $620 and $70.

68. *See* Calabresi, "Product Liability: Curse or Bulwark of the Free Enterprise System?" 27 *Clev. St. L. Rev.* 313 (1978).

69. E.g., 18 U.S.C. § 2520 (illegal wiretapping).

70. 28 U.S.C. § 2674. *See also* Carlson v. Green, 446 U.S. 14, 22 (1980).

71. 440 U.S. 332 (1979).

72. For an extended development of this argument, *see* concurring opinion of Brennan, J., in Quern v. Jordan, 440 U.S. at 349–66. For a state case interpreting *Quern* to preclude § 1983 coverage of states even where they have waived their Eleventh Amendment immunity, *see* State v. Green, 633 P.2d 1381, 1382 (Ala. 1981).

73. *See* B. Bittker, *The Case for Black Reparations*, chap. 5 (1973).

74. Fitzpatrick v. Bitzer, 427 U.S. 445, 455 (1976); Hutto v. Finney, 437 U.S. 678, 693–94 (1978). *See also* Field, "The Eleventh Amendment and

Other Sovereign Immunity Doctrines: Congressional Imposition of Suits upon the States," 126 *U. Pa. L. Rev.* 1203 (1978); Schnapper, "Civil Rights Litigation after *Monell,*" 79 *Colum. L. Rev.* 213, 254 n.222 (1979); Frug, "The Judicial Power of the Purse," 126 *U. Pa. L. Rev.* 715, 784–87 (1978). Another, more indirect approach would be for Congress to condition states' participation in federal grant-in-aid programs on their willingness to waive their Eleventh Amendment immunity. *See* concurring opinion of Stevens, J., in Florida Dept. of Health v. Florida Nursing Home Assn., 450 U.S. 147, 151 (1981).

75. See appendix 2. An example of the anomalies that the current system creates is that social service agencies performing identical functions are liable for damages or immune from suit, depending upon whether they are established at the county or state level. This varies from state to state.

76. *See* chap. 4.

77. E.g., Polk County v. Dodson, 102 S. Ct. 445, 453 (1981).

78. *Id.;* Owen v. City of Independence, 445 U.S. 622, 655 (1980).

79. 423 U.S. 362 (1976).

80. 436 U.S. at 694 n. 58. For a view more sympathetic to *respondeat superior* liability under § 1983, *see* Carter v. Carlson, 447 F. 2d 358 (D.C. Cir. 1971), *rev'd* on other grounds *sub nom.*, District of Columbia v. Carter, 409 U.S. 418 (1973).

81. *Id.* at 694, 701 n.66, 713. *See* opinion of Mr. Justice Stevens concurring in part. *Id.* at 714.

82. *See* Schnapper, *supra* note 74, at 215–16.

83. 436 U.S. at 693–94 and 692 n. 57.

84. *Id.* at 692 n. 57. For other critiques of the Court's treatment of the *respondeat superior* issue in *Monell, see,* e.g., Schnapper, *supra* note 74, at 215–40; Note, *Section 1983 Municipal Liability and the Doctrine of Respondeat Superior,* 46 *U. Chi. L. Rev.* 935 (1979). Given the weakness of the Court's decision, it is perhaps to be expected that lower courts would grow restive under it. *See,* e.g., Rhodes v. City of Wichita, 516 F. Supp. 501, 502 (D. Kans. 1981), which eliminates the remaining restrictions upon municipal liability by grafting a *Bivens* theory onto Fourteenth Amendment and § 1983 claims. On the other hand, some courts have gone so far as to deny *respondeat superior* liability under § 1983 even when the employer is a *private corporation. See* Powell v. Shopco Laurel Co., 678 F.2d 504 (4th Cir. 1982).

85. *See* Monell v. Dept. of Social Services of City of New York, 436 U.S. 658 (1978); and Owen v. City of Independence, 445 U.S. 622 (1980).

86. State of Maine v. Thiboutot, 448 U.S. 1 (1980).

87. City of Newport v. Fact Concerts, Inc., 453 U.S. 247 (1981).

88. See chap. 4.

89. For one recent case upholding such a procedure, *see* Pennsylvania v. Porter, 659 F.2d 306, 313–19. (3d Cir. 1981) (*en banc*). Compare, United States v. City of Philadelphia 644 F.2d 187 (3rd Cir. 1980). For a somewhat analogous provision, see the Institutionalized Persons Act of 1980, 42 U.S.C. § 1997; Pub. L. 96–247, 94 Stat. 349, May 23, 1980, which authorizes the Dept. of Justice to seek equitable relief, but not damages, on behalf of institutionalized persons from violations of § 1983.

## Part III Introduction

1. *See*, e.g., Graetz, "Assessing the Distributional Effects of Income Tax Revision," 4 *J. Legal Stud.* 351 (1975); Schuck, "The Politics of Regulation," 90 *Yale L. J.* 702, 720 (1981).
2. See chap. 1.

## Chapter 6

1. E.g., G. Sykes, *The Society of Captives* (1958).
2. E.g., Weatherley and Lipsky, "Street-Level Bureaucrats and Institutional Innovation: Implementing Special-Education Reform," 47 *Harv. Educ. Rev.* 171, 192–93 (1977).
3. *See*, e.g., Clark and Wilson, "Incentive Systems: A Theory of Organizations," 6 *Adm. Sci. Q.* 219 (September 1961).
4. Weatherley and Lipsky, *supra* note 2, at 172–73. See also sources cited in introduction, notes 15 and 16.
5. *See*, e.g., D. Mazmanian and J. Nienaber, *Can Organizations Change? Environmental Protection, Citizen Participation, and the Corps of Engineers* (1979); Wilson, "The Changing FBI—The Road to Abscam," 59 *The Public Interest* 3 (Spring 1980).
6. C. Barnard, *The Functions of the Executive* 167–69 (1946). This concept is similar to my notion of a "duty threshold," discussed in chap. 3.
7. Elmore, "Organizational Models of Social Program Implementation," 26 *Public Policy* 185 (1978).
8. *Id.* at 207.
9. *Id.* at 215.
10. *See* D. Yates, *Bureaucratic Democracy: The Search for Democracy and Efficiency in American Government*, chaps. 3, 6 (1982).
11. Wilson, *supra* note 5. *See also* Wilson, *The Investigators* (1978).
12. M. Derthick and P. Quirk, *The Politics of Deregulation* (forthcoming).
13. Mazmanian and Nienaber, *supra* note 5.
14. J. Mashaw, *Bureaucratic Justice* (1983).
15. Yates, *supra* note 10.
16. E.g., Handler, "Controlling Official Behavior in Welfare Administration," in J. ten Broeck, ed., *The Law of the Poor* 155, 179 (1966).
17. For a general discussion of the principal variables affecting implementation of statutory changes, *see* Sabatier and Mazmanian, "The Implementation of Public Policy: A Framework of Analysis," 1980 *Pol'y. Stud. J.* 538 (1980). For a similar discussion with regard to regulatory changes, *see* P. Schuck, "Regulation: Asking The Right Questions" (Washington, D.C.: American Enterprise Institute, 1979). See also sources cited *supra* chap. 1, note 1.
18. *See*, e.g., discussion of the Senate Antitrust and Monopoly Subcommittee's inaction after six years of hearings on industrial concentration, in P. Schuck, *The Judiciary Committees* 72 (1975).
19. E.g., R. Bauer, I. Pool, and L. Dexter, *American Business and Public Policy* (2d ed., 1972).

20. *See,* e.g., Schuck, "The Graying of Civil Rights Law: The Age Discrimination Act of 1975," 89 *Yale L. J.* 27 (1979); B. Ackerman and W. Hassler, *Clean Coal/Dirty Air,* chap. 1 (1981).

21. M. Lipsky, *Street-Level Bureaucrats* 85–86 (1980).

22. Borus, "Deinstitutionalization of the Chronically Mentally Ill," 305 *New Eng. J. Med.* 339 (August 6, 1981).

23. E.g., the Legal Services Corporation. Federal employers may choose from among the top three eligible candidates for a position. 5 U.S.C. § 3317.

24. W. Lippmann, *A Preface to Morals* 264–65 (1929).

25. 20 U.S.C. § 1601.

26. A. Bickel, *The Least Dangerous Branch: The Supreme Court at the Bar of Public Opinion* 29 (1962).

27. *Id.* at 30–31.

28. General Electric Company v. Gilbert, 429 U.S. 125 (1976).

29. U.S. v. Nixon, 418 U.S. 683 (1974); Shabacoff, "President Bows: But St. Clair Indicates There May Be Delay in Yielding Data," *New York Times,* July 25, 1974, at 1.

30. Dames & Moore v. Regan, 453 U.S. 654, 101 S. Ct. 2972 (1981).

31. The amount of literature on the nature and sources of political influence is enormous. *See,* e.g., E. Banfield, *Political Influence* (1961); J. Q. Wilson, *Political Organizations* (1974); R. Dahl, *Who Governs?* (1961).

32. *See,* e.g., D. Mayhew, *Congress: The Electoral Connection* (1974); M. Fiorina, *Congress: Keystone of the Washington Establishment* (1977); J. Buchanan and G. Tullock, *The Calculus of Consent* (1965).

33. *See* J. Q. Wilson, ed., *The Politics of Regulation* (1980); Schuck, "The Politics of Regulation," 90 *Yale L. J.* 702 (1980) (reviewing *The Politics of Regulation*).

34. For a summary of this research, *see* N. Milner, *The Court and Local Law Enforcement: The Impact of* Miranda 19–21 (1971).

35. J. Q. Wilson, *Varieties of Police Behavior,* chaps, 6, 8 (1968). *But see* Friedrich, "Police Use of Force," 452 *Annals* 82, 92 (1980).

36. Milner, *The Court and Local Law Enforcement,* at 204–05, 206 n.7, 219–20.

37. E.g., B. Ehrenreich and J. Ehrenreich, *The American Health Empire: Power, Profits, and Politics,* chap. 18 (1970); H. Levy and D. Miller, *Going to Jail: The Political Prisoner* (1970).

38. Sherman, "Perspectives on Police and Violence," 452 *Annals* 1, 9–10 (1980). *See also* Reiss, "Controlling Police Use of Deadly Force," 452 *Annals* 122, 126 (1980) (citing the New York City study and one conducted in Los Angeles and confirming the findings in three others). These findings were brought to my attention by Russell Hanlon, Yale Law School, class of 1982.

39. *See,* e.g., W. Muir, *Prayer in the Public Schools: Law and Attitude Change* (1967).

40. *See* Buder, "More Officers Are Turning in Colleagues Believed Corrupt," *New York Times,* April 11, 1982, at 43.

41. E.g., Wilson, *Supra* note 35 at 148, 285–88; J. Skolnick, *Justice without Trial: Law Enforcement in Democratic Society* 245 (1966); P. Chevigny, *Police Power,* 219, 248 (1969).

42. Ralph Nader is an example. *See* C. McCarry, *Citizen Nader* (1972);

Schuck, "The Nader Chronicles," 50 *Tex. L. Rev.* 1455 (1972) (reviewing books about Nader).

43. *See* Carlson v. Green, 446 U.S. 14, 21 n.8 (1980), citing Attorney General Griffin Bell's testimony to that effect in 1978.

44. See chap. 1.

45. *See*, e.g., U.S., Congress, House, Judiciary Committee, Subcommittee on Administrative Law and Governmental Relations, *Federal Tort Claims Act: Hearings on H.R. 24*, 97th Cong., 1st sess., November 5, 1981 (testimony of Burt Neuborne, professor, New York University School of Law).

46. On the history of and experience under these boards, see J. Hudson, "Police Review Boards and Police Accountability," 36 *Law & Contemp. Probs.* 515 (1971); Note, *Grievance Response Mechanisms for Police Misconduct*, 55 *Va. L. Rev.* 909 (1969); Note, *Reviewing Civilian Complaints of Police Misconduct*, 48 *Temp. L. Q.* 89 (1974); Brent, "Redress of Alleged Police Misconduct," 11 *U.S.F.L. Rev.* 587 (1977).

47. Note, *Grievance Response*, *supra* note 46, at 943.

48. Sheppard, "New Police Complaint Unit in Chicago Quits in Quarrel," *New York Times*, December 22, 1980, at A16.

49. Interview with Phillip Michael, first deputy commissioner, New York City Dept. of Investigation, July 16, 1980.

50. *See* 5 U.S.C. §§ 1204–08. The types of misbehavior that this office can prosecute are narrowly specified and include (1) "prohibited personnel practices" (primarily relating to impermissible grounds for taking action against an employee); (2) actions taken against employees who disclose information on official wrongdoing or mismanagement ("whistleblowers"); and (3) unlawful political activity by public employees.

51. *Supra* note 49.

52. *See* Pub. L. 94-305, 90 Stat. 668 (1976). Telephone conversation with David Voight, deputy chief counsel for advocacy, Small Business Administration, August 4, 1980.

53. Interviews on July 17, 1980, with James Lauer, assistant counsel, Subcommittee on Administrative Law and Governmental Relations, House Judiciary Committee; and Michael Dolan, deputy assistant attorney general, Office of Legislative Liaison, U.S. Dept. of Justice.

54. E.g., U.S., Congress, House, Judiciary Committee, *Hearings on Amendments to the Federal Tort Claims Act*, 96th Cong., 1st sess. (1979), at 45 (testimony of ACLU). *See also* Kaplan, "The Limits of the Exclusionary Rule," 26 *Stan. L. Rev.* 1027, 1050 (1974); Project, "Suing the Police in Federal Court," 88 *Yale L. J.* 781, 810–13 (1978).

55. A similar scheme, limited to constitutional torts, was included in proposed legislation (H.R. 2659) during the 96th Congress to bring *Bivens* actions under the FTCA by substituting the United States as defendant.

56. See chap. 5.

57. U.S., *Constitution*, Article VI.

58. *See* H. Kaufman, *The Forest Rangers* (1960); *see also* J. Q. Wilson, *The Investigators* 166–82 (1978).

59. For an empirical study of this mix and the reasons for its suboptimality in a very different bureaucratic context, see Schuck, "When the Exception Becomes the Rule: Regulatory Exceptions and the Formulation of Energy

Policy" (*Report to the Administrative Conference of the United States*, forthcoming).

60. Perhaps the fullest elaborations of this position may be found in K. Davis, *Discretionary Justice* (1970); and Amsterdam, "Perspectives on the Fourth Amendment," 58 *Minn. L. Rev.* 349, 414–29 (1974).

61. 28 C.F.R. § 59.

62. Buder, "High Police Official Loses Command Post," *New York Times*, November 1, 1980, at A1.

63. J. Fyfe, *Shots Fired: An Examination of N.Y.C. Police Firearms Discharges* (Univ. Microfilms Internatl. 1978).

64. *See* Bulletin no. 30, "Standards for the Removal and Return of Children by the Connecticut Department of Children and Youth Services," issued December 13, 1980.

65. *See,* e.g., Salinas v. Breier, 517 F. Supp. 1272, 1276–77 (E.D. Wis. 1981), and cases there cited.

66. Amsterdam's proposed linkage of police rulemaking to the operation of the exclusionary rule is an elaboration of this notion. *Supra* note 60, at 416.

67. *See,* e.g., United States v. Caceres, 440 U.S. 741 (1979).

68. Payton v. United States, 636 F.2d 132, 139–42 (5th Cir. 1981).

69. *See* A. Downs, *Inside Bureaucracy,* chap. 13 (1967).

70. P. Blau, *The Dynamics of Bureaucracy,* chap. 3 (rev. ed., 1963).

71. For a general discussion of these and other social changes encouraging challenges to official wrongdoing, *see,* e.g., Schuck, "The Politics of Regulation," *supra* note 33, at 714–15 (1981), and sources there cited.

72. *See* "Civil Service Reform Act Bringing a Rise in Dismissals," *New York Times*, November 12, 1980, at A1. Perhaps the most prominent example of a state-level public advocate is New Jersey's Office of the Public Advocate, § 52:27E-1, N.J. Stat. Ann. (West, 1980 Supp.).

## Chapter 7

1. Calabresi and Hirschoff, "Toward a Test for Strict Liability in Tort," 81 *Yale L. J.* 1055, 1060 (1972).

2. O. Fiss, *The Civil Rights Injunction* 75–80 (1978).

3. Until the amount-in-controversy requirement for federal question jurisdiction was abolished in 1976, Pub. L. 94–574, 90 Stat. 2721, the federal courts were often obliged to value, at least for this limited purpose, such rights. *See generally,* Note, *A Federal Question Question: Does Priceless Mean Worthless?* 14 *St. Louis U. L. J.* 268 (1969).

4. E.g., O'Shea v. Littleton, 414 U.S. 488 (1974); Stump v. Sparkman, 435 U.S. 349 (1978).

5. *See,* e.g., Rizzo v. Goode, 423 U.S. 362, 383 (1976) (Blackmun, J., dissenting).

6. *See,* e.g., Holmes v. N.Y.C. Housing Authority, 398 F.2d 262 (2d Cir. 1968).

7. E.g., Gautreaux v. Chicago Housing Authority, 342 F. Supp. 827, *aff'd,* 480 F.2d 210, *cert. denied,* 414 U.S. 1144 (1974).

8. *See*, e.g., paragraph 34 of decree in Wyatt v. Stickney, 344 F. Supp. 387, 403 (M.D. Ala. 1972).

9. *See generally* O. Fiss, *Injunctions* (1972).

10. E.g., Chayes, "The Role of the Judge in Public Law Litigation," 89 *Harv. L. Rev.* 1281 (1976); Special Project, *The Remedial Process in Institutional Reform Litigation*, 78 *Colum. L. Rev.* 784 (1978); Fiss, "The Forms of Justice," 93 *Harv. L. Rev.* 1 (1979); Eisenberg and Yeazell, "The Ordinary and the Extraordinary in Institutional Litigation," 93 *Harv. L. Rev.* 465 (1980), and sources cited at nn. 1 and 2; Diver, "The Judge as Political Powerbroker: Superintending Structural Change in Public Institutions," 65 *Va. L. Rev.* 43 (1979); symposium issue at 32 *Ala. L. Rev.* (1981); D. Horowitz, *The Courts and Social Policy* (1977), especially chap. 4; Frug, "The Judicial Power of the Purse," 126 *U. Pa. L. Rev.* 715 (1978); Nagel, "Separation of Powers and the Scope of Federal Equitable Remedies," 30 *Stan. L. Rev.* 661 (1978); Mishkin, "Federal Courts as State Reformers," 35 *Wash. & Lee L. Rev.* 949 (1978); Cox, "The New Dimension of Constitutional Adjudication," 51 *Wash. L. Rev.* 791 (1976).

11. Eisenberg and Yeazell, "The Ordinary and Extraordinary in Institutional Litigation," 93 *Harv. L. Rev.* 1281 (1976).

12. For example, the federal judge who authored some of the earliest and most controversial of these orders contends that they are "not new" but rather are "conventional judicial tools" used "in an unconventional setting." Johnson, "The Role of the Federal Courts in Institutional Litigation," 32 *Ala. L. Rev.* 271, 274–75 (1981).

13. For a detailed analysis of one court's hapless efforts to do so, *see* Horowitz, *supra* note 10, at chap. 4.

14. *See*, e.g., Diver, *supra* note 10.

15. I am indebted to Geoffrey Hazard for suggesting this point.

16. *See generally* Frug, *supra* note 10; Nagel, *supra* note 10.

17. *See* Mishkin, *supra* note 10. Eisenberg and Yeazell, it must be said, are singularly unimpressed by these constitutional tensions, viewing them as little more than vestigial reminders of quaint "historical circumstances" that no longer exist. They doubt whether these concerns are "realistic" and only reluctantly agree to "treat them seriously." *Supra* note 10, at 495.

18. E.g., sources cited *supra* note 10.

19. *See*, e.g., Pennhurst State School and Hosp. v. Halderman, 453 U.S. 1 (1981).

20. Fiss, *supra* note 2, at 92.

21. *Id.* at 35–44.

22. For one long-term effort, *see* "Longitudinal Study of Court-Ordered Deinstitutionalization of Pennhurst," prepared by Human Services Research Institute for Dept. of Health and Human Services under Contract no. 130-81-0021. On the effects of the school desegregation and busing orders, *see*, e.g., "School Desegregation: Lessons of the First Twenty-Five Years," 42 *Law & Contemp. Probs.*, pt. 1 (1978); G. Orfield, *Must We Bus? Segregated Schools and National Policy* (1978). Other studies, such as those of the school prayer decision—e.g., W. Muir, *Prayer in the Public Schools: Law and Attitude Change* (1967); K. Dolbeare and P. Hammond, *The School Prayer Decisions: From Court Policy to Local Practice* (1971); and Milner's study of the *Miranda*

decision, *The Court and Local Law Enforcement: The Impact of* Miranda (1971)—tend to focus upon rulings that narrowly proscribe a particular practice. Even those studies are largely confined to Supreme Court decisions, which may well be *sui generis;* systemic studies of how lower court decrees are implemented are virtually nonexistent. Another methodological problem is that those few studies tend to define judicial impact as "compliance" or "noncompliance"; broader second and third-order consequences, which are inevitable with structural orders, are generally ignored. *See* Horowitz, *supra* note 10, at 287.

23. *See,* e.g., Note, *The* Wyatt *Case: Implementation of a Judicial Decree Ordering Institutional Change,* 84 *Yale L. J.* 1338, 1352–60 (1975); Drake, "Judicial Implementation and *Wyatt v. Stickney,*" 32 *Ala. L. Rev.* 299, 307 (1981); other sources cited at M. McLaughlin, "The Courts and Social Change" (discussion draft, RAND Corporation, March 1981), at notes 1–4a; Note, *Mastering Intervention in Prisons,* 88 *Yale L. J.* 1062, 1073 (1979); Cox, *supra* note 10, at 827–28.

24. A favorable judgment may be found in M. Rebell and A. Block, *Educational Policymaking and the Courts: An Empirical Study of Judicial Activism* (1982), chap. 10. For a discussion of claimed success in a quasi-structural setting, see Harris, "The Title VII Administrator: A Case Study in Judicial Flexibility," 60 *Cornell L. Rev.* 53 (1974).

25. Note, *Implementation Problems in Institutional Reform Litigation,* 91 *Harv. L. Rev.* 428, 431 (1977).

26. Harris and Spiller, *After Decision: Implementation of Judicial Decrees in Correctional Settings* (1977), at 21–29.

27. E.g., Bell, "The Dialectics of School Desegregation," 32 *Ala. L. Rev.* 281, 295–96 (1981); Rebell and Block, *supra* note 24; Kalodner and Fishman, eds., *Limits of Justice: The Courts' Role in School Desegregation* (1978).

28. Chayes, *supra* note 10, at 1309.

29. Eisenberg and Yeazell, *supra* note 10, at 517.

30. Fiss, *supra* note 10, at 54–55.

31. *Id.* at 57–58.

32. *Id.* at 17. Later in the same article, Fiss acknowledges that the demands of structural cases transform the role of the judge. *Id.* at 50–57.

33. Chayes, *supra* note 10, at 1309.

34. *Supra* note 12, at 274.

35. *See,* e.g., Fiss, *supra* note 10, at 5–17.

36. Chayes, *supra* note 10, at 1296.

37. Horowitz, *supra* note 10, Horowitz, at 45. This dichotomy owes much to Davis's distinction between "legislative" and "adjudicative" facts. K. Davis, *Administrative Law Treatise* § 7.02 (1958) and § 12.8 (1982 Supp.).

38. Increasingly, exceptions are occurring even in the private law context, as in certain product liability litigation. E.g., Sindell v. Abbott Laboratories, 26 Cal. 3d 588, 607 P.2d 924 (1980).

39. E.g., Columbus Board of Educ. v. Penick, 443 U.S. 449 (1979).

40. *See,* e.g., *supra* note 10, at 45–56; Baum, "The Influence of Legislatures and Appellate Courts over the Policy Implementation Process," 8 *Pol'y Stud. J.* 560, 563–65 (1978).

41. *See,* e.g., Altman, "Implementing A Civil Rights Injunction: A Case

Study of *NAACP v. Brennan,*" 78 *Colum. L. Rev.* 739, 752–56 (1978); Note, *The* Wyatt *Case, supra* note 23, at 1370–71; Note, *Mastering Intervention, supra* note 23, at 1080–81.

42. See, e.g., Horowitz, "The Judiciary: Umpire or Empire?" 6 *J. Law & Human Behav.* 129 (1982).

43. *See* Horowitz, *supra* note 10, at 276.

44. *Id.* at chaps. 4, 5.

45. Mishkin, *supra* note 10, at 966. *See also* Glazer, "Should Judges Administer Social Services?" 50 *The Public Interest* 64, 78–79 (Winter 1978), which distinguishes between practical and theoretical knowledge in this context.

46. In devising a test for strict liability in private tort law that differs from the more intrusive "Learned Hand test" for negligence, Calabresi and Hirschoff have addressed just this problem. *Supra* note 1, at 1074–76.

47. *See generally* B. Ackerman et al., *The Uncertain Search for Environmental Quality* (1974). *But cf.* Weinberger v. Romero-Barcelo, 102 S. Ct. 1798 (1982).

48. Chayes, *supra* note 10, at 1307–08.

49. Fiss, *supra* note 10, at 14.

50. For a development of this point in the context of educational reform cases, *see* Rebell and Block, *supra* note 24.

51. E.g., Note, *The* Wyatt *Case, supra* note 23; Note, *Mastering Intervention, supra* note 23; Harris, *supra* note 24; Berger, "Away from the Court House and into the Field: The Odyssey of a Special Master," 78 *Colum. L. Rev.* 707 (1978).

52. In one school desegregation case, for example, the master proposed a housing reform so bold that the court rejected it and deprived the master of much further influence. Berger, *id.*

53. *See* Schuck, "Litigation, Bargaining, and Regulation," 3 *Regulation* 26 (1979); Note, *Rethinking Regulation: Negotiation as an Alternative to Traditional Rulemaking,* 94 *Harv. L. Rev.* 1871 (1981).

54. See Horowitz, *supra* note 10, at 276.

55. See Berger, *supra* note 51, at 733.

56. Fiss, *supra* note 10, at 56–57.

57. Note, *Implementation Problems, supra* note 25, at 447.

58. *See* McCree, "Bureaucratic Justice: An Early Warning," 129 *U. Pa. L. Rev.* 777 (1981).

59. Fiss, "The Social and Political Foundations of Adjudication," 6 *J. Law & Human Behav.* 121 (1982).

60. E.g., Berger, *supra* note 51.

61. Note, *The* Wyatt *Case, supra* note 23, at 1367 n.179; *see also* Fiss, *supra* note 10, at 54 n.108.

62. *See* Horowitz, *supra* note 10; Burt, "Pennhurst: A Parable" (unpublished manuscript, 1982).

63. Altman, *supra* note 41, at 745–46. *See also* Burt, *supra* note 62.

64. *See generally,* Special Project, *supra* note 10, at 870–927.

65. *Supra* chap. 1.

66. *Id.*

67. *See,* e.g., the case discussed in Altman, *supra* note 41.

68. *See*, e.g., M. Derthick, *The Influence of Federal Grants* (1970).

69. Elmore, "Organizational Models of Social Program Implementation," 26 *Public Policy* 185, 197–98 (1978), citing a study by Herbert Kaufman.

70. *See*, e.g., J. Peltason, *Fifty-Eight Lonely Men: Southern Federal Judges and School Desegregation* (1961); R. Elmore and M. McLaughlin, *Reform and Retrenchment: The Politics of California School Finance Reform* (forthcoming).

71. Miranda v. Arizona, 384 U.S. 436 (1966).

72. Baum, *supra* note 40, at 565–67.

73. *See*, e.g., the decree in Wyatt v. Stickney, 344 F. Supp. 387, 395–407 (M.D. Ala. 1972).

74. Note, *The* Wyatt *Case, supra* note 23, at 1368–69. Lawyers within the defendant agency may be able to facilitate compliance. *See*, e.g., Muir, *supra* note 22, at 120–21.

75. The exception is when Congress specifically vests the appointment power in the courts. U.S., *Constitution*, Article II, § 2, cl. 2. *But see* Reed v. Rhodes, 635 F.2d 556 (6th Cir. 1980), upholding a court mandate to a school board to employ a court-selected "administrator of desegregation."

76. *See*, e.g., *supra* note 73, at 405–06; decree in N.Y.S. A.R.C. v. Rockefeller, 357 F. Supp. 752, 768–69 (E.D.N.Y. 1973).

77. Harris and Spiller, *supra* note 26, at 18–19.

78. Diver, *supra* note 9, at 63 n.108.

79. *Id.* at 100.

80. Special Project, *supra* note 10, at 838–41.

81. E.g., Note, *Reading the Mind of the School Board: Segregative Intent and the De Facto/De Jure Distinction*, 86 *Yale L. J.* 317 (1976).

82. *See* Smith case study in Kalodner and Fishman, *supra* note 27, at 75–81; Clendenin, "Boston City Schools, Once Beacons, Losing Students and Pride," *New York Times*, September 20, 1981, at A32. *See also* Diver, *supra* note 10, at 100.

83. H. Rodgers and C. Bullock, *Coercion to Compliance* (1976), at chap. 3. *See*, e.g., United States v. Hall, 472 F.2d 261 (5th Cir. 1973).

84. *See* P. Samuelson, "The Pure Theory of Public Expenditures," 36 Rev. Econ. & Stat. 387 (1954).

85. *See* Clark and Wilson, "Incentive Systems: A Theory of Organizations," 6 *Adm. Sci. Q.* 219 (September 1961).

86. For an application of this notion to the question of educational reform, *see* R. Murnane, "Interpreting the Evidence on School Effectiveness," 83 *Teachers College Record* 19, 28–32 (1981).

87. One scholar has noted a similar effect when judges undertake an active role managing pretrial proceedings in certain kinds of cases. Resnik, "Managerial Judges," 96 *Harv. L. Rev.* 374 (1982).

88. Fiss, *supra* note 2, at 95.

89. E.g., Baker v. Carr, 369 U.S. 186 (1962); Wesberry v. Sanders, 376 U.S. 1 (1964); Reynolds v. Sims, 377 U.S. 533 (1964).

90. *See* A. Bickel, *The Least Dangerous Branch: The Supreme Court at the Bar of Politics* (1962); Mishkin, "The Reforming Judiciary," in G. Gunther and W. Moore, eds., *Judicial Power in the U.S.: What Are the Appropriate Constraints?* (Washington, D.C.: American Enterprise Institute, forthcoming).

91. Kalodner and Fishman, *supra* note 27, at 8.

92. Note, *The* Wyatt *Case, supra* note 41, at 1360–64; cases cited at Altman, *supra* note 41, at 741 nn.16–17.

93. *See* Diver, *supra* note 10; Special Project, *supra* note 10.

94. *See* Smith, *supra* note 82; Burt, *supra* note 62.

95. Diver, *supra* note 10.

96. *See*, e.g., R. Dahl, *Who Governs?* (1961); E. Banfield, *Political Influence* (1961).

97. Note, *supra* note 25, at 456.

98. E.g., Note, *id.;* Note, *The* Wyatt *Case, supra* note 23; Burt, *supra* note 62; Kalodner and Fishman, *supra* note 27: Special Project, *supra* note 10.

99. Diver, *supra* note 10, at 89.

100. *See*, e.g., Smith, *supra* note 82; Burt, *supra* note 62.

101. For several examples, see Rebell and Block, *supra* note 24.

102. For what seems to me to be essentially an articulation of this view, *see* Eisenberg and Yeazell, *supra* note 10, at 516–17.

103. *See generally,* B. Ackerman, *Social Justice in the Liberal State* (1980).

104. *See* Bickel, *supra* note 90, at 29–30.

105. *See* Henderson and Parsons, trans., and T. Parsons, ed., *Max Weber: The Theory of Social and Economic Organization* 126–32 (1947).

106. *See*, Bickel, *supra* note 90; Fiss, *supra* note 10, at 16.

107. E.g., Stewart, "The Reformation of American Administrative Law," 88 *Harv. L. Rev.* 1669 (1975); Freedman, "Crisis and Legitimacy in the Administrative Process," 27 *Stan. L. Rev.* 1041 (1975).

108. E.g., J. Buchanan and G. Tullock, *The Calculus of Consent* (1962); sources cited *supra* note 106.

109. Fiss, *supra* note 10, at 15.

110. *Id.* at 51–52.

111. *Id.* at 58.

112. *Id.*

113. *Id.* at 12–14.

114. *Id.* at 53–58.

115. *Supra,* chap. 1.

116. Fiss, *supra* note 10.

117. Fiss, *supra* note 2, at 55–56 (emphasis supplied).

118. Fiss, *supra* note 10, at 52–53.

119. *Id.* at 53.

120. *Id.* at 52.

121. *See*, e.g., R. Dworkin, *Taking Rights Seriously* 269–78 (1978).

122. The Supreme Court has managed to avoid passing on the merits of broad structural decrees outside the school desegregation area. *Supra* note 19.

123. Bickel, *supra* note 90, at 69.

124. Fiss, *supra* note 10, at 58.

125. *Id.* at 16.

126. E.g., Hutto v. Finney, 437 U.S. 678, 685–86 (1978); Estelle v. Gamble, 429 U.S. 97, 102 (1976).

127. *See*, e.g., the description of conditions in Arkansas prisons in Holt v. Sarver, 300 F. Supp. 825, 309 F. Supp. 362, *aff'd*, 442 F.2d 304, *on remand*, 363 F. Supp. 194, *rev'd*, Finney v. Arkansas Bd. of Corrections, 505 F.2d 194, *on remand*, 410 F. Supp. 251, *aff'd*, 548 F. 2d 740 (8th Cir. 1974).

128. For an exploration of analogous discrepancies between "myth system" and "operational code," *see* W. Reisman, *Folded Lies: Bribery, Crusades, and Reforms,* chap. 1 (1979).

129. Shakespeare, *The Merchant of Venice,* act I, scene 2.

130. Tribe has developed this metaphor into a conception of judicial function. Tribe, "Constitution as Point of View," paper presented to Legal Theory Workshop, Yale Law School, October 1981.

131. Youngstown Sheet & Tube Co. v. Sawyer, 343 U.S. 579, 635 (1952) (concurring opinion).

132. Ex parte Milligan, 71 U.S. 2 (1866).

133. *See,* e.g., W. Murphy, *Congress and the Courts* (1962); Diamond, "Containing the Least Dangerous Branch: From Founding to Civil War," in *Judicial Power in the U.S., supra* note 90; McDowell, "Curbing the Courts: Responses to Judicial Activism, 1857–1981," in *Judicial Power in the U.S., supra* note 90.

134. *See* United States v. Will, 449 U.S. 200 (1980).

135. For a sampling of this debate, *see Judicial Power in the U.S., supra* note 90.

136. U.S., *Constitution,* Art. I. § 6. *But see* Hutchinson v. Proxmire, 443 U.S. 111 (1979).

137. Cited at W. Berns, *The First Amendment and the Future of American Democracy* 53 (1976).

138. For one devastating dissection of positivism, *see* Leff, "Unspeakable Ethics, Unnatural Law," 1979 *Duke L. J.* 1229, 1233–37 (1979).

139. Resnik finds this to be true of intrusive pretrial orders as well. *Supra* note 87.

140. Bickel, *supra* note 90, at 251 (emphasis supplied).

*Chapter 8*

1. E.g., *see* Glazer, "Black English and Reluctant Judges," 62 *The Public Interest* 40 (Winter 1980).

2. Fiss, "The Forms of Justice," 93 *Harv. L. Rev.* 1, 53–55 (1979).

3. *Id.* at 58.

4. *See generally,* G. McDowell, *Equity and the Constitution* (1982); Special Project, *The Remedial Process in Institutional Reform Litigation,* 78 *Colum. L. Rev.* 784, 858–70 (1978).

5. *See* G. Gunther and W. Moore, eds., *Judicial Power in the U.S.: What Are the Appropriate Constraints?* (Washington, D.C.: American Enterprise Institute, forthcoming). *See also* R. Bork, *Constitutionality of the President's Busing Proposals* (1972).

6. Swann v. Charlotte-Mecklenburg Board of Educ., 402 U.S. 1, 16 (1971). For a critique of this principle, *see* Fiss, *supra* note 2, at 46–50.

7. *See generally,* Nagel, "Separation of Powers and the Scope of Federal Equitable Remedies," 30 *Stan. L. Rev.* 661 (1978); Frug, "The Judicial Power of the Purse," 126 *U. Pa. L. Rev.* 715 (1978).

8. ". . . the nature of the violation determines the scope of the remedy." Swann v. Charlotte Mecklenburg Board of Educ., 402 U.S. 1, 16 (1971).

9. Chayes, "The Role of the Judge in Public Law Litigation," 89 *Harv. L. Rev.* 1281, 1294 (1976).

10. *See* Administrative Procedure Act, 5 U.S.C. § 557(c) (hearings) and § 553(b) and (c) (rulemaking).

11. At least one court has issued such a decision in an exceedingly complex case. *See* Alabama Power Co. v. Costle, 606 F.2d 1068, 1093 (D.C. Cir. 1979), superseded 636 F.2d 323 (D.C. Cir. 1979).

12. *See*, e.g., Allison, "Implementation Analysis: 'The Missing Chapter' in Conventional Analysis. A Teaching Exercise," in R. Zeckhauser, ed., *Benefit-Cost and Policy Analysis 1974* (1975); Chase, "Implementing a Human Services Program: How Hard Will It Be?" 27 *Pub. Pol'y* 385 (1979); W. Williams, *The Implementation Perspective* 89–91 (1980); E. Bardach, *The Implementation Game* 264–66 (1977); Elmore, "Backward Mapping: Implementation of Research and Policy Decisions," 94 *Pol. Sci. Q.* 601 (1980); E. Hargrove, *The Missing Link: The Study of Implementation of Social Policy* (1975).

13. National Environmental Policy Act, 42 U.S.C. § 4332.

14. *See*, e.g., Executive Order 12291, February 17, 1981.

15. E.g., 15 U.S.C. § 2058(f)(1)(D).

16. E.g., Baram, "Cost-Benefit Analysis: An Inadequate Basis for Health, Safety, and Environmental Regulatory Decisionmaking," 8 *Ecology L. Q.* 473 (1980); Sax, "The (Unhappy) Truth about NEPA," 26 *Okla. L. Rev.* 239 (1973); Bardach and Pugliaresi, "The Environmental Impact Statement vs. the Real World," 49 *The Public Interest* 22 (Fall 1977).

17. E.g., Schaumburg v. Citizens for Better Environment, 444 U.S. 620, 637 (1980) (First Amendment); Siegel v. Chicken Delight, 448 F.2d 43 (9th Cir.), *cert. denied*, 405 U.S. 955 (1972) (antitrust); Halderman v. Pennhurst State School & Hosp., 612 F.2d 84, 103–08 (3d Cir.), *rev'd*, Pennhurst State School & Hosp., 451 U.S. 1, 18 (1981) (deinstitutionalization). The criterion has been imposed upon decisionmakers by at least one regulatory statute. *See* Consumer Product Safety Act, 15 U.S.C. § 2059(f), as amended. For application of a similar concept to the field of child welfare, *see* J. Goldstein, A. Freud, and A. Solnit, *Before the Best Interests of the Child* (1980).

18. E.g., Weinberger v. Romero-Barcelo, 102 S. Ct. 1798 (1982). Fiss vigorously criticizes the traditional doctrine but seems to accept it as applied to at least some structural injunctions. *The Civil Rights Injunction* 92–94 (1978).

19. For an analogous set of guidelines focused upon the separation of powers dimension of structural remedies, *see* Nagel, *supra* note 7.

20. *See*, e.g., Burt, "Pennhurst: A Parable" (unpublished manuscript, 1982).

21. See, e.g., chap. 7, notes 73 and 76.

22. *See*, e.g., C. Schultze, *The Public Uses of Private Interest* (1977); B. Ackerman and W. Hassler, *Clean Coal/Dirty Air* (1981). *See also* the emissions trading policy of the Environmental Protection Agency, 47 Fed. Reg. 15076 (April 7, 1982).

23. For a historical analysis of the declaratory remedy, *see* E. Borchard, *Declaratory Judgments* 87 (2d ed., 1941).

24. 347 U.S. 483, 494–95 (1954).

25. E.g., discussion of lower court remedial procedures in Hutto v. Fin-

ney, 437 U.S. 678, 683–84 (1978).

26. E.g., Jaynes, "Parole of Haitians Ordered; U.S. Balks and Sets Appeal," *New York Times,* June 30, 1982, at A16.

27. Frug, *supra* note 7, at 728.

28. For an example of a conditional injunction in nuisance law, *see* Boomer v. Atlantic Cement Co., 26 N.Y. 2d 219, 257 N.E. 2d 870 (1970).

29. See discussion in chap. 6.

30. Wilson, *The Investigators* (1978).

31. Wilson, *Varieties of Police Behavior* (1968).

32. B. Cardozo, *The Nature of the Judicial Process* 165 (1921).

33. Fiss, *supra* note 2, at 58.

34. U.S., Congress, Senate, Judiciary Committee, *Hearings on S.584 and S.585,* 97th Cong., 1st sess, (1981).

35. See, e.g., chap. 4; Owen v. City of Independence, 445 U.S. 622, 680–83 (1980) (Powell, J., dissenting).

36. *See,* e.g., 28 U.S.C. § 2675(a).

37. *See* Fuller, "The Forms and Limits of Adjudication," 92 *Harv. L. Rev.* 353 (1978). Indeed, the Court recently observed that the need to make such trade-offs is a reason for congressional leadership regarding the design of public tort remedies. Ferri v. Ackerman, 444 U.S. 193, 205 (1979).

38. There may well be constitutional inhibitions of Congress's power to prescribe uniform state indemnification or insurance practices with respect to officials found liable under § 1983, but its power to achieve similar results by imposing governmental liability directly seems clear. See chap. 5.

## Appendix 1

1. Note, *Limiting the § 1983 Action in the Wake of* Monroe v. Pape, 82 *Harv. L., Rev.* 1486, 1487 n.12 (1969).

2. *Federal Judicial Workload Statistics,* 1979–80, Administrative Office of the U.S. Courts, Washington, D.C., at 6.

3. *Annual Report of the Director, Administrative Office of the U.S. Courts, 1970,* Washington, D.C., at 92.

4. *Id.* at 98.

5. *Federal Judicial Workload Statistics,* 1979–80, *supra* note 2, at 2.

6. Whitman, "Constitutional Torts," 79 *Mich. L. Rev.* 5, 6 n.6 (1980).

7. U.S., Congress, House, Judiciary Committee, Subcommittee on Agency Administration and Government Relations, *Federal Tort Claims Act: Hearings on H.R. 24,* 97th Cong., 1st sess., October 13, 1981 (statement of Edward C. Schmults, deputy attorney general); November 16, 1981 (statement of William H. Taft IV, general counsel, Dept. of Defense).

8. U.S., Bureau of the Census, *Statistical Abstract of the United States: 1980* (101st ed., 1980), table 519, at 318.

9. U.S., Congress, Senate, Judiciary Committee, Subcommittee on Agency Administration, *Federal Tort Claims Act: Hearings on S.1775,* 97th Cong., 1st sess., November 13, 1981 (statement of Edward C. Schmults, deputy attorney general).

10. *Hearings on S.1775, supra* note 9, 97th Cong., 2d sess., March 31, 1982 (statement of J. Paul McGrath, assistant attorney general).

11. *Id.*

12. *Id. See also Hearings on S.1775, supra* note 9, 97th Cong., 2d sess., March 31, 1982 (statement of Donald J. Devine, director, U.S. Office of Personnel Management).

13. *Hearings on S.1775, supra* note 9, 97th Cong., 2d sess., March 31, 1982 (statement of William H. Webster, director, FBI).

14. Letter to the author from John Euler, Esq., assistant director, Torts Branch, Civil Division, U.S. Dept. of Justice, March 25, 1982.

15. Statement of Donald J. Devine, *supra* note 12.

16. *Id.*

17. Statement of J. Paul McGrath, *supra* note 10.

18. *Id.*

## Appendix 2

1. Peter Schuck, "Suing Our Servants: The Court, Congress, and the Liability of Public Officials for Damages," 1980 *Sup. Ct. Rev.* 281, 317 n.117 (1981).

2. E.g., Quern v. Jordan, 440 U.S. 332, 337 (1979).

3. *Id.* at 349, citing Milliken v. Bradley, 433 U.S. 267, 290 (1977).

4. Edelman v. Jordan, 415 U.S. 651, 676–77 (1974); the scope and meaning of Edelman have recently been cast into doubt by Cory v. White, 102 S. Ct. 2325, 2328–29 (1982). *See also id.* at 2332 (Powell, J., dissenting).

5. Edelman v. Jordan, 415 U.S. 651.

6. Owen v. City of Independence, 445 U.S. 622, 657 (1980), relying upon Monell v. Dept. of Social Services of City of New York, 436 U.S. 658, 690 (1978). Since *Monell* on its facts "unquestionably involve[d] official policy," *id.* at 694 and 701 n.66, the Court's rejection of *respondeat superior* as a basis for § 1983 liability, *id.* at 691, is *dictum. See also* Polk County v. Dodson, 102 S. Ct. 445, 453 (1981).

7. *Supra* note 6; Rizzo v. Goode, 423 U.S. 362, 376 (1976).

8. City of Newport v. Fact Concerts, Inc., 453 U.S. 247, 259, 101 S. Ct. 2748, 2755 (1981).

9. Barr v. Matteo, 360 U.S. 564, 575 (1959).

10. 435 U.S. 349, 356–57 (1978). *See* Schuck, *supra* note 1, at 318 n.126.

11. Wood v. Strickland, 420 U.S. 308, 321 (1975). The "outer perimeter" and type-of-act limitations apply to qualified immunity as well.

12. Harlow and Butterfield v. Fitzgerald, 102 S. Ct. 2727 (1982).

13. *Id.* at n. 30.

14. *See* William Casto, "Innovations in the Defense of Official Immunity under Section 1982," 47 *Tenn. L. Rev.* 47, 102 (1979).

15. E.g., Stump v. Sparkman, 435 U.S. 349 (1978) (judicial); Tenney v. Brandhove, 341 U.S. 367 (1951) (legislative). *See also* Lake Country Estates, Inc. v. Tahoe Regional Planning Agency, 440 U.S. 391, 405 (1979) (regional legislators); Imbler v. Pachtman, 424 U.S. 409 (1976) (prosecutorial).

16. Butz v. Economou, 438 U.S. 478, 512–13, 515, 516–17 (1978). The Court has also conferred absolute immunity upon judges when they were "exercising the State's entire legislative power" to regulate the bar. Supreme Court of Virginia v. Consumers Union, 446 U.S. 719, 734 (1980).

17. E.g., Butz v. Economou, 438 U.S. 478, 501 (1978); Scheuer v. Rhodes, 416 U.S. 232, 247–48 (1974).

18. Supreme Court of Virginia v. Consumers Union, 446 U.S. 719, 736–37 (1980).

19. Butz v. Economou, 438 U.S. 478, 507 (1978).

20. Scheuer v. Rhodes, 416 U.S. 232, 249 (1974).

21. Butz v. Economou, 438 U.S. 478 (1978).

22. State of Maine v. Thiboutot, 448 U.S. 1 (1980); Parratt v. Taylor, 451 U.S. 527, 101 S. Ct. 1908 (1981).

23. Carey v. Piphus, 435 U.S. 247, 257 n.11 (1978). *But see* Carlson v. Green, 446 U.S. 14, 22 (1980) (Rehnquist, J., dissenting).

24. City of Newport v. Fact Concerts, Inc., 453 U.S. 247, 101 S. Ct. 2748, 2760, 2761, 2762 (1981).

25. 42 U.S.C. § 1988.

26. *See* cases cited at Schuck, *supra* note 1.

27. Harlow and Butterfield v. Fitzgerald, n.30, 102 S. Ct. 2727 (1982); Butz v. Economou, 438 U.S. 478, 496–504 (1978).

28. Nixon v. Fitzgerald, 102 S. Ct. 2690 (1982).

29. Carlson v. Green, 446 U.S. 14, 22 (1980) (*dictum*); see *id.* at 504 (Rehnquist, J., dissenting).

30. *See* 28 U.S.C. § 2412 and 28 U.S.C. § 1920.

31. 28 U.S.C. §§ 2674, 2680(h).

32. 28 U.S.C. § 2680; see discussion in chap. 5.

33. Carlson v. Green, 446 U.S. 14, 23 (1980).

## Appendix 3

1. 2 T.R. 667, 673, 100 Eng. Rep. 359, 362 (K.B. 1789). Several commentators have pointed out the then long-standing doctrine that the only remedy for breach of a public duty was by indictment. *See,* e.g., Borchard, "Government Liability in Tort," 24 *Yale L. J.* 1, 42 n.171 (1924).

2. Mower v. Inhabitants of Leicester, 9 Mass. 247 (1812).

3. For a description of the state of affairs at the turn of the twentieth century, *see* 13 R.C.L. 306–07 nn. 2, 3; 2 A.L.R. 721. For one of the few rejections of *Mower, see* Anne Arundel County v. Duckett, 20 Md. 468 (1864).

4. Throughout his judicial career, Holmes maintained that immunity from suit was a fundamental aspect of political sovereignty. He frequently cited Thomas Hobbes, Jean Bodin, and other like-minded political philosophers for propositions based on an ultimately positivist view of the meaning of sovereignty. *See,* e.g., Kawanakoa v. Polyblank, 205 U.S. 349 (1907): "A sovereign is exempt from suit, not because of any formal conception or obsolete theory, but on the logical and practical ground that there can be no legal right against the authority that makes the law on which the right depends." *See also* The Western Maid, 257 U.S. 419, 433 (1921): "The United States has not

consented to be sued for torts, and therefore it cannot be said that in a legal sense the United States has been guilty of a tort. For a tort is a tort in a legal sense only because the law has made it so." The theory on which Holmes proceeded is vigorously criticized by Borchard, "Government Liability in Tort," 36 *Yale L. J.* 757, 758–66 (1926).

5. Miller v. Horton, 152 Mass. 540 (1891).

6. Raymond v. Fish, 51 Conn. 80, 96–97 (1883). For similar justifications, *see*, e.g., Valentine v. City of Englewood, 76 N.J.L. 509 (1908); Beeks v. Dickinson County, 131 Iowa 244 (1906).

7. This line begins with Bailey v. Mayor of the City of New York, 3 Hill 531 (N.Y. 1842).

8. Borchard, *supra* note 1, at 43–45; compare the majority and dissenting opinions in Owen v. City of Independence, 445 U.S. 662 (1980).

9. For immunity: e.g., Clark v. Waltham, 128 Mass. 567 (1880); Blair v. Granger, 24 R.I. 17 (1902). Against immunity: e.g., State v. Sweickhardt, 109 Mo. 496 (1891); Denver v. Spencer, 34 Colo. 270 (1905). *See also* cases cited in Borchard, *supra* note 1, at 229–30, 239.

10. Smith v. State of New York, 227 N.Y. 405, 409 (1920).

11. 22 U.S. 720 (1824). See discussion *supra* in chap. 2.

12. E.g., State v. Hill, 54 Ala. 67 (1876); Davis v. State, 30 Idaho 137 (1917); Smith v. State, 227 N.Y. 405 (1920).

13. Owen v. City of Independence, 445 U.S. at 683 n.27 (Powell, J., dissenting).

# INDEX

Absolute immunity, 42, 92; treatment in federal courts, 38; treatment in state courts, 38–39, 206–07; Learned Hand's approach to, 40; denied governor, 49; application, allocation and claim of, 88–92; distinguished from qualified immunity, 90; application to judges, 90; current state of, 204. *See also* Immunity; Qualified immunity

Activist state: and official illegality, xii–xv; and official liability, xii–xv, 111, 168

Administrative Procedure Act, 192

Agencies: ability to deter, 104–06; incentives, 106–07, 108; measures to deal with official illegality, 108; impediments to organizational change, 126–29; control of low-level employees, 128, 136–37, 143–44, 183, 193–95; role of, 129–31, 163; control of resources, 132; ability to generate support, 135; capacity to control misconduct, 142–46

—constituency building techniques: enforceability, 42; professionalization, 136–37; building political alliances, 137; disciplinary reforms, 137

Agency resources: information, 129–30; communication, 130–31; behavior shaping incentives, 131–34; political and public support, 134–35

Amsterdam, Anthony: on official discretion, 66

Aristotle, 112

Attorneys' fees, 164; under section 1983, 49, 50, 196; under Federal Tort Claims Act, 117–18

Bacon, Francis: on sovereign immunity, 31

*Bankers' Case*, 32, 33

Bardach, Eugene, and Kagan, Robert: on official self-protection tactics, 75

Barnard, Chester: "zones of indifference," 126

*Barr* v. *Matteo*, 40–41, 42, 43

Bickel, Alexander: on legitimacy, 133–34, 181; "principled flexibility," 178

*Bivens* v. *Six Unknown Agents of Federal Bureau of Narcotics*, 70, 100, 117, 141, 144; expansion of damage remedy, 52; officials' vulnerability to suit, 57; risk of harm, 64; emergence of, 69; complications under, 98–99; and amendments to Federal Tort Claims Act, 115; creation of action under, 196–97; volume of litigation under, 201–02; current liability-immunity doctrine under, 205

Blackstone, William: on English legal doctrine, 30–31, 32

Blau, Peter: on formalism, 74–75; risk taking, 76; on organizational change, 145

Bobbitt, Philip, 117

Borchard, Edwin: analysis of immunity doctrine, 39

Boston school case, 164, 168

*Brown* v. *Board of Education*, 50, 164, 167, 168, 191

Bureaucratic decisionmaking: economic models of, 59

*Butz* v. *Economou*, 69; extension of qualified immunity, 42–43, 90, 91

Calabresi, Guido: deterrence categories, 17; on social costs, 77, 80; on strict liability, 103–04; "cost of costing," 117

Cardozo, Benjamin, 195

*Carlson* v. *Green*, 42, 50
Chayes, Abram: implementation of
    structural injunction, 155, 156, 157,
    158
*Chisholm* v. *Georgia*, 36, 37, 44–45
Civil Service Reform Act of 1978, 140,
    146
Clifton, Robert de: petition of right, 31
Coase, Robert: on Coase theorem, 83
Compensation principle, 22–23, 56, 94,
    111–13, 197; and official liability
    remedy, 98; of nonmonetizable rights,
    117
Congress: and sovereign immunity,
    37–38; establishment of Court of
    Claims, 37–38; role in deterring
    official misconduct, 108, 197; power
    over courts, 179–80, 186; role in
    remedial reform, 197
Cost-shifting. *See* Indemnification;
    Insurance
Courts, 103, 129, 157, 167; influence on
    statutory amendments to Federal Tort
    Claims Act, 42; control of official
    conduct, 52; recent section 1983
    decisions, 118; expansion of public
    tort liability, 145. *See also* Injunction;
    "Least restrictive remedy";
    Remedies; "Structural" injunction

Damage remedy: compared with other
    remedies, 14–16; effect on purposes of
    tort law, 68–81, 98–100; against
    individual official, 79; good faith
    defense, 89, 92–99, 116
—absolute and qualified immunity,
    88–98, 149; damage action against
    federal official, 20, 38–43, 203–05;
    damage action against state and local
    officials, 143–51
"Deep-pocket" defendant. *See*
    Governmental liability
Deterrence, 16–22. *See also* General
    deterrence; Specific deterrence
Discretion: of low-level officials, 66, 67,
    98, 100, 127, 128, 143

*Economou*. See *Butz* v. *Economou*
Eisenberg, Theodore, and Yeazell,
    Stephen: on structural injunction,
    151–53, 155
Eleventh Amendment, 182, 183,
    203–04; relief against states, 45–46,
    50, 53, 88, 112, 118–19; immunity

from damages, 118–19; Congressional
    refusal to review, 196
Elmore, Richard: organizational models,
    126–29, 135, 193
Emergency School Assistance Act, 133
English common law tradition, 30,
    32–35. *See also* Public tort law;
    *Respondeat superior;* Sovereign
    immunity
Enterprise liability, xviii, 30; in English
    public law, 30, 32, 33–35; in private
    tort law, 51; consequences of, 100–02
—in American public law, 37–38, 53,
    118, 119–20; extension of, 56, 101;
    refusal to accept, 82, 83, 100, 182. *See
    also* Governmental liability;
    *Respondeat superior*
*Ex parte Young*, 38, 45–47

Federalism, 118–19, 153, 161–62
Federal Tort Claims Act (FTCA), 43,
    100; history of, 39, 41–42, 115–16,
    196–97; provisions of, 40, 41, 113–18,
    182–83; fourth amendment violations,
    42; tactical considerations, 84;
    indemnification, 85; waiver of
    sovereign immunity, 113; specific
    proposed reforms of, 113–18, 141;
    attorneys' fees, 117; volume of
    litigation under, 201–02; current
    liability-immunity doctrine under,
    205
Fiss, Owen: on structural injunction,
    153, 155, 158, 160; on legitimacy, 167;
    on "judicial interpretivist"
    conception, 174–78, 185; on future
    role of judge, 195
FTCA. *See* Federal Tort Claims Act

General deterrence, 77, 124, 147, 148,
    190, 194; and judicial intrusiveness,
    17–18; in remedial continuum, 20;
    effect on officials, 79; role of
    legislatures and courts, 103;
    constituency building techniques,
    135–42; expansion of, 182–83. *See
    also* Specific deterrence
*Goldberg* v. *Kelly*, xv, 95
"Good faith": immunity, 43, 72, 79, 94,
    98; construed by courts, 49; Supreme
    Court on, 72; defense, 89, 92–99, 116;
    standard, 93–98; objective test,
    94–95; subjective test, 94–97
Governmental immunity. *See* Absolute

immunity; Federal Tort Claims Act; Governmental liability; Qualified immunity; Section *1983*

Governmental liability: history of, in England, 30–35; Fourth Amendment violations, 42; effect on purposes of tort law, 100–09, 123; "deep-pocket" defendant, 102, 111, 118; structural models of, 109–11; per se, shortcomings of, 110–11; "compensation principle," 111–13; and strict liability, 112; implementation of, 123–24; future expansion of, 184, 197

—bureaucratic locus of, 104–08; suboptimization problems, 106–08; enforceability problems, 107–08

—history of, in United States: federal government, 35–43; state and local government, 38–39, 206–07

—proposed reforms of, 113–21, 184; in claims against United States, 113–18; in claims against state and local government, 118–21

*Gregoire* v. *Biddle*, 40

Hamilton, Alexander: on immunity of state governments in federal courts, 44

Hand, Learned: on absolute immunity, 40

*Harlow and Butterfield* v. *Fitzgerald*, 89, 94

Hirschoff, Jon, 103

Holmes, Oliver W.: on *respondeat superior*, 33; on individual activity, 64; on *Miller* v. *Horton*, 206–07

Holt, Sir John: transformation of *respondeat superior*, 33–34; enterprise liability, 34

Horowitz, Donald: on "social" and "historical" facts, 156; courts and social science, 157

Immunity: state and local government, 43–46; and vigorous decisionmaking, 88, 89; rules governing, 89–93, 203–05; judicial, 90–91

Implementation. *See* Governmental liability; "Street-level" agencies; "Structural" injunction

Indemnification, 98, 109*n*, 110, 183; state and local laws on, 85–88; cost-shifting model, 109

Injunction, 50, 53, 119, 149, 184; prohibitory, 14, 15, 16, 151, 162, 169, 184, 192, 195; mandatory, 14, 15–16, 151, 169, 170, 182, 192, 195; declaratory relief, 14, 49, 53, 191, 195; structural, 14, 147, 150, 151, 153, 171–85; federal court power overstates, 46; protection of nonmonetizable rights, 116; specific deterrence, 150; resistance to, 170; conditional, 191. *See also* "Structural" injunction

Insurance, 70, 82, 85. *See also* Indemnification

Jackson, Robert: on "institutional competition," 179, 181

Jacobs, Clyde: on government immunity, 44

Jay, John: in *Chisholm* v. *Georgia*, 36, 45

Johnson, Frank, 168; on structural remedies, 155

Judicial interpretivism: Owen Fiss on, 174–78, 185

Judicial intrusiveness, 126, 168; in remedial continuum, 14, 20; relation to remedial forms, 14–25; and injunction, 150–54, 185; least restrictive remedy, 189–96

Kaufman, Herbert, 143

Ku Klux Klan Act. *See* Section *1983*

*Lane* v. *Cotton*, 34

*Langford* v. *United States*, 38

"Least restrictive remedy," 186, 192; guidelines, 190–96; and declaratory judgment, 191, 192; and remand, 191–92; and prohibitory injunction, 192–93; and mandatory injunction, 193; factors to consider, 193–95

Legislatures: ability to generate support, 134; legitimacy of, 173; intervention of, 184

Legitimacy: of rules, 9–11, 133, 162; of institutions, 10–12, 133–34, 154, 164–69, 172–73; of courts, 158, 163–69, 181, 198. *See also* Remedies

Lincoln, Abraham, 180; on self-governance, 1

Lippman, Walter, 133

Lipsky, Michael, xviii, 4; on official inaction, 72–73; on "coping strategies," 131

Loss-spreading, 100–01, 103, 116; and compensation, 22–23

Madison, James: on immunity of state governments in federal courts, 44
*Maine* v. *Thiboutot*, 85
*Marbury* v. *Madison*, 36
Marshall, John: and *Osborn* v. *Bank of the United States*, 38, 45; on immunity of state governments in federal courts, 44
Mashaw, Jerry: on formalism, 74
Merton, Robert: on formalism, 74
*Miller* v. *Horton*, 206
Milner, Neil, 136
*Miranda* v. *Arizona*, 8, 10, 136
Mishkin, Paul: on judges, 158
*Monell* v. *Dept. of Social Science of City of New York*, 85, 120
*Monroe* v. *Pape*, xviii, xix, 48–49, 120

*Nathan* v. *Virginia*, 36
Nonmonetizable rights, 116–17, 148–49

Official illegality, xii-xiv, xviii–xix; and activist government, xii–xv; types of, xviii–xix; defined, 3; personal tort liability, 34; liability for, 34, 38, 56, 183; qualified immunity, 41–43; government-provided representation, 43, 84; risk aversion, 70, 77, 97, 105; self-protection, 79–81, 183; cost-shifting, 82, 83; legal defense, 83–85; indemnification, 85–88; and section *1983*, 121; remedies for, 183–96
—causes of, xix, 3–13, 60–68; comprehension, 4–6, 128–29; capacity, 6–8, 128–29; motivation, 8–12, 128–29; negligence, 12–13, 50, 128–29
—and immunity, 88; discretionary errors, 38; critics of, 39; state law exceptions, 39; burden of proof, 49. *See also* Damage remedy
*Osborn* v. *Bank of United States*, 38, 46
*Owen* v. *City of Independence*, 85

*Parratt* v. *Taylor*, 49, 50
*Pawlett* v. *Attorney General, Hardres*, 32
*Pennhurst State School and Hospital* v. *Halderman*, 168
Personal liability: legal defense, 82, 83–84; insurance, 82, 85; official

protection against, 82–83
—indemnification, 63, 82, 87–88; under federal law, 85; under state and local law, 85–87
Petition of right, 31–32, 44
*Pierson* v. *Ray*, 90
Pressman, Jeffrey, 5
Price theory: and street-level behavior, 60
Private tort law, 30, 56, 62, 66, 67–68
Public tort law, xiv-xix, 51−53, 101, 123, 183, 196; types of remedies, xiv, xviii−xix, 14−20, 51−53, 65, 183, 198; compared with private tort law, xviii, 30, 51, 56–57, 60, 76–77, 78–79, 82–88, 100; purposes of, 13, 16–25; American and English traditions compared, 35

Qualified immunity, 49, 92, 94, 204; applied to nonprosecutorial officers, 42–43; imprecise application of, 88; allocation of, 89–92; distinguished from absolute immunity, 90; scope of, 92; burden of proof, 93. *See also* Absolute immunity; Section *1983*
*Quern* v. *Jordan*, 118–19

*Reapportionment Cases*, 167, 168, 194
Remedies: judicial intrusiveness, 14–20; implementation of, 25–28, 123–24; distinguished from rights, 25–28, 175–78, 186–88; role of Congress in designing, 42, 53, 103, 108, 118–19, 196–98
—deterrence, 100, 102–09; specific, 77, 79, 100, 103, 125, 147–50, 182, 184; general, 77, 79, 124, 182
—particular forms, 13–20; declaratory judgments, 53, 191; injunctions, 53, 192; damages, 55, 82–99, 148–50, 169, 183, 195. *See also* Injunction; "Structural" injunction
—particular purposes: institutional competence and legitimacy, 16, 23–24; compensation and loss-spreading, 22–23, 24, 98, 100–01, 116; moral exemplification, 23, 24, 100–02; system efficiency, 24–25, 102; vigorous decisionmaking, 40, 71–81, 100–01
*Respondeat superior*, 31, 37, 82, 104, 118, 203; in private tort law, 30, 33–34, 51; in public tort law, 30, 34, 51, 83, 214; English roots, 32–35;

rejected by Supreme Court, 38, 119–21. *See also* Governmental liability; Sovereign immunity

*Rizzo* v. *Goode*, 120

Rose-Ackerman, Susan: on corruption as cause of official illegality, 8

*Russell* v. *Men of Devon*, 206

Schelling, Thomas: on individual incentives, 101

*Scheuer* v. *Rhodes*, 49, 69, 89, 90, 91, 92–93

Section 1983, 69, 117, 144, 153, 196–98; text of, 47; history of, 47–51; growth and volume of litigation under, 48–51, 199–201; recovery of attorneys' fees under, 50, 196; indemnification under state and local law, 85; current liability-immunity doctrine under, 203–04. *See also* Federal Tort Claims Act

Self-protection tactics of officials. *See* "Street-level" officials

Shakespeare, William, 179

Smith, Adam: on state intervention, 35

Sovereign immunity, 34, 182; English roots of, 30–32; American history of, 35–41; Court of Claims established, 37–38; erosion of, 39. *See also* Federal Tort Claims Act; Governmental liability; *Respondeat superior*

Specific deterrence, 77, 100, 109, 124,159, 182; contrasted with general deterrence, 17, 19, 124; in remedial continuum, 20; effect on officials, 79; role of legislature and court, 103; intrusive forms of, 147; superiority of social valuations, 148; nonmonetizable costs, 148–49; immunity, 149; prevention of harm, 149–50; injunction, 150

State and local government, 44, 47, 118; vulnerability to suits, 119. *See also* Eleventh Amendment; Section 1983

Stone, Christopher: on remedies for corporate misconduct, 104; on indemnification, 109*n*

Story, Joseph, 37

"Street-level" agencies, 125–26; role in reforming public tort remedies, 198

—control of low-level conduct: agency motivation, 135–36; professionalization, 136–37; political alliances, 137; disciplinary systems,

137–42; lay and victim participation, 139–42; rulemaking, 143

—resources for organizational change, 123–25; information, 128–30; communication, 130–31; incentives, 131; political support, 134–35

"Street-level" officials, 44, 91, 106, 144; defined, xvii, 59; compared with higher-level officials, xvii–xviii; vulnerability to suits, xvii–xviii, 57, 60–68, 70; reasons for illegality, xix, 3–13; risk-aversion of, 55, 56, 69–70, 76, 97, 98; behavioral response of, to tort remedies, 55, 57, 59, 69–81, 97–98; work environment of, 60–67; discretion, 66, 67; constraints, 67–68; "duty thresholds" of, 68, 70, 143; decisional calculus of, 68–81, 97–98

—self-protection by: types, 71–77; possible tort remedy for, 77–79; magnitude of, 79–81, 97–98

"Structural" injunction, xx, 16, 182, 190, 191, 192, 195; distinguished from earlier intrusive judicial interventions, 151–53

—implementation problems, 154–56; information, 156–61; negotiated decrees, 159, 160–61, 168–69; special masters, 159–60, 161, 168–69; communication, 161–63; incentives, 163–67; political support, 167–69

—legitimation problems, 169–70; "pure rights" conception, 171–73, 174, 181; "judicial interpretivist" conception, 173–78, 181, 185; "institutional competition" conception, 178–81, 185. *See also* Injunction

*Stump* v. *Sparkman*, 204

Sykes, Gresham: study of prison life, 9

System efficiency, 100, 101, 102, 183; as a remedial goal, 24–25

Tax Injunction Act, 49

*Thiboutot, Maine* v., 85

*United States* v. *Kirkpatrick*, 207

*United States* v. *Nixon*, 36

Vigorous decisionmaking, 79, 82, 89, 104; as remedial goal, 21–22; importance of, 40; chilling of, 55, 56, 83, 87, 98; undervaluation of, 80; promotion of, 88, 101, 149, 183; and "good faith" standard, 94; and official liability, 98; and Federal Tort Claims

Vigorous decisionmaking *(continued)*
  Act, 114, 116; and disciplinary reform,
  137–38

Wildavsky, Aaron, 5

Wilson, James Q., 67; on official
  behavior, 59–60; study of police
  behavior, 136, 193–94
Wizard of Oz: analogy, 166
*Wood* v. *Strickland,* 49, 72, 94–97
*Wyatt* v. *Stickney,* 160, 162–63, 168